The Political Construction of Business Interests

Many societies use labor market coordination to maximize economic growth and equality, yet employers' willing cooperation with government and labor is something of a mystery. *The Political Construction of Business Interests* recounts employers' struggles to define their collective social identities at turning points in capitalist development. Employers are most likely to support social investments in countries with strong peak business associations that help members form collective preferences and realize policy goals in labor market negotiations. Politicians, with incentives shaped by governmental structures, took the initiative in association building, and those that created the strongest associations were motivated to evade labor radicalism and to preempt parliamentary democratization. Sweeping in its historical and cross-national reach, the book builds on original archival data, interviews, and cross-national quantitative analyses. The research has important implications for the construction of business as a social class and powerful ramifications for equality, welfare state restructuring, and social solidarity.

Cathie Jo Martin is Professor of Political Science at Boston University and former chair of the Council for European Studies. She is the author of *Stuck in Neutral: Business and the Politics of Human Capital Investment Policy* (2000) and *Shifting the Burden: The Struggle over Growth and Corporate Taxation* (1991) and has held fellowships at the Radcliffe Institute and the Russell Sage Foundation.

Duane Swank is Professor of Political Science at Marquette University and Vice President/President-Elect of the American Political Science Association Organized Section in Comparative Politics. He is the author of *Global Capital, Political Institutions, and Policy Change in Developed Welfare States* (Cambridge 2002) and has held fellowships with the German Marshall Fund and at the Australian National University.

Cambridge Studies in Comparative Politics

Other Books in the Series

Ben W. Ansell, *From the Ballot to the Blackboard: The Redistributive Political Economy of Education*
David Austen-Smith, Jeffry A. Frieden, Miriam A. Golden, Karl Ove Moene, and Adam Przeworski, eds., *Selected Works of Michael Wallerstein: The Political Economy of Inequality, Unions, and Social Democracy*
Andy Baker, *The Market and the Masses in Latin America: Policy Reform and Consumption in Liberalizing Economies*
Lisa Baldez, *Why Women Protest: Women's Movements in Chile*
Stefano Bartolini, *The Political Mobilization of the European Left, 1860–1980: The Class Cleavage*
Robert Bates, *When Things Fell Apart: State Failure in Late-Century Africa*
Mark Beissinger, *Nationalist Mobilization and the Collapse of the Soviet State*
Nancy Bermeo, ed., *Unemployment in the New Europe*
Carles Boix, *Democracy and Redistribution*
Carles Boix, *Political Parties, Growth, and Equality: Conservative and Social Democratic Economic Strategies in the World Economy*
Catherine Boone, *Merchant Capital and the Roots of State Power in Senegal, 1930–1985*
Catherine Boone, *Political Topographies of the African State: Territorial Authority and Institutional Change*

(Continued after Index)

For Jim, Julian, and Jack. I love you with all my hearts (CJM)
For Melanie, Rob, Jennifer, and Mary Lou (DHS)

The Political Construction of Business Interests

Coordination, Growth, and Equality

CATHIE JO MARTIN

Boston University

DUANE SWANK

Marquette University

CAMBRIDGE UNIVERSITY PRESS
Cambridge, New York, Melbourne, Madrid, Cape Town,
Singapore, São Paulo, Delhi, Mexico City

Cambridge University Press
32 Avenue of the Americas, New York, NY 10013-2473, USA

www.cambridge.org
Information on this title: www.cambridge.org/9781107603646

© Cathie Jo Martin and Duane Swank 2012

This publication is in copyright. Subject to statutory exception
and to the provisions of relevant collective licensing agreements,
no reproduction of any part may take place without the written
permission of Cambridge University Press.

First published 2012

Printed in the United States of America

A catalog record for this publication is available from the British Library.

Library of Congress Cataloging in Publication data
Martin, Cathie J., author.
  The political construction of business interests : coordination, growth, and equality /
  Cathie Jo Martin, Boston University, Duane Swank, Marquette University, Wisconsin.
    pages cm. – (Cambridge studies in comparative politics)
  Includes bibliographical references and index.
  ISBN 978-1-107-01866-2 – ISBN 978-1-107-60364-6 (pbk.)
    1. Industrial policy–Case studies. 2. Industrial relations–Case studies. 3. Manpower
  policy–Case studies. 4. Corporate state–Case studies. I. Swank, Duane. II. Title.
  HD3611.M375   2012
  338.9–dc23   2011047477

ISBN 978-1-107-01866-2 Hardback
ISBN 978-1-107-60364-6 Paperback

Cambridge University Press has no responsibility for the persistence or accuracy of URLs
for external or third-party Internet Web sites referred to in this publication and does not
guarantee that any content on such Web sites is, or will remain, accurate or appropriate.

Contents

Figures

Tables

Acknowledgments

We have worked on the central questions of this book for roughly a decade and, as a result, have accumulated many debts and obligations to the institutions and colleagues that have helped us. We are extremely pleased to acknowledge these invaluable contributions here. For financial and logistical support of this project, we wish to thank the following institutions: The Baker Library (Harvard Business School), the Danish Social Science Research Council, the Danish Study of Power and Democracy, the Erhvervsarkivet (Aarhus Denmark), the German Marshall Fund of the United States, the Helen Way Klingler College of Arts and Sciences and the University Committee on Research at Marquette University, the Institute of Advanced Study at Warwick University, the Mugar Library (Boston University), the Modern Records Centre (Warwick University), the National Archives of Scotland, and the Radcliffe Institute (Harvard University).

Numerous colleagues have offered very valuable criticisms, suggestions, and support; although we are fully responsible for the book's shortcomings, our arguments and analyses have been improved in dramatic ways by their comments. We extend our heartfelt thanks to Peri Arnold, Lucio Baccaro, Brian Balough, Uwe Becker, Suzanne Berger, Hartmut Berghoff, Patrick Bernhagen, Mark Blyth, Brian Burgoon, Walter Dean Burnham, Marius Busemeyer, John Campbell, Giovanni Capoccia, Jonathan Chausovsky, Peter Munk Christiansen, David Coates, David Coen, Bob Cox, Thomas Cusack, Bodil Damgaard, Charlie Dannreuther, Frank Dobbin, Patrick Emmenegger, Jeffrey Fear, Jørgen Fink, Walter Friedman, John Gerring, Peter Gourevitch, Wyn Grant, Christopher Green-Pedersen, Justin Greenwood, Jørgen Goul Andersen, Jacob Hacker, John Hall, Peter Hall, Bob Hancke, Hal Hansen, Niamh Hardiman, Gary Herrigel, Alexander Hicks, Helle Holt, Martin Höpner, Martin Jes Iversen, Lawrence Jacobs, Kurt Jacobsen, Geoffrey Jones, Desmond King, Carsten Kjærgaard, Elizabeth Knoll, Jette Steen Knudsen, Tim Knudsen, Bob Kuttner, Jørgen Kvist, Michele Lamont, Morten Larsen, Johannes Lindvall, Richard Locke, Peter Løhmann, Rodney Lowe, Jørgen Stein Madsen, Per Kongshøj Madsen, Mikkel Mailand, Peter May, Sara Jane McCaffrey, Sophie Meunier, Jim Milkey, Sid Milkus, Thomas Paster, Ove Kaj Pedersen, Sofia Perez, Klaus Petersen, Jonas Pontusson, Gerhard Ritter, Neil Rollings,

Anders Rosdal, Bo Rothstein, David Rueda, Ken Scheve, Vivien Schmidt, Lyle Scruggs, Hilary Silver, Steven Skowronek, Mark Smith, John Stephens, Wolfgang Streeck, Lise Togeby, Christine Trampusch, Peter Trubowitz, Gunnar Trumbull, Judy Vichniac, Albert Weale, Erik Wibbels, Mark Wickham-Jones, Graham Wilson, Søren Winter, Christina Wolbrecht, Steve Wuhs, McGee Young, Daniel Ziblatt, Nick Ziegler, and the anonymous reviewers of our work. In addition, we extend our sincere thanks to Eric Crahan, Political Science and History Editor at Cambridge; the book has been improved in innumerable ways as a result of the feedback provided by Cambridge University Press. Finally, we wish to extend a special thanks to our colleagues Torben Iversen of the Department of Government at Harvard, David Soskice of Oxford and Duke Universities, and Kathleen Thelen of the Political Science Department at MIT. Torben, David, and Kathy read the entire manuscript (as well as many of our earlier papers) and offered superb counsel on virtually every aspect of the book, and our manuscript has been improved greatly by their suggestions.

We also extend our thanks for many helpful commentaries to participants on panels at multiple meetings of the American Political Science Association, the Council for European Studies, the Midwest Political Science Association, and the Society for Socio-Economics as well as to participants at seminar series at Aalborg University, Aarhus University, University of Aberdeen, Amsterdam University, University of Bergen, Boston University, CIDE and University of Texas Austin (cosponsored conference), University College Dublin, University College London, Copenhagen Business School, Danish National Institute for Social Science Research, Dartmouth University, Duke University, German Historical Institute, Georgetown University, Goethe Institute, University of Gothenborg, Harvard Business School, Harvard Center for European Studies, Harvard Kennedy School, Maison des Sciences de l'Homme de Paris Nord, Massachusetts Institute of Technology, University of Massachusetts Lowell, Max Planck Institute Cologne, University of North Carolina, University of Notre Dame, Northwestern University, Oxford University, Radcliffe Institute, Southern Danish University, Tampere University, Wake Forest University, University of Warwick, University of Washington, Wissenschaftzentrum Berlin, and Yale University.

In addition, we want to acknowledge two important contributions to our research. First, we have benefitted enormously from the exceptional research assistance of several graduate students. At Marquette University, Jason Charrette, Emanuel Coman, Bowie Hall, Mujtaba Ali Isani, David Ruigh, and Craig Shockley provided invaluable research support. Samantha Fang was deeply involved with the project; Ben Ansell, Rhoda Bilansky, Peter Løhmann, and Thomas Pasteur provided very helpful assistance at critical junctures. Second, we wish to offer a special acknowledgment of the seminal work of Colin Crouch on the origins and evolution of employers' organizations and labor and industrial relations systems. Professor Crouch's work, especially *Industrial Relations and European State Traditions* (Oxford 1993), significantly influenced our thinking and aided us notably in building our historical quantitative data set.

We also wish to acknowledge and thank the Cambridge University Press journals, noted below, for permission to use material previously published in the following articles: Cathie Jo Martin and Duane Swank: "Does the Organization of Capital Matter?" *American Political Science Review* 98 (No. 4, 2004): 593–611; "The Political Origins of

Coordinated Capitalism: Business Organizations, Party Systems, and State Structure in the Age of Innocence." *American Political Science Review* 102 (No. 2, 2008): 181–98; "Gonna Party Like It's 1899: Party Systems and the Origins of Varieties of Coordination." *World Politics* 63 (No. 1, 2011): 78–114. Cathie Jo Martin: "Sectional Parties, Divided Business," *Studies in American Political Development* 20 (No. 2 2006): 160–84; "Corporatism from the Firm Perspective." *British Journal of Political Science* 35 (No. 1 2005): 127–48; "Reinventing Welfare Regimes." *World Politics* 57 (No. 1 2004): 39–69; and (coauthored with Kathleen Thelen) "The State and Coordinated Capitalism: Contributions of the Public Sector to Social Solidarity in Post-industrial Societies," *World Politics* 60 (No. 1 2007): 1–36.

Finally, we wish to express our deep gratitude to our nonacademic support teams. I (Cathie Martin) wish to acknowledge my family and friends who have contributed in so many ways that I can't begin to count them. My husband, Jim Milkey, has made me incredibly happy for 25 years and everything good in my life reflects his love and support. My brilliant sons, Julian and Jack Milkey, are a constant source of insight and amusement: Their skeptical challenging of the conventional wisdom has made me a better scholar. I thank my very wonderful family for putting things into perspective over the years: Mary MacKenzie, Patty and Ike Skelton, Mary and Jim Kozlowski, Robin and John Hanley, Jimmy Martin, Julie and John Sheerman, Ruth and Bob Milkey, John Milkey and Lindley Boegehold, Joanne and Michael Ertel, Mike, Joe, Christina, Kate and Mike, Patty, Jay, Carly, Sidney, Lindsey, Emma, Tess, Camille, Thomas, Dean, Tom, Patsy, Ralph and Lucy Lightbown, and Cassie. My dear friends have also helped to see me through the tough spots: Kari Moe, Cathy Boone, Nora Dudwick, Elisabeth Møller, Bent and Lone Schou, Tim and Birgit Knudsen, Maryse Igout, Peter Munk Christiansen, Mike Lipsky, Susan Eckstein, Paul Osterman, Sarah Robinson, Sal D'Agistino, Michele Lamont, Frank Dobbin, Vivien Schmidt, David Palumb, Peter Erichsen, Michael Segal, Cathy Dunham, Guy and Lisa Molyneux, Kuniko Shiotani, Jim Pope and Nancy Marks, and my fabulous book group: Kari, Rebecca, Sarah, Jo, Rachel, Julie, Susan, Shara, and Marcella. Finally, I want to thank Duane Swank for being such a wonderful coauthor and friend!

I (Duane Swank) wish to thank my wife, Melanie, for her unwavering support and encouragement throughout this project. I also wish to thank Melanie as well as step-son Rob Baker, daughter-in-law Jennifer Baker, mother-in-law Mary Lou Rutledge, and our friends in southeast Wisconsin and central Illinois for the many opportunities to get away from scholarly pursuits and have some real fun. Last, I wish to thank Cathie Jo Martin for her inspiring work ethic, constant good humor, and friendship throughout our labors on this book.

Introduction

On one of the darkest days of the year, an author made her way by multiple trains to a small, wind-swept village in northern Jutland and continued on foot to a factory on the outskirts of town. Battered by relentless wind and sleet (albeit fortified by a piece of Danish pastry en route), she felt like a science fiction protagonist when she suddenly stepped into a utopian vision of the twenty-first century. The factory floor was a hotbed of experimental methods and collaborative spirit, what with its use of the raging winds for power, state-of-the-art technology, and teams of managers and workers striving for continuous productivity improvements. Perhaps most surprising to the uninitiated, however, was the firm's means for obtaining a skilled workforce, the linchpin of the system. Many employees came from the ranks of the long-term unemployed, who had been trained by the government's active labor market program – Denmark's version of welfare reform. Through an elaborate job rotation scheme, the firms' own workers went to school for retraining and the trained unemployed (subsidized by the state) took their places on the shop floor to gain practical experience. Eventually, the unemployed were moved into regular jobs and the cycle began once again.

This happy story of cooperation raises obvious questions: What factors go into the development of dynamic cooperative and relatively egalitarian societies and, in particular, how do governments convince employers that social investments will better their bottom line? High levels of business cooperation were essential to the success of the active labor market programs that sustained the hiring strategy in our wind-swept Danish village. Firms viewed the programs as "win-win" arrangements, that expanded employment, greatly reduced the welfare rolls, allowed companies to fill unproductive positions (with subsidized workers), and maintained labor stability and wage equality (as low-wage positions were subsidized by the state). Yet, whereas the benefits of the programs might seem compelling in hindsight, the great puzzle is how employers came to believe in this win-win logic.

The central goal of our book is to reveal how employers form their social preferences and develop their capacities to act collectively in support of broad social goals. We suggest that employers are social animals and, as such, develop their policy interests in packs; consequently, their business organizations are deeply determinative of

wonderful

I

how they think about the world in general and welfare state programs in particular. For instance, Denmark has centralized, peak employers' associations, which help member firms develop policy positions addressing shared economic, political, and social concerns. The Danish associations inspire greater attention to collective goals than less-organized, comparable organizations in other countries, because the Danish groups facilitate regular meetings with government and labor leaders, and expose members to ideas about the benefits of social policies for productivity growth and labor market stability. Working through these associations, Danish employers helped the state to develop the labor market policies in the early 1990s to attack unemployment: managers participated in designing the programs, protected them from political attacks by the right, and implemented them by hiring the long-term unemployed. Some firms were motivated by a sense of corporate social responsibility, but there was also a strong sense that the changes were important to securing high rates of economic growth. In marked contrast, both American and British employers are hampered in realizing collective concerns, because their weak and fragmented umbrella interest groups fail to act on members' preferences.

The pivotal role of institutions in nurturing employers' social policy preferences raises additional questions. Where did these peak organizations come from and why did rather similar national economies develop such different forms of associations for business representation? Are institutions for coordination really responsible for shaping employers' views of social policy or are these institutions themselves evidence of some deeper cultural predispositions that have brought employers both to organize collectively and to view social interventions in a more benign light? How are these organizational forms being sustained and, perhaps, transformed with the transition to the postindustrial economy? Of course, small countries have an easier time producing high levels of coordination than large ones; therefore, it is not surprising that larger countries – lacking geographically-concentrated social networks – would rely more on anonymous markets to facilitate economic exchange. Yet great diversity exists even in the set of relatively small countries; for example, Sweden and Switzerland have very different competitive strategies, social policies and industrial relations systems. We search for the deep roots of this divergence.

We begin our story of employers' struggle for political self-definition with the origins of national, multisectoral employers' associations in the period between the 1890s and World War I. This was a moment of shifting political identities in which increased industrialization, global trade, and the emerging factory system motivated employers to seek *national* industrial development policies to further their ambitions in global markets and to manage the chaos associated with rapid economic change. Employers everywhere moved away from their attachment to free market liberalism to pursue national policy solutions to the challenges of industrial development and, to this end, formed national employers' associations to facilitate unified action for collective goals. Yet, while these peak associations had remarkably similar ambitions, their ultimate forms varied widely across countries. In some nations, national business associations were highly organized, encompassing a large share of the potential membership and facilitating routinized engagement on the issues of the day. These highly structured groups enabled employers to cooperate with each other and with representatives from labor and government. In other countries, these national associations remained loosely-organized and fragmented, and there was little cooperation either within business or among employers and other social actors.

Countries' varying capacities to produce highly organized employers' associations came not from dramatic differences in business desires, culture, and attitudes toward government, but rather reflected the interplay of party politics and the governmental structures that set the rules of the game. Politicians eager to woo business support for their own party ambitions were (often secret) leaders in the formation of these encompassing associations and, consequently, the interplay of party competition mattered enormously to the ultimate signature forms of the organization (a fact largely overlooked in the academic literature). In particular, the number and centralization of political parties mattered enormously to politicians' willingness to nurture strong associations. Countries with multiple parties created incentives for right party leaders (sympathetic to business) to delegate high levels of policy-making authority to the private associations representing employers and workers because they believed that their business allies would win more in negotiations with labor than in legislative battles facing both worker and agricultural interests. With time, associations in these countries developed as the legitimate representatives of their business communities and gained significant capacities for self-regulation and political engagement with the economic and social agendas of their governments.

The structure of two-party systems held no such incentives for the delegation of power or the strengthening of the collective business voice; consequently, the peak associations gained little control over policy making. The early disappointment of employers anxious to evolve a system of self-regulation led to the formation of new groups hoping to solve the problems of business representation; this proliferation of groups eventually produced a highly fragmented system of representation with limited coordination among diverse sectors of the economy.

Today, these peak employers' associations face an uncertain future in the postindustrial world, and, once again, their fate lies largely in political hands. An essential question of the twenty-first century is whether the institutions for coordination established during the golden age of manufacturing will persist and whether states can continue to build social pacts and new coalitions of broad majorities for social needs. Postindustrial production often requires a highly skilled workforce, yet global competition demands greater efficiencies and flexibility: Whereas the one might necessitate a strengthening of collective labor market institutions, the other might well precipitate the atomization of social life. Given employers' associations' centrality in shaping corporate responses to social needs, much hangs on the survival of these coordinating institutions.

Countries' capacities to sustain coordinating associations to respond to the challenges of the postindustrial age are influenced, in fact, by the very same features of government that enabled states to create coordinated responses to the advent of advanced industrialized capitalism. Again, the structure of partisan competition matters greatly to the endurance of business institutions for coordination and the state continues to be crucial to class formation. Countries with centralized governments and multiparty systems have produced stronger, larger welfare states and bureaucrats in these robust public sectors have an easier time of sustaining business organization. Big government has had a positive impact on institutions for coordination and has helped to sustain processes of consensual negotiation and cooperation between the state and the labor market partners; in turn, these processes have helped participants to find in the postindustrial economy a new equilibrium between growth and equity.

This book comes at an uncertain point in the trajectory of advanced capitalism. While coordination as a political and economy philosophy has been at odds with the fundamental premises underlying public policymaking in America for the past thirty years, it may be precisely what is needed with the faltering of finance capitalism, the glaring defects of deregulation as a political philosophy, and the evident need for collective redirection at this critical economic juncture. Politicians of the recent past glorified laissez-faire individualism, promoted (if not achieved) small government, repudiated social spending, and sought to release the free market to work its magic on everything from home mortgages to air traffic control; however, deregulation lost something of its sheen after the financial crisis in 2008 and wise men are casting about for new models of capitalism. Political coordination has been viewed by some as necessary to collective redirection at critical junctures in capitalist development.[1] At issue is how countries can best manage the transition from one period of relative economic stability to the next, what role do mechanisms for coordination play in facilitating this transition, and how can this transition be managed with the least damage to the social fabric.

We are persuaded that political coordination helps to produce the social supports that enable a transition to a new stage of capitalist development: The capacity for organization has an important impact on the emergence of new forms of economic productivity and on the state's ability to sustain relative equality and some measure of redistribution. As the Danish example suggests, coordination and social harmony can lead to economic prosperity *and* productivity: In some cases, what's good for society is good for General Motors. Fearing that the transition to services would bring declining productivity growth rates and threaten the fiscal solvency of the state, Danish government actors and their private sector allies have sought to create a new, green encompassing economy that would have room for nearly all – including the old, unskilled, and disabled – as productive workers. Evidence suggests that this strategy has produced high levels of economic growth, while accelerating industrial restructuring and protecting higher levels of social solidarity. For example, Denmark ranked third on the Global Competitiveness Index's top ten economies in 2007–2008, had the lowest level of inequality in disposable family income, and had a very high rate of employment among the working-age population.[2]

In offering insights into the determinants of coordination, our book has implications for struggles to sustain equality and growth in the real world. While our venture is rooted in substantial scholarship – we offer extensive original research and theory to back up our somewhat controversial assertions – we also wish to speak to everyone who is concerned with the fate of collective societies. We hope to capture the voices of the men and women who are struggling to figure out how to make a buck, to cultivate productive workers, *and* to foster a fair and just society. At the dawn of the twenty-first

[1] Gamble 2009.
[2] Economy Watch; OECD 2006.

century, life in even some advanced industrial countries often feels frightening, atavistic and mean. The United States is trapped in severe economic distress and political disunity. A thirty-year political commitment to unbridled free market individualism has torn asunder the social fabric: Guarantees of social protection against impoverishment are gone, and wages as a percentage of the GDP have reached an all-time low. Life is grim for many American workers, and employers often share these worries, especially those in the growing service sectors who are unwilling or unable to move production offshore.

Our work also has relevance for the understanding of equality and for why advanced economies at very similar levels of national income exhibit stark differences in their distribution of resources. We believe employers to be critical actors in these distributional struggles: Managers may sway politics to the right toward individualistic, deregulated solutions, yet employers may also endorse higher levels of economic and social coordination. In the former case, the state may well be captured by narrow sectarian concerns – a story all too vividly revealed in the saga of finance capitalism; yet in the latter case, employers may give crucial support to state coalitions in support of social solidarity. Thus, the question of employers' ability to retain high levels of coordination in the face of dramatic social and economic change is relevant to social science theory and social solidarity alike.

I

Collective Political Engagement and the Welfare State

> What counts in making a happy marriage is not so much how compatible you are, but how you deal with incompatibility.
>
> Leo Tolstoy

Introduction

What magical ingredients create societies that seem to have it all, in achieving their policy goals with a balance of efficiency and equality, economic growth, and social security? Is there something in the bubbling brew of civic engagement that permits some countries to obtain collective goals with benefits for a broad cross section of society? Why are some nations better able than others to reinvent their institutional commitments to growth and equality at points of major economic transformation? Can business managers be persuaded to develop strategic preferences for public policies and to sign onto the social deals that seek to balance economic growth and social protections? If so, what factors bring employers to cooperate with workers and other social groups, rather than to view the world as a stage for pitched economic strife?

Tolstoy's quote about happy marriages at the beginning of this chapter captures a central theme of this book: Processes of collective engagement matter. The signature way that people come together to solve problems has enormous impact on whether they make it through the trials and tribulations of marital life. In like manner, nations evolve characteristic processes of collective political engagement among citizens and groups; and while these processes are themselves a work in progress, a characteristic manner of problem solving seems to endure, even as it evolves, across epochs.

 We believe that the mystery of productive *and* egalitarian societies lies, in some measure, with the attitudes and social identities of business, and most critically, with the structures of collective political engagement – the political party systems and encompassing peak employers' associations – that incorporate societal interests into the policy-making process. The ways that actors come together to grapple with joint

6

concerns (i.e., the dimensions of collective decision-making forums) set boundaries for subsequent solutions. Divergent business (and labor) aptitudes for coordination are a major factor underlying variations in countries' capacities to fend off the tragedy of the social commons while sustaining economic performance. Other factors matter to national performance on social measures, and we emphasize the crucial contributions of the power of organized labor to demand social protections and of employers' needs for workforce skills. Yet we believe that the political-organizational story of employers' struggles to grasp their social interests is a vital but relatively unknown contributor to the rise of labor market coordination, national skills systems and modern welfare states. Our book tells the tale of the development of encompassing employers' associations; the effect of these associations on employers' views toward social policies; the impact of labor market coordination on equality, redistribution, and economic growth; and the mechanisms for social institutional renewal at points of economic transformation.

Advanced industrial economies sort into three types of labor market coordination with distinctive encompassing peak associations that unify diverse sectors of the economy and that provide an interface between managers, government, and workers. In the *macrocorporatist* model countries, such as Denmark, employers are organized into hierarchically ordered groups, and the peak association negotiates broad political agreements with labor and the state through collective bargaining and tripartite policy-making committees. In countries with *sectoral coordination*, such as Germany, employers wield power largely at the industry level: Employers' associations within specific industries engage in significant coordination with corresponding labor unions but the encompassing, multisector, peak associations are much weaker, and the state is largely absent from these negotiations. In *pluralist* countries, such as the United States, employers are represented by a panoply of conflicting groups, with many purporting to aggregate business interests and with none having much policy-making authority.

These varied types of encompassing peak employers' associations are the dependent variable in the first part of our book, as we determine why some countries produce highly coordinated groups while others do not. Around the onset of the twentieth century, party leaders and bureaucrats on the right created peak, multisector business associations to preserve their political control against rising democratization and to garner support for their industrial development agendas. Encompassing associations were deeply influenced by the structure of party competition: Government actors led in the formation of these associations, and their willingness to cede power to these groups reflected their own electoral and policy goals. The path to cooperation was paved with subtle ironies and unintended consequences: Countries creating the strongest associations did so, initially, for undemocratic reasons – to evade labor radicalism and to sidestep the parliamentary process. Yet high levels of coordination eventually produced the most egalitarian of societies, and the structure of party competition contributed to the ongoing renewal of these associations, particularly at points of major economic change.

In the second part of the book, different types of encompassing peak employers' associations become an independent variable that helps to explain the social preferences of employers as well as cross-national distinctions in socioeconomic outcomes. Employers' positions depend on the way they are brought into political debates, therefore variation in firms' social preferences reflect diverse types of peak encompassing employers' organizations. Somewhat surprisingly, more positive business views toward social policies are found in countries with more highly organized business associations, while countries with weakly organized business groups fail to aggregate employers' collective preferences and diminish business support for the welfare state.

The expression of employers' political preferences, in turn, has a profound impact on societal spending on social protections and on nations' capacities to develop efficacious policies to create human capital infrastructure, to augment economic growth with productive labor, to expand employment, to protect citizens from social risks, and to create the relative equality that contributes to labor market peace. Under some conditions, employers can be induced to join political coalitions in support of social programs and relatively egalitarian outcomes because they believe that these policies will contribute to higher levels of economic growth. High levels of coordination that bring together expansive political coalitions of actors address the needs of a broader cross section of society and are less likely to exclude significant portions of the population from the benefits of skills, employment, and economic self-reliance. Countries with higher levels of coordination between the labor market partners and with the state have a greater capacity to maximize cooperation between left and right, to focus on practical needs rather than ideological conflict, to avoid contentious zero-sum warring over distributional outcomes, to minimize concessions to special interests, and to adapt quickly to economic crises.

Finally, the structures for collective political engagement have powerful implications for the life cycle of political and societal institutions – their births, reinvention in response to shifting economic challenges, and capacities to resist decay. Recent theories of institutional variation and change have fruitfully gravitated toward two ideal types: (a) punctuated equilibria models of discontinuous change in which path dependencies are set into place at critical junctures and (b) incremental adjustments that add up to long-term significant change, as emergent political coalitions convert institutions to new purposes or allow former functions and constituencies to fade away.[1]

We applaud the strong analytic salience of these models but suggest that structures of collective political engagement have a significant impact on both types of change. At moments of historical contingency, possibilities for radical reform and new path dependencies are shaped most profoundly by the political rules of the game that help us to construct our collective, political selves. These forums set boundaries on the range of political coalitions that are influential to processes of incremental institutional change. Thus, our book's major theoretical contribution is to reveal the primacy of the political in formation of the business class, in processes of capitalist development, and in broader questions of institutional change.

Our Scholarly Inspirations

Scholars dating back to the Enlightenment have recognized the centrality of forums for political engagement in the evolution of modern societies, yet diverse modes of engagement have taken a back seat to other explanations for cross-national variation

---

[1] Skocpol 1985; Cappocia and Ziblatt 2010; Streeck and Thelen 2005; Hacker 2002.

across advanced, industrial economies. We seek to reaffirm the primacy of political institutions and, in particular, the centrality of those institutions that foster collective *lovely* decision making in economic and social policy. We draw inspiration from three lines of social science inquiry that are relevant to the cross-national variations in employers' organization, social preferences, welfare state outcomes, and national capacities for institutional renewal.

First, scholars of business history and the varieties of capitalism recognize that (1) employers sometimes articulate preferences for social protections, particularly when these policies are linked to investment in skills and the human capital of workers. Second, students of social construction, networks and corporatism suggest that employ- (2) ers' views about social protections and industrial cooperation are deeply influenced by their business associations and firm-level institutions. Third, historical institutionalists (3) recognize that the agency of political leaders and state structures have been crucial to the organization of societal interests in issues related to the political economy.

Labor Activism, Skills, and Varieties of Capitalism

A distinguished group of scholars rightfully emphasize the dimensions of the working class – activism and skills – to account for cross-national variations in the emergence of social protections, relative equality, and the organization of employers. Employers may organize collectively and/or accept limited social provisions to resist labor activism, in the form of highly organized unions or powerful left parties. Managers generally reject policies that increase costs of production in wages or taxes; yet when faced with strong labor opposition, they may organize to bargain collectively or tolerate social concessions to labor. Therefore, degrees of union organization and left party control have a significant impact on welfare state outcomes.[2] Moreover, some individual firms are more willing to make concessions to labor, due to greater harm by disruptions in their (highly mechanized) production processes, lower wage costs as a percentage of total production costs and interest in governmental benefits that impose comparable costs on competitors.[3] Ethnic and religious diversity reduces working class unity and dampens the organization of labor market partners and welfare state development.[4]

Firms also recognize a positive contribution to firm productivity of social provisions that nurture worker skills, health, or other aspects of human capital. The elegant, highly influential "varieties of capitalism" model argues that social protections are *(CMEs)* particularly relevant to employers in "coordinated market economies" (CMEs), where production strategies for high-end market niches rely on blue-collar workers with specific skills that require extensive training programs. Employers promote social benefits that guarantee the provision of these specific skills, guard against turnover, and protect their investment; moreover, workers are more likely to defer employment to develop specific skills when offered unemployment and employment protections. In "liberal *LMEs* market economies" (LMEs), Fordist production strategies rely on less highly skilled workers, labor-management relations are contentious, and social protections are spotty,

---

[2] Korpi and Shalev 1979; Korpi and Palme 2003; Huber and Stephens 2001; Scruggs and Lange 2002; Castles 1998; Paster 2011; Kuo 2010; Hyman 2001, Schrank 2009, Block 1977; Lindblom 1977.
[3] Jaccoby 1998; Ferguson 1995; Gordon, 1995.
[4] Davis 2000; Manow and Van Kersbergen 2009; King 2007.

as neither workers nor employers have incentives to invest in specific skills.[5] Insights into the linkages between social protections and skills are immensely important in helping us to understand employers' material interests in social policies and in driving organization for collective benefits. In addition, even though debates over the relative contributions of business and labor have been periodically a bit heated, many scholars recognize that positive business support for the welfare state does not negate the central role of labor leadership in the development and maintenance of strong social protection systems.[6] Firms' development of social benefits for their own workers also contribute to the evolution of public sector welfare states.[7]

This highly stylized, parsimonious model is less adept at capturing diversity at the national, regional, sectoral, and firm levels, and at providing insights into institutional evolution and change. Critics are troubled by the concept of institutional complementarities and by the view that institutions are robust determinants of strategic action. Nations within models vary on multiple dimensions and have diverse types of complementarities; thus, while Scandinavian countries have high levels of both coordination and equality, continental nations such as Germany are highly coordinated but much less egalitarian. Models mask significant subnational diversity: sectors and institutional domains are shaped by different historically specific economic orders. Dualism rather than a singular strategy of economic competition characterizes some countries. Even firms within the same industry hold to radically different patterns of cooperation, reflecting their historical legacies and institutional capacities. The proliferation of transnational rules and structures also shape firms' competitive environments and strategic choices. Nor do the two static categories suggest much about institutional change, the origins of diverse systems, and their future capacities to sustain high levels of coordination against the game-changing rise of the postindustrial economy.[8] Questions abound about the future capacity of labor market coordination to resist the disorienting impacts of deindustrialization. While defenders of VOC theory see persistence, critics note an erosion of coordination and drift toward "liberalization." The model's theoretical difficulties in accounting for institutional change contribute to this lack of consensus.[9]

The approach is also criticized for neglecting political influences on firms' strategies for coordination, although recent scholarship crucially emphasizes the complementarities between proportional party systems and coordinated market economies, grounded in the mutual interests of both employers and party leaders in high specific

[5] Hall and Soskice 2001; Martin 2000; Iversen 1999; Estevez-Abe et al. 2001; Thelen 2004; Manow 1998; Ebbinghaus and Hassel 2000; Martin and Swank 2004; Gourevitch and Shin 2005; Wood 2001; Regini 1995. The varieties of capitalism categorization are closely connected to the conception of welfare regimes (Esping-Andersen 1990), in which the structure of policy rather than the firms' competitive strategies influence employers' use of the welfare state. See also King 1995.

[6] See Korpi 2006; Swenson 2002 on the former, Chapman 2007 on the latter. Moreover, macrocorporatism, by definition, entails sustained engagement between densely organized, centralized labor and employers' organizations (Hicks and Swank 1992).

[7] Baldwin 1990; Osterman 1995; Martin 2000; Hacker 2002; Mares 2003; Leimbruper 2008.

[8] Martin and Thelen 2007; Höpner 2007; Lane and Wood 2009; Morgan 2005; Deeg and Jackson 2007; Amable 2003; Busemeyer and Trampush 2011; Martin 2000; Berk and Schneiberg 2005; Whitley 1999; Ackers and Wilkinson 2003; Herrigel 1996; Djelic and Quack 2003; Hancke et al. 2007.

[9] Swank 2002; Hall and Gingerich 2004; Pontusson 1997; Howell 2003; Campbell and Pedersen 2007.

skills. Politicians in PR party systems represent well-organized economic interests, do not poach voters from other parties, and participate in coalition governments; therefore, they have a less acute need to focus solely on short-term electoral interests and are better positioned to work toward longer-term goals and urge capitalists to do the same.[10] Yet questions remain about the origins and diversity of these interlocking political economic arrangements. We turn to other analytic traditions to grasp how employers' preferences for skills, social protections, and coordination evolve and change; why these preferences vary across nations, industries, and firms; and the role of political structures and agency in these processes.

Networks, Associations, and the Construction of Preferences

Literatures on economic sociology and corporatism emphasize the impact of institutions on the social construction of business interests. These models recognize that a firm may have multiple objectives, several positions are conceivably in its interests, and its decision making is constrained by bounded rationality; consequently, even firms with the same structural characteristics often diverge in their expressed preferences for public policy. This differs from the VOC literature, which views firms' preferences as grounded in material incentives arising from political economic institutions. Perception is important to when companies view social supports as contributing to their bottom lines, and when they believe that the benefits of social programs (in added productivity) outweigh their additional costs to the production process.

Economic sociologists investigate the organizational structures and networks that introduce new ideas, and help employers to form political identities and policy preferences.[11] When organized collectively, managers from diverse sectors come to identify with one another, to set a priority on shared concerns, and possibly to take action. Thus, business associations both represent members' interests and shape preferences.[12]

Yet, not all groups will make employers favor social policy: Belonging to the Federalist Society or the Hell's Angels, for example, is not likely to draw one to look favorably on state intervention. Certain structural characteristics of groups are more likely to engender positive views of collective social solutions among their members than others, and scholars divide industrial relations institutions into two broad groupings: corporatist and pluralist associations. Institutional characteristics of scope, exclusivity, and degree of centralization distinguish these "pluralist" and "corporatist" models of association and influence how employers engage politically to achieve collective goals. Corporatist groups, found in many continental European countries, are centralized, functionally specific, hierarchically ordered, encompassing, and have a unitary peak employers' association, that unites firms and cooperates closely with labor and with government. Pluralist groups (e.g., in America) overlap in function, are narrow in scope, are not exclusive representatives of their members, and are not hierarchically organized into a centralized peak association.[13]

---

[10] Swank 2002; Iversen and Soskice 2007; Martin and Swank 2008.

[11] Penrose 1959; Fligstein 1990; Dobbin 2009; DiMaggio and Powell 1991; Hillman and Hitt 1999; Best 1990.

[12] Moe 1987, 277; Granovetter 1985, 481; Mansbridge 1980; Friedland and Robertson 1990, 32; Martin, 2000; Turner, 1982.

[13] Katzenstein 1985; Schmitter 1981; Liphardt and Crepas 1991; Wilson 1990; Grant 1989.

Scholars of corporatism initially focused on labor and on the articulation of broad group concerns in wage setting and collective bargaining processes, yet variations in ideal types also have an impact on employers' preferences for welfare state programs.[14] As discussed later, corporatist groups are more likely than pluralist groups to promote collective action because they direct participants' attention to broader, shared concerns. Although significant material cleavages divide employers in all advanced, industrialized countries and business interests are not a priori less diverse in countries with a high level of corporate organization, a corporatist aggregation of interests allows employers more easily to find common ground.[15]

Critiques of the corporatist literature parallel those of varieties of capitalism in that the bimodal structure hardly seems equipped to capture the range of diversity among advanced capitalist democracies. Moreover, in its initial formulation, corporatism suggested a functionalist response to the "ungovernability" of modern societies and a non-zero-sum solution to class conflict. Yet the creation and renewal of collective institutions is not always functional in solving dislocations of capitalist development and nations demonstrate different capacities for constructing and renewing institutions for coordination.[16] Corporatist theory is also somewhat static, and tells us little about the origins of high levels of coordination or the capacities of some national peak employers' associations to endure. Industrial restructuring, deindustrialization, and the growing gap between skilled and unskilled sectors complicate economywide collective bargaining and associational capacities to reconcile the diverse interests of industrial and service sectors.[17] Yet some corporatist institutions are surprisingly resilient.[18] Thus, while groups and networks shed light on the processes by which employers develop their preferences, one needs a theory of institutional change to explain the origins and renewal of diverse types of interest representation.

Historical Institutionalism and the State in the Construction of the Social Classes
Finally, we are inspired by historical institutional analysis, and our interest in "society building" draws from important work on "state building," punctuated equilibria models, the role of agency at critical junctures, and slow processes of incremental institutional change. Scholars of institutional change utilizing punctuated equilibria models suggest that the resolution of political conflicts at critical junctures create enduring path dependencies and analyze the specific political issues and agency at the points of institutional and policy creation. Outcomes are often unpredictable at an early point in time, yet choices taken at critical junctures establish paths with increasing returns.[19] The strategic interventions of government bureaucrats and party leaders have great significance at these moments (when both the range and impacts of possible outcomes

---

[14] Streeck 1992; Martin 1995; 2000; Swank and Martin 2001; Visser and Hermerijck 1997; Trampusch 2010.
[15] Berger 1981; Katzenstein 1985; Crouch 1993; Rothstein 2000; Bernhagen 2007; Offe 2003.
[16] Schmitter 1981; Goldthorpe 1984; Streeck 2009; Martin and Thelen 2007.
[17] See Colin Crouch 1993 on origins. On pressures, see Crepaz 1992; Huber and Stephens 2001; Pontusson 1992; Wallerstein, Golden, and Lange 1997; Scruggs and Lange 2002; Coates 1999.
[18] Wallerstein and Golden 1998; Swank 2002; Traxler 2000; Treu 1998.
[19] Pierson and Skocpol 2002; Weir 1992; Orren and Skowronek 2004.

Is this financial crisis a critical juncture?

are expanded) and foster the evolution of democratic institutions.[20] Ideas may also play a transformational role at these critical junctures in inspiring radically new directions in policy.[21] Business historians have produced fascinating work on the importance of agency at critical junctures to the origins of the institutions underlying modern capitalist models. Criticizing theories that overstate the historical economic and labor market differences between the liberal and coordinated countries, they emphasize the specific historical political context and importance of agency in the evolution of capitalism and the creation of skills systems.[22]

Another strand of analysis points to the incremental shifts underlying apparent stability through processes such as drift and conversion and suggests that punctuated equilibria models explain continuity more successfully than change. Endogenous change may threaten extant systems of coordination: Institutional rust, erosion, and decay result from shifting actors, new priorities, and new purposes, and change transpires through erosion, conversion, and layering. The advent of neoliberalism was, itself, a response to the endogenous erosion of state capacity rather than to the exogenous pressures of globalization. Policy systems can be hijacked by new political coalitions, which transform goals and impacts, even while formal structures prevail.[23]

We ascribe to these theories but suggest that variations in the collective processes of political engagement shape the manner in which policy legacies are reinterpreted at critical junctures and delimit the range of political coalitions that might contribute to incremental institutional change. Certainly, agency at critical junctures establishes new paths, and new political coalitions capture existing institutions for their own political purposes, yet political structures of engagement constrain strategic action. Countries have characteristic ways of solving social and economic problems, and these reflect the ways that social actors come together with government actors to negotiate new policies or even institutional arrangements. These rules of political engagement exert a strong influence on institutional adaptation, for example, in reinventing welfare state regimes for the needs of the postindustrial economy. Thus, within the set of institutions governing the political economy, we give preference to those that bring actors together in collective negotiation – industrial relations organizations together with political parties – as most essential to processes of institutional change.

In the following pages, we offer our own models to account for cross-national distinctions in the organization of social class and public policy outcomes, keeping in mind the political economist's attention to skills, the network sociologist's attention to groups and the historical institutionalist's attention to state agency and structures. We emphasize the following key points.

First, cross-national comparisons should differentiate between the public sphere of policy making (through legislation and party politics) and the private sphere of industrial self-regulation, coordination and representation by the social partners, embodied

[20] Berger 1981; Gourevitch 1986; Martin 1991; Capoccia and Ziblatt 2010; Berman 2006; Bermeo and Amoretti 2004; Ahmed 2010.

[21] Hall and Taylor 1996; Schmidt 2002; Blyth 2001; Campbell and Pedersen 2007; Culpepper 2003.

[22] Kocka 1981; Berghahn 2007; Blackbourn 1998; Jones 2000; Fear 2005; Herrigel 1996; Fellman et al. 2008; Iversen 2011; Abelshauser 2005; Anderson 2000; Dunleavy and Welskopp 2007; Rollings 2008; Andersen and Jacobsen 2008.

[23] Hacker 2002; Thelen 2004; Streeck and Thelen 2005; Mahoney 2010.

in the encompassing peak employers' associations and their labor counterparts. Indeed, what sets the coordinated European economies apart is the enormous import of their private systems of policy making vis-à-vis public legislative processes; these matter enormously to policy outcomes and have powerful impacts on preferences for social policy and redistribution.

Second, there are, never the less, strong complementarities between these public and private spheres, and in particular, between proportional representation party systems and coordinated market economies. Political economists root these complementarities in the strong motivations of both politicians and the social partners to restrain short-term preferences for electoral victory and rent-seeking rewards in favor of longer-term interests in the production of high specific skills that are necessary to a high-growth equilibrium.[24] But following sociologists, we also emphasize the collective action and cognitive impacts of diverse institutional arrangements that facilitate the realization (or not) of longer-term economic interests. The institutional design characteristics of party systems and encompassing labor market associations for the social partners have a substantial impact on the probabilities of groups constructing and realizing their material interests in various ways. For example, a key reason why coordinated countries tend to produce a more favorable balance between growth and equality is that well-organized social partners as stakeholders have world views molded by their representative organizations. Highly coordinated associations aid in the resistance to rent-seeking behavior by both individual capitalists and the state.

Third, our work emphasizes the primacy of the political in processes of institutional evolution and change. The state constitutes the location of political conflict over the evolution of the political economy: the rules and structures of political competition set the boundaries of contestation and influence the incentives of both politicians and managers. The nation state is also important because models of coordination become institutionalized at the end of the nineteenth-century, when national systems of labor market coordination first developed to cope with the expansion of global economic exchange. Pockets of coordination existed in most countries at the local and regional level before this critical juncture; however, countries' diverse rules of political competition had vastly different implications for coordination. Thus, while the various models of capitalism cannot account for all diversity at the firm and sectoral levels, national systems of representation and collective bargaining do have a special impact on the provision of collective social goods.

Finally, this is decidedly not a functionalist process: Although both party leaders and social partners sometimes take measures to achieve policy ends, they almost always act to maximize their power and control. For example, when party leaders on the right initially encouraged the development of strong encompassing employer organizations around the end of the nineteenth century, they were motivated by desires both to secure industrial development policies and (perhaps more importantly) to resist democratization and to secure political control against a possible coalition of farmers and labor. Employers participated in active labor market policies in the 1990s, in part, to retain their jurisdictional policy control against a possible invasion by the state. Thus, these models evolved less because party leaders and employers pursued functional

---

[24] Garrett 1998; Swank 2002; Iversen and Soskice 2007; Martin and Swank 2008.

solutions to their needs for certain types of skills than for political reasons, although the positive impacts of these political economic arrangements became more apparent with time. The *political* underpinnings of these institutional arrangements account for why countries have rather different political economies at various points in time and why one sees dysfunctional behavior even in high equilibrium societies.

Varieties of Encompassing Employers' Associations

Our book delves into the recurring struggles among employers to define their collective social entities and to nurture institutional capacities at critical turning points in the evolution of modern capitalist democracies, and into the impact of these struggles on social and economic outcomes. We articulate and investigate four dependent variables: (a) the origins of peak, multisector associations and attendant labor-market coordination during the rise of industrial capitalism, (b) the adaptation of these associations during the transition to the postindustrial economy, (c) the impact of the diverse types of associations and labor market coordination on employers' preferences for welfare state spending at the firm level and cross-national variation in spending at the aggregate level, and (d) the impact of diverse types of labor market coordination on equality and redistribution.

The empirical underpinnings of our story about business organization and public policy are sweeping in both their historical and cross-national reach, as we use a mixed-methods approach that combines broad cross-national quantitative analyses with historical archival case studies and extensive interviews with firms. First, we utilize large-N statistical analysis to test hypotheses on the causes of our dependent variables. With techniques such as pooled time-series cross-sectional analysis, we conduct "variable-oriented" analysis, using quantitative measures of political economic phenomena to generate probabilistic assessments of theoretical propositions. Large-N tests of hypotheses have substantial capacity to generalize findings about important theoretical assertions; yet these frequently reveal little about the actual preferences, motivations, and interpretations of events by political actors or the exact causal sequences that undergird theoretical relationships of interest.[25]

Second, to reveal underlying processes and to bolster our findings about the formation of employers' associations, we engage in intensive, historical analysis using primary source material to investigate the formation of employers' associations in four model countries: Denmark, Germany, United Kingdom, and United States. Our four polities represent "ideal types" of levels of employer organization and forms of coordination as determined by mixes of our core independent variables (discussed later). These case investigations allow us to demonstrate that the causal argument had its intended effect using process tracing, or the careful temporal reconstruction of the cases. We identify intermediate steps between cause and effect and use our qualitative data to construct analytic narratives to reveal the underlying incentives that produce action.

[25] Ragin 1987; King, Keohane, and Verba 1994; Brady and Collier 1994; Lieberman 2005; Mjøset and Clausen 2007.

Third, we conduct interviews with 107 randomly selected firms in Denmark and Britain to understand the microlevel dynamics by which employers come to support and to participate in state social programs (in this case, for the long-term unemployed). We also cite Moira Nelson's findings for the German case, in which she replicated our Danish study. We match independent variables at the cross-national and firm levels; therefore, our firm-level findings bolster our quantitative analysis of the contribution of business organization to welfare state spending and shed light onto the microprocesses of business preference formation.

We begin with a discussion of the peak employers' associations at the center of our story: These multisector business organizations encompass many industries and often include sectoral trade associations among their members; thus, they typically claim to represent the highest aggregation of business interests in the land. Encompassing employers associations potentially encourage three types of nonmarket coordination: between *employers and labor* in industrial relations, between *business and government* (with labor) in political engagement, and cooperation among *firms* on production issues.[26] Systems differ in the formality and centrality of their cooperative linkages among actors in the degree and level of coordination (peak, sector, firm), and in the degree to which the same group covers all functions.

First, industrial relations between *employers and labor* may entail collective bargains coordinated across sectors and covering virtually all workers, but collective bargains may also be devolved to the industry level or pursued by individual firms with their workers. Second, in *business-government* relations, employers may enter the policy-making process through formal, centralized tripartite commissions or ministry boards that set a wide range of public policies, or through informal, ad hoc and individualistic interventions as when individual firms provide expertise, lobby, and donate campaign funds to legislators but make no promises to abide by subsequent policy outcomes. Third, nonmarket cooperation within the business community may be quite low or quite high; in the latter case, individual firms engage in a great deal of formal collaboration – even with their competitors – on economic activities that promise to enhance the productivity and competitiveness of all (such as technology transfers, R & D, or vocational training.) These functions may be located in a single encompassing employers' association (which coordinates a hierarchy of sectoral industry associations) or in several such groups. Some countries have functionally divided peak multisector employers' associations, with one devoted to intraindustry cooperation on trade, technology sharing, and policy making and the other with formal authority over collective bargaining and industrial relations.

We sort encompassing employers' associations and their associated forms of labor market coordination into three ideal types. First, macrocorporatist systems of business representation have centralized, functionally specific, highly organized groups that focus on broad collective concerns in strong, nonlegislative channels for cooperation with labor and government. In Scandinavia, for example, very strong peak associations have considerable influence over industrial sector groups in a hierarchical,

[26] Soskice 1990; Traxler 2000; Traxler, Blaschke, and Kittle 2001; Traxler and Huemer 2007; Treu, 1992.

functionally specific system. The peak employers' associations and unions are highly centralized (with a high level of power by peak federations over members), coordinated among collective bargaining units, and integrated in national policy forums. These encompassing associations cooperate closely with government and labor at the highest level and firms are more likely to induce policies through the collective bargaining process or in tripartite advisory commissions of administrative governmental agencies than through the legislative process. The state plays a strong coordinating role in sustaining national collective bargaining, and the highly organized associations offer governments an institutional vehicle through which to build business support and compliance for social welfare initiatives.[27]

A second ideal type, "sector coordination," predominantly entails cooperation between firms and workers (or among firms) at a more intermediate, sectoral level, and this cooperation may operate without sustained state participation. This form of coordination, found in Germany and elsewhere, entails tightly coordinated connections among firms and investors, cooperation among competing firms within the same industrial sector for research and development, long-term relations between purchasers and suppliers, and enterprise-based labor-management cooperation. Whereas both countries with strong macrocorporatist institutions and sector coordination may have relatively high levels of coordinated collective bargaining and tripartite negotiations, countries with sector coordination have a smaller role for the state in policy development and less-encompassing structures. Countries with sector coordination also tend to have a greater division of labor between the realms of industrial relations and interfirm cooperation over trade and other business-related policies at the peak level. Thus, Germany has preserved dual sets of organizations – for business promotion and industrial relations – since the early twentieth century, while in the macrocorporatist Denmark, an encompassing employers' association quite early gained formal responsibility for unifying employers in various spheres. Although macrocorporatism and sector coordination have often been lumped together, we draw this distinction because highly cooperative engagement between employers and labor can occur at various levels of the economy (sector versus peak), and the associations for industrial relations and politics/economic activities may be unified or separated and may include varying degrees of guidance by the state.[28]

Third, in pluralist systems of business representation, the encompassing employers' associations (and usually there are more than one) are very weak and engaged in limited cooperation with other actors. In the United States and other liberal countries, firms belong to multiple groups and the groups overlap in function, are narrow in scope, are not the exclusive representatives of their members, and are not hierarchically organized into a centralized peak association. Few formal channels for coordination join business in consultation with unions and government, and employers' input into public policy is largely limited to the legislative process.

---

[27] Katzenstein 1985; Martin 1991; Soskice 1990, 43.
[28] See also Hicks and Kenworthy 1998; Martin and Swank 2004; Martin and Thelen 2007; Höpner 2007.

Some firms cooperate with their workers in work councils and shop-floor production teams; however, these strategies are seldom found above the firm level.[29]

While peak employers' associations were everywhere relatively weak at the end of the nineteenth century, divergence among nations along paths of macrocorporatism, sector coordination, and pluralism were already pronounced by the 1920s and more so in the 1930s.[30] Table 1.1 documents this divergence in employer organization and overarching modes of coordination in the early and latter decades of the twentieth century for sixteen (now advanced industrialized) nations. First, the Scandinavian polities of Denmark, Norway, Sweden, and the Benelux nations displayed increasingly strong macrocorporatist organization of employers (with moderate sector coordination). Second, the Germanic nations and Italy exhibited moderate organization of national peak associations and strong sector coordination during this period. Third, Anglo nations (with Finland and France) had pronounced pluralist employers' organization: Encompassing centralized and integrated national peak associations and sector coordination remained limited in these systems from the turn of the century until World War II. With rare exception, these 1920s-to-1930s patterns of employer organization and coordination persist at the end of the twentieth century, despite significant evolution in the functions of the organizations in response to changing economic conditions and political coalitions. Thus, one wonders why these diverse types of associations arose and evolved along separate paths.

Partisan Origins of Encompassing Employers' Associations

Our initial task is to understand how different types of encompassing employers' associations were created and how these institutions have been reconfigured for changing economic times. Countries ultimately diverged in developing encompassing associations in the mold of macrocorporatism, sectoral coordination, or pluralism; yet somewhat surprisingly, industrial development movements initially articulated quite similar preferences for highly organized peak employers' associations and nonmarket labor coordination. Employers and their government collaborators sought cooperation to secure national industrial development policies, to enhance performance in global markets, to transform regulatory privilege from agriculture to industry, and to preserve their political control against rising democratization.

The structure of partisan competition – the primary vehicle for collective political engagement in the nineteenth century – is a major reason for this game-changing divergence in business organization. Two features, in particular, shape the strategic choices of the government and business actors who participate in the development of national, encompassing, multisector employers' organizations. First, party structure is a significant determinant of the type of encompassing employer association and this structure is initially defined by the number of political parties: Two dominant parties seek electoral control in some countries while multiple parties compete in others. In the 1910s and 1920s, proportional representation is introduced in some countries and the variation in PR versus winner-take-all electoral rules reinforces the early paths toward divergent types of employer organization. Multiparty systems with PR (particularly in centralized

[29] Schmitter 1981; Wilson 1990; Grant 1989.
[30] Crouch 1993.

TABLE 1.1. *Patterns of Employer Organization and Coordination at the Dawn of the Twentieth and Twenty-First Centuries*

	Early-Twentieth-Century (1920s–1930s)			Late-Twentieth-Century (1980s–2000s)		
	Employers' Organization	Macrocorporatism	Sector Coordination	Employers' Organization	Macrocorporatism	Sector Coordination
Low Organization by 1920s and 1930s						
Australia	−.93	−.39	−.91	.15	.06	−.95
Canada	−.93	−.81	−.91	−1.94	−1.45	−.95
France	−.93	−.69	−.57	.12	−.41	−.27
New Zealand	−.53	.46	−.57	−.14	−.51	−.95
United Kingdom	−.53	.03	−.91	−.17	−.92	−.85
United States	−.93	−.81	−.74	−1.94	−1.56	−.83
Moderate Organization by the 1920s and 1930s						
Belgium	.49	.60	.44	.23	.58	.28
Finland	−.16	−.50	−.03	.82	.57	.87
Italy	−.42	−.58	.78	.05	.33	1.01
Netherlands	.36	.46	.10	.12	.16	−.35
High Organization by the 1920s and 1930s						
Austria	.87	.92	1.11	.23	.49	.62
Denmark	1.65	1.46	1.11	.23	.86	.28
Germany	1.13	.65	1.79	.76	.21	.58
Norway	1.39	1.13	.43	.99	1.08	.42
Sweden	1.39	1.43	1.28	.66	.79	.45
Switzerland	1.00	.57	1.11	−.05	−.16	.28

See text for descriptions of measures of employer organization and coordination; see Chapters 2, 7, and 8 as well as historical and contemporary ancillary materials (available at www.cambridge.org/9781107018662) for more measurement details and data sources.

governmental systems) are more likely to represent employers in a single party and this helps to focus business attention on common goals; in comparison, two-party systems tend toward catch-all units with employers dispersed across parties.[31] Moreover, leaders of right parties in multiparty systems have greater incentives to delegate policy-making authority to private channels, because they are unlikely to win electoral majorities and their constituents are more likely to secure favorable policy outcomes in direct negotiations with workers than in parliamentary processes. We note that these business parties almost never contained *only* employers and industrialists struggled within the party with other factions, such as aristocrats or landowners (Germany, Denmark, and Britain), national liberals (Germany, Denmark, and Britain) and/or workers (Britain and the United States). Yet in multiparty systems, the majority of employers were more likely to gravitate to a single party than in two-party systems.[32]

Second, the level at which political competition is organized – central versus federal – also matters to the formation of peak employers' associations. Because political action takes place at the national level, centralized governments produce national, centrally organized and regionally homogenous parties and (in multiparty systems) well-organized corporatist associations as well. In federal systems of government with decentralized political authority, parties are more likely to be cross-class and regional in scope; the electorate is more likely to divide along regional, religious and/or ethnic lines; and employers' associations remain regionally fragmented.[33] Chapter 2 goes into the arguments in greater detail.

The characteristics of partisan representation – the number of parties and their degree of centralization – lead us to a rather simple way of parsing out the worlds of business politics. Centralized, multiparty systems tend to produce highly coordinated macrocorporatist associations and national cooperation among business and labor along with a high level of state involvement. Federal, two-party systems tend to produce *pluralist* employers' associations and competitive strategies that largely rely on market competition. Federal, multiparty systems tend to produce *sectoral coordination*, with significant levels of nonmarket coordination at the industry level without extensive state involvement. Table 1.2 captures the relationship among party system structure, governmental centralization and varieties of employers' associations.

Other factors (tested in Chapter 2) certainly influence employer organization, and may be wholly responsible for the evolution of sector-level (as opposed to national, multisector) business groups. Industrialization broadly accounts for the general timing of coordination and both labor activism and preindustrial traditions of nonmarket coordination rooted in skills traditions make employers more likely to organize collectively. Yet the formation of *industry-level* groups and *national peak* associations rely on substantially different processes, and political factors become particularly pertinent to the national story. Even though economic structures, labor activism, and preindustrial

---

[31] Cusack et al. 2007. Of course, party leaders (often also businesspeople) have economic interests that are related to their class, but here we focus on the specific interests of certain types of parties that transcend the interests of individual actors.

[32] In the United States, for example, while the Republican Party was very much a party of business, manufacturers in the south and west did not belong and largely lacked a partisan home.

[33] Coleman 1987; Hawley 1966; Amorin and Cox 1997; Manow and van Keesbergen 2009.

TABLE 1.2. *The Impact of Party System and State Centralization on Patterns of Coordination in Capitalist Democracies*

Number of Parties	Level of Centralization	
	Centralized system unitary polity; national parties, high coverage of specific interests	Federal system fragmented polity; regional parties, low coverage of specific interests
Multiparty system dedicated parties, high coverage of specific interests	**Danish** full-blown macrocorporatism	**German** sectoral coordination; cooperation without much state involvement
Two-party system catch-all parties, low coverage of specific interests	**British** pluralism with periodic efforts at state-led, top-down coordination	**U.S.** pluralism with market competition, segmentalism

cooperation may be sufficient to explain the creation of *sectoral* or *regional* employers' organizations; national, multisectoral, associations require a moment of disconnect in social life and presuppose political will in order to overcome the high transaction costs of group formation beyond the industry level.

One might protest that strong parties evolve from strong interest groups and, indeed, in some cases, the two forms are quite interconnected (think of labor unions and social democratic parties). Yet parties form for varied reasons (in top-down fashion from legislative factions as well as from the bottom-up) and many parties are in place before the evolution of the encompassing business and labor organizations. Moreover, the formation of diverse party profiles reflects the idiosyncrasies of agency and social construction at key historical junctures.[34] Thus, we recognize a dynamic and mutually reinforcing relationship between the spheres of industrial relations and political party competition during this period of early industrialization and democratization, and test with appropriate quantitative methods and process tracing the impact of party structure on interest group development.[35]

Chapter 2 assesses our political theory of business organization with a cross-national quantitative analysis of sixteen nations over four decades, using historical data on labor markets, economic structures, political institutions, early employers associations and patterns of coordination. Chapters 3 through 6 present historical case studies based on extensive primary source material of the development of national employers' associations in Denmark, Germany, the United States, and Great Britain.

---

[34] Whereas the origins of parties are beyond our mandate, parties form in diverse fashion: Some from the bottom-up are closely connected to the labor movement; others from the top-down emerge from factions in the legislature. Still others are linked to other social (religious or ethnic) cleavages and have a more tenuous connection to the labor market partners (Rokkan 1999; Manow and Van Keesbergen 2009; Duverger 1954; Eldersveld 2000.)

[35] Martin and Swank 2008, 14; see also Iversen and Soskice 2009. While scholars link some political party development to the structure of societal cleavages (Duverger 1954; Lipset and Rokkan 1967; Bartolini 2000); we emphasize that parties also influence the construction of class cleavages.

We show that although a slightly different problematic confronted party leaders in each country, the structure of political competition contextualized conflict and shaped the way that state, business, and labor actors resolved their struggles over industrial modernization and labor peace.

Coordination among employers, once established, did not become a static, enduring artifact, and the various modes of encompassing peak associations and their related forms of coordination evolved, ebbed and flowed over the course of the twentieth century. Macrocorporatism was *not* a constant cure for the dislocations of capitalist transformations, and by century's end, coordinating institutions came under particularly severe stress with the rise of the service economy. Postindustrial production has been associated with lower productivity growth and greater diversity in the interests of business and labor, making coordination, social spending, and relatively egalitarian arrangements harder to sustain.[36] But industrial restructuring has also enhanced the need for coordination because this can help to reallocate productive resources for the new trajectories of capitalist development.

Thus, we also explore the mechanisms by which institutions are reworked at a second critical juncture, the transition to the postindustrial services economy, and the requirements for survival of highly organized associations (if, indeed, they can survive). At issue is how countries can best manage the transition from one period of relative economic stability to the next, what role do mechanisms for coordination play in facilitating this transition, and how can this transition be managed with the least damage to the social fabric.

Chapter 7 presents an empirical snapshot of efforts to sustain coordination at this second critical juncture in the evolution of modern capitalism, the transition from industry to services at the end of the twentieth century. We find that the structure of political competition that was so crucial to the evolution of diverse types of employers' associations is also a significant determinant of the reinvention of coordination for the postindustrial age. Deindustrialization has certainly taken its toll and formal structures of corporatism have been eroded even in the strongest macrocorporatist countries. But there has been significantly less drop-off in the formal labor market institutions and even new institutional innovations in collaboration in some countries, as politicians and labor market partners grapple to sustain coordinating capacities. Somewhat paradoxically, two-party systems are supposed to vie for the median voter, which should make them more centrist; however, parties in multiparty systems need to make coalitions with other parties and actors, and this facilitates accommodation. Thus, our quantitative analysis finds that proportional multiparty systems and centralized government sustained high levels of coordination in macrocorporatist countries, while labor market coordination was eroded in federal systems with winner-take-all electoral rules.[37] We take up this theme in Chapters 9–11, as we explore the role and fate of employers' associations in adaptation to postindustrial pressures in Denmark, Britain, and Germany.

---

[36] Pontusson 2005; King and Rueda 2008; Brandolini and Smeeding 2008.

[37] Scholars on the left and right agree that capitalism suffers periodic setbacks, but disagree about the severity of the causes of and solutions to crisis moments. The left believes that capitalism has seeds of its own self-destruction: competition is inherently unstable due to the falling rate of profit (associated with

Impacts of Peak Employers' Associations on Policy Preferences

We next investigate how employers form their preferences for social policies; in particular, we explore how employers are brought into political debates through their encompassing peak associations. Somewhat paradoxically, more positive business views toward social policies are found in countries with highly organized business associations than where employers are weakly organized. As we lay out in Chapter 8, the structural characteristics of encompassing employers' associations have an impact on employers' views of social policies and relative levels of equality due to political economic, collective action, and cognitive effects.

Macrocorporatist forms of association make employers' more likely to express support for collective social goods for *political economic effects*, in that these groups foster highly centralized, coordinated collective bargaining, that leads to wage compression and motivates employers to eliminate low-skilled jobs and to support skills training.[38] These highly organized systems of coordination solve *collective action* problems for social goods (or those in which the benefits cannot be restricted to those who bear the cost of provision). The broad scope of the groups enable them to adjudicate among the demands of diverse industrial sectors, to bind members to negotiated decisions, and to cultivate norms of trust that a broad cross-section of business will comply with identified outcomes. Macrocorporatist associations are also associated with proportional party systems, which allow politicians to restrain their short-term electoral concerns for long-term interests in a reputation for good economic management. These party leaders help firms in coordinated market economies realize their collective interests in skills training systems.[39] Macrocorporatist associations have a *cognitive* impact on their members in educating employers about the benefits of social policies, exposing managers to the ideas of government and labor policy experts, focusing participants' attention on broader concerns, nurturing norms of "social partnership," and allowing employers to participate and have a say in the formation of public policy.[40]

Fragmented, *pluralist* interest groups do not have these effects on employers, as the groups do not foster collective wage setting and compete with one another for members. These structures encourage concessions to the particularistic self-interests of members and work against agreements to solve collective action problems. In countries with *sector coordination*, one is likely to find deals between business and labor at the sectoral level, which offer core workers high levels of social protections but which neglect the interests of labor-market outsiders. From the perspective of collective action theory, industrial sector-based organizations simply have few if any incentives

the changing organic composition of capital) and while countries may thrive during economic bubbles, these bubbles ultimately burst, putting an end to prosperous times. Long waves of capitalist production are punctuated by short bursts of crisis, or Kondratiev waves, when the organizing technologies become exhausted (Brenner 2001). The right has a more narrow view of capitalist limitations; for example, Schumpeter views creative destruction as necessary to rid the world of outdated production in order to utilize resources more efficiently in new industries.

[38] Wallerstein 1989.
[39] Olson 1965, 1982; Streeck 1992, 265–84; Katzenstein 1985; Visser and Hemmerijck 1997; Wilensky 2002; Henley and Tsakalotos 1992; Crepaz 1992; Streeck and Schmitter 1985, Crouch 1993; Hicks and Kenworthy 1998; Cusack et al. 2007.
[40] Crouch 1993; Katzenstein 1985; Rothstein 2000, 2005.

to significantly contribute to the costs of programs that address the needs of marginalized workers.

A caveat is in order: one might surmise that the higher levels of business support for social policies and welfare state spending simply reflect the distinctions among welfare state regimes. The Social Democratic welfare state regime clearly entails a more universal distribution of social benefits (and broader group of beneficiaries) than either the Christian Democratic or Liberal regimes.[41] We argue, however, that structures of political engagement have an independent impact on cross-national differences in social spending, which is most readily apparent at moments in which policy reforms are broadly similar across regime types and policy legacies play a more muted role in innovations in social intervention. For example, the active labor market reforms of the 1990s borrowed from each welfare state type, diverged in significant ways with the various regimes, and on paper appeared quite similar across advanced, industrialized countries. Yet implementation of the reforms was quite uneven, with the Scandinavian countries both spending more and demonstrating higher rates of business participation. This divergence represented, to a great extent, fundamentally different processes of collective political engagement, which induced cross-national deviation in the interests and capacities of the implementing agents (such as employers.)

We investigate the impact of encompassing employers' associations on employers' preferences for social policies. Chapter 8 offers a quantitative analysis of national-level cross-section time-series data to demonstrate that the presence of corporatist peak associations, and the associated institutions of national coordination, is positively associated with the amount of national resources devoted to active labor market programs and the level of social protection for workers. Our interviews with randomly selected firms in Denmark and Britain further help us to understand the microlevel processes of business preference formation.

Business Organization, Equality, and Economic Growth

Finally, we evaluate how diverse types of peak employers' associations contribute to cross-national variations in social and economic outcomes, such as redistribution, relative levels of equality, employment and economic growth. We find that well-ordered societies – with high levels of organization among business and labor – are best positioned to reconcile diverse goals of economic growth and relative equality. One might expect to find the opposite. Encompassing groups might be unable to reconcile the conflicting interests of their diverse memberships or to make zero-sum choices: In this case, large encompassing groups might easily sink to a least-common-denominator decision rule, in which little is accomplished, or might seek to gratify the self-interests of their various members, without concern for the general will. Moreover, coordination has come to be associated with rigidity and calcification in the modern love affair with the market, and we might anticipate that more highly coordinated societies would have greater difficulty in reworking their economic and social institutions at major turning points in capitalist development. Yet countries that are coordinated at the highest level, in fact, have an easier time engaging in significant restructuring of

[41] Esping-Andersen 1990; Castles 1993.

their social and regulatory institutions at moments in which economic change makes the old systems obsolete.

Because firms have somewhat indeterminate interests, employers may be attracted to different types of political projects, and their encompassing peak associations influence their strategic choices. For example, in some circumstances, firms in the core manufacturing sector – which compete in exposed sectors – may endorse segmentalist social protections that advantage their own highly skilled workers but that do little for the skills needs of marginally employed workers. In other cases, these firms might prefer solidaristic policies with significant investments in low-skilled workers, both because they view these low-skilled workers as a potential labor pool and because they need high levels of training to cope with industrial change. In like fashion, firms hiring low-skilled workers might support state policies to subsidize their workers social needs or they might resist such protections as driving higher taxes.

We argue that the forms of peak employers' associations create different possibilities for government policy entrepreneurs to build political coalitions in support of social investments and redistribution. Societies with the most collective processes of political engagement ease government policy entrepreneurs' task of constructing broad political coalitions around policy goals and give social actors responsibility to negotiate pragmatic solutions. Macrocorporatist employers' associations and related forms of labor market coordination increase business support for social provisions both for their own workers and even for the long-term unemployed. These highly coordinated associations offer political entrepreneurs a platform for reaching firms, produce wage restraint and increase employment, curb passive welfare state interventions, enhance active social spending on skills and reduce dualism. Finally, strength in business organization bolsters labor's ability to secure egalitarian policies such as state fiscal distribution across working-age families. In this way, macrocorporatism blunts the rise of income inequality, labor market dualism and irregular and long-term unemployment.

Certainly the partisan composition of government and party structure also contribute to a country's likelihood of building coalitions to compensate low-skilled workers for rising inequality; for example, strong Christian Democratic parties (with their cross-class constituencies) pull politics to the right and countries with strong social democratic party leadership are more likely to support the low-skilled workforce.[42] Proportional representation and centralized governance have also contributed to the growth of a large public sector. High levels of public sector employment have increased total employment, which makes it more likely that the low-skilled will work often in the public sector itself and which strengthens public bureaucrats' incentives to raise the skills of this labor source. The growth of the welfare state has also expanded female labor force participation, which increases women's demands for social protections.[43] Yet, coordinated market economies with strong macrocorporatist institutions and associated modes of labor market organization have an independent impact on equality and redistribution, in part, because substantially less policy is created through legislative, electoral channels than in liberal countries. This delegation to private policy-making channels reduces the impact of parties and increases the involvement of stakeholders. Today, when party systems are

---

[42] Iversen and Stephens 2008.
[43] Martin and Thelen 2007; Huber and Stephens 2001.

in significant disarray (even in the havens of social democracy), the delegation of policy making to the social partners has served to stabilize welfare states.

Thus, encompassing labor market organizations are – more than ever – a pivotal institution in systems of collective political engagement and these have tremendous impacts on the capacities of policy entrepreneurs to build enduring coalitions targeted on the needs of the long-term unemployed. In Chapter 12, we find that macro-corporatism has a strong positive impact on direct fiscal redistribution by the state, wage equality, and features of labor market dualism such as irregular employment. We also find clear evidence that coordination, for all its importance in maintaining solidaristic policies and outcomes, does not impede economic growth.[44] Case studies in Chapters 9–11 document policy entrepreneurs' efforts in Denmark, Britain, and Germany to build support for skills initiatives among low-skill workers.

Conclusion

While coordination was once celebrated as the warp of the social fabric, a fondness for free-market neoliberalism in the late twentieth century diminished the popularity of cooperation as a central organizing principle for societies. In parallel fashion, the structures of collective political engagement – at the center of democratic theory and the social contract – have faded in recent studies of cross-national policy variations. We return structures of collective political engagement to center stage as a linchpin of democratic societies, and put forth that society building is as important as state building in the evolution of modern capitalist democracies.

First, the book emphasizes the essential role of political structures and agency in the formation of the business class; in particular, our political institutional view of the origins of employers' associations is a radical departure from prior research. With our (hitherto untold) story about the political origins of national associations, we reveal that stylized facts and an absence of dialogue between business historians and students of party politics have made us rather blind to the enormous importance of political structures in the evolution of corporate coordination. The strategies of politicians and state bureaucrats, heavily informed by the structure of party competition, are a determinative element in the evolution of varieties of business associations and associated modes of economic coordination. In addition, the same features of the polity are profoundly important to the renewal of these associations with the transformation from industrial capitalism to the postindustrial economy. Work on contemporary parties recognizes that alternative forms of interest intermediation may develop in response to representational gaps in party politics, and it follows that politics as well as economics would also have a role in the origins of systems of business representation.[45]

Second, we link the origins of varieties of capitalism to employers' varying capacities for collective preference articulation, and in particular, to encompassing peak employers' associations. Fascinating work has recently grounded diverse types of industrial

---

[44] This quantitative assessment, drawing on 1973 to 2003 annual data from eighteen nations, utilizes pooled time-series cross-section models of these policy and outcome variables.
[45] Lawson and Merkl 1988.

capitalism in employers' preferences for skills and suggests that these skills strategies are heavily shaped by legacies of preindustrial guilds.[46] We ascribe to the importance of guild traditions, but also view interests as socially constructed and receptive to politics. Political structures had a feedback impact on skills and economic development, in that two-party systems with little incentives to nurture strong national employers' associations rewarded employers who engaged in low-skills competition and hampered future collective skills-building institutions. The relationship between electoral and industrial relation systems is dynamic and we stress the coevolution of political representation and economic organization. An encompassing business organization (and coordinated capitalism) has difficulty surviving without a consensual PR party system; thus, business representation varies systematically with the party system.[47] Our intensive investigation of the historical circumstances surrounding the emergence of national patterns of business organization helps to unravel the *reciprocal influences* of movement in the two spheres, and highlights the element of historical contingency that may be overlooked in less historically grounded studies.

Finally, our work offers insights into the processes of renegotiating the social contract in the postindustrial age and debates about the durability of models of capitalism. A new watershed moment is upon us, and an essential concern is whether the institutions for coordination developed during the golden age of manufacturing can survive. When Maytag is moving operations from Newton Iowa to Mexico, when Starbucks is hiring more Americans than Ford, and when hedge funds are busting up long-time corporations for salvage, will coordinated employers stick with the social program? The recent threats to organized capitalism are widely debated, with broad disagreement between those who forecast an end to coordination and a convergence on neoliberal policies, and those who envision a continuation of managed capitalism and a divergence of models.[48]

We believe that structures for collective political engagement delimit national options at moments of institutional change, when the architecture of capitalism is reworked. Sustaining institutions of coordination may depend on state capacity to renegotiate social pacts, to build new coalitions of broad majorities, and to develop new institutional forms. Political institutions and state strategies and capacities are crucial for sustaining coordinating institutions against postindustrial decline and to the reworking of collective organizations for new skills and challenges in the postindustrial economy. Better-organized, encompassing and centralized organizations do more to educate members about the benefits of social policy, to help members define common ground, and to solve the transaction costs of collective action. Thus, the survival of egalitarian social protections depends, in part, on whether well-organized groups can continue to bring employers together and on the structures and strategies of the state to bolster the institutions of coordination.

---

[46] Thelen 2004; Iversen and Soskice 2009.
[47] Martin and Swank 2008; Iversen and Soskice 2009.
[48] Hall and Gingerich 2004; Howell 2003; Campbell and Pedersen 2007; Glyn 2006; Streeck 2009.

2

The Political Origins of Coordinated Capitalism

Introduction

At the dawn of the twenty-first century, varieties of capitalist democracies seem worlds apart. Despite globalization and industrial restructuring, the Scandinavian countries have largely retained "macrocorporatism." In Germany and other continental European countries, economy-wide negotiations are on the decline, although economic sector-based coordination is resilient. Finally, an aversion to cooperation appears bred in the bone in the Anglo-liberal lands of the United States and Great Britain: "Pluralist" associations organize employers and workers, and the representation of business interests remains a highly individualistic affair.

Whereas it is tempting to conclude that these patterns of cooperative engagement versus laissez-faire individualism are indelibly imprinted on national psyches, a century ago they were much less distinct. Employers and their political allies across the west shared many beliefs about developmental capitalism and national movements struggled in parallel fashion to develop highly coordinated peak business associations to push these industrial policy agendas. The late nineteenth century was a period of enormous political transformation, as capitalist development and the first wave of globalization created pressures for national industrial policies. Even in the United States, communities were noteworthy for their Tocquevillian patterns of cooperation, and the movement for national business organization sought to emulate these community efforts in nonmarket coordination. Yet in the process of nationalizing political engagement, the "virtuous circles" of coordination failed to thrive beyond the community level in the Anglo countries, even while they ultimately took hold in continental Europe.

This chapter explores the origins of employers' associations to investigate why some countries develop full-blown macrocorporatism, others disproportionately rely on sectoral coordination, and others fail to move beyond market modes of coordination and pluralist organization of interests. Our extensive archival and quantitative analyses lead us to a somewhat surprising discovery: how employers organized nationally was influenced more by the strategic scheming of their political leaders and the interplay of party politics than by employers' ideological convictions. Marx had it right when it came to the formation of the business class – employers require an executive manager (of the bourgeoisie) to help them organize their interests and forge their collective political identities. Party system characteristics and norms of power sharing among levels of government affect the political incentives of both public and private sector leaders, and shape the evolution of employers' organizational capacities.

The dance of party politics does not tell the whole story of why employers in some countries were able to set aside internecine squabbles to coordinate while capitalists elsewhere remained mired in interindustry conflicts. Industrialization generally drove business organization and preindustrial patterns of collectivism (e.g., guilds) created legacies for nonmarket coordination and skills production.[1] Yet cross-national skills levels were more similar at the end of the nineteenth century and diverged after experiments in employers' organization moved in fundamentally different directions. Thus, the electoral context was critical to the evolution of cooperative institutions during industrialization and encompassing business associations failed to thrive on the hostile ground of two-party political systems.

Chapter 2 tests our argument that political competition and state structures shape the evolution of peak business institutions and associated forms of coordination. We draw upon a rich data bank of historical indicators of political economic development and employ large-N quantitative analysis of 1900 to 1930s variation in employers' organization and nonmarket coordination. Chapters 3–6 offers detailed historical case analyses of the causal processes that link political institutions, employers, and economic coordination in Denmark, Britain, the United States, and Germany. This effort to trace institutions' political inception helps us to reject an alternative possibility that culture explains all and that high levels of both business coordination and social protection simply reflect a deep cultural collectivist impulse. Thus, we show that institutions, once in place, have a truly independent effect on the preferences of social actors.

Theories of Business Organization

Whereas advanced economies today exhibit disparate levels of coordination, the impulse for nonmarket coordination seemed ubiquitous in the decades surrounding 1900, when national employers' associations with quite similar goals developed in many countries. Rising labor activism and advances in industrial life – with their attendant concentration of production in factories, urban migration, and global marketing – were the precipitating events that prompted a "search for order" and business organization across the western world.[2] Employers bitterly resented the enormous policy privilege granted to agriculture over industry and wanted their governments to develop industrial supports for competing in world markets, to make workers' skills commensurate with the remarkable technological advances of the era, to protect against new social risks, and to protect home turf from invasive imports with tariffs. As early capitalism was largely unregulated, advances in industrialization prompted firms to form sector trade associations or multisector umbrella organizations to manage competition and

---

[1] Thelen 2004; Hall and Soskice 2001; Cusack et al. 2007.
[2] Wiebe 1967.

to assist in rapid industrial growth.[3] With the consolidation of regionally dominated and diverse economies into national economies and with growing global exchange, manufacturers also came to recognize their collective interests in forming *national* encompassing associations to lobby for national policy solutions.

Sectoral industry groups were created for many reasons, yet the early multisectoral associations shared remarkable similarities in their positions and organizing principles. They sought legal licensing, extraparliamentary private powers for self-regulation (in conjunction with labor), and government departments of commerce. Finally, they aimed to become umbrella associations with powers superceding sectoral organizations.

Yet success varied wildly. By the onset of World War I, employers in the Nordic and Germanic nations had begun to establish relatively broadly organized and centralized associations, while employers in the Anglo nations remained more fragmented and decentralized, and these differences grew in the 1920s and 1930s. Danish employers developed a highly organized association to negotiate labor market policy deals with unions and government that prefigured the "macrocorporatist" institutional structures still in place. Germany developed an early peak employers' association but with limited capacity for national negotiation, and coordination remained stronger at the sectoral level. British and American employers' associations were denied formal licenses for business representation and produced multiple, pluralist peak associations. (See Table 2.1.)

By World War II, nations with a low articulation of employers' associations in the early twentieth century (the Anglo countries and France) had market-based modes of economic organization.[4] These countries had fragmented employers' and labor associations, decentralized labor and industrial relations systems, and minimal levels of sectoral cooperation to solve business' collective goods problems.[5] Nordic nations continued to have macrocorporatist institutions (with moderate or high sectoral cooperation). The Germanic nations and Italy developed relatively moderate levels of macrocorporatism, but high levels of sectoral coordination. Benelux nations developed above average levels of nonmarket coordination by World War II, but macrocorporatism also tended to predominate in these nations. (See Table 2.2.)

From the standpoint of the present, nothing may seem particularly surprising about these levels of coordination, as each country has its own foundation myth of

---

[3] Hayes 1937; Bensel 2000; Baldwin 1990; Tedlow 1988; Lynn and McKeown 1988, 2–3.

[4] We introduce our conceptualization and measurement of macrocorporatism and sectoral coordination in Chapter 1. We infer types of broader coordination from employers' organization: Thus, we associate macrocorporatist modes of coordination with highly organized peak association (i.e., corporatist employers' associations). We associate moderately organized employers' associations with more sector-based coordination. Yet, we can refine our analysis of employers' organization and directly measure overall macrocorporatist and sectoral coordination in the early twentieth century. To confidently and comprehensively assess our theoretical arguments, especially on the political causes of coordination, we conduct separate analyses of employers' organization and dimensions of overall coordination.

[5] France is an exceptional case. In the mid to late 1800s, the French political economy exhibited elements of sectoral coordination in the form of, for instance, universal banking and related forms of industrial cooperation. Yet, after the collapse of the Crédit Mobilier in 1867, patterns of coordination began to take on a more market-oriented character; state organization of finance and, ultimately, dirigism increasingly structured the French economy (e.g., Bussiere 1997; Lescure 1995a; 1995b; Marmefelt 1998).

TABLE 2.1. *Patterns of Employers' Organization in Developing and Democratizing Nations, 1900–1938*

Nations	1900	1914	1925	1938
Low organization by 1920s–1930s				
Australia	3.0	3.0	3.0	3.0
Canada	3.0	3.0	3.0	3.0
France	3.0	3.0	3.0	3.0
New Zealand	3.5	3.5	4.0	4.0
United Kingdom	3.5	4.0	4.0	4.0
United States	3.0	3.0	3.0	3.0
Moderate organization by 1920s–1930s				
Finland	3.0	3.0	4.5	4.5
Italy	3.0	3.0	4.5[a]	na
Netherlands	3.0	3.5	5.0	6.0
High organization by 1920s–1930s				
Austria	4.0	4.5	7.0	na
Belgium	3.0	3.0	4.0	7.5
Denmark	5.5	6.5	7.0	9.0
Germany	4.5	5.5	7.0	na
Norway	4.5	5.0	6.0	9.0
Sweden	4.5	5.5	6.5	9.0
Switzerland	4.5	5.0	6.0	7.5
Mean – All nations	3.6	4.0	4.8	5.6

Note: The table displays our additive index of (1) scope of employers organization (i.e., the share of employers organized in peak national associations); (2) the centralization of power (e.g., control over strike/lockout funds, bargaining strategies) in peak national associations; and (3) integration of peak associations into national policy-making forums. (See Historical Ancillary Materials for detail.)
[a] Employers organization measured circa 1921–2.

(handwritten margin note: pushes Belgium into high coord)

exceptional circumstance that accounts for its peculiar trajectory in the pantheon of national permutations. Thus, Britain's liberalism and regard for individual agency is traced back to the Magna Carta; Germany's interests in social coordination reflects a dogged affection for preindustrial, authoritarian values; and Scandinavian collectivism is traced back to the agrarian philosophy of Grundvig.[6] Yet ideological determinacy minimizes the shared features of preindustrial social expectations across Europe and neglects the peculiar ironies of national trajectories. Germany had no monopoly on collectivist thought: Similar intellectual legacies from the ancien regime persisted in Burkean ideals of old Tory England and in German conceptions of organic society. The British-conceived National Industrial Council after World War I inspired coordination across advanced societies. Liberal philosophy had a robust following in many countries in the mid 1800s; For example, liberals were major proponents of German nation building. Danish liberals supported free trade, whereas the Right Party endorsed tenets similar to those of the British Tories.[7]

[6] Bowen 1947.
[7] Blackbourn and Eley 1984; Mayer 1981; Lowe 1978.

TABLE 2.2. *Patterns of Nonmarket Coordination in Democratizing Nations, 1900–1938*

Nations	Macrocorporatism			Sector Coordination		
	1914	1925	1938	1914	1925	1938
Low employer organization, 1920s–1930s						
Australia	−.47	−.30	−.25	−.91	−.91	−.91
Canada	−.77	−.68	−.74	−.91	−.91	−.91
France	−.78	−.73	−.43	−.57	−.57	−.57
New Zealand	−.51	−.34	.26	−.91	−.57	−.57
United Kingdom	.03	.06	.04	−.91	−.91	−.91
United States	−.77	−.69	−.73	−.91	−.91	−.57
Moderate employer organization, 1920s–1930s						
Finland	−.84	−.49	−.25	−.57	−.16	.10
Italy	−.84	0.37[a]	NA	.44	.78[a]	NA
Netherlands	−.37	.44	.91	.44	.10	.10
High employer organization, 1920s–1930s						
Austria	−.33	1.22	NA	1.11	1.11	NA
Belgium	−.75	.25	1.40	.10	.11	.78
Denmark	.85	1.19	2.34	1.11	1.11	1.11
Germany	.01	.87	NA	1.79	1.79	NA
Norway	.16	.44	2.41	−.23	.10	.77
Sweden	.01	.86	2.53	.78	1.12	1.45
Switzerland	−.11	.47	1.12	.77	1.11	1.11

The index of macrocorporatism adds the employers' organization index, union organization (density and centralization of powers in peak associations), and the centralization of collective bargaining. The sector coordination index combines producer-finance linkages and the extent of enterprise cooperation to provide collective business goods (training systems, export market, and industrial strategies). See Historical Ancillary Materials for details.

[a] Coordination measured 1921–2.

The new coordinating institutions were inspired by an emergent organizing principle advocated by technologically advanced sectors whose interests differed from old ideological liberals, the landed gentry and handicraft trades. Nationalist industrial development ideology supplanted liberalism as the hegemonic philosophy at the end of the nineteenth century, just as liberalism had replaced mercantilism a century before.[8] Although the success of this new public philosophy partly depended on its congruence with older traditions, it both fundamentally differed from prior thought and was broadly similar across nations. The dual impact of continuity and change is apparent in the motivations for the first German peak employers' association, the Centralverband (CVDI). Bismarck imagined industrialists as constituting a new estate (following the ancient regime tradition), yet the CVDI was founded on the economic ideas of nationalist industrial development authored by Henry C. Carey (who also inspired Lincoln).[9]

[8] Fellman et al. 2008.
[9] Wehler 1970, 140; Craig 1978.

How, then, can one account for the cross-national variations in the organization of national business communities and institutions of nonmarket coordination? Two sets of arguments suggest that employers across nations simply had different needs for coordination: one related to their levels of development and the other to the organization and skills levels of workers.

Industrialization

First, variation in employer organization may reflect differences in stage and type of capitalist development – levels of industrialization, openness of the economy, and regional economic diversity – although the literature makes contradictory predictions about these impacts. Leaders of *industrialization* may have the greatest need to organize to achieve economic order; hence, higher per capita income or higher manufacturing shares of total economic output should produce higher levels of business organization. Yet late industrializers might organize more rapidly to catch up with their competitors and might also develop other institutions for nonmarket coordination such as long-term bank-industry cooperation.[10] (Formal hypotheses are presented in Table 2.3; see #1 and #2).[11]

Variations in *exports* might contribute to divergent levels of organization, as countries with large export sectors might have greater need to coordinate their efforts to survive in international markets than those producing for domestic consumption. Alternatively, employers in countries with lower exports might experience fewer pressures to constrain wages, be more willing to grant labor higher wages in exchange for industrial stability, and form associations to bargain collectively.[12] (Table 2.3, #3.)

High levels of *economic regional diversity* should work against the development of encompassing, centralized employers' associations and extensive nonmarket coordination because pronounced regional diversity makes it difficult for employers to identify common ground; therefore, countries with more diverse, regionally specific economies might develop less-centralized employers' associations and more limited nonmarket coordination.[13] (Table 2.3, #4.)

Labor Activism

A second set of explanations for variations in coordination points to features of the workforce: Employers organize either to stunt labor activism or collectively to develop skills for highly productive workers. Employers may be most motivated to coordinate when confronted with *highly organized unions*; moreover, industrial unions are more likely than craft unions to produce encompassing, highly centralized national labor and employers' associations. Industrial unions reinforce solidarity among workers of various skills levels and create capacities to cooperate with employers over training and wages, whereas craft unions pursue self-interested strategies benefitting upper strata workers and motivate workers to control skills.[14] (Table 2.3, #5.) Strong ethnic

---

[10] Wilensky 2002; Gershenkron 1962; Gourevitch 1986.
[11] To avoid excess hypotheses, where theory supports both positive and negative effects of causal forces, we stipulate only the one that we believe is stronger or conventionally supported.
[12] Gourevitch 1986; Katzenstein 1985; Galenson 1952.
[13] Tolliday and Zeitlin 1991.
[14] Korpi and Shalev 1979; Crouch 1993; Stephens 1980; Kuo 2010; Clegg et al. 1964; Thelen 2004.

TABLE 2.3. *Hypotheses on the Origins and Development of Employers' Organization*

Economic Needs Variables

#1: *The higher the level of industrialization as evidenced by per capita GDP, the higher the corporatist organization of employers (and nonmarket coordination).*

#2: *The higher the level of industrialization as evidenced by manufactures' share of total economic output, the higher the corporatist organization of employers (and nonmarket coordination.)*

#3: *The greater the trade openness of the economy, the higher the corporatist organization of employers (and nonmarket coordination).*

#4: *The lower the levels of regional diversity, the higher the corporatist organization of employers (and nonmarket coordination).*

Response to Labor Organization Variables

#5: *The higher the level of labor mobilization, the higher the level of corporatist employer organization.*

#6: *The greater of degree of religious and ethno-linguistic fragmentation, the lower the corporatist organization of employers (and nonmarket coordination).*

#7: *The stronger the traditions of coordination, the higher the corporatist organization of employers (and nonmarket coordination.)*

Party and State Structure Variables

#8: *The higher the level of proportionality in voting, the higher the corporatist organization of employers (and nonmarket coordination).*

#9: *The lower the level of state centralization (i.e., more federalism), the lower the corporatist employers' organization (and nonmarket coordination).*

#10: *In proportional/multiparty systems, the greater the federalism, the higher the sector coordination.*

---

and religious *cleavages* diminish both worker organization and employers' incentives to organize.[15] (Table 2.3, # 6.)

Firms' *skills* needs may also influence employers' preferences for coordination because firms relying on highly skilled workers have greater need for collective training mechanisms that prevent "free-rider" companies from raiding the talented workforce of other firms. Skills at the dawn of industrialization reflected preindustrial guild traditions: Guilds facilitated vocational training systems, allowed firms to develop specific assets, and enabled the evolution of a skills-based export sector. For example, German guilds created a legacy of cooperation over skills development among small firms, skilled masters and unskilled journeymen; however, with the decline of British guilds, skilled workers formed craft unions, pursued self-interested strategies to control skills to augment wages and hurt unskilled workers' interests.[16] (Table 2.3, # 7.)

We find much merit in arguments about industrialization and workforce profiles; yet, we consider these insufficient to explain the diversity of national associations. The arguments make somewhat conflicting predictions, which suggests that employers

---

[15] Stephens 1980; Manow and Van Kersbergen 2007.

[16] Hall and Soskice 2001; Crouch 1993; Thelen 2004; Galenson 1952; Unwin 1966; 2004; Cusack et al. 2007. "Traditions of coordination" (e.g., guilds) are associated with proportional representation and employers' organization. Cusack et al. (2007). Thus, the absence of a theoretical accounting and a statistical control for past coordination may well lead us to accept a spurious relationship between proportionality/multipartism and employers' organization.

make strategic choices in organizing collectively. The labor-oriented explanations of activism and collectivist skills traditions rely on different underlying processes for arriving at cooperative industrial relations and it is hard to reconcile pitched warfare on the one hand with cosy coordination on the other. Guilds certainly nurture cooperation in their *economic* impact of producing high skills and nonwage competition by employers. Thus, the decline of British guilds (which once reinforced social solidarity among preindustrial laborers) reduced both skills and solidarity. Yet guilds also have a *political* impact of fragmenting political identities and inhibiting organization above the sectoral level: thus Danish guilds failed repeatedly to organize before a Right Party leader induced them to join the manufacturers' new multisectoral organization.[17] Sweden's industrial unions differ from Denmark's craft unions, yet both have macrocorporatist employers' groups.[18]

Moreover, the formation of business sectoral groups and national peak associations relied on substantially different processes. Diverse motivations – efforts to export, to control wages, to generate collective skills – prompted organization at the sectoral and regional levels. But the formation of national group required political will to cross the enormous gulf from a pluralist network of industry associations to a highly centralized, capacious peak organization with substantial power over its constituent groups. With the emergence of national industrial economies, local traditions for cooperation needed to be reworked on a grand scale and political arrangements had a powerful impact on these great transformations. Timing was important in that national patterns were solidified at the point in which regional economic and political communities became incorporated into national and even global structures. Thus, the political context molded the incentives for collective action of both employers and political actors.

Party Systems and State Structures

The similarities in associational ambitions and differences in outcomes lead us to consider a third broad set of explanations: the structure of political competition, which set the stage for the struggle over industrial development. Organizing employers presents a collective action problem, as firms are motivated to enjoy benefits of organization without contributing to the group effort to secure these benefits.[19] Employers in 1900 had many reasons to seek nonmarket coordination – associated with promoting trade, securing favorable industrial policies, generating skills, and restricting capitalist competition – yet their capacities to organize varied with the political context. An outside agent may facilitate organization, and party leaders and governmental bureaucrats may play this role when they have independent political needs for business organization. Political leaders have electoral incentives to organize employers' associations to expand their constituent base, gain political support for legislation, and help with implementation.[20]

---

[17] Unwin 1966, but see Zeitlin 1990; Agerholm and Vigen 1921. Guilds themselves originate with the expansion of the local state, developing to engage in self-regulation or to act as an agent of municipalities. William Kahl, intro to Unwin, 1966, p. xxvxxxvii.

[18] Det faglig arbejdsbevaegles, Sisson 1987; Davis 2000; Galenson 1952.

[19] Olson 1965.

[20] Martin 1994; Torcal and Mainwaring 2003; Maier 1975.

Political leaders sympathetic to employers also have incentives to delegate power to private forums, when they believe that their policy ambitions and social class constituency's interests will be met more readily in nonlegislative arenas. These incentives may be even more important in predemocratic regimes, where political authority is not transferred through democratic elections, but where premodern political parties remain important in parliaments.[21] Just as state building is shaped by the bureaucratic goals and interests of its executors, "society building" (the timing of, motivations for, and forms of business political action) reflects similar impulses. Key periods of corporate organization have occurred when state actors have particularly activist agendas.[22]

Whereas agency at critical junctures is important to subsequent institutional outcomes, the struggle for political power plays out in an institutional context; therefore, the structure of political competition affects outcomes as well. Students of comparative politics generally root political party development in societal cleavages[23] and have largely neglected the reciprocal influence of parties and electoral systems on the historical evolution of business organization and social class. Yet, parties and interest organizations both represent societal interests, and it is not surprising that party systems shape interests organizations. When parties inadequately represent a societal group's interests, an interest organization might form from the bottom up in order to address this gap in representation. Alternatively, party strategists might create a business group from the top down to serve their political needs of rallying societal support for the party's agenda or to develop corporate capacity to implement the policies of the business party. Thus, whereas close ties link some parties to some interest groups, the broader party system emerges for various reasons that may well have little to do with interest groups, reasons such as governmental structures and electoral rules. Once in place, this system has an independent effect on the evolution and organization of social organizations.[24]

Two structural characteristics of political engagement manipulate how employers develop their encompassing associations. First, electoral rules and the number of parties have an impact on employer organization because multiparty systems with proportional representation are more likely than two-party, majoritarian systems to produce dedicated business parties, to inspire cooperation among social actors, and to delegate policy-making power to the social partners. Multiparty systems have higher coverage of specific groups; therefore, employers are likely to belong to a single party. (But in federal systems of government, these dedicated business parties are likely to remain at the *regional* level.) The dedicated business party inspires coordination because it focuses attention on common goals among its constituents and makes credible commitments to policy platforms (rather than changing course to capture the

[21] Differences between democratic and authoritarian regimes were rather subtle during this period. Thus, democratic Britain and authoritarian Prussia both legislated major expansions of suffrage in 1867 (Anderson 2000, 406), while the United States effectively denied suffrage to many African Americans until 1964. The Danish government was not allowed to act if both bodies of parliament opposed a proposal; the lower body held budgetary responsibility and was democratically elected by proportional representation.
[22] Martin 1991; 1994; Schneider 2004; Garon 1987; Grant and Marsh 1977; Hawley 1966.
[23] Lipset and Rokkan 1967; Daadler 1966; Bartolini 2000.
[24] Torcal and Mainwaring 2003; Martin 1991; 1994; Octavio and Cox 1997; Chhibber and Kollman 2004.

median voter.)[25] Other interests may be included in the party, and these factions may have different policy demands from those of employers; however, the crucial issue is that employers are not dispersed across parties. Coalition governments – the norm in multiparty systems – further encourage cooperation among competing interests (often present through successive elections) and stability in policy outcomes.[26] Leaders of business parties have incentives to delegate policy-making authority to private channels because they are unlikely to win electoral majorities and constituents are more likely to secure policies in direct negotiations with workers than through parliamentary processes.

In comparison, two-party systems deliver catch-all parties – with diverse constituencies and less coverage of specific interests – and employers are often dispersed between parties. Even though the parties may attempt to cultivate competing business associations, employers in competing parties may feel that they have no partisan home to represent them politically, which makes them wary of government regulation. Employers in catch-all parties are reluctant to believe politicians' promises, because platform positions fluctuate to attract the median voter and electoral change brings radical policy reversals.[27] Politicians in two-party systems realistically can hope to win absolute electoral majorities and are, consequently, less willing to delegate policy-making authority. (Table 2.3, #8.)

Second, the distribution of authority across levels of government – centralization versus federalism – should influence the degree to which employers produce corporatist associations; indeed, democratic theory generally concludes that the organizational representation of interests follows constitutional structure.[28] Federal systems have greater levels of regional diversity in policy outcomes and employers' associations will have similarly diverse concerns across these regions. Federal systems also have less-centralized political parties, and parties dominated by local elites have less need for centralized business organizations than parties with strong, national leadership. Federalism exacerbates the incomplete coverage of specific economic interests by magnifying ethno-linguistic and religious cleavages, and intensifying regionally-based sectoral divisions within the economy, which reduce the salience of class cleavage.[29] Thus, we hypothesize that the degree of federalism should be negatively associated with employers' organization and nonmarket coordination. (Table 2.3, #9.)

These characteristics of partisan representation and state structure – the number of parties and the degree of centralization of the polity – have a salient impact on the extent and nature of employer organization and patterns of cooperation, ranging from highly coordinated corporatist groups to highly fragmented pluralist groups. First,

---

[25] Kitschelt 1993; Cusack et al. 2007.
[26] Proportional representation accelerated the emergence of distinctive party memberships by unlinking voting from regional districts and encouraging socioeconomic cleavages to replace regional cleavages.
[27] Downs 1957; Shefter; Steinmo, and Tolbert 1998.
[28] Coleman 1987. We tested additional hypotheses about political factors and found limited support. For instance, governmental control by collectivist social democratic and communitarian Christian democratic parties might enhance coordination. Korpi 2006; Hicks 2008; Wilensky 2002. (See our analyses in the ancillary materials at www.cambridge.org/9781107018662.)
[29] Amorin and Cox 1997; Chhibber and Kollman 2004.

centralized multiparty systems tend to produce encompassing and highly coordinated corporatist associations with a high level of coordination with state involvement (macrocorporatism). These party systems delegate significant policy-making authority to the social partners, but industrial relations systems retain a crucial role for the state, as employers trust that their dedicated business parties will represent their interests in political channels.

Second, federal multiparty systems are likely to produce high levels of employer coordination at the industry level (sector coordination), but have weaker peak associations and less state involvement. Federal multiparty systems have difficultly producing dedicated national business parties, because sectional cleavages remain salient; moreover, even though business-oriented politicians have incentives to delegate political authority to social partners, the absence of a single national business party makes employers more resistant to state oversight. Whereas federalism should, ceteris paribus, impede the development of nonmarket coordination and macrocorporatist associations, in combination with high multipartism, federalism should foster relatively high sectoral cooperation.

Third, centralized two-party systems tend to produce pluralist systems with periodic episodes of coordination, in which government officials seek to impose greater coordination from the top down, but which is refuted when the opposing party takes office. These countries may exhibit greater levels of coordination than countries with federal two-party systems, but experiments in coordination are time-limited.

Fourth, countries with federal two-party systems tend to produce pluralist employer representation, in which no unitary peak group speaks for collective business interests. Party strategists might nurture business groups to rally societal support or to further electoral ambitions by reaching out beyond their party's constituency base; but these groups are unlikely to evolve into singular, encompassing peak associations.[30] Representation gaps may inspire group formation; however, business organizations will be subject to the same vulnerability that prompted their initial development. Moreover, party leaders will not delegate much policy-making authority to organized business and labor because, even when one party becomes significantly linked to business (e.g., the U.S. Republican Party in 1896), the business-oriented party can hope to win an outright majority. Thus, different combinations of the party system and unitary-federal dimensions are likely to result in divergence in the predominate mode of nonmarket coordination. (See Table 2.3, #10.)

Cross-National Quantitative Analysis

Methodology

We assess our hypotheses on the origins of employers' organization and types of coordination through both the quantitative analysis of historical data and comparative case studies. After outlining the measurement and estimation procedures for the quantitative work, we report our findings from analysis of 1900 to 1930s data from sixteen nations on hypothesized causes of highly organized employers and nonmarket

---

[30] When major parties insufficiently cover societal interests, alternative political organizations may emerge to fill these representation gaps. Lawson and Merkyl 1988.

economic cooperation. We deepen our understanding of causal mechanisms through our comparative historical case analysis (Chapters 3 through 6), and consider quantitative findings in light of case evidence to conclude this chapter.

Measurement for Historical Quantitative Analysis

Our central goals are, first, to explain why employers in some nations had organized encompassing and centralized interest associations by the years immediately proceeding World War II (while organizations in other nations remained pluralist). Second, we wish to address the closely related question of why some nations had established the institutions for national (macrocorporatist) coordination and others sectoral coordination before World War II. To these ends, we use our measures of employers' organization, macrocorporatism, and sectoral coordination reported and discussed in Tables 2.1 and 2.2. These measures are based on data for circa 1900, 1914, 1925, and 1938 for sixteen nations. (Extensive measurement details and data sources for all variables are reported in ancillary materials at www.cambridge.org/9781107018662).

For general economic determinants of coordination, we follow standard practice and measure the level of industrialization as (log) per capita Gross Domestic Product (hereafter GDP). We also construct measures of the concentration of economic activity in manufacturing (percentage of GDP from manufacturing). We measure trade openness by computing exports as a percentage of GDP (both in 1990 US dollars). We proxy regional dispersion of economic activity by taking the log of area (expressed in square miles). For the labor and industrial relations system, we measure labor mobilization as union membership as a percentage of the work force. To proxy traditions of coordination for skills and other business goods, we sum dichotomous measures of the presence (1.0) or absence (0.0) of guilds, rural cooperatives, industrial (versus craft) unions, and a large skills-based export sector.[31] To measure nonclass cleavages, we utilize the number of nonclass (religious, ethno-linguistic, urban-rural) cleavages present at the beginning of the century.

With respect to political hypotheses, we measure proportionality/multipartism in the electoral system by an ordinal scale of proportionality of electoral rules where 0.0 designates low proportionality (e.g., the United States), 1.0 signifies semiproportionality (e.g., France in 1919, 1924) and 2.0 designates high proportionality (e.g., Denmark after 1915) in electoral outcomes. Empirically we emphasize the proportionality of the electoral system and not the number of effective parties. As highly proportional systems are multiparty systems, measures of effective number of parties inherently tap features of the cleavage structure of society.[32] Thus, proportionality incorporates our theoretical logic on multiparty system dynamics but avoids problems associated with measurement of additional features of cleavage structures. Finally, we measure state (de)centralization by a federalism-unitary ordinal variable (where 0.0 designates a unitary polity, 1.0 signifies a federalist system, and .5 represents an intermediate or quasi-federal institutional structure).[33]

---

[31] These historical indicators were developed by Cusack et al. 2007; see Kreuzer 2010 for a critique.
[32] Lijphart 1999.
[33] We use a number of alternative indicators of electoral/party systems and state centralization; tests with alternative measures reported in the ancillary materials do not differ from the results reported in Table 2.4.

All of the above measures are computed as lagged levels of designated factors where the lag is typically the annual mean for five years before the point of measurement of coordination. For example, for any country in 1910's decade (where employer organization is measured circa 1914), union mobilization is mean union density at two or more time points between 1908 and 1913 (where the number of time points is a function of data availability or historical considerations).

Estimation

Following our theoretical arguments, we specify empirical models of the degree of nonmarket coordination. Our models for employers' organization and macrocorporatism are:

[Eq. 1]   Employer Organization$_{i,t}$ = α + β_1(Proportionality of Electoral System)$_{i,t-1}$ + β_2(Federalism)$_{i,t-1}$ + β_3(Union Mobilization)$_{i,t-1}$ + β_4(Nonclass Cleavages)$_{i,t-1}$ + β_5(Traditions of Coordination)$_{i,t-1}$ + β_6(Log Area)$_{i,t-1}$ + β_7(Openness)$_{i,t-1}$ + β_8(Log Per Capita GDP)$_{i,t-1}$ + $\varepsilon_{i,t}$,

[Eq. 2]   Macrocorporatism$_{i,t}$ = α + β_1(Proportionality of Electoral System)$_{i,t-1}$ + ... + β_7(Log Per Capita GDP)$_{i,t-1}$ + $\varepsilon_{i,t}$,

where Eq. 2 is equivalent to Eq. 1 but deletes Union Mobilization and where *i* designates nation; *t* designates decade, 1900s, 1910s, 1920s, and 1930s as discussed above; and $\varepsilon_{i,t}$ is the error term. With regard to the "*it*," we delete country decades from analysis where fascist regimes are in power (i.e., Austria, Germany, and Italy in the 1930s) and where democratic competition is not yet in place (e.g., some nations for 1900).[34]

With respect to sectoral coordination, we estimate the same model with one major exception: we add a test for the interaction of proportionality and federalism. This specification allows us to assess whether greater federalism in the context of proportional, multiparty systems promotes sectoral coordination. Thus, our core specification of the model for sectoral coordination is:

[Eq. 3]   Sectoral Coordination$_{i,t}$ = α + β_1(Proportionality of Electoral System)$_{i,t-1}$ + ... + β_7(Log Per Capita GDP)$_{i,t-1}$ + β_8(Proportionality of Electoral System × Federalism)$_{i,t-1}$ + $\varepsilon_{i,t}$,

We estimate our models with ordinary least squares (OLS) with panel corrected standard errors computed for unbalanced panels. To further account for the sources of possible spuriousness, we also estimate our final models with a lagged dependent variable. Cusack, Iversen, and Soskice's argument suggests that past levels of employer organization and attendant conditions (e.g., cospecific assets of capital and labor) lead employers to choose highly proportional electoral rules to guarantee parliamentary representation.[35] Thus, a control for past employers' organization (macrocorporatism or sector coordination) should further assuage fears of spuriousness of our findings for electoral-party system variables. Moreover, a lagged dependent variable explicitly accounts for autocorrelation dynamics in the dependent variable;[36] its presence also effectively shifts the dependent variable to a change measure and, in turn, allows assessment of explanatory variables effects on changes in employer organization.[37] In addition, we assess the robustness of our results to a variety of alternative specifications, estimators, and country decade exclusions. (These analyses are fully reported in the book's ancillary materials.)

Findings

Employers' Organization. We report the findings for employers' organization in the first two columns of Table 2.4. The results do indeed suggest that the proportionality of the electoral system is significantly related to the degree of employer organization. The substantive magnitude of this effect (β = .9172) is also large (see column I): an increase from minimal to moderate, or moderate to high proportionality is associated with an increase of roughly 1.0 on our (3 to 9) scale of employer organization. On the other hand, the coefficient for the effect of federalism (although correctly signed in the negative direction) falls short of statistical significance at conventional levels. (Federalism is, however, significant in some key model specifications for macrocorporatism and sector coordination.)

For labor and industrial relations factors, the relationship between employer organization and past union mobilization is highly significant in virtually all specifications of our models. In terms of substantive magnitude, an increase in unionization rates of 10 percent of the workforce would, all else being equal, result in a .6 increase on our (3 to 9) scale of employer organization. Traditions of coordination, as hypothesized, are also significantly and positively associated with employer organization; a shift of 1.0 on our (1 to 4) scale of traditions of coordination results in a .76 point change in the index of employer organization. This finding adds support to the argument that guild traditions and associated cooperative legacies are related to employers' organization and promote the further development of coordination.[38] It is also important to note that in the presence of this control, our central measure of proportionality remains significant. As discussed above, the presence of this variable, itself an important correlate of proportionality and corporatist organization of employers, should minimize concerns that the significant relationship between proportionality and employer's organization is spurious.[39]

With respect to economic forces, geographic size and trade openness are not significantly related to employer organization; but (log) per capita GDP is modestly associated with employers' organization in Column I. Economic concentration in manufacturing – our main alternative measure of development – even though correctly signed, is largely insignificant and dropped from further models.

---

[36] Beck and Katz 1995.
[37] Recall that an equation of the following form, Employers Organization$_{i,t}$ = α + (1+φ)(Employers' Organization)$_{i,t-1}$ + $\beta_j(X)_{i,t-1}$ + $\varepsilon_{i,t}$ is equal to Employers' Organization$_{i,t}$ – Employers' Organization$_{i,t-1}$ = α + φ(Employers' Organization) $_{i,t-1}$ + $\beta_j(X)_{i,t-1}$ + $\varepsilon_{i,t}$. Only the coefficients for the lagged dependent variables are different.
[38] Cusack et al. 2007; Iversen and Soskice 2009.
[39] We delete the insignificant religious, ethnic, and regional cleavages variable to make sure we get good estimates of federalism; its inclusion makes no difference to the results for employer organization.

TABLE 2.4. The Underpinnings of Nonmarket Coordination, 1900s–1930s, in Sixteen Nations

Variables	Employers' Organization		Macrocorporatism		Sector Coordination	
	I	II	III	IV	V	VI
Proportionality of	.9172**	.4166**	.3997**	.2129**	.7245***	.2500**
Electoral System	(.4350)	(.2466)	(.1972)	(.1105)	(.1838)	(.1161)
Federalism	−.5959	.1507	−.1743	−.1876**	−.3556	−.2660*
	(.4953)	(.3119)	(.1955)	(.1103)	(.4182)	(.2032)
Federalism ×					.5451***	.2438**
Proportionality					(.2328)	(.1217)
Union Mobilization	.0607***	.0329***				
(Union Density)	(.0195)	(.0125)				
Religious, Ethnic,			−.5660***	−.1651*	−.3044***	−.0426
Regional Cleavages			(.1372)	(.1121)	(.1231)	(.0822)
Traditions of	.7647***	.2625*	.5314***	.2698***	.1829*	.0596
Coordination	(.2224)	(.1762)	(.1316)	(.1079)	(.1210)	(.0725)
(Log) Area	.2544	.0357	.1522**	.1166**	.1379	0831
	(.1533)	(.1094)	(.0728)	(.0439)	(.1088)	(.0510)
Openness (Exports	.0223	.0004	−.0016	−.0002	−.0176**	.0014
as % of GDP)	(.0197)	(.0160)	(.0107)	(.0072)	(.0068)	(.0047)
(Log) Per Capita	1.9546**	−.0583	1.6953***	.6770**	.5577*	.1266
GDP	(.9453)	(.5652)	(.4751)	(.3512)	(.3821)	(.1556)
Nonmarket		.9257***		.9560***		.7446***
Cooperation $t-1$		(.1504)		(.1419)		(.0796)
Constant	−4.6702	−.4527	−4.1767	−2.3756	−2.8181	−1.5056
R2	.8007	.9127	.8000	.9080	.8754	.9573
N	36	36	36	36	36	36

All models are estimated with ordinary least squares with panel correct standard errors. Cases are thirty-six country decades for the sixteen nations defined in the text. Each model includes time period dummies for 1900s, 1910s, and the 1920s.
* probability < .10
** probability < .05
*** probability < .01

Finally, the shift to the lagged endogenous variable model reported in Column II – a formulation that controls for past levels of employers' organization and shifts to an assessment of explanatory factors' impacts on changes in employers' organization – does not alter this pattern of results. In fact, all core findings except the one for economic development hold. In sum, historical quantitative data analysis of pre–World War II variations in employers' associations suggests that electoral/party systems, union mobilization, traditions of coordination, and (perhaps) economic development largely explain why some nations experienced extensive organization of employers.

Macrocorporatism. A complimentary analysis of the inception of macrocorporatist coordination is presented in the third and fourth columns of Table 2.4. Proportionality is significantly and positively associated with macrocoordination: The substantive impact of moving from disproportional to semiproportional, or from semiproportional to highly proportional electoral systems is roughly .4. Keeping in mind that macrocorporatism (and sectoral coordination) is a standard score index (i.e., mean = 0.0, standard deviation = 1.0), this finding suggests that moving from (dis)proportionality (0.0) to a proportional system (2.0) would change the score of corporatism by .8 or the equivalent of moving from 1930s New Zealand to the 1920s Austria or Denmark (see Table 2.2). On the other hand, federalism – even though correctly signed and registering a t-test of -1.0 – is not significant.

We also offer tests for the effects on macrocorporatism of features of industrialization and labor and industrial relations systems. Recall that union density itself is a component of macrocorporatism and, thus, is excluded from the explanatory model. As highlighted in column III, nonclass cleavages retard the development of macrocorporatism, whereas traditions of coordination exert an independent, positive and significant effect on the evolution of national coordination. The level of economic development is significant and positively associated with macrocorporatism as hypothesized. But, the openness of the economy to international trade, commonly cited as causal to early macrocorporatism, is surprisingly unrelated to pre–World War II national coordination.[40] Finally, (the log of) area, as a proxy for economic diversity, is significantly and (surprisingly) positively associated with macrocorporatism.[41]

In the lagged dependent variable model in column IV, all determinants of macrocorporatism that receive support in the earlier specification of column III are significant and correctly signed. The only exceptions are that, first, the substantive magnitudes of core causal factors are reduced in size and, second, the (insignificant) federalism variable of the basic model is significant. In sum, the development of early twentieth-century macrocorporatist modes of coordination is positively affected by late nineteenth-century traditions of coordination and the course of economic development. Nonclass cleavages serve to weaken corporatism; so too might federalism, although the evidence is limited. Most centrally, electoral proportionality/multipartism consistently promoted macrocorporatism in the early decades of the twentieth century.

Sectoral Coordination. Our parallel analysis of pre–World War II sectoral coordination is presented in columns V and VI of Table 2.4. With respect to our core arguments on electoral and party systems, we find substantively large, correctly signed, and significant effects on sectoral coordination of the proportionality of the electoral system. For instance, in a model without the interaction of federalism and proportionality (full model results in ancillary materials), a shift from disproportional (0.0) to highly proportional (2.0) electoral systems would result in a change of roughly 1.5 (2 × .7689, the regression coefficient for proportionality) on our standard score index of sectoral cooperation. This would be the equivalent of moving from the moderately market-driven economic context of New Zealand in the 1920s (sectoral coordination −.57) to the moderately high sectoral coordination of Switzerland in the 1930s (sectoral coordination 1.11).

---

[40] Cameron 1978; Katzenstein 1985.

[41] Although positive and significant here, the effect of area on macrocorporatism is inconsistent in alternative model specifications and estimations. Thus, we do not make much of this finding. See ancillary materials for full results.

As to federalism, recall that our theory anticipates a significant interaction between federalism and proportionality: A move from centralization to fragmentation of authority in proportional/multiparty systems fosters sectoral coordination. The table, indeed, reveals a significant interaction between these factors. Moreover, the computed effect of federalism in proportional/multiparty systems, given by the equation, $-.3356 + (.5451 \times 2)$, is correctly signed and highly significant.[42] Specifically, the marginal effect on sector coordination of shifting from a unitary polity to federalism in highly proportional electoral systems is .7346.

With respect to industrialization and labor factors, nonclass cleavages and traditions of coordination all have significant and correctly signed effects on pre–World War II patterns of sectoral coordination. As to the remaining factors, we find that even though economic development is positively and significantly associated with sector coordination, international openness is significantly and (incorrectly) negatively associated with sector coordination; country size is unrelated to sector coordination.

With respect to our lagged dependent variable model of column VI, past levels of sectoral coordination, as well as proportionality, federalism, and their interaction largely explain the evolution of sector coordination; nonclass cleavages, traditions of coordination, and economic development – all significant in the basic model – fall short of conventional levels of statistical significance in the dynamic model of column VI. Overall, the quantitative historical analysis suggests most clearly that the political context of proportional electoral rules and a federal polity is strongly conducive to the development of sectoral driven coordination.

Quantitative Findings and Historical National Experiences

Industrialization

These quantitative findings gain added salience when considered in light of the historical case analyses of the formation of peak employers' associations in Denmark, Britain, the United States, and Germany (presented in greater detail in Chapters 3 through 6). First, industrial development was clearly the fundamental motivation for employer organization at the national level, as employers everywhere wanted policies to support business expansion in world markets and to protect home turf. The American National Association of Manufacturers' goals for industrial development included the extension of domestic and foreign markets, reciprocal tariffs, the Nicaragua Canal, expansion of a merchant marine, and expansion of waterways.[43] The Federation of British Industry claimed to mark "a distinct state in the evolution of capitalism. It meant that the old ideas of nineteenth-century commercial capitalism, with its insistence on free trade and the natural play of economic forces, had finally passed away... The attitude to industrial policy, to trade rivals and to the working class was to be carefully planned."[44]

---

[42] The interaction of X_1 (federalism) and X_2 (proportionality of electoral rules) when the dependent variable is Y (sectoral coordination), will tell us whether the effect of X_1 on Y varies with levels of X_2. The interaction term itself, when multiplied by a value of X_2 and added to the coefficient of X_1, becomes the slope, or the marginal effect, for X_1 on Y at that level of X_2. Friedrich, 1982; Kam and Franzese 2008.

[43] NAM 1926.

[44] FBI's Labour Research Department 1923, 5.

Yet, differences in types of industrial development were less important to cross-national variations in employer organization. For example, shares of total economic production in manufacturing were higher in pluralist Britain (39 percent in 1920) and coordinated Germany (48 percent) than in the pluralist United States (29 percent) or coordinated Denmark (23 percent). Similarly, greater trade openness did not correspond either to higher or to lower levels of nonmarket coordination: Exports constituted 14 percent of the GDP in 1920 in both the United Kingdom (a pluralist country) and in Germany (a coordinated one), while the United States (a pluralist country) and Denmark (a corporatist one) trailed behind with 4 and 11 percent of the GDP devoted to exports, respectively. All employers wanted to export more, but whereas early laggard status may have prompted German organization, Germany was a formidable industrial power by 1880 and Britain had begun to experience significant trade pressures by the 1890s.[45]

Sectoral diversity existed in all our countries, but structures of federalism politicized these conflicts differently across nations, and efforts to overcome the diversity fared better in some settings than others. Certainly, intrabusiness divisions between manufacturing and finance – over tariff reform in particular – made the national, multisector organization of employers in Britain difficult to achieve.[46] Yet other countries had impressive intra-industry conflicts; for example, German employers in heavy and light industrial sectors profoundly disagreed about tariffs, played out organizationally in the dueling Centralverband der Deutsche Industrie and the Bund der Industriellen. British elites were, by some measures, more unified than German ones, due to the commercial needs of the landed gentry and British public education.[47] Danish manufacturers were also deeply divided over tariff protection, with exporters of specialty agricultural products particularly opposed to any constraints on free trade.[48] Regional diversity certainly constrained coordination in the United States (e.g. northern and southern employers had different interests in collective training systems), yet again federalism played into how these divided interests were politicized.[49]

Labor Mobilization as a Cause of Employer Organization
The qualitative cases reinforce the quantitative finding that both highly mobilized labor organizations and highly skilled workers facilitated the development of early associations into corporatist organizations. Employers everywhere feared the power of the working class, and many calculated that stable industrial relations would forestall the rise of socialism. Thus, Danish employers' intense hostility to labor became more accommodating after a vitriolic conflict in the metal industry in 1885. A decade later, the national multiindustrial association lobbied for a joint committee (with labor) to

---

[45] Klug, 2001.

[46] Burgess 1975, 305; Turner 1984, 6–7; Marrison 1983, 148; Platt 1968. Manufacturing and financial interests diverged over trade protections (with finance committed to unrestricted capital flows) and fiscal policy (with finance desiring fiscal austerity).

[47] Fear 2005; Maier 1975, 41. A key difference was that British party competition was organized around home rule: This, with limits on suffrage and electoral rules, defeated the drive for protection in the British election of 1906. Klug, 2001, 223–5.

[48] Galenson 1952.

[49] Berk 1994; Piore and Sabel 1984; Bureau of Labor 1911; Hansen 1997.

oversee collective bargains; the episode demonstrates both the power of labor resistence and the importance of strategic calculations.[50]

Germany and Britain both considered the creation of a highly organized system of industrial relations after World War I in response to labor activism, and one may argue that the greater threat from German workers enabled a stronger form of coordination to emerge. Facing the postwar revolution, competing multisector associations formed the Reich Association of German Industry (RDI) and a new framework for industrial relations was created. Even though industrial peace motivated the Federation of British Industry, British employers ultimately ceded less power to unions.

Yet a labor peace explanation does not explain all cross-national variation in employers' organization. Early German umbrella groups were motivated by needs for policy supports for industrial competition and whereas the RDI sought labor peace, moves toward greater coordination began in Germany even before the revolution. One also wonders why employers behaved so differently toward craft unions: Assertive Danish craft unions brought firms to organize nationally to cooperate with labor in the 1890s, while strong British craft unions brought employers to fight workers by shedding skilled labor. Weak American craft unions allowed employers to fight labor individually and organization remained fragmented.

Legacies of coordination and skills also influenced the emergence of employer' associations as predicted: nations with preindustrial guilds (and associated cooperation) were less likely to form fragmented pluralist employers' associations. Yet the handicraft sectors were not leaders in the creation of the peak employers' associations in our model countries, and organizers came from more technologically advanced industrial sectors with radically divergent policy goals. Even though the Danish guild tradition was undeniably collectivist, guilds had largely disappeared before their repeal in 1852; their intellectual heirs – the handicrafts sectors – favored economic cooperation to restrict competition but had little aptitude for political cooperation.[51] These sectors were quite reluctant to join the encompassing employers' association and caved only when threatened by a workman's compensation insurance reform. German handicraft sectors were also among the most aggressively anti-union, even while they developed collective skills-training institutions for their workers.[52] Moreover, skills in the United States and Britain were not appreciably lower during this period than in Denmark and Germany and even in liberal countries, employers and unions sought to improve skill formation before the 1920s. Germany had significant concerns at the turn of the century about the shoddy quality of its products in some sectors, causing one contemporary observer to note: "the German executes commissions of the same kind so faultily that he is seldom able to secure a second order."[53]

Party System Characteristics
Most importantly, the cases reveal that party politics had a significant impact on the type of peak employer representation that developed around the beginning of the

[50] Due et al. 1994, 78–9.
[51] Asbjorne Nørgaard 1997, 120; Due et al. 1994, 75; Galenson, 1952, 70–72; Bruun 1938, 409.
[52] Thelen 2004.
[53] Hansen 1997; Zeitlin 1990; Dawson 1904, 13–14.

twentieth century. In all our countries, top-down interventions by party activists were largely responsible for employer organization at the national level. Nevertheless, major differences in partisan competition sent the associations down radically divergent tracks, as the business parties in multiparty systems had a motivation to delegate authority. This motivation was absent in two-party systems.

In Denmark, a country with both multiple parties and centralization, a dedicated business party developed to unify employers, to cultivate their collective identity, and to foster their trust that their views would be represented in government. The party feared a center-left coalition, recognized that employers would win greater victories in private channels of self-regulation with labor than in parliamentary forums, and sought to allow significant policy-making authority to develop within private channels. The Danish right party, Højre, helped to create the Employers' Confederation of 1896 (subsequently, the Dansk Arbejdsgiversforening, DA) in order to consolidate its power at a time when it was being threatened by parliamentary reform.[54] The adoption of PR and reorganization of Højre into the Conservative Folk Party in 1915 increased the employers' share of the right party's membership and strengthened the identity of Danish manufacturers as a national business community. Regional differences among industrialists gradually began to disappear, enabling the functional reorganization and centralization of authority within DA, and full-blown macrocorporatism was achieved.[55]

In a country with multiple parties but a federal governmental structure, German employers were scattered across parties and significant regional infighting persisted well into the early twentieth century.[56] No single dedicated business party developed to nurture the firms' collective identity; rather politicians from different parties courted business organization to bolster their political and policy agendas. Wilhelm von Kardorff (a Free Conservative member of Parliament, employer, and close friend to Bismarck) created the Employers' Association in 1876 to help Bismarck construct an industrial-economic cleavage within German society. The Bund der Industriellen was later organized by free-traders (and liberal party leaders) to offset CVDI influence. Finally, wartime need for cooperation and the postwar desire of employers to regain political power led to the merger of these associations into the Reich Association of German Industry (RDI), with state actors highly involved in its inception.[57] Employers and their political allies sought self-regulation with labor rather than navigate the fragmented legislative/party system and economic democracy was an alternative to socialism. Yet business remained disunified and dispersed across parties after the war, and the RDI remained ineffective with real decision making devolved to lower, industrial sector groups.[58]

In a country with two dominant parties and a centralized governmental structure, Britain, employers were divided between the parties and had no partisan home. An early industrializer, Britain developed vigorous sectoral unions and employers'

---

[54] Agerholm and Anders 1921.
[55] Galenson 1952, 79–82; Beretningen om Dansk Arbejdsgiversforenings Virksomhed 1927–1928.
[56] Pollock 1929, 860; Chanady 1967, 65–71.
[57] Clagget et al. 1982; Brady 1942, 72; Gatzke 1954, 51; Mierzejewski 2002, 202.
[58] Bunn 1958, 284; Maier 1975, 15, 40; Rogers and Dittmar 1935, 483–4.

associations before other advanced industrialized countries; yet, there was no political incentive for state entrepreneurs to organize a peak employers' association from
the top-down to support party's ambitions at the end of the nineteenth century. Only
when World War I finally created a sufficiently strong imperative for coordination did
the Conservative-dominated British Foreign Office aid in the creation of a national
peak association, the Federation of British Industries. But the FBI failed to realize
its corporatist ambitions for two reasons related to party politics. First, the British
Liberal Party cultivated a separate group of employers and the dueling groups were
used in political battles between the parties. Second, neither party had an incentive to
delegate policy-making authority to business or labor, as each hoped to win outright
victories in parliamentary and electoral contests. Parties refused to share power with
the social partners, when both business and labor asked for self-regulation during the
National Industrial Conference, and the social partners became more confrontational
when this cooperative experiment failed.[59]

Finally, in the United States, party competition was enormously important both
to the initial formation of the National Association of Manufacturers (NAM) and to
its subsequent evolution into pluralism. In a country with two dominant parties and a
federal structure of government, party competition was organized along regional lines:
The Republican Party in the northeast held interests closely allied with business, but
industrialists in other parts of the country lacked a partisan home as manufacturers
in the south and west were forced to choose between voting Democratic or joining a
party with African Americans. The Republicans organized NAM as a extraparty channel to appeal to these employers and to improve McKinley's chances of gaining the
Republican nomination at the convention (to get votes from Democratic states).

NAM's slip into pluralism reflected its highly-partisan origins and the reluctance
of Democratic opponents to grant NAM's policy wishes. NAM's corporatist goals
made it lobby for a department of commerce and for a license to speak for employers in business-government cooperative arrangements. But its policy ambitions were
thwarted by its deep connections to electoral politics, and Democratic legislators
rejected its legislative proposals. In addition, neither party had incentives to delegate
policy-making authority to the social partners. Left without its anticipated central role
in managing industrialization, NAM started to wither away at the end of the century
and only gained new life when it reconstituted itself after a decade as an organization
devoted to fighting organized labor in 1903. This critical juncture signaled a setback
for coordination in the political economy and strengthened the liberal impulse among
U.S. employers: with the failure of coordination, American industrial relations turned
toward laissez-faire liberalism and pluralism evolved.

Conclusion

The end of the Nineteenth Century was a watershed moment in the evolution of modern political economies. National business communities together with their political
leaders sought to develop cooperative capacities in order to nurture industrial capitalism, even in countries like the United States that would become bastions of neoliberal

[59] Lowe 1978.

thought. Yet in this search for order, some nations constructed nonmarket institutions for managing the chaos of industrial capitalism, whereas in other countries early experiments with coordination evolved into less structured, more pluralist forms of employers' associations. This chapter applies the wide-angle lens of quantitative comparative historical analysis to assess why nations moved down these divergent paths.

Our quantitative investigation supports our core hypothesis that macrocorporatist business representation and associated nonmarket coordination is most likely to evolve in a centralized, multiparty, proportional representation political system. As predicted, party competition, levels of federalism, and historical labor market legacies all had bearing on the development of managed capitalism. In our comparative analysis of historical quantitative data, the absence of proportionality and attendant two-party system is systematically associated with low levels of employers' organization and low levels of nonmarket coordination – both macrocorporatism and sectoral coordination – in the early decades of the twentieth century. There is also evidence (though less strong) that federalism and associated fragmentation depressed employer organization and macrocorporatist coordination. The interaction of electoral proportionality and federalism is strongly associated with the evolution of sectoral coordination. Features of industrialization and industrial relations systems (levels of union mobilization, traditions of coordination, and economic development) also each foster encompassing and centralized employers' associations. Traditions of coordination and economic development promote macrocorporatist institutions. Yet, the strategic context of employers' choices differed across countries and core features of party politics directly determined the character of employers' collective actions, so important to the ultimate capitalist trajectory.

The following chapters present historical studies of Denmark, the United Kingdom, the United States, and Germany to delve deeper into the dynamic and mutually reinforcing relationship between the spheres of industrial relations and political party competition. With process tracing and historical archival analysis, we reveal the causal mechanisms that link political institutions to the development of employers' organizations and modes of nonmarket coordination.

3

Party Conflict and the Origins of Danish Labor Market Coordination

It is almost more important to have a good employers' association than a good government.

Niels Andersen

Introduction

The exceptionally high levels of equality in Scandinavian today are underscored by equally impressive levels of social and economic coordination. For example, for much of the post-war era, the peak associations for the social partners – the Confederation of Danish Employers (DA) and the Danish Confederation of Trade Unions (LO) – negotiated broad collective bargains and engaged in corporatist tripartite discussions with government to develop a wide spectrum of public policies. Although collective bargaining was decentralized to sectoral level cartels in the 1980s, wage setting remains relatively coordinated even at the decentralized level and policy making continues through tripartite channels.[1]

This institutional exuberance for consensus is attributed to various causes: Perhaps cultural exceptionalism explains the high levels of coordination, as citizens of the frozen north simply have a more collective esprit des corps. Modern cooperation may reflect historical patterns of industrial conflict, because well-organized and aggressive Scandinavian labor movements wrested power away from an upper class divided between agricultural and industrial elites. As a late industrializer, Denmark may have been motivated to develop high levels of coordination and cooperation in order to catch up to other advanced nations.[2] Tales of cultural harmony and class warfare,

[1] Traxler 2004; Mailand 2002. Although DA's member associations also engaged in sectoral collective bargaining and gave political advice with Danish Industry as the leading industrial association, DA had formal responsibility for participating in tripartite negotiations and for organizing collective bargaining, and the other groups were technically subordinate to DA's jurisdictional authority.

[2] Knudsen 2002; Østergård 1992; Castles 1993; Gershenkron 1962.

however, are a bit difficult to reconcile, and one wonders how employers cast their lot with cooperation over conflict.

We suggest that the dynamics of party politics are essential to understanding Danish employers' ability to obtain a high level of industrial self-regulation and cooperation at the end of the nineteenth century. The Right Party (Højre) contained most industrialists; however, the urban industrial wing was in frequent conflict with the provincial aristocratic wing over both policies and strategies for retaining power against the threats of a farmer-labor alliance. Even though the party had been allowed to rule without a parliamentary majority in the lower chamber before the system change in 1901, growing democratization made this arrangement unlikely in the future. The business wing leaders of the Right Party created the peak employers' association, in part, to solve party problems and to move policy making to a venue where employers were more likely to win. Niels Andersen, Right Party leader and entrepreneur, founded the Danish Employers' Federation of 1896 (subsequently to become DA) to compensate for the party's growing weakness, to develop a second front for representing the business voice, and to nurture extra-parliamentary channels for self-regulation, collective bargaining, and policy making.

The Right Party evolved into the Danish Conservative Party with a new constitution in 1915. The new Conservative Party continued to be factionalized between an industrial wing and a middle-class wing, but the new party consolidated more thoroughly the employer vote. Moreover, the introduction of proportional representation meant that employers' minority vote shares in districts would still count toward parliamentary seats. This electoral consolidation helped to strengthen the national interests of employers and the internal organization of DA subsequently became less regional in focus as well.

The Danish story testifies to the importance of party structure to the delegation of policy-making power to the private sector: when right parties with large business constituencies have little hope of winning legislative majorities, they will be more willing to allow for the self-regulation of business, rather than pursuing regulation through political channels. Moreover, the case demonstrates that changes in the party system (i.e., the move from the Højre to Conservative Party and the introduction of proportional representation) produces changes in the encompassing employers' associations and associated institutions for nonmarket coordination. Thus, the historical analysis of the Danish case furthers our core argument that party system structure adds a crucial step in nation's diverging paths toward economic coordination or liberalism.

Theories of Danish Business Organization

Industrialization

Three aspects of the Danish political economy contributed to the rise of a highly organized business community: economic modernization of the economy, the character of labor, and the dynamics of party competition. Employers in the burgeoning manufacturing sector sought policies to nurture industrialization, as merchandise production and trade grew rapidly in the 1890s and industrial sectors were becoming more capital-intensive. Employers sought to cooperate, in part, to alter the policy landscape, as regulatory policies stayed true to the political and economic power of agriculture.[3] The small size of firms and small population undoubtedly contributed to the formation of employers' associations, because employers lacked the option of forming internal strategies for managing labor relations and sought collective solutions to protect against social risks.[4]

Yet, the diversity of economic interests worked against easy business compromise and the structure of the Danish economy had a somewhat complex impact on employers' capacity to organize. Despite its small size, the Danish economy was historically deeply polarized between agriculture, industrial and handwork enterprises, with particularly sharp divisions on tariffs. Agriculture was the largest sector of the Danish economy until well into the twentieth century and in 1890 two-thirds of the Danish population lived on farms, with the other third equally distributed between Copenhagen and the provincial cities. Yet by the end of World War I, industry was the fastest growing sector of the Danish economy and, by 1921, 33 percent of citizens were farmers, 29 percent worked in handwork or industrial sector, and 17 percent engaged in trade or transportation. Danish farmers cultivated an aggressive export sector and in 1914 agricultural products were 85 percent of Danish exports. Danish manufacturers, a cross-national laggard among industrial countries, were generally anxious to protect their domestic markets and battled against the tariffs; however, even here pronounced sectoral differences separated manufacturers from artisans.[5] Tariffs were a particularly intense battleground; for example, an 1893 act split the Right Party between the artisan wing that desired protection and the free-trade industrial wing that rejected it. In the Tariff Bill of 1908, farmers feared that tariffs protecting Danish industrial products would prompt retaliatory tariffs on Danish specialty agricultural exports. Industrial exports remained under 10 percent of GDP during this period, and a widespread push to export did not bring industrialists together in Denmark, as it did in some other countries. In fact, the domestic focus of Danish firms may have fostered cooperation: firms worried less about their wage costs because they did not compete in world markets.[6]

Labor: Activism and Skills

The features of Danish labor also motivated high levels of employer association, but in a rather contradictory way, as both trade union antagonism and guild collectivism reputedly drove the business response. Destroying unions was a clear motivation for the organization of employers at the sectoral level in the 1870s and 1880s, when skilled workers in the metal and building sectors, in particular, sought to alter the balance of power between labor and capital. Employers' violent opposition to unions peaked with

---

[3] Between 1880 and 1910, per capita real Gross Domestic Product rose from 2,181 to 3,705 (1990 international dollars). Agriculture's share of GDP fell from 42 to 30 percent during this period. In addition, exports as a percentage of GDP increased from 21 to 30 percent when measured in current Koner; when computed in constant 1990 international dollars, the 1880 and 1910 values are roughly half these totals. During these decades of development, and reinforcing the perception that mid-sized Danish industrial enterprises focused on domestic markets, the agricultural share of exports remained close to 90 percent. (For sources of these and all historical data used, see the Historical Ancillary Material.)

[4] Scheuer 1992: 169; Baldwin 1990.

[5] Fink 1988, 51–4.

[6] Dybdahl 1969; Hyldtoft 1999, chapters 13–14; Gourevitch 1986; Galenson 1952, 71–2; Due et al. 1994, 73–90.

an acrimonious battle in the iron industry in 1885, an episode that established the right of workers to organize collectively. When smiths at Borch & Henriksen began a strike, S. C. Hauberg led iron manufacturers to form the Association of Manufacturers in the Copenhagen Metal Trades (Foreningen af Fabrikanter i Jernindustrien i Kjøbenhavn). The trade unions retaliated with a series of successive strikes and firms began a five-month lockout to stop labor organization. Ultimately the business and labor sectoral associations negotiated a collective agreement and employers recognized labor organizations, when employers felt that they had no other options.[7]

Although employers organized at the sectoral level in response to high levels of labor militancy, their decision to develop a national employers' association required articulation of their strategic interests in coordination and a sea change in collective action. Niels Andersen recalled the industrial battle of 1885 as a precipitating motivation for later business organization, yet the Danish craft unions were weaker than Swedish industrial unions and drew their inspiration from Britain. Multisector employers organization developed earlier than multisector unions in most towns, as employers were better able than workers to overcome the limitations of industrial and craft-based divisions. Labor only organized a peak association two years after the Employers' Federation of 1896 joined employers throughout the land, and labor did so at the employers' instigation. Thus reflecting on the first twenty-five years of LO, J. S. Hansen credited the Employers' Association of 1896 with the emergence of a strong encompassing labor association.[8]

Guild collectivism also paved the way for cooperative industrial relations, although again the impact of the guilds was complicated. Certainly, employers' embrace of cooperation was fully congruent with the collectivist, preindustrial guild system; the national employers' association emerged less than fifty years after the official end of the guilds; and a large share of workers were skilled craftsmen. Danish collectivism had deep roots in the ideological/spiritual writings of N. F. S. Grundtvig, the Lutheran church, the peaceful revolution of King Frederick VII, and the agricultural cooperatives (which produced 80 percent of milk by 1903). Yet, Grundtvig's collectivism had more purchase in the agricultural world than among city dwellers, just as the somewhat comparable Populist tradition was largely confined to rural America. Employers' social concerns were inspired by Germanic workplace stability more than by Social Democratic values of equality and business sought social protections to limit class mobility. Denmark retained a variant of serfdom through the seventeenth century, and this early history is difficult to reconcile with the later cultural norms of equality.[9]

Moreover, the impact of the guilds on the specific organization of the employers' federation was limited and its formation signaled both continuity and change in business history. The guilds' repeal in 1857 was largely "a codification of changes in economic life which had already taken place over decades."[10] Although guilds largely focused on restricting competition, the peak employers' association sought to expand

[7] Due et al. 1994, 73–4; Galenson 1952; Bruun, 1938; Sisson 1987.

[8] Agerholm and Vigen 1921, 4; Nørregaard 1943, 362; Hansen 1922, 261; Due et al. 1994, 91.

[9] Galenson 1952, 195; Due et al. 1994; Knudsen 1991; 2002; Østergård 1992, 16; Andersen and Jacobsen 2008, 8; Levine 1978.

[10] Bruun 1938, 409; A Nørgaard 1997, 120–92.

trade; and the impetus to organize a national, multisector peak association came from the technologically advanced industrial sectors rather than from the handicraft sectors with ties to former guilds. Although guilds separated handicraft sectors from large firms and reinforced working class solidarity in Germany, they created deep hostility between skilled and unskilled workers in Denmark and significantly weakened the labor movement. In economic terms, guilds discouraged price cutting and wage competition and encouraged strong social connections; however, in political terms, handicrafts had great difficulty organizing above the sectoral level and industrial firms took the lead in collective bargaining.[11] Indeed, the guilds' demise made employers less fiercely opposed to worker organization:

This position [of opposition to collective bargaining] might have seemed natural and obvious in the old system, where masters were almost as numerous as smiths. When large-scale operations developed, it was harder to uphold. Therefore, industrial employers essentially became more willing than old handwork employers to bargain with the new employers' organizations.[12]

Thus, at the dawn of coordination, neither labor activism, cultural predispositions, nor postguild legacies of coordination can completely capture employers' endorsement of the peaceful, cooperative demeanor that became the signature of Danish business in later years. The great transformation occurred because employers lacked other ways to control labor, yet even this rational calculation of self interests was not enough to evolve high levels of coordination. A commission first proposed an industrial cooperation strategy in 1878, but the two major political parties were at a stalemate, and it was only with the shift in party composition that the Right Party advanced a new system of private coordination with labor.[13]

The Structure of Party Competition and Danish Employers

Our central contention is that the creation of the Danish peak association – initially called the Employers' Federation of 1896 and later the Confederation of Danish Employers (Dansk Arbejdsgiverforeningen or DA) – can only be fully understood in light of the backdrop of partisan struggle. Democratization was on the horizon (with a big system change in 1901), and the Right Party fought to retain its power in the face of demands for full political and industrial rights. A faction of the party determined that a politics of coordination – in which a cooperative employers' association was key – could offset socialism and demonstrate the party's relevance to a middle-way politics. Because the anticipated reforms threatened the right's political hegemony, it had incentives to delegate as much authority as possible to private institutions for negotiation between the social partners. Politically, the Right Party had to fight both the workers and the farmers; however, in private channels, employers had only the workers to beat. Thus, the particular structure of party politics made employers aware of strategic and collective interests in the creation of an encompassing and centralized peak organization.

---

[11] Due et al. 1994, 75; Galenson 1952, 69–72.
[12] Bruun 1938, 381.
[13] Jacobsen and Pedersen 2009.

The party system developed over the latter part of the nineteenth century in the wake of the Second Schleswig War, which cost Denmark a third of its territory and prompted an acute national political identity crisis. Two loose political groups evolved into a Liberal Party (Venstre) for wealthy farmers and a Right Party for the nobility, bourgeoisie and some urban workers. The Liberals usually gained majorities in the lower chamber of parliament (Folketinget) with members elected by voters, but the Right and aristocracy dominated the upper chamber (Landstinget). The king had the right to form a government as long as both chambers did not oppose, the Right Party was able to rule for many years with the support of the king and the upper chamber, and the government was deeply undemocratic.[14] Emergent Social Democrats increasingly claimed the loyalties of the working man in the 1880s and politics was divided by strong left-right and urban-rural splits, but lines were fluid until the 1890s.[15]

The Right Party's campaign for political power transpired in three stages: a battle between the Right and Liberal parties, a center-right coalition against social democracy, and a move by the Right to nurture private avenues for policy making. First, intense competition between the Right and Liberal parties motivated the Right to build constituency organizations beyond its elite core. Divided government – with Liberals controlling the lower chamber and the executive and upper chamber controlled by the Right – produced legislative stalemate, and Prime Minister Estrup created a series of contentious provisional budgets in the 1880s and 1890s.[16]

This uneasy balance was upset with the rise of social democratic sentiment in Copenhagen and growing Liberal Party opposition. Fearing that an alliance of Liberals and Social Democrats (SDs) would throw the Right out of power, the Right Party decided to expand its constituency base beyond its elite core and to make up for its shortcomings with a stronger organization. To this end, the party created local voter and worker committees among the mass electorate to mobilize the support of working class constituents and to offset rising radicalism. When the SDs got 40 percent of the vote in Copenhagen's Blågård district in 1881, retailer E. H. Ryssel promoted worker committees, which had 29,000 members by 1887. By 1887, membership had risen to 29,000 members, and the group offered sickness and free legal advice to members.[17] The Right Party also created regional Conservative Clubs in 1885, which began as discussion groups for activist party members, but became magnets for new members with

[14] The National Liberal Party, damaged by the German war, moved into the Right Party after the war. The bourgeoisie in towns (including many National Liberals) were dissatisfied with this arrangement and briefly formed a Middle Party (Mellempartiet), but the Right Party consolidated its membership after Liberal Party landslides in the 1872 and 1876 elections. The alliance between nobility and bourgeoisie continued to be uneasy, however, as the "stock market opposition" had different interests from the aristocracy, especially in industrial development policies. When Prime Minister Estrup twice dissolved the Folketinget, the "stock market opposition" complained that such instability was bad for the needs of industrial development. Petersen 1979–, 217. Twenty percent of the upper chamber MPs were appointed by the king and high tax payers over 40 had increased voting privileges. Jacobsen and Pedersen 2009; Hyldtoft 1999.

[15] Fink 2000, 14–17; Nørgaard 1979, 136 .

[16] The Liberal Party accused Prime Minister Estrup and the Right Party of running a dictatorship and pursued a "withering politics" to stop government by refusing to pass budgets and other laws, prompting Estrup's provisional budgets. Jacobsen and Pedersen 2009.

[17] Fink 2000, 21–5; Dybdahl 1969, 88; "Historisk Tilbageblik I glimt."

parties, choruses, and carnivals. At their more politically oriented gatherings, the clubs welcomed speakers from the segment of the population from which Højre's leadership was drawn. Thus, in the first year, party leader Lars Dinesen shared the stage with a manufacturer, a retailer, and handicraft employers. The Right Party portrayed itself as a cross-class party with mass appeal, and worker committees and conservative clubs were essential to this agenda.[18]

A second stage in the passion play of party politics was an era of center-right alliance against the rise of social democracy and growing inevitability of parliamentary reform. In the 1890 election, Social Democrats gained seats in the lower chamber and economic cleavages (especially on trade) surpassed attitudes toward political liberalism as the central issue of the day. Economic cleavages divided the population into rich and poor farmers, employers and workers and the growing diversity of interests created possibilities for shifting party alliances.[19]

The Right Party's leadership was split on how to revive its fortunes: The moderate, urban parliamentary wing (including most industrialists and led by Lars Dinesen) advocated a voting alliance with the Liberal Party to stop socialism, whereas the conservative clubs opposed cooperation.[20] At an 1890 delegate meeting, Dinesen argued that the Liberals and Social Democrats had little in common besides their attack on the Right Party, and proposed a counteralliance with the Liberals. He also sought to centralize the party, by strengthening executive committee control, and giving the central parliamentary committee oversight over candidate selection. This move would greatly curb the power of the local conservative clubs, which Dinesen viewed as shortsighted. The Right Party participated in extensive electoral collaboration with the Liberals in April 1892, but lost about 15 percent of its vote.[21]

The conservative club faction of the Right Party, led by Jacob Scavenius, resisted collaboration with Liberals, blamed moderates for the electoral setback, and favored a strong national defense and moral rectitude. Scavenius inspired a string of attacks on Dinesen in the newspaper "København" in the fall of 1892. Dinesen retained support of the Right representative council, but conservative clubs resolved to run candidates against those Liberal officeholders, who had won in the earlier cross-party alliance.[22] Conflict between the factions played out over the national defense; indeed, the issue inspired a center/periphery split among both parties. Prime Minister Estrup and the parliamentary wing proposed ramparts to defend Copenhagen until outside aid materialized, whereas Scavenius and Conservative Club activists insisted on protection for the entire nation. Around 1890, the Right's parliamentary wing and its Liberal allies moved to defend Copenhagen with the construction of Middelgrundfortet.[23]

---

[18] Dybdahl 1969, 91, 115–17.

[19] Fink 2000, 23.

[20] Bindslev 1937–8, 57.

[21] Dybdahl 1969, 14–15. The Liberal Party was also divided between a wing committed to a "withering politics" (visnepolitiken), to wear down the power of Council President Estrup, and a wing, led by Frede Bojsen, that favored compromise with the Right Party (forligpolitiken). Nørgaard Petersen 1979, 218.

[22] Blindslev 1937–8, 57–8; Nørgaard Petersen 1979–, 219–23; Dybdahl 1969, 14–15; Bindslev 1937–8; Berlingske Tidende, December 18, 1894, "De forenede konservative klubbers delegeretmøde."

[23] Kiilerich 1975, 115–17, 128.

The centrist wings of the Right and Liberal Parties also pushed budget deals in the lower chamber.[24]

The April 1895 election was a make or break moment for the Right and Liberal compromise wings and the Right moderates suffered dramatically, when the party lost over a quarter of its voters in 1892 and 1895.[25] Conservative Clubs proposed to ban further negotiations with Liberals; a Right finance law was voted down in May 1895; the Right Party leader resigned; and executive council rules were proposed to give provincial members more influence.[26]

The Formation of the Danish Employers' Confederation of 1896

Right Party's Interests and Niels Andersen's Role

The Right Party next determined that its best bet for retaining political influence and stopping socialism was to coopt the working class; to this end, it cultivated a private system of industrial policy making. According to its official history, the Right Party's involvement in the creation of the Employers' Federation must be viewed against the backdrop of the party's fight for rule against the Liberals and nascent Social Democratic Party.[27] After losing constituents to the Social Democratic and Liberal parties, the Right was increasingly solely comprised of its two dominant (uneasily united) wings, industrialists and aristocrats. Just as the party had used organization to cement working class support in the 1880s, it sought to strengthen its political position with the creation of another organization, the employers' association, in the 1890s. Associational politics was a strategy by employers to augment their political influence in both industrial relations and public policy. Manufacturers were both uncomfortable with aristocrats within the Right Party and concerned that the party would be overwhelmed by a Liberal–Social Democratic alliance, and transferring political authority to private channels was a way to escape the rising democratic tide. Thus the organizer of the Danish Employers Federation, Niels Andersen, recalled at the time he stepped down as chairman of the DA in 1911, "It is almost more important to have a good employers' association than a good government."[28]

---

[24] In 1890–1 Bojsen (Liberal) developed an extensive reform program that included reducing sugar taxes and introducing a beer tax, a tariff reform, a new poor law, a law for elderly support, state support of a sickness fund, and accident insurance. The vote in 1892 strengthened Bojsen's political standing and compromise on many of these measures seemed possible. A key point of compromise occurred in the development of a finance law that would replace the provisional laws that Estrup had created during periods of stalemate between parties and branches of Parliament. After much negotiation in the fall of 1894, Right Party in Folketinget gave the Liberals the repeal of the earlier provisional law; in return, Liberals supported the fortification of Copenhagen (an important issue for Right Party moderates) with the stipulation that military recruits would be kept at the current number and that the overall defense budget would be reduced (Jørgensen 1962, xi–xii, 45; Brøndsted 1925, 146–54; Kiilerich 1975, 114.) The Liberals had also hoped to secure Estrup's resignation, but this did not occur, and Estrup did not include any Liberal men in his cabinet; and with this, the compromise faction of the Liberals lost standing.
[25] Dybdahl 1969, p. 11, chapter III.
[26] Nørgaard Petersen 1979–81, 224–5; Right Party Delegate meeting 1895, 5.
[27] Agerholm and Vigen 1921.
[28] Agerholm and Vigen 1921, 211–12.

Niels Andersen (a Right Party member of parliament and a construction/ railroad magnate) and Vilhelm Køhler (director of the Frederiksholms Teglværker brick factory, head of the bricklayer guild, and a master builder) created the Danish Employers' Federation of 1896. A building trades strike in February 1896 precipitated the organization's development: Andersen and Køhler proposed an employers' association committed to restraining industrial conflict and to securing labor peace through collective action. Køhler and Andersen held a meeting in Copenhagen attended by representatives from industry sectoral associations and narrowed the agenda to a simple, limited program: members of the future employers' association would not hire workers from other member companies during permitted strikes or lockouts and a committee with representatives of the union and firms would negotiate the industrial incident.[29]

Andersen was a leading Right Party legislator as well as captain of industry, and had participated in past constituency-building exercises; for example, he spoke at the party's second Constitution festival to build Conservative Clubs in 1886. By definition, Andersen came from the business and parliamentary wing of the Right Party; yet, he was a born negotiator, was known within Parliament as being "knowledgeable, eloquent and politically independent" and seemed able to cross sides. He was even chosen as a spokesman for the Liberals on the Railroad law in 1892. Andersen was personally involved in the defense of Copenhagen, in acquiring and donating the land for the first permanent fort in Copenhagen, Gardehøjfortet, and in supervising the construction of Middlegrundsfortet (the fortification that prompted the parliamentary compromise between the moderate wings of the Right and Liberal parties in 1890). When the Right lost a major vote in 1898, the party nearly broke apart due to bitter divisions between the two wings; but the factions finally agreed on Andersen as party speaker in the lower house.[30]

Political Ambitions: Unifying Business Policy Positions and Self-Regulation

Whereas the Employers' Federation was specifically created to respond to the building strike, Andersen worked to transcend the immediate concerns attending the dispute and to build the association into a vehicle for unifying Danish industry, for attaining industrial peace, and for achieving the policy ambitions of the Right Party. The Employers' Federation focused on two central goals: to unify the business political voice with an aim at nurturing industrial development and self-regulation, and to achieve industrial peace.

First, its founders viewed the DA as a vehicle for the political unification of Danish industry, so that employers could themselves set the agenda for labor market reforms. Shortly after its formation, the leadership sought regional diversity and gathered

---

[29] Agerholm and Vigen 1921, 10–13.

[30] Dybdahl, 1969, 115–17; Neergaard, N. "Niels Andersen." *Salmonsens konversationsleksikon,* http:// runeberg.org/salmonsen/2/1/0764.html; Nørgaard Petersen, 1979, 219–20; Nielsen, "Ydby skriver i Sydthy Årbog om:Polarforskeren Knud Rasmussen, Etatsråden og Ydby Missionshus" cites Niels Andersen letter to "De kongelige ordenes kapitel," http://www.cmi.dk/Charles.html; Ministry of Transportation, "Niels Christensen Monberg," http://www.trm.dk/sw14784.asp; Kiilerich, 1975, 128; Rambusch 1988, 232–3. Andersen also supported the expansion of taxes over military cutbacks, and was part of a group favoring "self-taxation" Blangstrup 1915, 720.

information from industrial firms in the provinces, as the association was particularly interested at building links to companies outside of Copenhagen.[31] Whereas much is often made of DA's role in organizing collective bargaining, the importance of its political function is revealed in the retrospective written to commemorate the first twenty-five years of DA's existence: "the most important evidence of the organization's energy and vision was its contribution to the solution of the question about insurance against workmen's accidents." The law demonstrated that "employers' legitimate interests could get expressed in the law."[32]

Worker's accident insurance was the first major political issue for the employers' federation and the case demonstrates the employers' ambition for self-regulation and its great success in obtaining a voluntary self-financed program, monitored by a private corporatist board. The first Industrial Injuries Insurance Act of 1898 gave firms responsibility for accidents but allowed them to take out private insurance, excluded agricultural employers and established a "Workmen's Compensation Board" to self-regulate the program. The Right Party strongly favored an English voluntary model over the German version (demanding compulsory participation in a worker fund). Ludvig Bramsen, the Right Party Director of Insurance (and member of the board for the DA) made his fortune in the private insurance industry and may have believed that the German version would have driven private plans out of business.[33] Social Democrats wanted a universal, tax-financed bill, fearing that workers would bear the burden of social insurance.

Employers recognized that they would have to pay one way or another, sought to retain as much control as possible, and therefore, favored a voluntary plan with significant business oversight. They proposed a deal to major agricultural export interests who were overly represented in Parliament and who wanted to avoid expanded labor costs in their international markets. Industrialists would support exempting agriculture from the bill (suggesting that it apply only to "high risk," i.e., manufacturing industries) if the rich farmers would support a voluntary measure in which employers could choose to purchase private insurance and which would be governed by a board for determining compensation composed of the social partners.[34] Denmark became the only country to vest control over a social insurance program in a corporatist board. Bramsen had not included a corporatist body in his initial sickness insurance proposal; rather, Niels Andersen was responsible for introducing the idea of a Works Council as a governing body.[35]

The DA leadership used the insurance reform to build its membership base and, most importantly, to persuade the handicraft sectors to join; thus, the offensive helped to unify the political voice of business. The employers' federation feared that the financial burden of this insurance in its initial form would largely fall on employers,

---

[31] DA-Korrespondence 1897_25 (20/2/1897).
[32] Agerholm and Vigen 1921, 5, 16, trans. by author.
[33] Bramsen had been invited by Kaiser Wilhelm II to be one of three Danish representatives at a Worker's Protection Congress in Berlin. (Bramsen 1964, 106–30).
[34] Andersen 2010, 514–56, 102.
[35] Former Prime Minister Estrup, now a member of Landstinget, aggressively and successfully pushed the proposal in the upper chamber, where supporters feared that it would be opposed by conservative aristocratic members of Right Party. A. Nørgaard 1997, 168.

and held a meeting in September 1896, inviting representatives from the crafts manufacturing associations, to develop proposals for parliament on the bill. Over the course of the coming months, Andersen reached out to many sectoral handicraft associations, and proposed that industry and handicrafts jointly develop a system of self-regulation, as an alternative to the Liberal-dominated government plan. This would both avoid a government-imposed economic burden and build cooperative linkages to other social actors. In March 1897, the federation sent a circular encouraging recipients not to endorse the state insurance, and offering to build a common insurance concern with other employers.[36] This would "prevent the negative economic effects of a law that requires employers to pay support for work accidents ... But this concern, as contemplated, will also be able to create the foundation for another Collaboration between trade and association with common interests."[37]

The circular initially spawned the disapproval of the Union of Danish Industry and Handicraft, which warned their members against letting themselves be ensnared by the employers' association. An exchange of notes between the two organizations ended with both seeking to find common ground, and finally in 1898, the Handicrafts sectors joined the newly titled Confederation of Danish Business, a move that unified all kinds of employers. The endeavor offered a lasting lesson for employers, in showing that cooperation on social legislation could benefit both employers and workers.[38]

Industrial Peace

The second central goal of the employers' association was to achieve industrial peace. Thus, Niels Andersen stated "our purpose and only wish is to be a future obstacle to strife between workers and employers" and the leadership, in particular, wished to avoid debilitating strikes at all costs.[39] A federation regulation stated: "No inequality between employers and workers concerning the work relationship (including, for example, wages and performance) should give rise to work stoppages from either side. This inequality should, instead, be settled with a compromise or an arbitration."[40] The trade associations determined that organizational members of the peak association would each elect a representative and pay 30 kroner in dues. If the association's governing body recognized an ongoing strike as illegitimate or an ongoing lockout as legitimate, members would have to pledge not to hire workers or purchase materials from the plant that had the strike or lockout.[41]

This vision of industrial peace did not come easily to all employers, and the iron industry, led by S.C. Hauberg, initially was the most skeptical. Andersen sought arbitration; however, the metal trades employers favored a politics of confrontation to stop organized labor's challenge to management's prerogatives. The Employers' Federation of 1896 and the iron manufacturers began resolving their differences on industrial

---

[36] These included the Handiwork Union, the Industrial union, Handwork Representatives Group, and the Collective Representation of Danish Handiwork and Industry. Arbejdsgiverforeningen af 1896, 8/3/1897; Galenson 1952.

[37] Arbejdsgiverforeningen af 1896. 8/3/1897. Italics in original, trans. by CJ Martin.

[38] DA Korrespondance, 1897_25 (20/2/1897); Sophus and Vigen 1921, 15–16.

[39] Agerholm and Vigen 1921, 2.

[40] "Vedtægter for Arbejdsgiverforeningen af 1896."

[41] Agerholm and Vigen 1921, 11–14.

relations during a major metal-industry conflict in 1897. An industrial conflict began in Aalborg when worker demands for a significant wage increase were rejected and the provincial factory employers appealed to Copenhagen industrialists for support. A lockout began in the provinces in March, Copenhagen employers factories promised to lock their factories on April 1st if the provinces didn't solve the dispute, and the battle threatened to become both encompassing and difficult. A voluntary agreement involving the mayor and the national bank director was almost reached in March but fell through and the labor unrest continued.[42]

This provided the Employers' Federation of 1896 with an opening to offer its assistance, in return for a recognition of its jurisdiction. DA sent a confidential letter to the Association of Manufacturers in the Iron Industry in Copenhagen (Foreningen af Fabrikanter i Jernindustrien i Kjøbenhavn), which included a draft plan for avoiding future strikes: A Labor Court (Arbejdsdomstol) would include a member of the Danish Supreme Court, two members of the Ministry of the Interior, two members from the Employers' Association of 1896, and two members from the predecessor to LO (De Samvirkende Fagforeninger). The letter stressed the importance of cooperation with the union and proposed a procedure for dealing with employers reluctant to accept the Labor Court's rulings.[43] Andersen stressed the confidentiality of the letter, writing:

> The points mentioned, of course, must be the object for closer negotiations with the associations that have joined the "Employers' Federation of 1896," and will also allow us to put forth that this letter can be interpreted as a pledge.[44]

The employers' federation also sought to organize labor during this episode and scholars credit these actions for being largely responsible for the centralized form of the Danish LO. Danish employers sought a more centralized labor federation, in part, in order to ask unions to refuse to work for free-riding firms who stayed out of the business group.[45] Thus, DA's interest in centrally organized labor unions partially reflected its desire to exert jurisdictional control over its own sectoral association members. On July 12, 1897, Andersen wrote to De Samvirkende Fagforeninger (DSF) to solicit its impression of the progress in the iron industry conflict and to imply that DA wished to participate as an agent of negotiation. The breakthrough in the negotiations, in fact, reflected a strong role for DA, which obtained an initial compromise in the iron industry conflict, with the iron industry sectoral association negotiating its own resolution thereafter. In March 1898, DA wrote again to DSF, bemoaning the fact that no one currently played a mediating role in industrial conflict on the labor side, which meant that DSF's member associations were contributing to the undermining of work effort. DA encouraged DSF to play the same leadership role in negotiations that DA was attempting to do on the employers' side.[46] De Samvirkende Fagforeninger then formed a new encompassing labor organization, De Samvirkende Fagforbund (LO) in 1898, and workers and employers both obtained encompassing peak organizations to represent their political interests.[47]

[42] Agerholm and Vigen 1921, 17–19.
[43] 1897, 46–8, 23/6/1897, DA Korrespondance, General udgående 1896 6 30 til 1899 9 21.
[44] Andersen to Foreningen af Fabrikanter i Jernindustrien' i Kjøbenhavn, trans. by C. J. Martin.
[45] Due et al. 1994, 78–9; Galenson 1952, 2–8, 58, 69, 72, 9.
[46] Andersen to DSF. 7/12/1897; DA to DSF, 3/1898; Agerholm and Vigen, 1921, 20.
[47] Jacobsen and Pedersen 2009.

On August 20, 1898, Niels Andersen sought to bring the political parties more forcefully into the negotiation process, by proposing that he and the union man in parliament, J Jensen, jointly lead the mediation process. The negotiations resulted in a proposed collective bargain on August 26; however, the firms opposed the proposal. But this setback motivated Andersen to increase the stakes, and he appealed to the Iron Industry Association's governing body, urging the industry association to pledge in advance to stand by the negotiated results and stating that the same offer would be made to labor. Both sides agreed to commit to the outcome whether they won or lost, and a collective bargain was subsequently negotiated on September 8, 1897, which represented the first agreement between the Employers' Association of 1896 and the peak union. The union, in fact, gained very little by the lengthy strike and managed to obtain only one concession from employers that was not offered before the lockout.

S. C. Hauberg had vehemently opposed Andersen's conciliatory tactics in the initial stages of the conflict; however, the iron industry leadership began "wandering over to the Employers' Association's camp," in recognizing the attractions of a permanent court for industrial arbitrations that would adjudicate guilt in breakdowns of wage bargaining. Hauberg, met with Andersen and Køhler in June and the DA and the iron industry sectoral group agreed upon a simply formulated proposal for a permanent negotiating body, which paved the way for a lasting union and moved the iron industry toward industrial cooperation. The proposal for a mandatory arbitration board was put for a vote on the Employers' Federation's rules: "No disagreement between the employer and workers concerning the work relationship ... should bring about a strike from either side, but this disagreement must without exception go to negotiation." The Joint Committee of 1898 (Fællesudvalget af 1898) was, thereby, established as a joint body to rule on violations of collective agreements and the employers' federation won a significant victory in its effort to control labor with a politics of coordination.[48]

The September Compromise and the Danish Model

The fundamental outlines of the Danish model of industrial relations were established in 1899 with the famous September Compromise after a huge, three-month, labor market battle. The employers staged a "Great Lockout" and its resolution induced employers and workers to engage in their first general negotiation (hovedaftalen), between DA and LO. The Great Lockout (Storlockouten) began with a rather minor strike in Jutland, but the employers quickly responded with a far-reaching lockout, that extended across the economy and lasted three months. Indeed, evidence suggests that employers drove the lockout in order to push toward a national system of collective bargaining, as DA's leadership had discussed the possibility of a grand lockout with the textile manufacturers association and with the iron manufacturers in the years before. Yet the Liberal Party cut short Right Party's plans to use industrial conflict to set up national collective bargaining, by giving aid to the striking workers; consequently, the anticipated quick resolution failed to materialize and the battle turned bitter. At the onset of the industrial conflict, the employer federation's members included both hawks and doves, but the majority (and certainly the leadership) held to

---

[48] Agerholm and Vigen 1921, 20–1; Due et al. 1994, 79.

a moderate position. The objective of the battle was to strengthen the DA's "own equal rights vis-à-vis the labor union (De Samvirkende Fagforbund) at a time when it was on its way to getting the upper hand. It should be a defensive battle before the labor movement became too strong."[49] The employers' demands made sense in light of these broader institutional ambitions: DA sought to centralize collective bargaining by vesting authority in DA and LO and demanded managerial prerogatives over work.[50]

States Minister Hørring in an informal meeting with Niels Andersen threatened to intervene if the two sides were unable to find a solution. But employers and labor associations ended the stand-off with the September Compromise (September Forlig), which established a system of collective bargaining.[51] Although business had the upper hand in the battle, it stopped short of seizing complete victory, causing an observer to note:

Had the employers really been convinced of winning, it seems odd for them to have abstained from dictating humiliating terms ... The main outcome of the conflict of 1899 was, in reality, that both parties became equally strong. They had tested each other's power and developed respect for one another. This realization meant that workers also became less dissatisfied with the result, maybe not at first, but after they saw what had come out of the settlement.[52]

The institutionalization of the Danish model, following the lockout of 1899, had benefits for both business and labor, but employers enjoyed the greatest victory. The compromise established employers' control over the organization of work, significantly devolved power to the social partners, and set up a permanent court of arbitration. Thus, by 1900, DA had successfully contained industrial conflict at a national, multiindustrial level and orchestrated the formation of a joint committee to oversee collective agreements.[53]

Further Consolidation and Centralization of DA's Power

Even though the September Compromise put into place a system of collective bargaining, it did not produce a permanent centralization of employers' power within the DA. The September Compromise had established employers' control over the organization of work, yet participation in industrial relations systems remained voluntary, decentralized, and organized along trade lines. The empowerment of DA came only with its subsequent reorganization and centralization.

With regime change in 1901, the Liberal Party gained control of government and reinforced agriculture's political hegemony in public policy. Thus, a 1903 tax act shifted the tax burden from land to a personal and corporate income tax, even while (largely rural) cooperatives continued to be excused from taxation. Employers sought a ministry for industry with powers equal to the parallel ministry for agriculture, and like their British counterparts, wanted to vest power over international trade (export supports) in the foreign ministry. Instead, a Ministry for Trade and Shipping was created

[49] Nørregaard 1943, 513.
[50] Due et al. 1994, 80–1.
[51] Due et al. 1994, 80–1.
[52] Nørregaard 1943, 525–6, trans. by C. J. Martin.
[53] Nørregaard 1943, 529; Fællesudvalget af 1898; Due et al 1994.

64 *The Political Construction of Business Interests*

(which favored unrestricted trade) and the economic development concerns of industrialists and artisans remained a responsibility of the Domestic Ministry.[54]

Although both industrial and handicraft employers resented the Liberal Party's preferences to agriculture, centrifugal forces associated with evolving industrialization increasingly divided the DA's various constituencies. Industry increasingly aimed for foreign export (and sought trade supports), while construction and some handicraft sectors largely produced for an internal market, and retail sectors wanted free trade. While large industrialists wanted to hold firm against threats of inflation in 1907, the construction industry worried more about the possibility of economic downturn. Small handicraft firms were more open to peaceful labor market negotiations, whereas the iron manufacturers were "gripped by permanent lockout sickness." Iron manufacturers' dissonant voices earned them the moniker of the "unruly corner." Although dominated by handicraft and construction industry workers in the early years, the DA steering committee added a sizable number of representatives from manufacturing in 1907.[55]

These trends led to a solidification of the distinctive industrial subgroups within DA, with none more important than the divide between the industrial and handicraft sectors. The industrial sector developed the Industrifagene, when SC Hauberg and textile industry leaders convened a meeting of about fifty industrialists in October 1906 to develop closer cooperation among industrial sectors, to gather trade statistics, and to combat the perceived domination by the handicraft sectors. The group was careful to state that the committee would have no decisive authority, would work completely within the DA framework and would, of course, keep DA fully informed of its activities. In 1910, the Industrifagene and the older Industriforeningen formed the Industriraadet, which later became the powerful Danish Industry (DI). Four divisions had evolved within DA by 1910, representing industry, commerce, agriculture, and handicrafts (which included construction, carpenters, and masons).[56]

Niels Andersen publicly declared that DA had full confidence in the loyalty of the new independent Industrifagene, but was privately skeptical, in part, because Hauberg initially resisted Andersen's vision of coordination and there was much jockeying for power between the two. Yet the leaders of the new industrial group were active within the DA as well – Hauberg both organized the Industrifagene and served as director of DA from 1911–20 – and sought to construct their subgroups in a manner that would not detract from DA's larger mechanisms for cooperation. The Industrifagene stated that it would have no decisive authority, would work completely within the DA framework and would keep DA fully informed of its activities.[57]

[54] With the 1901 system change, no longer could government rule with a majority in the lower chamber against it. Andersen and Jacobsen 2008, chapter 13.
[55] Andersen and Jacobsen 2008; Agerholm and Vigen 1921, 27.
[56] "Industrifagene under Arbejdsgiverforeningen," 10/17/1906, 326; "Industrifagenes Fælleskommission," 12/5/1906, 384–5; Henriksen, 11/9/1910, 569–572; For a fascinating account of these organizational efforts, see Andersen and Jacobsen 2008.
[57] Agerholm and Vigen, 1921, 161; Members expressed concern at the October 1910 general meeting that the newly formed handicraft association would seek to limit competition. Henriksen, 11/9/1910 569–72; "Industrifagenes Fælleskommission," 12/5/1906, 384–5.

Deep geographical differences also persisted within the DA, as it was largely an association of associations, and even within the same industrial sectors, employers in Jutland might have quite different opinions from those in Copenhagen. Much time was spent in the early years dealing with the regional organizations, and the national headquarters begged the regional groups to provide statistical information about the behaviors of the regional groups' member firms' on issues such as dues and contributions to the strike insurance. In this vein, on March 25, 1914, the central administration sent a letter to regional Aarhus employers' organizations ("Foreningen af Arbejdsgivere i Aarhus" og "Foreningen af Arbejdsgivere ved Aarhus Haven"), asking them to deposit into a strike insurance account a figure based on wages paid out by individual members. The letter acknowledged that it was often difficult to get the local organizations to pay their dues and to get updated information about the activities of individual members. The DA headquarters asked for a report on wage statistics, in order to improve its strike insurance for 1914, and noticed that not all firms were on the list, making it "virtually impossible to the research."[58]

Given the regional and sectoral splits within the DA, one wonders how the association managed to assert centralized control and to unify the business voice, and to some extent, the DA never completely succeeded in reconciling its diverse elements. The association established by Hauberg grew into Danish Industry, a member of DA that remained something of a separate identity and stronger than the parent organization.[59] Yet several factors worked to strengthen and to sustain the coordinating powers of the peak association.

First, the regional fragmentation within DA was greatly mitigated by the expansion of proportional representation and the reorganization of Right Party into the new Conservative People's Party. The Conservative Party was formed in 1915, when a group of young conservatives, the "June Association," sought to shift the power base of the conservatives from the aristocracy to the bourgeois middle class, and threatened to leave Right Party, if their demands were not granted. Breaking formally with Right Party, the June Association reintegrated the Free Conservatives (who had split with the party in 1899), and some members of the spinoff Social Liberal Party (Radicale Venstre). The new Conservatives more exclusively represented employers and the middle class and focused more narrowly on the interests of its core constituencies.[60]

The Conservative Party was less of a cross-class party than the old Right Party, yet infighting persisted, largely between the big business wing (led by Alexander Foss, who also presided over DI) and the middle-class wing (led by editor Asger Karstensen). The middle-class, petite bourgeois elements mistrusted the "smokestack barons," and wartime (and postwar) economic policy was often a point of contention. The most dramatic episode was the battle between Foss and Karstensen over the Max Bellin affair. Foss and Karstensen sat on a price control commission, together with Bellin and Lauritz Vilhelm Birch. Birch accused Bellin of using his position on the commission to engage in unsavory speculation (that ultimately had wide-ranging impacts on the Danish economy) and while Karstensen supported Birch, Foss sided with Bellin. An

[58] DA Arbødigst to Hr. Grosserer, 25 Marts 1914; DA to Hr. Grosserer, 28 Oktober 1915.
[59] The Industrial Council (Industrietraadet) was another predecessor of DI.
[60] Dybdahl 1969, 12; Bindslev 1937–8, 264–71; Hatting 1966.

infuriated Birch began an anti-trust campaign against Big Business in the next finance law debate, and Foss responded with a vigorous defense of industrial self-regulation, pointing out that employers generally enjoyed an excellent relationship with government and that self-regulation was necessary for international competitiveness. The conflict became more muted due to more pressing postwar concerns and to the party's deeply pragmatic goals which were focused on seeking to join ruling coalitions and (in words of its official history) "driven more by tactical considerations than by ideas."[61]

Despite the continuing conflicts within the party on the right (now between industrialists and middle class, rather than between rich landowners and industrialists), the Conservative People's Party functioned like a more dedicated business party vis-à-vis employers. The creation of proportional representation was important to this evolution, as it consolidated employers' interests in the political sphere; this, in turn, produced a corresponding centralization of interests in the associational sphere and brought employers to transcend their regional bases. Denmark changed the constitution in June 1915, and this extended proportional representation in the electoral system, expanded the impact of employers' vote (because with PR votes constituting less than the majority within the district still contributed to parliamentary seats) and strengthened the identity of Danish manufacturers as a national business community. The Liberal Party held majorities in most districts and was, therefore, over-represented in parliament. Proportional representation, thus, allowed the right to gain greater political power. The political consolidation of the nations' employers with proportional representation permitted the gradual reduction of regional differences among industrialists, and encouraged the functional reorganization and centralization of authority within DA. In 1919, the Committee on Law Revisions (Lovenes Revision Udvalg) successfully recommended that DA be reorganized along functional instead of regional lines and eliminated the regional bases of membership.[62] The organization committee decided in February 1927 to further alter the representative composition of the organization so that individual firms would enjoy the same ratio of representation to dues as the organizational members in each of the four functional areas. Each of the four areas should also have at least one member in the Central Administration. This functional reorganization was eased by the receding distrust separating Copenhagen manufacturers from their regional counterparts – a shift made possible by the deepening political identity of employers.[63]

Second, the Danish state implemented reforms that fortified the employers' organization against the fragmentation of its authority. DA was strengthened in 1907, when the state delegated formal powers to the peak employers' association to intervene in sectoral disputes, if member organizations could not negotiate collective bargains. In 1910, a law created a penalty court (Den Faste Voldgiftsret) and a dedicated negotiator representing the state (Forligsmanden). The penalty court was viewed quite favorably by employers, as a guarantor of the private right for self-regulation. The negotiator guaranteed that although employers were given a right for self-determination, the

[61] Hattan 1966, 108–11; Fink 2000; Jacobsen and Pedersen, 2009; Bindslev 1937–8, 264–71.
[62] "Den ekstraordinære Hovedgeneralforsamling den 19. December," 12/26/1920: 450–1.
[63] DA Hovedkontoret, 1928, 62–6; Galenson 1952, 79. Finally, in 1931, a uniform bargaining policy was created that was mandatory for affiliates. DA Hovedkontoret, 1928.

state would remain involved in this process. These formal powers had policy feedback effects on employers' visions of cooperation, and, over time, even Hauberg's views on coordination evolved, ultimately landing him in the procoordination camp. The man who began his organizational career in 1885 as a militant foe of labor ended up being known as a great supporter of industrial coordination.[64]

Third, the employers' association was strengthened by the party's pragmatic attitudes toward social policy. When major social reforms were undertaken in the 1930s, the Conservatives were furious when they were shut out of the coalition supporting these reforms by a secretive agreement between the Liberals and Social Democrats. By the 1960s the Conservatives were to brag that they had played a major role in every "decisive step in this expansion" of the welfare state.[65] The cooperative vision of Niels Andersen and his allies was institutionalized in the September Compromise of 1899 and this has strengthened and structured Danish industrial relations (with some changes) down to the present day.

Conclusion

This chapter explores the role of political competition in shaping the organization of Danish employers and evolution of economic coordination during the formative decades of industrialization. As we found in Chapter 2, industrialization and labor activism fostered high levels of employer organization; yet these offer an incomplete explanation of Danish employer associational development and the emergence of national economic coordination. Economic modernization and industrialization served as an impetus for employer organization to manage the process of economic change; yet, industrialization and economic openness also exacerbated conflicts within and across sectors. In addition, central developments in the process of building a highly centralized, national employers' peak association were driven by relatively moderately sized, domestically oriented industrial enterprises. Similarly, labor disputes provided crucial impetus for the formation of sectoral level employers' organizations; yet, the strategic calculations of employers' associations and their leadership led to the promotion by employers of greater levels of union organization and the centralization of labor and industrial relations at the national level. Moreover, Even though guilds laid the groundwork for nonmarket coordination and high skills among the workforce, they had significantly declined in importance decades before the formative period of employer organization and leadership came from the industrial enterprises as apposed to the guild-based handicraft sector. Thus, one must explore the incentives set by the electoral and party system to grasp fully the emergence of high levels of employer association and nonmarket coordination in Denmark by the early twentieth century.

After failed efforts to forge a center-right partisan alliance, the employers' Right Party confronted the prospects of an ineluctable rise in the political power of social democracy and, in turn, of the improbability of electoral victory and parliamentary majorities. In this context, Right Party and its leadership (especially Niels Andersen) sought to organize the collective voice of business in national policy making, to

---

[64] Due et al. 1994, 76; Vigen 1946, 6–7.
[65] Møller 1994, 111–60; Friis 1969.

encourage politically the delegation of national policy-making power to private labor market institutions, and to foster within these institutions high levels of cooperation between labor and business; this cooperative framework would not only promote industrial peace, but maximize under the current electoral and political constraints the economic and political interests of Danish business.

The advent of proportional representation and the evolution of the Right Party into the Conservative Peoples Party (a more dedicated employers' party) had an important impact on the inner workings of the employers' organization in reinforcing the incentives for political and economic cooperation. Thus, political institutions, especially features of the electoral and party systems, fundamentally mattered for the construction of highly organized employers and of the overarching system of national economic coordination.

4

British Experiments in National Employers' Organization

> We are organised for nothing except party politics.
>
> Winston Churchill

Introduction

At first glance, Britain appears to be the quintessential pluralist country, gripped by antagonistic industrial conflict and committed to laissez-faire liberalism since early days of the industrial revolution. Until 1965, three encompassing associations purported to represent employers – the Federation of British Industries, the British Employers Confederation and the National Association of British Manufacturers; these finally merged into the Confederation of British Industry. Yet, Britain has periodically sought high levels of labor market coordination at various points in the twentieth century, and Margaret Thatcher's extreme liberalism seems at odds from the more collectivist sentiment in British public philosophy.[1]

This chapter explores how Britain came to create fragmented, pluralist employers' associations, punctuated by periods of corporatist experimentation. We argue that the failure of institutions for coordination reflect the limited incentives for cross-party cooperation in a two-party competition. Strong economic divisions (between free traders and protectionists, and financial and manufacturing interests) and the absence of a guild tradition (with craft-based unions seeking to control skills) also contributed to employers' inability to sustain lasting coordination. We consider the impact of bipolar partisan competition at two critical junctures in the evolution of employer representation. First, party structure helps to explain the failure of a national, multisector group to develop at the end of the nineteenth century, when employers elsewhere formed peak associations. Employers were distributed between the Conservative and

---

[1] Fulcher 1997; Runciman 1993; Rodgers 1988; Turner 1984; McDonald and Gospel 1973; Ringe and Rollings 2000; Middlemas 1990; Zeitlin 1990; Lowe and Rollings 2000.

Liberal parties and neither party would reap obvious rewards by rallying a strongly organized business association.

Second, the dynamics of two-party competition give insight into the limited attainments of Britain's first national encompassing association, the Federation of British Industries (FBI), and the proliferation of encompassing groups by the 1920s. The FBI was motivated by the wartime need for significant industrial cooperation and the group initially hoped to become the singular representative of business, to promote industrial development, to enhance international competitiveness, and to regulate the relations of the social classes. Ultimately, the FBI was forced to focus on foreign commercial trade, leaving labor and social policies to the National Conference of Employers' Organisations (which became the British Employers Confederation).

The FBI's grand corporatist aspirations were diminished by party politics, as diverse parties and warring governmental departments cultivated and listened to their own set of employers. Conservatives had a strong hand in the FBI's origins, with an important role played by Sir Arthur Steel-Maitland (MP from Birmingham, party chair in 1911, Under Secretary of State for the Colonies from 1915–17, and Secretary for Overseas Trade from 1917 to 1919). Liberals cultivated their own employers, who formed the National Conference of Employers' Organisations. Employers' conflicting political allegiances undercut corporate unity and as the would-be executive managers of the bourgeoisie were in competition with one another, a singular association failed to develop. Because no national, multisector association was formed at the end of the nineteenth century, collective bargaining developed fully at the industry level, and the industry associations resented FBI's efforts to assert jurisdiction over industrial relations.[2]

Moreover, neither party had an incentive to delegate powers to the social partners, which further dampened the potential for a highly coordinated employers' association. A dedicated business party did evolve after World War I, when the great majority of employers drifted to the Conservative Party. Yet even upon the emergence of more robust, class-based partisan cleavages, a corporatist-style system of industrial relations failed to develop because the state refused to delegate policy-making authority to organized business and labor. In Denmark, employers were motivated to work with labor because the industrial right feared an alliance of agriculture and labor in the triad of party politics. In Britain, industrialists felt a similar disparity of interests with wealthy agricultural export interests; however, political representatives of business had a real chance of winning electoral majorities. Thus, when the social partners sought self-regulation in the National Industrial Conference, Parliament refused to cede any powers of self-regulation, as politicians in both major parties hoped to win electoral majorities. Britain periodically tried to achieve greater coordination thereafter, experimenting with collective solutions in the years following World War II, and in the 1960s; yet, liberalism was renegotiated at each juncture.[3] Economic diversity, legacies of earlier failures in cooperation, and the absence of partisan incentives worked against social coordination.

---

[2] Blank 1973; Middlemas 1990, 113; Lowe and Roberts 1987.
[3] Lowe 1978; Zeitlin 1996; Ringe and Rollings 2000.

Theories of British Employers' Organization

Low levels of labor market coordination are often attributed to the strength of laissez-faire liberalism, which was, indeed, a powerful force in mid-nineteenth-century Britain. Yet, laissez-faire liberalism is not singular in the pantheon of British public philosophy; for example, the decidedly illiberal conceptions of mercantilism and the functional representation of interests in an organic society were important to eighteenth-century Britain and Burke attacked the theory of natural rights as failing to recognize "corporate personality."[4] Even in Britain, laissez-faire liberalism was falling out of vogue by the late nineteenth century, as employers looked with alarm at their competitors and sought industrial development policies to sustain their economic power. Thus, we consider three sets of explanations for limited labor market coordination: the patterns of industrialization, character of labor, and dynamics of party competition.

Patterns of Industrialization
Patterns of industrialization might work against coordination due to the country's early industrialization, high levels of exports, and deep divisions between financial and manufacturing concerns. As the leader of the industrial revolution, perhaps Britain had no need for coordination to catch up to other countries or to compete in world markets; certainly early nineteenth-century firms endorsed free trade, leading to the 1846 repeal of the Corn Laws. Yet by the end of the century, only a minority of British employers' favored unrestricted trade and while finance and cotton spinners flourished with the free movement of goods and capital, manufacturing interests in the iron and wool trades suffered. Moreover, the vocal opposition to protection accounted for a fairly small part of the total industrial economy; for example, cotton, wool, and other textile manufacturers hired only 3.4 percent of workers in 1901; compared with the 10.3 percent hired by protection-oriented producers of iron, steel, and machinery.[5]

Joseph Chamberlain began drawing attention to Britain's growing trade deficit in 1886 (as Liberal President of the Board of Trade) and joined the British Chambers of Commerce in proposing a Ministry of Commerce. Gladstone rebuked Chamberlain's efforts to raise public awareness, through circulars on public works, industrial cooperation and protection. Protectionist sentiments gathered steam after the McKinley Tariff Act of 1890 awakened employers to the resurgence of neo-mercantilism, and even some cotton industrialists wanted tariffs, although financial interests remained committed to unrestricted flows of goods and capital. Chamberlain ultimately left the party (over issues of Irish Home Rule and trade protection) to form the Liberal Unionists and continued to draw attention to the disconnect between free trade and British economic interests. In 1895, *The Chamber of Commerce Journal* cited Joseph Chamberlain's publication on competing in the Colonies as marking the "official abandonment of the principle of *laissez-faire*."[6]

---

[4] Beer 1957, 628, 617.
[5] Gershenkron 1962; Trentmann 2008; Klug 2001, 230–1, 236.
[6] Platt 1968, xxxiii, 81–2; Matthew 1995, 163–5; Trentmann 2008; Rempel 1972, 13; Cain and Hopkins 1980, 485; Ridings 2001; Quinault 1985, 634–5; Burgess 1975, 305l; Turner 1984, 9; Marrison 1995.

The diversity of business views on free trade brings us to another feature of British industrialization, the sharp divisions between financial and industrial interests. Finance was particularly sensitive to inflationary pressures (especially given the pound's special place in international monetary exchange) and although industrialists favored an aggressive postwar reconstruction policies, financial interests were much more cautious about setting off inflationary pressures. Manufacturers blamed the City's singular focus on protecting the value of the pound for a variety of ills: sustained underinvestment in manufacturing, restricted growth of firms, eroded competitiveness, and heightened unemployment. At the same time, the barriers between finance and industrial capitalism may be overstated, and in one study a larger percentage of employers were in finance in Germany than in Britain. Although financial interests sought to return to the gold standard after World War I, many felt that this would stimulate the international economy and expand staple industry exports. A deeper gulf separated the interests of landowners from those of productive capital and labor.[7] Moreover, other countries with significantly divergent interests – e.g. Danish export agricultural versus domestic manufacturing firms – organized at a high level during this period.

Labor Characteristics
Low levels of labor market coordination may also reflect characteristics of the British working class: the contentious impulses of craft-based unions to drive wages up by controlling skills, the ability of employers to contain industrial conflict to the sectoral level due to reduced solidarity between skilled and unskilled labor, and the absence of a vigorous, collectivist guilds tradition. The engineering lockout of 1897 illustrates how craft unions' efforts to control skills reinforced wariness between management and labor. In 1851, the Amalgamated Society of Engineers (ASE) began protecting skills by reducing labor market "redundancy," and firms responded with labor-saving capital investments. The Engineering Employers Federation (EEF) staged the Great Lockout of 1897 to resist demands for skilled operators, higher wages and an eight-hour day. The EEF ultimately recognized the union's right to bargain collectively, in exchange for employers' control over the skills content of jobs, overtime, and piecework arrangements. The conflict laid the groundwork both for industry-level bargaining and for a legacy of mistrust.[8]

Another argument attributes the failure of coordination to the early decline of guilds, a source of fraternity among preindustrial laborers. Whereas the German guilds fostered much cooperation among handicraft employers, skilled and unskilled workers; the British state did not shore up the guilds after 1800, skilled labor formed craft-based unions to regulate training, these strong craft unions controlled skills to drive up wages, and employers adopted labor-saving devices to deskilled workers. The absence of guilds also affected the apprenticeship system, by removing external

---

[7] Marrison 1995; Wilson 1990; Cain and Hopkins 1980; Daunton 1989, 127; Ross 2004; Bergholf and Möller 1994; Fear 2005; Rollings 2008. I am indebted to Neil Rollings for clarifying these points. Lazonick (1983) points to small firm size as diminishing cooperation, although small size drove collective action in Denmark (Galenson 1952).

[8] Fulcher 1991; Burgess 1975, 4; Clegg et al. 1964, 161–7; Zeitlin 1990.

monitoring mechanisms for punishing opportunistic behavior such as poaching, and firms began using apprentices for cheap labor.[9]

Craft unions and the early decline of guilds compel our attention in explaining the British case, yet the many parallels between Danish and British labor organization call into question the degree to which workforce characteristics and organization account for the full range of cross-national variation in employer organization. British engineering conflicts were much like the Danish metal industry battles and one wonders why the British did not seek to coopt labor with a national framework of industrial relations.[10] Moreover, in other sectors, British employers sought to organize labor much like their Danish counterparts; thus, employers' organizations in the iron and coal industries preceded the unions and urged workers to organize, and shipbuilding firms implemented a general lockout to force fitters and plumbers to come to a settlement. Unlike British employers, when Danish aggressive craft unions tried to wrest control over skills from employers, firms organized at a multi-industry, national level to reclaim their managerial prerogatives and to stabilize patterns of industrial engagement. Although the absence of guilds undoubtedly worked against skills production, apprenticeships and skills endured in metalworking and engineering, at least until the 1920s. In the 1940s and 1960s, employers and unions attempted frameworks for vocational training resembling those in other countries.[11]

Party Competition and the Evolution of British Employers' Associations

We suggest that the dynamics of party competition greatly contributed to the inability of British employers to develop strong national associations and to secure public policies enabling a higher degree of coordination. Political actors in this largely two-party system had less motivation to encourage cooperation among employers than their counterparts in multi-party systems, because employers had no partisan home. British employers were dispersed between the two major parties, the Conservatives and the Liberals (with some drifting into the Liberal splinter National Unionists); therefore, no party could help business identify its collective interests. Employers competed with other interests for power within both parties. Throughout much of the nineteenth century, a greater proportion of industrialists belonged to the Liberal party (and nearly half of the Liberal MPs came from business before World War I); however, the party also included many ideological liberals and some workers, who resisted employers' desired industrial development policies. A solid share of manufacturers also voted Conservative, but the land-holding aristocracy dominated the party, and industrial proposals were repeatedly blocked by agricultural interests. The partisan composition shifted at century's turn: When the Liberal Party was rent asunder in 1886 by the Irish Question of Home Rule, the splinter Liberal Unionists attracted many employers, whereas others migrated to the Conservative Party. But the Liberal Unionists never developed into a full-blown party, focused primarily on the Irish question, remained

---

[9] Unwin 1966; Clegg et al. 1964; Thelen 2004, 96–109.

[10] Lord Wemyss leading the right wing of British business did form a short-lived "Parliamentary Council" in November 1898 to fight labor. Yet few firms wished to be associated with Wemyss's extreme positions and the Council thwarted union legislation rather than offered detailed business alternatives. Bell 2008, 30–4.

[11] Clegg et al. 1964, 47, 129–30, 239; Zeitlin 1990.

divided over tariffs, and ultimately merged with the Conservative Party. During World War I, the two major parties (or factions thereof) formed coalition governments; yet these were marked by much jockeying of position and departmental infighting, as is discussed later.[12]

The major parties also had no reason to delegate policy-making functions to the private sector during this period; each thought that it had a chance for outright victory and could impose its political agenda in Parliament. Thus even when the Labour Party appeared on the scene and British partisan politics were organized more doggedly along class lines, two-party competition prevented the creation of vibrant associations among the social partners.[13] Employers were deeply frustrated by the reluctance of the parties to delegate, as Sir Charles Macara noted about the Board of Trade's refusal to delegate authority to a council on labor disputes:

The Industrial Council never had a chance to settle a single dispute. [This can be attributed to] jealousy on the part of the politicians ... They were afraid of the practical men holding controlling positions in industry becoming too powerful or popular in carrying out the work for which they were son eminently fitted.[14]

The importance of party structure – the dispersion of employers across parties and the reluctance to delegate authority to employers – shaped two episodes in the early organization of British employers. First, at the end of the century, British business organization remained firmly fixed at the industrial sector, even though employers in Denmark, Germany and the United States all formed national peak associations. Second, during World War I, the first national, multisector business organization, the FBI, fell far short of the corporatist ambitions of its organizers. To these cases, we now turn.

The Absence of a National Organization at Century's Turn

British employers did not create an encompassing employers' association at the end of the nineteenth century, rather firms organized at the sectoral level. This nonevent reflects political party dynamics, illustrated in failed efforts to create a Board of Arbitration and a Tariff Reform League. First, Charles Ritchie (president of the Board of Trade) sought a compulsory Board of Arbitration and a National Conciliation Board, to include both business and labor representatives and to act as an "appeal court" for local boards of trade, or something akin to the Danish-style industrial self-regulation. Ritchie encountered opposition both from the landed gentry in the Conservative Party, who had little interest in nurturing industrialists' influence, and from employers in the Liberal Party, suspicious of the Conservative government. Although Ritchie invited employers to a conference on the reduction of trade conflict, no broader effort was made by the Conservative Party to create more permanent multisector employers'

---

[12] Garst 1999, 800; Ridings 2001, 771; Phillips 1981, 167–8; Fraser 1962a, 60, 66–7; Dutton 1981, 879.
[13] At its inception, the logic of single-member districts led Labour initially to form an electoral alliance with the Liberals (in a Lib-Lab coalition) and Labor supplanted the Liberal Party after the war. Labour increasingly pursued catch-all party strategies and the middle class voter. Kirchheimer 1966. Just as state actions shaped workers' perceptions of interests in cooperation Cronin (2000), these shaped firms' interests.
[14] Macara 1921, 173.

association, and no such group existed to aid Ritchie with his ideas about industrial self-regulation. Employers at that time undoubtedly felt less pressure than in Denmark to seek the transfer of policy making to private channels because they did not anticipate significant political threats from democratization. Employers in industries most hurt by foreign imports recognized the attractions of Ritchie's proposal, but were dubious about the implementation, in large part because they felt that both business and labor were incompletely organized. Thus one participant acknowledged that the employers "took upon themselves very great responsibility when they rejected the overtures of Mr. Ritchie"; but felt that the institutional capacity for taking action at the national level was underdeveloped and that only local boards had the capacity to implement such coordination. Ultimately, however, the Board of Arbitration was given no compulsory powers but only the right and responsibility to oversee arbitration if both sides requested it.[15]

The constraints of two-party competition on multisectoral employers' organization surfaced again in the tariff battle beginning in 1903, when the diversity of interests within the Conservative Party prevented the party from cultivating employer coordination. Supported by many employers, Joseph Chamberlain (Liberal Unionist Colonial Secretary) asked Conservative Prime Minister Balfour to enact legislation for Imperial Preferences to cope with the Boer War, the German tariff of 1902, and the growth of most favored nation arrangements. As the representative of Manchester (and the free-trade-oriented cotton spinners), Balfour refused to take action. Chamberlain resigned his post, formed a Tariff Reform League to lobby for pro-tariff candidates, and tried to seize control of local Conservative Party organizations; this drew opposition from financiers, cotton industrialists, and Conservative and Liberal Unionist MPs from the landed gentry. The party was ripped apart, lost the 1906 election and Chamberlain's stroke put an end to efforts to organize employers for industrial development policies.[16]

The Federation of British Industries

The dynamics of two-party competition also shaped the origins and evolution of the Federation of British Industries, at a time when World War I made coordination essential to the national interest. The formation of the FBI reflected an effort to overcome the limits of two-party conflict, but its ultimate trajectory was doomed by the party structure.

Background Context for the Formation of the FBI
War was the great motivator for labor market coordination, which seemed suddenly necessary to save the British Empire. Centralized control and planning by government became a crucial feature of British economic life: Employers were asked to sustain high levels of production to defeat Germany and to consult with central government on economic and social policy. A munitions crisis instigated a furious round of attacks

[15] Clegg et al. 1964, 263–5; "British Iron Trade Association," 6/8/1899.
[16] Quinault 1985, 634–5; "Mr. Chamberlain on His Proposals," 6; Rempel 1972, 16; Gollin 1976, 84–8; Trentmann 1996, 1009–12, 1024; Coats 1968; Irwin 1994, 85; Middlemas 1990, 39.

on the Asquith government and led to a coalition government, which developed a new Ministry of Munitions and appointed as head Lloyd George, who told Winston Churchill that he was "in despair over the stupidity of the war office."[17] Lloyd George asked unions to give up restrictive practices and the right to strike (to be restored after the war) and the Ministry of Munitions developed tripartite committees of employers and workers to implement industrial change; however, it wanted to preserve its control over policy making, was reluctant to delegate substantive authority to the social partners and believed that it, alone, recognized the "national interest."[18]

The FBI's nascence also reflects unique political conditions: Even the political parties sensed the urgent need to cooperate and formed coalition governments marked, none the less, by significant jockeying for power.[19] Strong support for coordinated capitalism came more easily to the Conservative/Unionist Party, with its limited historical commitment to laissez-faire and theme of Disraeli's "one-nation," classless, commonality of interests. The Unionist Social Reform Committee recommended in 1911 a roster of social interventions and mechanisms for industrial arbitration. As Lord Hugh Cecil put it, "There is no antithesis between Conservatism and Socialism ... Conservatives have no difficulty in welcoming the social activity of the State."[20]

Yet even while concentrating on the war effort, the parties formed an uneasy partnership, especially in advance of the 1918 election. Lloyd George never got along with rank and file Conservatives, ignored Bonar Law (Chancellor of the Exchequer and Conservative Party head) when George became prime minister, mobilized the media to get his way, and alienated both business and labor. Arthur Steel-Maitland vented his frustration with the government: "Of course, I hate these selfish Whigs with whom we are leashed up."[21] Industrialist Dudley Docker complained to Steel-Maitland (who forwarded the complaint to Bonar Law):

It is a most disgraceful thing that George should make the speeches he does, as without the slightest question he is at the bottom of everything and is merely playing for his own hand. I do not know what our party may be doing – if we have one – to counteract these things, but certainly something ought to be done. The coalition was most unfortunate – probably the worst day's work our party has done.[22]

Most troubling to manufacturers and their Conservative Party allies were Lloyd George's close ties to financiers and the commercial insurance industry, and comparative neglect of industrialists. Bankers placed debt reduction above other taxing and spending priorities after the war, and this foreclosed a range of options vital for

---

[17] Hazlehurst 1971 199, 282. Sectoral Whitley Councils were created to negotiate agreements on wages and working conditions. Platt 1968.

[18] Rubin 1984, 318.

[19] The Liberal government fell in May 1915, due to its inadequate wartime preparation and to the broader failure of the party system to obtain coordination (Gollin 1983), and it was replaced by a bipartisan coalition including Liberals and some Unionists from the Conservative Party. This failed in December 1916, and a new grand coalition government was formed, unifying the Conservatives and the "Lloyd George Liberals," under David Lloyd George. Another coalition government was created in 1918. Hazlehurst 1971; Beaverbrook 1963.

[20] Cited in Dutton 1981, 881, 872.

[21] Maitland to Sanders 6/6/1916 . Morgan 1970: 129–31.

[22] Docker to Maitland 7/29/1915.

economic renewal and for postwar reconstruction. Alarmed by constraints on industrial policies placed by concerns about adverse balance of payments and exchange rates, Steel-Maitland suggested the creation of a new bank to help pay for the war.[23]

Conservative Party Constituency-Building Efforts

The FBI's formation should be viewed in the context of Conservative Party constituency-building efforts, began after the 1906 electoral loss and intensified during the war. Steel-Maitland had worked to expand the network of local conservative groups and to strengthen party organization when he became party chairman in 1911, and described himself as "a party manager with an intelligence service through the country!"[24] He sought to expand party influence through cross-class appeals in alliance with the British Workers' League, a centrist workers' political organization that the Conservatives hoped would stem the tide of labor activism. Steel-Maitland was drawn to the League's conception of pre-Keynesian, anticyclical interventions, with which "the Government should regulate the distribution of their contracts and public works so as to avoid intensifying periods of industrial boom and to mitigate periods of depression."[25] He repeatedly met with the League organizer, Victor Fisher, to help plan a conference on Industrial Reconstruction, following the Labour Party's annual meeting, "that would constitute another step towards the formation of a real national movement." Fisher cautioned Steel-Maitland that although "all the responsible men on your side should be made aware of our general tactics," the media's advance knowledge should be limited. Lord Milner suggested that this meeting be convened by a neutral third party, rather than by the League or the Unionists.[26]

Steel-Maitland instantly grasped the political advantages of cross-class alliance, yet he also seemed genuinely interested in social and economic coordination, had studied with Arnold Toynbee at Oxford, and remained close to the socialist Lord Milner. Steel-Maitland told Milner that he went to Birmingham to run for Parliament because "I believe the town is potentially capable of corporate effort more than any other town in the Kingdom." He favored government intervention in a range of spheres and wrote, "A number of the important social problems must be tackled by local action, either acting by itself or in conjunction with the central Government. Such are housing, Public Health, Education, Poor Law, etc."[27] He wrote to Bonar Law:

The war has obliterated many old Party distinctions ... Classes have joined in the prosecution of the war ... new groupings of men may arise, while those who have often combated one another over the old questions may find themselves largely in sympathy over the new.[28]

Steel-Maitland held to the Gramscian notion that ideological change must precede revolutionary change and tried to alter public opinion by cultivating Conservative Party media outlets. Seeking unsuccessfully to persuade Docker to purchase the *Daily Express,* Docker later bought the *Globe* at Steel-Maitland's suggestion to create an

[23] Maitland to McKenna 8/16/1915; Dando no date; Middlemas 1990, 30; Gilbert 1965; Daunton 1996, 132.
[24] Maitland to McKenna 8/16/1915; Middlemas 1990, 40.
[25] British Workers League 10/11/1917.
[26] Victor Fisher to ASM 11/22/1917; ASM to Victor Fisher 12/14/1917, 133.
[27] Maitland to Lord Milner 2/19/1910.
[28] Maitland to Bonar Law 11/16/1917.

organ for Conservative ideology.[29] Steel-Maitland was fascinated by American presidents' efforts to nurture a less hostile press and urged a similar strategy for British politicians.[30] In this vein, he wrote:

In previous great periods of change, such as the laisser [sic] faire movement, you know much better than I how opinion of the best kind had developed years before the practical movement began ... This seems much less the case at present ... Development of opinion, so far as it takes place, is concurrent with, not precedent to political action.[31]

The Formation of the Federation of British Industries

The creation of the Federation of British Industry clearly fits with Conservative's ambitions to expand party power and to solidify the voice of industry. The FBI was officially organized by Dudley Docker, a Birmingham chairman of the Metropolitan Carriage, Wagon and Finance Company and a leader in the business movement to regain British trade supremacy. Docker had created the British Manufacturers' Association (representing Birmingham's metal and engineering firms), and was active in the British Electrical and Allied Manufacturers' Association (BEAMA). In February 1916, Docker, Nettlefold, and Peter Rylands invited 100 employers to plan a new association and asked each to pledge one thousand pounds (which would allow them to become members of the Grand Council of the Association); early stages of planning were dominated by the Midland engineering sector, but most industrial sectors were ultimately included. Sir William Peat, chair of the initial meeting, said the association would "organise the manufacturing interests of the country so that they could speak with one voice by means of their representative or representatives" and constitute a "Parliament of traders." Another participant, Sir Algernon Firth, remarked, "Each trade has its own little Association – probably a great number of them – but their work is absolutely inefficient because they have never yet learned the value of adequate combination and of efficiently working together ... Now, gentlemen, that is exactly the spirit which we have got to overcome."[32] FBI included individual firms, but held that the "Federation is above all a 'Federation of Associations.'"[33]

The FBI's formation was enabled by Conservative Party's efforts, despite the public view that the FBI sprang up autonomously; Docker acted in close conjunction with Conservative politicians, especially Arthur Steel-Maitland, and had close ties to the Foreign Office.[34] Steel-Maitland described Docker as "one of the very ablest business men in the whole of the Kingdom."[35] Docker had been close to Steel-Maitland since the latter ran for office in 1906 and offered to lend Steel-Maitland one or two of his Daimler cars for the campaign.[36] Docker proposed a lucrative financial venture to Steel-Maitland, but the latter declined it as inappropriate "so long as I am at the

[29] Henderson to Maitland 6/12/1912; Davenport-Hines 1884, 55–6,79–80.
[30] Strachey to Maitland 2/24/1916.
[31] Maitland to Milner 2/19/1910.
[32] United British Industries Association 7/20/1916, 4, 16–18; Blank 1973, 14–16.
[33] Federation of British Industries 12/5/1916, 1.
[34] Blank 1973; Davenport-Hines 1984; Grant and Marsh 1977.
[35] Maitland to Steel 6/8/1916.
[36] Docker to Steel-Maitland no date.

Central Office."[37] Despite Docker's disillusionment with party politics after the 1906 election, he was the only "considerable subscriber" in Steel-Maitland's reorganized East Birmingham Conservative Association in 1914.[38] Steel-Maitland nearly joined the board of Docker's company, but was then offered the job of Under Secretary of the Colonies in 1915.[39] Steel-Maitland tried to save Docker's skilled workers from the draft, as Docker was "one of the most important business men in the Midlands" who was "doing really important work for the Government."[40] Docker was also close to Sir Victor Wellesley (controller of Commercial and Consular Affairs in the Foreign Office from 1916 to 1919), with whom he served on the Commercial Intelligence Committee. The Foreign Office was so determined to make the FBI succeed that it lent Guy Locock and particularly, Roland Nugent, who became the director and secretary of the organization.[41]

The FBI explicitly aimed to enhance capacities for coordination in the British economy, sought the powers for self-regulation, embraced a very corporatist organizational model, and desired a high level of industrial peace. Its organizers wanted "to afford a means for bringing the industrial interests of the country as a whole into closer touch with the Government, not in any spirit of hostility, but with the view of achieving complete and cordial co-operation between the State and industry for the national advantage."[42] Docker felt that if a Ministry of Commerce had existed upon the start of the war:

[There would have been] none of the scandalous wasted of men, money and brains...and but little of the labour trouble ... Such a Minister would have been in a position quickly to organise, with the aid of a comparably few men, the great resources of industrial Britain, and also the vast army of workers.[43]

Docker considered it incumbent to unify employers across sectors, dreamed of a "Business Parliament" for making industrial policy, bemoaned Britain's lack of a dedicated political party for manufacturers (sensing that Liberals, particularly, failed to respect industrialists), and sought "to transform Britain into a model corporatist state."[44] Even though Bonar Law expressed skepticism over an "Industrial Parliament," Steel-Maitland supported the employers, pointing to the existence of agricultural councils and asking his staff to gather evidence on this point.[45] The *Globe* (owned by Docker) stated in an editorial entitled "The Party or the State?": "The

---

[37] Docker to Maitland 11/30/1911; Maitland to Docker 12/3/1911.

[38] Maitland to Docker 1/10/1916. Even though he was born into a high Tory family, Docker became more closely attached to the Unionists, sat on Joseph Chamberlain's Tariff Commission, and lobbied vigorously for tariff reform in the great trade battle of 1903–6. Docker was deeply disappointed with the Unionist/ Conservative coalition when the Liberal Party won the election in 1906 and mused that he might even be tempted to join the Labour Party. After Steel-Maitland became chair of the Conservative Party, he sought to bring Docker back into Conservative Party politics. Davenport-Hines 1984, 55–6, 79–80.

[39] Maitland 5/24/1915; Davenport-Hines 1984, 55–6, 63.

[40] Maitland's secretary to Townroe, 11/9/1915.

[41] Davenport-Hines 1984, 86. "Company Meeting. Federation of British Industries," 3/12/1917, 12.

[42] Labour Research Department 1923, 7–8.

[43] Davenport-Hines 1984, 106–7, 71.

[44] Davenport-Hines 1984; Turner 1984, 33–9, 137.

[45] Maitland to WGS Adams 7/4/1916 .

party system has been carried on to unnecessary lengths" such as it has "become deliberative only in name … It is the reason why so much of our legislation is inefficient, even when not injurious, to our commercial interests, on which after all the country depends."[46] Dudley was also inspired by the Swedish employers' association:

As an illustration I cannot do better than relate to you a conversation I recently had with Mr. Wallenberg, who is president of the Swedish Federation of Industries. Mr. Wallenberg told me that they had had in his country for some six years a similar federation to ours, and that no action was taken by the Swedish Government which might affect industry without previous consultation with the Federation … They have got one association, and one association only, for the purpose of being recognized by the Government … for the purpose of dealing with the Government we must have one big Federation, with a constructive policy.[47]

The FBI also sought to promote peaceful labor-management relations; consequently, its initial rules pledged to support the "promotion and encouragement of free and unrestricted communication between masters and workmen with a view to the establishment of amicable arrangements…and to the avoidance and settlement of strikes and all other forms of industrial warfare between masters and workmen."[48] FBI supported the appeal to citizens by Neville Chamberlain (Director-General of National Service, son of Joseph Chamberlain and future Prime Minister) to join a new "Industrial Army" to help in the postwar unemployment and reconstruction. The proposals included setting up a Central Statutory Board to regulate and to redistribute employment.[49] Docker claimed that the "question of our relations with labour calls for all the patience, tact, and consideration we can command" and took credit for the meetings on the redistribution of labor after the war. "The welfare of the Empire is essentially dependent upon the existence of a satisfactory understanding between employers and employed, and I hope the Federation will play an important part in promoting such an understanding."[50]

In addition to these corporatist ambitions, the FBI was called upon to aide in political struggles and the employers' federation offered the Foreign Office a vehicle for influencing its Liberal Party coalition partners. Thus, before a deputation of employers from FBI met with the Prime Minister concerning the "Denunciation of Commercial Treaties," the Foreign Office sent a memo ("regarded as strictly private") to answer potential objections.[51] In planning for reconstruction, Steele Maitland wanted to develop closer co-operation with the colonies and organized a dinner between "Colonial Premiers" and representatives of the FBI. Thus, Director Nugent wrote to Fitzjohn Oldham:

[Docker] wants you to get into touch with Mr. Steele Maitland in regard both to the question of entertaining the Colonial Premiers, and bringing them in on the Consular matter. He wants to

---

[46] Davenport-Hines 1984, 83.
[47] "Company Meeting. Federation of British Industries," 3/12/1917, 12.
[48] Labour Research Department 1923, 42.
[49] "Army of Industry," 1/22/1917, 6.
[50] "Company Meeting. FBI," 3/12/1917, 12.
[51] Nugent to Vassar-Smith 10/26/1917.

know exactly what Mr. Steele Maitland would advice, but adds that...Steele Maitland is most anxious that he should not be brought into the matter in any way.[52]

In particular, the Conservatives wanted to get the right employers on advisory councils to government ministries and departments. Steel-Maitland felt that only the Finance Committee had been "appointed with proper consultation with the industries affected" (i.e. industrialists were much less represented than financiers).[53] Nugent viewed advisory committees as being "packed" by the politicians (and Liberal politicians, in particular, seemed to be a problem); moreover, when "views do not happen to be pleasing to the particular Department concerned," advisory reports tend to be ignored.[54] Relations with the Munitions Ministry had become particularly strained over time. Thus, Nugent appeared quite pleased when Christopher Addison, Liberal Minister of Munitions, agreed to "accept an Advisory Committee nominated by the Federation of British Industries ... It is also the first great test as to whether the Federation is capable of fulfilling the role which it has set out to fill, that of a body capable of advising the Government on Industry in general."[55] In an overture to E. F. Hiley, Ministry of National Service, the FBI asked to be the sole representative of business: "it will be of very little use for the Federation to undertake this duty unless it is it the only body in the Country which does undertake it." Hiley responded, "I do not understand why the Federation of British Industries should be the only Employers' Association to be consulted by the Director-General ... If you could arrange that the Federation should represent all the industries of the country, it would, I think, remove some of the difficulties."[56]

The Federation of British Industry's Downfall
The FBI's grandiose dreams never quite materialized, as its hoped-for consensus among employers and far-reaching goals for coordination and labor peace were dashed by both inter-industry conflicts and the interplay of party competition. First, the legacy of organization at the industrial sectoral level prevented the FBI from realizing its full ambitions, as the sectoral industry associations jealously guarded their own control over industrial relations. The Engineering Employers' Federation's chair, Allan Smith, viewed the FBI as seizing control over industrial disputes from the sector organizations, and refused to join the FBI as long as it sought to be "a single body dealing with both commercial and labour questions." The FBI executive council offered to create a separate "Labour Section" to meet Smith's objections, and Docker proposed a press statement, stating, "It is the earnest desire of the Federation of

[52] Nugent to Fitzjohn Oldham 3/20/1917. Steel-Maitland invited Nugent and other FBI insiders to a "small informal Committee of the Unionist Party" that was going "to work out a policy for the Party in regard to Nationalisation, his view being that it was useless to adopt a merely negative attitude and that some constructive policy in regard to the control of industry should be adopted by the Party." Nugent to Rylands. 19th December, 1919.
[53] Steel-Maitland to Bonar Law date 1916.
[54] Nugent to Peat 2/8/1917.
[55] Nugent to Caillard 3/14/1917. Nugent subsequently reported feeling ignored by the Ministry. Nugent to Hadfield 4/4/1917.
[56] Nugent to Hiley 2/19/1917; Hiley to Nugent 2/20/1917.

British Industries to assist and strengthen such Associations."[57] Nugent wrote Docker that, "This apparently sticks very badly in the gizzards of his [Smith's] Council, and he is most anxious for us to drop it."[58]

To meet these objections, the FBI created a separate National Advisory Council of Employers to handle all labor negotiations; yet, jurisdictional disputes persisted. The EEF opposed FBI's efforts to expand "the scope and functions of the National Advisory Council of Employers," when FBI sought to have that body accorded "executive powers instead of acting as had been originally decided upon in a purely advisory capacity." Smith sought to exclude the Advisory Council from an advisory committee at the Ministry of Munitions – and got assistance in his strategic campaign from the other employers' associations, such as those in shipbuilding, textiles, and building trades.[59] Finally, the EEF engineered a vote in the FBI Grand Council on a "self-denying ordinance," which stipulated that the FBI could not intervene in labor relations unless the member sector associations specifically requested help.[60] The Prime Minister requested one body of employers with whom to negotiate, and both groups sought this position. When the FBI Labour Sub-Committee issued a report on industrial cooperation after the war, the EEF worked hard to prevent the report and proposed the formation of a "Confederation of Employers Organisations for dealing with labour questions." The FBI should be informed of this plan immediately "with a view to preventing that Federation from proceeding further with the report prepared by its Labour Committee."[61]

Second, the FBI's goals for industrial cooperation, labor peace, and protectionist trade policies were constrained by cross-cutting economic interests, especially on trade protection. The FBI sought to be an encompassing organization and its goals for inclusion came in conflict with its policy ambitions. Employers did not fear an electoral coalition of center and left against the right, as did their peers in multi-party systems, and this produced fewer incentives to overcome sectoral conflicts. The stalemate is revealed starkly in FBI's merger with the free-trade Employers' Parliamentary Association (EPA), a group dominated by the cotton spinners and regional interests in Manchester and Lancashire. The EPA was organized by avid free-trader, Charles Macara (with significant involvement of government leaders from the Liberal Party) to fight protection and to support the National Insurance Act, and a dominant faction favored cooperation with labor.[62] The merger intimated that industry would finally be

---

[57] FBI 10/31/1916.

[58] Nugent. Excerpt letter to Docker 10/28/1916. The British Engineers' Association also volunteered to join only after the "technical difficulty caused by the Federation being a Trade Union was removed." (FBI 2/23/1917.)

[59] Engineering Employers Federation, 7/27/1917, 59; Engineering Employers Federation, 7/19/1917, 20; Turner 1984, 39–42. The Shipping Federation and Mine-owners refused to join the Advisory Council, despite repeated FBI pleas to do so, and the Shipping Federation evidently attempted to prevent the Advisory Council for making official recommendations to the government on workmen's compensation. Nugent wrote, "I do not see that they can very well expect the majority of the Employers of the country to wait indefinitely for the minority, who have, after all, been given every opportunity of discussing the thing jointly if they wish to do so." Nugent to Cleminson, 6/1/1917.

[60] FBI Bulletin, August 15, 1918, 385.

[61] Nugent to Rylands, 1/11/1918; Engineering Employers Federation 1/25/1918, 200.

[62] Rodgers 1988; "Employers' Parliamentary Association," 3/27/1914, 13; Macara resigned in protest after the merger. Davenport-Hines 1984 114–16.

unified and *The Times* wrote that this "close cooperation ... should result in the long-sought consummation of a complete and truly national association of employers."[63] Yet the union prompted continuous power struggles; for example, the EPA sought a FBI central office (in Manchester), to which Nugent concluded: "We cannot risk, say Manchester, getting to feel itself so independent that if it differs from the Federation on any point there will be any danger of its trying to split off." The alliance also compromised FBI's ability to take a position on trade protections, and Nugent reflected with some frustration that it was FBI's "duty as the principal manufacturers' association in the country to procure, and give to the Government, the views of manufacturers."[64]

On the other side, the FBI was challenged by the strongly protectionist British Manufacturers Association (BMA), which became the National Union of Manufacturers. Fearing the postwar "sudden dumping of German & Austrian goods," the BMA met in December 1915 "to secure the appointment of a Minister of Commerce," and "as high wages and free imports cannot go together, to promote such measures as may be necessary to protect the wages and interests of all our industrial workers." At a December 12, 1916 meeting, the BMA voted to join the FBI as a member; as Chairman George Terrell later remarked, the FBI "was now becoming such a powerful Body that it was necessary to fall into line with them." Yet the BMA remained a separate organization, because it did not want to abandon its campaign for protection.[65] The dual associations engaged in much subsequent competition; thus Nugent reported that the BMA was trying to "claim the whole credit for the Deputation [to the Ministry of Munitions]... They have been trying to steal our thunder for some time, and this must be put an end to, or they may develop into a serious nuisance."[66]

The FBI was also torn over whether to support the London Imperialists – which became the British Commonwealth Union – a political group with ambitions of becoming a party dedicated to protection. Nugent posed the issue as a choice between two bad options: between disappointing members who wanted to form a new political party and alienating a larger group who, while perhaps sympathetic to the protectionist goals, did not wish "to tie the Federation's hands in any manner in the future." Nugent who was, himself, a protectionist, concluded, "It is better to lose twenty Members now than half the Federation in a few weeks' time."[67] Nugent also feared that an association with the new party would compromise its influence with its existing political relationships (i.e. the Conservative Party).[68]

Third, the ambitions of the FBI were scaled back by the interplay of party and bureaucratic politics: Just as Conservative Party activists such as Arthur Steel-Maitland in the Foreign Office had encouraged the creation of the FBI, the Liberals nurtured financial interests and employers such as Sir Charles Macara from Manchester who listed toward the free-trade wing of business. FBI also found itself on the wrong side of Lloyd George and the Liberals in several policy disputes and interdepartmental battles

---

[63] "Our Trade Future," 1/11/1917.
[64] Nugent to Dixon 5/29/1917; Nugent to Dixon 2/8/1917, 143.
[65] Journal of meeting notes of the NUM. No page numbers or dates.
[66] Nugent to Caillard 3/20/1917.
[67] Nugent to Dixon 7/1/1917 .
[68] Nugent to Hadfield 5/14/1917.

during this period, which constrained its power and compromised its appearance of neutrality.

Most significantly, the federation was ensnared in a bureaucratic turf war over foreign commercial policy. Although British civil servants are required to be nonpartisan, the Foreign Office had enormous support from Conservative Party politicians. The Conservatives and Foreign Office wanted to locate control over foreign commercial policy in the economic department of the Foreign Office rather than in the Board of Trade, arguing that foreign policy and international economic policy were intrinsically linked. The Board of Trade deeply resented the movement of the Foreign Office into the trade area on jurisdictional grounds – before the war, it held the reins of power in economic affairs and had been primarily responsible for supporting British industrialists in their efforts to conduct foreign trade. The Asquith government's president of the Board of Trade president, Walter Runciman (a prominent Liberal), sought control over all foreign economic matters. Later Sir Warren Fisher (permanent undersecretary to the treasury and head of the civil service) proposed the incorporation of the Foreign Office into the Home Civil Service. Yet, the Board of Trade's assistance to British industrialists was minimized by its overarching philosophical committed to limited government intervention and noninterference with free trade. Frustrated with this position and with Trade Chairman Runciman, the Foreign Office created its own foreign trade department.[69]

Conservatives in the Foreign Office viewed the Board of Trade committees as "unrepresentative," with insufficient links to employers and "largely shut off from one another." Steel-Maitland argued to Bonar Law that all industrial matters should "be dealt with together and in connection with some representative body of employers and employed which would get the help and win the confidence of both."[70] When Conservative Unionist Arthur Stanley took over as President of the Board of Trade, there was some hope that the antagonism would be resolved. Robert Cecil (Foreign Office) proposed to Stanley (Board of Trade) a new Department of Overseas Trade with both ministries taking a role in oversight. Stanley responded, "while your proposal for divided responsibility is somewhat novel, I can see that it possesses many advantages, and I am quite disposed to agree to make the experiment." But consensus broke down over which ministry would lead. Cecil argued that making the head "Board of Trade official is altogether contrary to the spirit of the new Department." Stanley responded that making the head a Foreign Office official "would presumably be equally barred."[71]

The Foreign Office asked the FBI to intervene in the deliberations, sending a report outlining its vision of "the proper organization of the Government Service of commercial intelligence in foreign Countries," to Nugent, who passed it on to select members as "very confidential." The FBI recommended that all trade promotion policies be situated in the Foreign Office and a committee set up by the government, including Docker and Victor Wellesley, suggested a compromise: A Department of Overseas Trade would report jointly to the Foreign Office and the

---

[69] Watt 1997, xv; Maisel 1989, 169–75.
[70] Maitland to Adams 7/4/1916.
[71] Stanley to Cecil 7/25/1917; Cecil to Stanley 7/31/1917 ; Stanley to Cecil 8/2/1917.

Board of Trade.[72] The initially optimistic Steel-Maitland became the new Head of the Department of Overseas Trade; however, the bureaucratic division of labor between the units continued to rankle both sides. Although the FBI testified in favor of keeping a strong role for the Foreign Office in the oversight of foreign commercial policy, the office's influence was scaled back and sweeping reforms of the consular services failed to materialize.[73] Lloyd George sided with the Board of Trade, which is not surprising as he had been President of the Board of Trade from 1905 to 1908 and Chancellor of the Exchequer from 1908 to 1915, and Steel-Maitland ultimately resigned in protest.[74]

The parties and economic actors were also divided over wartime reconstruction and, again, the Conservatives and their industrial allies lost the battle. Financiers and the landed gentry desired a politics of deflation and significant public spending limits in order to protect the pound in foreign monetary exchange, and received political support from many Liberals for this course of action. Many conservatives and manufacturing interests joined the broader public in calling for vigorous reconstruction, lower interest rates and social and economy policies to bolster employment and trade. Thus Sir Auckland Geddes (Deputy Director-General of Munitions and then Director of National Service) worried that the postwar trade would pick up too slowly and promoted aggressive industrial conversion. Within the coalition government, the Tory reconstructionists tended to be men from industry rather than from finance, often came from "the Celtic fringe and most were not social equals of the City's Mandarins."[75] The FBI developed a "Reconstruction Memorandum" to submit to the Prime Minister, and planned, rather aggressively, to go to the press if he did not fall into line. Nugent suggested that Docker:

get a letter ready to send to the Prime Minister … The idea would be to let the Prime Minister have the scheme first, letting him know that we consider the matter most urgent and important. If he consented to set up such a committee, he would more or less have to take our nominees, at any rate for the Employers' representative … If he does not accept it, we could insert it in the papers, letting him know that we are doing so … the refusal to adopt the suggestion, and the publication of this refusal, backed by a good, stiff propaganda from the Federation … might give the Government a very bad jolt just at the time when everybody is beginning to complain that they are not looking ahead enough and laying their plans sufficiently carefully.[76]

The close connections between Conservative Party activists in the Foreign Office and the FBI harmed the FBI's bid to represent business in the National Industrial Conference, the major postwar effort to institutionalize industrial coordination and labor peace. The conference was held in February 1919, with cabinet ministers, bureaucrats, 600 trade unionists and 300 employers in attendance. The purpose was to form a "provisional joint committee" to guide British industrial relations for the foreseeable future and the *New York Times* (April 7, 1919) described the accord as a "new Magna Carta." Motivated by expanding suffrage in 1918, both business and labor participants in

---

[72] Nugent to Rylands 1/18/1917; "Commercial Counsellors," 12/16/1916, 5; Maisel 1989, 169–75.
[73] Steel-Maitland to Bonar Law 9/17/1917; Platt 1968, xxiv, 371–9.
[74] "Overseas Trade Departmental Differences," 7/26/1919, 147.
[75] Cline 1970, 168.
[76] Nugent Exerpt to Docker, 3/27/1917.

the provisional joint committee agreed to a quintessential social democratic bargain – unions would restrain industrial power in exchange for progressive government policy. There was great enthusiasm for this British revolution as an alternative to the Russian revolution; even the Webbs welcomed "home rule for industry."[77]

A unitary, encompassing employers' organization was required to speak for business in the National Industrial Conference process, and the victor was the National Confederation of Employers Organisations (NCEO), a group of staple producers with close ties to the Liberal Party. The NCEO had roots in two former organizations: the Confederation of Employers Organisations (developed by the Allan Smith and the Engineering Employers Federation after Lloyd George asked employers to speak with one voice in negotiating with labor) and a Manchester based group organized by Macara and WP Rylands, the "Central Association of Employers' Organisations."[78] Macara and Smith had both been deeply involved the Board of Trade's Industrial Council during the battle over the Liberal National Insurance Act of 1911, proposed by Lloyd George (then chancellor of the exchequer in the Liberal government of Herbert Henry Asquith). In fact, Macara took credit for the creation of the Industrial Council and the leading bureaucrat in the National Industrial Conference was Horace Wilson, who had been a top civil servant at the Industrial Council.[79]

The conference was initially considered a great success, and Lloyd George remarked about the provisional joint committee: "You may be making a model for civilization which all lands will turn to and say 'Let us follow Britain'" (*The Times* 5 March 1919). But the National Industrial Conference ultimately failed, as the full conference never met after April 1919, and key proposals of the provisional joint committee were abandoned – related to hours of work, rate of pay and, most critically, the establishment of a self-regulating national industrial council. The failure has been credited to improved postwar economic and political conditions, and labor representation not fully supported by the rank and file (as the TUC struggled with shop floor resistance). Moreover, Allan Smith and the NCEO – chosen to speak for employers – represented only a part of the business community: The NCEO was less interested in cooperating with unions than the FBI, and Smith was generally a difficult, uncompromising man. At the same time, both business and labor were committed initially to cooperative action; Smith had overcome his antagonism toward labor and was motivated to compromise, because employers were disillusioned by wartime controls and sought self-regulation.[80]

An interpretation rooting the problem with the social partners neglects the government's role in the fiasco: The fruits of this experiment were barren, in part, due to the absence of incentives to delegate by political leaders in two-party systems. The government ultimately rejected the recommendations of the provisional joint committee, perhaps because Lloyd George either had limited interest in the industrial project or had sought the process to postpone compromise with unions. The Prime Minister

---

[77] Lowe 1978, 649–53.
[78] Turner suggests that Manchester group was inspired by the German Central Association of Employers. Turner 1984, 34–44.
[79] Melling 1992, 473–4; Macara 1921, 170–2, 206, 240; Lowe and Roberts 1987; Rodgers 1988.
[80] Lowe 1978, 650–4, 668–71; Blank 1973; Rodgers 1988; Turner, 1984, 48, 150.

remarked, "It would have been a mistake if the fight had come sooner ... [there was] a dangerous element, which it is well we should have given time to quiet." Divisions within the Cabinet and hostility within parliament toward a private industrial council also played a role: The mechanisms for self-regulation were viewed as usurping the government's authority and raising fundamental questions about jurisdictional boundaries. Sir Robert Horne (Minister of Labour) argued that it was "impossible for the Government to surrender its freedom to any body of people however eminent." This caused a delegate to remark that employers "were under the impression that whatever we decided would be accepted by Government. I do not think – I know – I would not have given my time unless I were under the impression that our decision was to be accepted."[81]

The wartime experiments in cooperation came to an end with the downfall of the National Industrial Conference, and the government's refusal to delegate policy-making authority marked a turning point in the negotiations, as neither business nor labor would accept consensual politics without substantive power. The episode set off a period of intensive class conflict among business and labor and whereas 26.5 million days were lost in strikes in 1920, 85.8 million were lost by 1921. The episode left a legacy of "abortive futility" (according to the Ministry of Labour) for industrial cooperation during the Mond-Turner talks and the economic collapse after 1931.[82] After the failed NIC experiment, the FBI turned much more hostile to labor, and by 1922 the association was explicitly demanding that workers' standard of living be adjusted downward.[83]

British employers were so disgusted by party politics that coalitionists from both parties discussed forming a Centre Party to improve political representation. The inertia of majoritarian electoral rules prevented the emergence of a new party, but the experiment reflects the depth of disappointment with the current system.[84] In time, the British government ceded additional regulatory authority to interest groups, yet divided employer representation kept business input pluralist and fragmented.[85]

Conclusion

Periodic openings for cooperative strategies and collective organization among employers existed in Britain, as in other countries, but these strategies were undercut by the interplay of two-party competition as well as by the structure of industrial relations. Stark economic divisions and the characteristics of the labor movement contributed to Britain's failure to develop a national, multisector association by the end of the nineteenth century and to the curtailment of the FBI's corporatist ambitions. The pound's role as the world's leading currency made manufacturing take a back seat to finance in politics, constrained protectionist policies, and inhibited the formation of a national, multisector employers' organization. Craft unions and the absence of a

[81] Lowe 1978, 651, 657–62.
[82] Lowe 1978, 664, 674.
[83] Labour Research Department 1923, 42.
[84] "A Centre Coalition Party" 5/14/1919, 13; "Concern about Indemnities" 5/15, 1919, 14.
[85] Alderman 1984, 11–12; Turner 1984.

strong guild tradition limited labor market cooperation by depressing mutual interests in skills development.

These forces for fragmentation were greatly reinforced by the absence of incentives for politicians in two-party systems to nurture high levels of business organization and private policy-making channels. At the end of the nineteenth century, the dispersion of employers across parties made for limited political efforts to build a national association, apart from the periodic efforts of Charles Richie and Joseph Chamberlain.

World War I created fertile ground for national employer organization and greater coordination, yet the first British national, multisectoral organization – the Federation of British Industry – faltered in the environment of two-party competition. Electoral competition between the Conservative and Liberal Parties, bureaucratic battles between party-affiliated government departments, and sectoral divisions among employers undercut Steel-Maitland and Dudley Docker's initiatives to build the FBI into a singular and encompassing institution for business representation. The Conservative and Liberal parties each nurtured its own favored employers, and politicians in neither party had incentives to give the social partners any real power for self-regulation. Both parties could credibly hope to gain control of government and, in the absence of credible peak association capacities, few actors believed coordination would work above the sector level.

Ultimately, a corporatist employers' organization and institutions for nonmarket coordination failed to emerge. Party governments periodically experimented with the construction of cooperative institutions (e.g., more centralized wage bargaining in the 1970s) and the employers' groups finally merged into a single peak association, the Confederation of British Industry, in the mid-1960s. Yet, British employers remained fragmented and pluralistic in character, and institutional capacity for reaping the benefits of coordination remained weak. With the ascent of neoliberalism and a succession of market-oriented governments since the late 1970s, these historical patterns have been reinforced and significantly deepened.

5

Sectional Parties and Divided Business
in the United States

Introduction

American business organization appears exceptional from a cross-national perspective. Whereas most other advanced nations created a single peak employers' association to represent business interests, the United States developed two umbrella organizations by 1912 that have competed for power for the past 100 years. The first of these, the National Association of Manufacturers (NAM), initially sought to cooperate with labor and the state, and then led the corporate attack on its former allies. Thus, one wonders why America developed a pattern of fragmentation and redundancy with its multiple umbrella organizations – at a time when other countries were consolidating business representation into unitary organizations – and why NAM switched positions and used coordination to resist rather than to work with the state and labor.

As with Britain, the American experience initially seems easy to explain: A neoliberal, individualistic cultural imperative drove political and economic development. An immense and regionally diverse terrain complicated collective action by employers and a huge domestic market diminished the need for cooperative supports in foreign markets. Weak, craft-based unions did not motivate high levels of business coordination to resist labor, and the absence of an influential guilds tradition worked against the collective production of worker skills.[1] Yet NAM's puzzling early trajectory does not mesh with the foundation myth of the triumph of American exceptionalism: At its inception, NAM organizers sought to become an encompassing, corporatist peak association to represent all of business and held policy positions (for skills and non-market coordination) similar to those of contemporaneous European manufacturers. NAM's distrust of labor and the state developed only with a sea change, a decade into its organizational life.

We suggest that this rise and fall of the cooperative instinct among employers reflected efforts to solve a representation gap, created by the sectionally based and locally dominated U.S. two-party system. The McKinley campaign helped to create

[1] Hartz 1955; Davis 2000; Piore and Sabel 1984.

89

NAM to promote its industrial policies and to reach Southern employers who lacked a partisan home (resisting both post–Civil War Republicanism and Democratic economic policy). But NAM's corporatist ambitions were defeated by the very political structural conditions it was created to overcome, as neither party felt the need to compromise or to delegate power to private channels of policymaking for the social partners. Employers were dispersed across parties, and no coming democratization threatened business control. Democratic legislators from the south and west recognized NAM's political identity and limited its scope, by defeating its bids for a national charter and other legislative proposals. Left without a role in managing the transition to industrial capitalism, NAM began to wither away; finally, in 1903, NAM revised its core policy positions and chose new leadership with a decidedly antagonistic stance toward unions and state-led coordination.

The rise and decline of NAM's cooperative instincts are eerily echoed in the conception of the U.S. Chamber of Commerce, which had a similar institutional commitment to cooperation with labor and government and was created by political figures for electoral and bureaucratic reasons that bring to mind the NAM experience. The Chamber came of age later than NAM and enjoyed greater legislative success in expanding national administrative capacities, yet the Chamber met with frustrations reminiscent of NAM's in securing Congressional support for its coordinating public policies.

Theories of American Business Organization

Ideological explanations for American pluralism have difficulty accounting for the impulse for coordination revealed in NAM's early history. Moreover, the agriculture sector – nurtured by extensive developmental state policies – casts doubt on the American blanket philosophical rejection of coordination.[2] Therefore, we turn to three types of arguments for low levels of employer organization and labor market coordination: patterns of industrialization, character of labor, and dynamics of party competition.

Industrialization and the Evolution of U.S. Business Representation
The triumph of pluralism may reflect the particular trajectory of American industrialization – in particular, the nation's size and vast regional disparities, rise of internal strategies to manage coordination, and huge domestic market. Yet economic structural features have somewhat complicated impacts on business incentives to develop multisector groups.

Business organization was clearly complicated by sectional regional diversity, as southern, export-oriented, agricultural producers had vastly different interests from northern manufacturers. Yet, in the crucible of late nineteenth-century immense economic development, American manufacturers – like their European counterparts – had a collective interest (and self-interests) in a more favorable regulatory climate and sought to wrest economic privilege from agriculture to industry. By 1899 manufacturing was responsible for $5.04 billion of total value added, compared with only

---

[2] Ferleger and Lazonick 1993, 67–98.

$3.4 billion generated by agriculture.[3] Moreover, 85 percent of the largest industrial plants were located in the Northeast, which should lower the transaction costs of organizing. Similar conflicts of interest separated Danish export-oriented agricultural producers from domestic producers of manufactured good; yet these industrialists were able to develop an encompassing peak employers' association.

The development of a strong encompassing employers' organization may also have been hampered in the United States by the rise of the modern corporation, cartels, mergers, and other forms of collusion as an internal solution to managing labor markets and market instability. Depression in 1893 prompted a merger movement led by J. P. Morgan, as banks created centralized holding companies in one industry after another. The Sherman Antitrust Act deemed cartels illegal, and antitrust law's discouragement of economic collusion by employers may have increased business antagonism to public policy and cooperation in the social realm as well. Mergers helped firms to solve stability problems with corporate concentration. Although some nineteenth-century employers had tried to use labor organization to stabilize industry, as industries came to be dominated by a few large firms there was less need for labor to assist in stabilization. Yet the merger movement also unified bankers and manufacturers behind industrial policies such as the reciprocal tariff, because financiers acquired deeper interests in manufacturing concerns.[4]

The huge U.S. domestic economy may have worked against employers' need for coordination to nurture competitiveness in world economies. Yet, by 1900 U.S. firms exported nearly as much value in goods as Britain, Germany and France combined and exports of manufactured products greatly exceeded exports of raw materials.[5] Moreover, in Denmark, the domestic focus of manufacturing enabled higher levels of coordination because employers could afford higher wages to secure labor peace. Finally, none of these explanations can account for NAM's strange journey from an instrument for cooperation to an agent of liberalism.

Labor and American Employers
Features of labor may also contribute to the fragmented, decentralized representation of American business, as weakly organized unions and the absence of extensive specific skills reduce incentives for corporate cooperation. Enfranchised by the 1840s, white, male American workers obtained political rights without a social democratic party and their organization into craft unions worked against working class unity. Compared with CMEs, firms in LMEs use workers with lower skills and have fewer incentives to nurture collective mechanisms for training, workforce stability, and non-market coordination.[6]

Yet, whereas American workers were more weakly organized than countries with industrial unions, many firms developed segmentalist labor market strategies to cooperate with labor, paying higher wages and benefits to attract a productive, stable workforce. 1898 to 1902 marked a high point of trade agreements, trust formation and

---

[3] U.S. Dept of Commerce 1961, 139; see Bensel 2000; Wiebe 1962; Trubowitz 1998.
[4] Josephson 1940; Sklar 1988; Ferguson 1995.
[5] Werking 1977, 21.
[6] Shefter 1986; ; Hall and Soskice 2001; Thelen 2004.

other combinations; firms frequently sought union assistance with these processes, by negotiating trade agreements with unions and asking labor allies to pressure firms to join the combinations. Moreover, in 1895, many manufacturers resembled their European counterparts in skills levels, competitive strategies, and content of production processes. The munitions "armory practice" with interchangeable parts laid the groundwork for mass-production but was not widespread. Demands for workers skills increased with the expansion of metal production and firms sought mechanisms for addressing an enormous skills deficit. Old forms of apprenticeship training declined because paid labor became a more viable way to supply workers, rather than because skills were downgraded. Thus, states and communities developed extensive vocational training programs, and some employers entered into private, collective arrangements to meet skills needs. It was at the point when regions were integrated into a national economy, that the United States failed to develop a *national* vocational training scheme, despite a major push by business before the 1917 Smith Hughes Act and the 1926 High School Reform Act. Employers lobbied hard against the location of vocational training in general education programs – lacking standards, occupational definitions, skills benchmarks, certificate procedures or ties to the labor market – but employers were insufficiently well-organized to obtain a collective training system. The decline in specific skills came after NAM failed to establish itself as a singular, unity peak association, and large firms began developing their own in-house training programs.[7] NAM's interest in coordination is consistent with the need for high skills, yet NAM's retreat from coordination is a greater mystery.

Party Competition and Employers' Associations: Segmented Parties, Divided Business

Our central argument is that the dynamics of two-party competition channeled both NAM's move to coordinate and subsequent turn toward pluralism. The American story differs somewhat from the British case, in that the Republican Party was more dominated by business than either British party. The Republican Party was a business party in the *policy* sense, but a significant representation gap existed in the *electoral* realm, as no party represented southern and western manufacturers, who counted beyond their electoral strength at the nominating convention stage.[8] Party strategists (most notably Marcus Hanna, McKinley's campaign manager) sought to broaden the Republican base beyond its northeast/midwest stronghold, and NAM was created at the behest of the McKinley campaign as an alternative political organization to fill this representation gap, to rally support for McKinley's nomination and to further the party's industrial agenda.

Yet, NAM was also afflicted by the political features of a federal, two-party system in which significant authority is devolved to lower levels of government, ill-equipped

[7] Jacoby 1998; Gable 1959, 539; Bensel 2000; Trubowitz 1998; Berk and Schneiberg 2005; Piore and Sabel 1984; Hounshell 1978; Bureau of Labor 1911; Hansen 1997, 266–8, 5489; Margo 1990.
[8] Even though southern states delivered all electoral college votes to Democrats, they wielded considerable power in the nomination; lacking their own favorite sons, they provided important support to contenders from other regions. Leech 1959, 62. The GOP was more completely dominated by business due to the strong sectional concentrations of economic activity, which permitted economic elites in each region to control their parties.

to address national issues. Weak polities with fragmented political authority, under-developed national bureaucracies, and high levels of regional diversity are likely to produce neither parties nor interest groups that represent coherent national constituencies. The federal devolution of authority to the state level combined with party localism and sectional domination in the United States worked against the materialization of employers' associations with a national focus. Democratic legislators voted against most NAM policies, which they viewed as advantaging Eastern and Midwestern manufacturers, and GOP strategists had no reason to collaborate with Democrats in this bipolar electoral competition. Because the parties did not face a threat from a center-left coalition, it had no reason to delegate policy-making authority to a private system of business and labor representation. The Republicans controlled government, yet the separation of powers in the U.S. government allowed the Democratic opposition to derail the NAM agenda. NAM abandoned its quest for cooperation, defeated by the party politics that inspired its organization.

Rise and Decline of the National Association of Manufacturers

The Republican's Strategic Interests in Business Organization
William McKinley was the candidate for industrial development, and the northeastern industrialists represented the most powerful bloc in the party; yet deep sectional divisions (regional, sectoral, and urban/rural) complicated the Republicans' efforts to attain their national economic goals. To avoid sectional disputes, McKinley and Hanna focused the 1896 campaign on manufacturers' core concern of the reciprocal tariff and dodged the divisive silver question. Hanna colorfully proclaimed: "Our sole cry will be McKinley and protection. St. Louis will ring with it and the birds will sing it." McKinley and Hanna sought to delay taking a formal position on silver and Hanna hid McKinley's support for the gold platform from the silver states, even while he secretly making commitments to the gold states.[9] The *Macon Telegraph* reported:

[I]t is generally doubted here that Governor McKinley has put himself on record from Thomasville, Ga., as being unalterably opposed to the free coinage of silver. He would hardly take a stand, they say, against the unmistakable wishes of the people among whom he intended to go in furtherances of his interests in the presidential nomination.[10]

Political tensions about the balance between national and regional governments hampered Republican efforts to create national public policies. Democrats opposed the Republican Party's push for industrial development (viewed as shifting privilege to manufacturers), enacted policies to benefit export farmers rather than industrialists, and largely opposed the expansion of national state capacity. The Democratic Party platform proclaimed that the Union needed saving: "From a corrupt centralism, which, after inflicting upon ten states the rapacity of carpet-bag tyrannies, has honeycombed the offices of the Federal Government itself with incapacity, waste, and fraud."[11] Republican national policy goals were also hampered by the party system's

---

[9] Wiebe 1962; Cleveland Press 3/23/1986; Kohlsaat 1923, 33–6; Stern 1963, 21–30.
[10] "M'Kinley's Tour," 3/27/1895, 1.
[11] Bensel 2000; Olcott 1916, 213.

domination by corrupt local party bosses, who were often committed to "native son" candidates and demanded patronage for political support. Hanna considered deals bosses in New York, Pennsylvania and elsewhere, but McKinley determined that the patronage costs were too high.[12]

McKinley and Hanna creatively undercut urban bosses with campaign techniques usually associated with twentieth-century politics: grass-roots mobilization, polling, advertizing, a Southern strategy, and businessmen committees. Organization depended on money, and Hanna solicited many $5,000 contributions from large manufacturers for McKinley's gubernatorial run in 1891, and he himself contributed $100,000 to the presidential campaign in 1896. The campaign of 1896 relied on business organization *and* money, rather than on party bosses.[13]

A key tactic was to establish independent power bases in localities, beyond party boss control. Hanna hoped to secure the nomination for McKinley on the first ballot and this required securing pledges from other states. An early victory in a big northern state was essential: Illinois was the first state to choose convention delegates, and Charles Dawes (later vice-president) led the McKinley attack on the Illinois machine (and native son Shelby Cullan), using political outsiders such as businessmen, Union vets, and retired Republicans. Illinois delivered forty-six out of forty-eight delegates to McKinley and Dawes noted in his diary, "It is McKinley against the field – against the bosses – against everything that the bosses can bring to bear."[14] In Indiana, the campaign feared that McKinley's enemies would push Harrison to run as a favorite son "merely for the purpose of rallying the anti-McKinley sentiment." McKinley aide, G. H. Grosvenor, asked William Holloway "to organize thoroughly a movement" and to identify the leading man in each county "who will take charge of the business of securing a straightforward vote."[15] In a grass-roots operation, each voter in Indiana was assigned to a Republican Party loyalist, called the "blocks of five" system, and the campaign unleashed "an army of campaigners" who distributed 120,000 pamphlets with slogans such as "good money never made times hard." Critics feared that this "free use of money on the part of manufacturers" would lose "thousands of votes."[16]

Another institutional innovation to garner business support was the Republican club, created by Hanna in 1880 with the "Cleveland Business Men's Marching Club." The clubs were amalgamated into a National Republican League "for active party service, originated in Ohio in the interest of Major McKinley." The League was a vehicle for business leaders to sell the party to voters, and the "merchandising approach" to politics became especially important with the rise of independent voting.[17]

The campaign's southern strategy sought to alter geographically determined political identities among Southerners, who repudiated a Republican Party dominated by African-Americans but who deplored the Democrats' free silver policy. W. W. Brown of Macon Georgia expressed wanting nothing to do with a Republican "negro-bossed

[12] Olcott 1916: 300–1.
[13] Olcott 1916, 298; Stern 1963, 7, 13; Croly 1912, 184.
[14] Croly 1912, 182; Dawes 1950, 66.
[15] Boyle to Holloway, 4/5/1895; Grosvenor to Holloway, 3/21/1896.
[16] White 1928, 7–8; Olcott 1916, 324; Cleveland Press 3/25/1896, 6.
[17] Lauer 1901, 101; White 1928, 201; Burk 1904, 10; Jensen 1971, 164–5.

organization," but offered to bet $10,000 on a McKinley victory.[18] Charles Dick and Joe Smith traveled throughout the south to secure endorsements for McKinley and to reposition the party along class rather than sectional lines. McKinley used a three-week "social" visit to Hanna's Georgian winter home to greet key Republicans from the state, and met with a half-dozen protectionists to discuss the formation of a local Protection League. The election of 1896 produced the largest percentage of Republican votes in the south since reconstruction; indeed, Atlanta very nearly went Republican.[19]

The Formation of the National Association of Manufacturers

NAM officially credits its inception to Thomas H. Martin, who proposed a national convention for displaying American manufactures in his Atlanta-based trade publication, *Dixie Manufacturers*. Martin then allegedly proposed forming a multisector association to represent manufacturers' policy interests to Thomas Egan and the Cincinnati Manufacturers' Association. The Cincinnati manufacturers initially responded with a poorly attended meeting, but Egan subsequently held a banquet for 450 employers at the Grand Hotel to raise $10,000 fund for the initiative. A group called "the Big 50" organized the convention, with Egan in charge as "the father of the project" Manufacturing organizations all over the country were urged to attend because "manufacturing interests of the entire country may be best promoted by concerted action." The invitation described the meeting as "non-political, nonpartisan and nonsectional.[20]

At the time, NAM denied that McKinley had any role in its inception, but the association later admitted that McKinley assisted in its origins, and the effort fit well with Republican's other institutional experiments.[21] Considerable overlap united the NAM organizing effort and McKinley Republican campaign. In Ohio, McDougall served as chair of the Committee on Resolutions at the initial NAM convention, was the keynote speaker at NAM's second convention, and had been among the group of McKinley's closest friends that struggled with Robert Walker's financial crisis.[22] McDougall visited McKinley for a week shortly before the NAM organizing convention, and although we have no record of their discussions, newspapers charged that McKinley had "an 'authorized organ' in Cincinnati." McKinley complained to McDougall about the

---

[18] "$10,000 to bet on M'Kinley," 7/15/1896, 9.

[19] Olcott 1916, 305–7; "They Welcomed M'Kinley," 3/18/1895, 1; Bacote 1959, 220. Hanna was also accused of buying African Americans' delegates' votes for McKinley. Bacote 1959, 220; White 1928, 168.

[20] Martin was inspired to hold a series of conventions in South America by the Cotton States and International Exposition in Atlanta, which displayed local industrial products for an international audience. He realized that even though the upper middle class came to these exhibitions, the expositions did little to advertize American goods to mass consumers. NAM 1926, 61; "The Cincinnati Convention," 1/27/1895, 19; "Dixie the Toast," 1/28/1895, 7; "Tomorrow in Odd Fellow's Temple." 1/21/1895. The association also offered Atlanta business leaders a vehicle for promoting their goods and regional attractions for industrial development – a warm climate, a lower wage rate, and cheap real estate. "To Cotton Mill Men."1–27, 1895, 19.

[21] NAM 1926; Gable 1959. The funding for the Grand Hotel meeting is a mystery, and one wonders if Hanna were involved.

[22] NAM 1895. McKinley helped to subsidize Walker's enterprises and was almost lost in scandal when Walker threatened to declare bankruptcy. Olcott 1916, 290.

newspapers being "full of every manner of suggestion of conspiracy and strategem" and told a Tribune reporter that "you [McDougall] were acting on your own responsibility and sense of duty."[23] NAM treasurer, D.D. Woodmansee, also led the Ohio League of Republican Clubs.[24]

The first president of NAM, Thomas Dolan of Pennsylvania, was curiously elected to office without attending the convention. "Delegates were entirely in the dark as to who would be recommended [by the nominating committee], and when the name of Mr. Thomas Dolan of Philadelphia was announced by Chairman Fish, there was a moment of silence and then a burst of applause." Yet although distant from NAM's organizing efforts, Dolan was chosen by the McKinley family to serve as a trustee for the president's monument after his death. Dolan with three other men was accused of contributing $100,000 to a McKinley campaign fund in 1900, and recovering the money from the Metropolitan Street Railway Company.[25] The McKinley campaign worried that Quay and Platt would derail McKinley's candidacy in 1896, and W.M. Osborne recommended contacting Dolan to coordinate a "fight in Penn. for every delegate."[26]

The three Georgian employers attending the NAM organizing convention were also deeply involved with the McKinley campaign (and with coordinating McKinley's visit to Georgia in 1895). Martin, credited for conceptualizing NAM, served on the organization's constitution and bylaws committees and was the president of the Atlanta McKinley Club. Colonel J. .F Hanson (owner of the *Macon Telegraph*) was both the NAM vice-president from Georgia and the major speaker at the meeting of the Southern Republican Party convention before the 1896 convention. Hanson met with McKinley in Atlanta in March 1895 during his southern sojourn and discussed campaign strategy. Colonel AF Buck recommended potential Republican delegates for the nominating convention and served as a liaison to African American Republican leaders in the state.[27]

At NAM's organizing convention, McKinley was first to speak after Cincinnati's mayor. A host of marching businessmen meet McKinley upon his arrival, escorted him through the streets of Cincinnati, and McKinley's keynote address drew a standing ovation from the crowd. The *National Industrial Review* highlighted these political overtones, predicting that NAM "will be in future a great factor in our National elections."[28] NAM's second annual meeting in January 1896 offers deeper evidence of the association's role in McKinley's presidential ambitions. The meeting was originally scheduled for the fall of 1895, "just about the time when the campaign for the Republican nomination for the Presidency will open, and McKinley will be there."

---

[23] McKinley to McDougall,12/19/1894/; McKinley to W. Heath, 2/5/1895.

[24] "Woodmansee Is Once More Chosen," 2/13/1895, 8.

[25] "It's President Dolan," 1/25/1895; "For the McKinley Monument,"10/6/1901, 3; "Metropolitan Cash Used for M'Kinley," 4/4/1908.

[26] Osborne to McKinley. When Dolan suggested that businessmen had done a mighty service in the campaign and proposed that a businessmen's league be formed "in every county in Pennsylvania," Quay presciently opposed the conception: "Its basic theory is that organized wealth shall dictate high office, and so take possession of the Government" ("Mr. Quay Takes a Stand").

[27] "Manufacturers in Convention," Bacote 1959, 218; McKinley to Col. J. F. Hanson, February 27, 1896; McKinley to R. E. Wright. 1/4/1896; Col A. F. Buck to McKinley, 1/8/1896.

[28] Steigerwalt 1964; Gable 1959, 536; *The National Industrial Review*, May 1895.

But it was put off until January 1896, shortly before the series of state conventions to choose the nominee. NAM organizers promised in advance that the convention would be nonpartisan, yet the organizers also predicted that the critical issues to be taken up meant that "a greater significance attaches to the outcome of this convention and its ultimate results, than to that of any other convention, either commercial or political, that has ever been held on this hemisphere." According to *The New York Times*, the most significant event was "the applause which greeted a mention of the name of Major McKinley. This applause told as plainly as could a preamble and resolution the real purpose of the delegates."[29] In his keynote address, McDougall mentioned McKinley repeatedly and blamed business paralysis on lack of statesmanship:

While you have been devoting your energies to the building up of this marvelous industrial and economic system, you have not been organized for its protection ... I do not unduly criticise our modern legislators when I say that not one man out of fifty, either in a State Legislature or in a Federal Congress, possesses the qualifications, the knowledge and the experience that entitle him to wisely legislate on such a marvelous system. Now, this Association is formed for what purpose? To speak, as representing those vast interests, to the legislators of this country ... We do need statesmen. (Prolonged applause.) ... Party politics make a foot-ball of the interests of this country ... And nothing but the voice of our united manufacturing industries will be able to compel these so-called statesmen to act.[30]

Shortly before the election of 1896, NAM's *National Industrial Review* went further in abandoning its alleged nonpartisan neutrality to lobby for the Republican policies of tariff protection and reciprocity. Asserting that "there are certain questions embodied in the platforms of the two great political parties that are of vital interest and importance to the manufacturer," the *Review* urged members to support these policies whether they be Republicans or Democrats. Moreover, the *National Industrial Review* repeatedly urged southern manufacturers to form local chapters of manufacturing associations in order to focus employers' minds on national issues.[31]

NAM's Goals for Industrial Coordination, Labor Peace, and Corporatist Representation

NAM's official goals highlight employers' interests in industrial development policy, rather than the association's later anti-labor orientation. First, in its manifesto, NAM's policy objectives all stressed industrial development: the extension of domestic and foreign markets, reciprocal tariffs, the Nicaragua Canal, expansion of a merchant marine, and expansion of waterways. NAM's Committee on Resolutions proposed a general principle: "To the largest possible extent our home market should be retained and supplied by our own producers and our foreign trade relations should be extended in every direction."[32] NAM sought to rise above sectional economic disputes in this national

[29] "A High-Tariff Republican President"; National Association of Manufacturers, 7/6/1895, 148; "Manufacturers Cheer for McKinley."
[30] McDougall 1896, 3–8.
[31] National Association of Manufacturers 1896; *National Industrial Review* VI (#7 August; National Association of Manufacturers, 7/6/1895, 154.
[32] NAM 1926; "Reports of Officers: Annual Address of President Edgerton"; "Delegates Got Down to Business."

endeavor to be the first "general organization of manufacturers exclusively embracing all trades, conditions, sections, and sizes of industrial units": "The Association is not in any respect a competitor of any other organization"; rather it "occupies a position of complete independence and fills a field that is distinctively its own."[33]

Second, NAM identified industrial cooperation among agents in business, labor and the state as necessary to economic development. NAM's vision of industrial development was far from neutral on the balance of class power, as it sought to quiet labor militancy after a twenty year recession producing shocking episodes of labor unrest.[34] Yet before opposing labor in 1903, NAM's leaders viewed stable, cooperative labor relations as essential to firms' export ambitions, which President Edgarton later noted when deploring the misconceptions about the origins of NAM and lack of attention to the organization's "biography."[35] President Search stated in 1901 that industrial development created new labor problems and suggested that NAM could make recommendations about social conditions of the workplace with "industrial betterment ideas":

Organized capital is confronted by organized labor and it is exceedingly gratifying to note that instead of more determined antagonism there is a larger disposition to consider the points at issue with calm deliberation and intelligent judgment ... There is an economic value in such ideas in addition to the interest which attaches to them from the humanitarian standpoint, and profit can be derived in many ways ... in those modern establishments where progressive ideas have been applied in full force.[36]

Third, NAM aimed to become a peak association for sectoral industry groups with a proto-corporatist organizational structure, and hoped to formalize collaboration with government and labor to give the association a privileged role in shaping public policy. NAM purported to embrace "a broader field" than other organizations, to represent "the entire manufacturing interests of the country," and not to constitute "a competitor of any other organization."[37] Initially, only associations were permitted to belong to peak organization and individual members were required to represent their associations. The executive committee sought "to consolidate into one great powerful representative body the total force and influence of American industry, so that when any question of any large national industry shall present itself, American manufacturers will speak and act with a positive assumption that they will be heard and heeded ... At present the power of manufacturers is diffused through many minor organizations."[38] NAM sought legislation to obtain a "federal act of incorporation" or a national charter and lobbied for the creation of a new cabinet-level Department of Commerce (finally established in 1903), to act as a clearing house for technical expertise, to rationalize business-oriented regulation, and to represent business in the new vision of coordination.[39]

[33] Wilson 12/1/1898: 1.
[34] Josephson 1940, 28. 169.
[35] NAM 1926, 61–2.
[36] Search 1901, 23–4.
[37] Steigerwalt 1964, 33. Organizers were inspired by Germany and Canada. "The National Association of Manufacturers and other Organizations," 148.
[38] "Proceedings of the First Meeting of the Executive Committee of the National Association of Manufacturers of the United States of America," 4/1/1895, 67.
[39] Search 1900, 12–13.

The Failure of Coordination

NAM was formed to overcome the electoral and institutional incapacities of section-ally dominated two-party competition and to foster McKinley's nationalist economic and presidential ambitions; however, the group nearly floundered on the circum-stances motivating its rise. Created to overcome sectional tensions, these were never fully resolved: NAM's leadership was dominated by medium-sized firms in the East and Midwest and member companies employed only about a third to half of the nation's manufacturing workers.[40] In 1898 the top dues-paying states were New York, Pennsylvania, Ohio, Illinois, New Jersey and Indiana. Only the states with the most members could send representatives to the executive committee and a Tennessee man protested that this clause "shut out from your Executive Committee every State south of Mason and Dixon's line."[41] Delegates to the 1903 annual convention voted to expand the scope of NAM to include employers beyond manufacturing, but the executive committee rejected this resolution, explaining that reconstituting NAM as a broad-based employers association would lose the special emphasis on core manufacturing interests.[42]

As NAM strove to become more encompassing, economic divisions on trade policy increased. The association struggled to present itself as "a body of leading manufac-turers whose efforts are united in work that will promote the general welfare of the manufacturing interests of the country." The *American Statesman* bemoaned the "widely prevailing impression that the National Association of Manufacturers is an organization composed exclusively of those who are interested in foreign trade." NAM's pro-trade reputation became particularly problematic after 1900, when prosperity expanded the domestic market for U.S. goods and interest in exporting to foreign markets subsided.[43] Strong import retail interests in San Francisco held their own "Industrial Convention" to express the multiplicity of employer interests in that city, and the San Francisco Chamber of Commerce opened a Washington office to lobby Congress.[44]

NAM's dubious reputation (as a partisan political agent of the Republican Party seeking to establish a base in Democratic states) ensnared it in legislative infighting and its bills to secure a position as the central business representative were postponed or rejected. NAM repeatedly sought a license to be incorporated as the central orga-nizational body representing business. But this was rejected by Democratic legislators who viewed NAM as acting for Republican and sectional interests.[45] After the 1896 election, the organization viewed the creation of a commerce department as immi-nent and a member of NAM's Resolutions Committee, George Johnson, leaked a story to the *New York Times* that a commerce department bill was about to be passed by the Senate, that President-elect McKinley had already selected John Converse to head the new department, and that Converse had NAM's unconditional endorsement. Yet this legislation repeatedly faltered in Congress and by 1898 Search was to comment wearily, "There is scarcely another government in the civilized world that does not

[40] Yet this rate was comparable to initial membership in other countries' peak associations. Brady 1943.

[41] NAM 1898, 35; 1895, 48–50, 65–6.

[42] Steigerwalt 1964, 121–2.

[43] "Home Interests and Foreign Trade," 12 3/15/1899: 92.

[44] "San Francisco Industrial Convention" 1895, 94; Steigerwalt 1964.

[45] Search 1901, 13.

possess a governmental department ... to observe a solicitude in behalf of trade and industry."[46] NAM reported on its lobbying efforts:

it will require considerable active work on the part of the merchants and manufacturers of the country to show the representatives from the Granger States the urgent necessity for the passage of this bill ... Our representatives in Congress now realize that the creation of a Department of Agriculture was beneficial to the entire country, to manufacturers and merchants as well as the farmer; likewise, a Department of Commerce and Industry will serve to promote general prosperity throughout the country.[47]

NAM also lobbied for an extension of the Dingley Tariff Act of 1897 to ease the creation of reciprocal tariffs, but to no avail. The association then pressured the Senate to approve treaties for commercial reciprocity, but the Senate refused to consider these treaties, even with successive Presidential requests and the State Department's creation of a process to negotiate international treaties. NAM's frustration with the failure to pass reciprocity treaties prompted it to organize a National Reciprocity Convention in 1902. The NAM leadership (dominated by would-be exporters) sought to champion tariff reduction and to send a clear message to Congress that business as a group supported this position. Members of the American Protective Tariff League descended on the conference in large numbers, "captured the convention for regular Chinese wall protection," and significantly scaled back the initial resolution.[48]

NAM's legislative disappointments contributed to its failure to establish itself as the central representative of business and left the association with little purpose by century's end. Whereas European corporatist organizations played a large part in policy development and implementation but their electoral functions remained limited, NAM achieved its electoral goal with McKinley's victory but its postelectoral engagement with policy was minimal. Members derived little from the meetings and the biggest challenge was to stay solvent. The organizers decided to allow individual firms – in addition to organizations – to join, but membership had dropped to under 1000 members by 1902.[49]

The association's failure to expand scope and membership explains its ultimate conversion to an antilabor platform in 1903, and sheds light on the larger question of why American employer associations drifted into neoliberalism. The precipitating cause for NAM's adoption of an antilabor stance was the proposed Congressional legislation mandating an eight-hour work day and prohibiting employers' use of injunctions against collective actions by workers. NAM's negative position represented a profound about-face, and as late as 1901 President Search continued to assert that the "relations between manufacturers and their employees has never been regarded as one of the proper functions" of NAM. But the campaign against

---

[46] "A Ninth Cabinet Member," 2/23/1897, 1. Search admired the British and French departments for commerce and industry that shaped technical education, patents, strikes, inspections, and trade. Search 1898, 13–14.

[47] "Committee on Commerce and Industry," 1898, p. 46–7, 173.

[48] NAM Proceedings 1901, 8, 66, 109; "Will Discuss Reciprocity," 8/17/01, 7; "Reciprocity Convention Meets in Washington," 11/20/1901, 8; Scheinberg 1973, 225.

[49] NAM 1902, 32; NAM 1926, 59–62, 174.

the eight-hour day gave the association new life and, in the profound absence of more positive goals, NAM's antilabor position enabled membership to reach 2742 by 1907.[50] Thus, history moved in a different direction and we can only speculate about NAM's trajectory had national governmental capacity been greater, sectional conflicts been less acute, and the party system not been dominated by two major parties.

The U.S. Chamber of Commerce

The origins of the U.S. Chamber of Commerce echo the NAM story, as the Chamber was developed to accomplish all that the NAM failed to do. Even though it is beyond the scope of this chapter to develop fully this parallel story, we offer the Chamber's tale as a shadow case to fortify the claims made about NAM's genesis and strange trajectory. Once again a president (now Taft) led industrialists in his effort to further coordination, to unify employers across sectional divides, and to build an electoral constituency. The Chamber's goals were much like NAM's: to consolidate and to represent employers' political interests, to facilitate economic coordination, to build export capacity, to create industrial infrastructure, to offer political support for the expansion of the administrative state, and to aid in Taft's electoral ambitions. Overall, the Chamber fared somewhat better in realizing its preferred public policies, as it developed in a later era when national governmental power was on the rise and when its ambitions for representing employers in public/private forums could more easily be gratified by governmental processes. But the Chamber suffered legislative setbacks comparable to those of NAM's, and its objectives were defeated by sectional and partisan rivalries.

First, the Chamber's trajectory resembles that of NAM's in the processes by which the Chamber was formed: Government officials took the lead in its organization and both political and electoral ambitions provided motivation. In the early twentieth century, it became clear that NAM failed to represent a broad cross-section of business, never built a broad constituency beyond its core regions, and remained focused on small and medium-sized manufacturers. Soon after NAM's abrupt policy reversals, state actors endeavored to create an encompassing employers' organization to facilitate cooperation among business, labor and the state; the Chamber was the culmination of these experiments in coordination.

Steps leading to the Chamber's formation began with Oscar Straus, the secretary of the Department of Commerce and Labor, finally created in 1903. Straus asked department aides in the department's Bureau of Manufactures' to study the German system of export promotion, and Naham Stone wrote an extensive report on British and German data collection on tariffs, patents, foreign investments, and treatment of commercial interests abroad. Stone was impressed by foreign departments' administrative capacity to offer extensive technical advice to business and by the system of collaboration between the public and private spheres:[51]

---

[50] NAM 1902, 23; NAM 1926, 59–62.
[51] Kaufman 1972, 23; Stone 1978, 22–4.

So far we have no equipment comparable to that in foreign countries ... In view of the rapid growth of our foreign commerce, the work of this Department in connection with foreign tariffs is relatively of as great importance to the country as the work of the Treasury Department ...

Above all it is highly important that the people for whose benefit the work of the Department is to be done be kept in close touch with it. To-day there is no provision for systematic cooperation between the Department and the various commercial and trade associations which are most affected by its work. Except for the correspondence which goes on between the Department and individual business firms, and occasionally also some commercial organization, there is no medium by which regular interchange of opinion and active cooperation on a comprehensive scale could take place.

Impressed by Stone's research, Straus invited chambers of commerce and boards of trade from forty cities to meet in Washington, DC, in December 1907. Participants agreed to form a National Council of Commerce composed of representatives of commerce organizations throughout the country and to appoint an Advisory Committee to act as a liaison between government and local chambers. But the National Council of Commerce was never widely endorsed by business, perhaps because of its $100 membership fee and the suspiciously close ties of Council's leader, Gustav Schwab, to the German shipping industry.[52]

Straus's successor, Charles Nagel, also sought business organization support for his activist economic policy, but believed that employers' efforts to organize themselves had been inadequate and together with Albert Baldwin (Commerce's Bureau of Manufactures) met with chambers across the land to solicit business interest in a broader group. The Chicago Chamber attempted to organize a national association on its own, but the limited response convinced organizers that they needed government assistance to succeed. Baldwin found that "many alert businessmen" were convinced of the need for closer relations between business and government in competition against "foreign trade rivals" and advocated something like the German model.[53]

In December 1911, President Taft proposed a bill to Congress establishing a new encompassing organization. In February, Baldwin and two colleagues met with six sectionally diverse employers to plan and to invite (from President Taft) a cross-section of employers to an April 1912 conference creating the U.S. Chamber of Commerce. About 700 delegates attended, representing 392 organizations and most states. After Taft's welcoming speech, Secretary Nagel offered a testimonial to the power of business-government cooperation and to the importance of transcending sectionalism. The group's structure exemplified its ambition to become a peak association representing business, as it was to have only organizational members, such as local chambers of commerce, boards of trade, and other commercial organizations.[54]

The political ambitions of the state actors driving the Chamber's creation were striking. The Commerce Department sought in the business association a "mobilized constituency" that would help lobby Congress for funds. Baldwin sought to assist the

[52] Sturges 1915, 59–61; Wiebe 1962.
[53] Childs 1930; Werking 1978; Baldwin 1912.
[54] Shreve 1949; Wiebe 1962; State caucuses chose members of the nominating committee for the Chamber's board of directors. "Organization and Purposes of the Chamber of Commerce of the United States," 8; Baldwin 1912.

nascent group by sending conference proceedings to a broad group of employers and to reaffirm that the Bureau of Manufactures would seek to help the new group "in every legitimate way." Internecine battles with the State Department (which also promoted export trade) fueled the Commerce Department's desire to bring in outside allies. Nagel feared that the State Department's cultivation of cultivate commercial interests would diminish the bureaucratic power of the Commerce Department and told Secretary of State Huntington Wilson that this was to be a Commerce Department event.[55]

The Chamber's creation was also motivated by the Taft's electoral ambitions. In August 1911, Nagel calculated that Taft's leadership in establishing the group would garner considerable goodwill among employers in advance of the 1912 election. But once formed, the Chamber's President Harry Wheeler wrote to Taft, saying that "contrary to his original purpose" he could not participate in the campaign, as the organization feared that an overly political connection between the Chamber and the Republicans would compromise the groups other goals. The Chamber also made it clear that, while cooperating with "every executive and legislative department," it would refuse no federal support to preserve its neutrality.[56] Perhaps the Chamber realized the danger of linking its fortunes to a candidate that might well lose in a three-way presidential race. Had Theodore Roosevelt not run against his former party, one wonders if the Chamber might have played a more explicitly political role in the campaign.

Second, the Chamber shared NAM's goals of seeking to be a liaison for governmental relations, a vehicle for promoting industrial development, and a "clearing house" for information about state-of-the-art business methods. The Chamber's *Nation's Business* lamented "the general failure throughout the nation to use the multifarious service which the government is ready to perform, and which it can better perform than any private organization." The Chamber planned to gather monthly polling data on employers' policy views and to provide "by means of referendum vote an intimate knowledge of the business sentiment of the United States on all important subjects affected by national legislation." It sought to represent business views to government and promoted a message of "commercial patriotism," arguing that "the interests of each are the interests of all." To ensure that legislators were apprised of business views, the organization developed a legislative committee to analyze issues before Congress.[57]

As with NAM, the Chamber organizers hoped to aggregate business opinion into a single formidable voice and, in particular, to overcome the limitations of the sectional party system. In this vein, the *Globe Democrat* disparaged organizations "which call themselves 'national,' but which include bodies in only a few states"; and noted that the Chamber's proponents wanted "to form an organization broadly representative of the whole country and of all commercial and industrial interests." Wheeler credited the Chamber's creation to the "vital necessity ... to impel business men to forget competition, to obliterate sectional lines, and to forego selfish gain in their desire for its creation." The *Nation's Business* pointedly asked its readership, "Can the business

[55] Werking 1978, 322, 338–9; Baldwin 1912.
[56] Wiebe 1962; "No Federal Support," 9/22/1912.
[57] "Organization and Purposes of the Chamber of Commerce of the United States," 1912, 8; "The Chamber's Field," 9/2/1912, 1–2; "Committees on National Legislation," 9/2/1912, 2.

organizations and the business interests that are scattered over forty-eight States and our possessions be brought into one cohesive body that shall ultimately be able to bring to a focus the entire constructive thought of the entire nation." The leadership sought to overcome sectionalism by forming committees with an equal number of members from each of the four regions: Eastern, Western, North Central and South Central.[58] At the first annual meeting of the Chamber, Charles Nagel (Secretary of Commerce) bluntly confronted the problem of unifying manufacturing interests in a sectionally divided party system:

> We are confronted with this difficulty, that politically speaking we are still divided on sectional lines. Industrially speaking we do not recognize those lines ... Politically we are a house divided against itself and industrially we are one union. We need the intelligence, the judgment and the experience of the whole country to solve the problems that confront us, without bias and without prejudice, with that brotherly co-operation that we boast of having sustained ... What is your difficulty? I say you have been divided. Agriculture is one large interest in the United States that has been permitted to speak for itself ... The labor unions know what they want and ask for it ... You ought to know your mind, and to find the way to register your opinion ... It will not take long for the people of the nation to understand that the laborer and the proprietor belong together."[59]

At the heart of the Chamber's economic vision were proposals to expand the national, administrative state in order to augment American firms' trading capabilities vis-à-vis foreign competitors. Hence it held a referendum documenting tremendous member support for a permanent tariff commission or "permanent body of experts to gather, investigate, and tabulate technical and statistical facts of all kinds pertinent to the tariff schedules." The Chamber supported proposals to double government spending on the Commerce Department's Bureau of Foreign and Domestic Commerce and to increase the Bureau's administrative capacity in the form of consular commercial attaches and translators. The association supported a national budget, reasoning that the United States was one of the few countries lacking a centralized accounting of national government.[60] The group promoted the Owen-Glass banking and currency reform, which led to the U.S. Federal Reserve Bank, and a "Legislative Reference and Bill Drafting Bureau" within Congress, that would provide Congressional commit-tees with information about legislation and ensure that bills are drafted correctly.[61] The Chamber supported rationalizing and expanding national and state highways and joined Progressives in viewing the proposed federal trade commission as a "constructive and timely aid to business." Finally, the Chamber expressed considerable interest in

---

[58] "Businessmen to Be Brought into Closer Touch with Government," 1912; Wheeler 1913; "Organization and Purposes of the Chamber of Commerce of the United States" 1912, 8; "The Method for Selection of Committees in the Chamber of Commerce of the United State of America," 1/20/1913, 8.

[59] "Secretary Charles Nagel Speaks Encouragingly,": 1/28/1913, 3. Despite the Chamber's ambitions to reach out to businessmen across sections, the organization remained most heavily represented in the Northeast and upper Midwest. ("Membership Map of the National Chamber," 5/15/1913, 8.)

[60] Kaufman 1971, 347; "Two Important Decisions," 6/16/1913, 1; "Permanent Trade Commission," 1/28/1913, 3; "Promoting Foreign and Domestic Commerce," 5/15/1913, 3; "Opinions of Leaders in Business World and in Education," 11/18/1912, 2.

[61] "Referendum on Banking and Currency," 10/15/1913, 1; "Legislative Reference and Bill Drafting Bureau," 11/15/1913, 4.

the Wisconsin income tax experiment, especially because an income tax would shift the burden off property taxes.[62]

The Chamber also mirrored early NAM positions in promoting peaceful labor relations. NAM's move to the far right on labor issues had put off employers who were less radical on the subject or for whom other issues were more important; and both Roosevelt and Taft considered NAM's antiunionism a political liability.[63] Chamber President Wheeler envisioned the organization as cooperating with both labor and agricultural interests in order to "find a proper solution of the problems which now vex the nation." Wheeler believed that this cooperative stance was absolutely essential to the country's economic ambitions and wrote, "The interdependence of their interests is so positive that antagonism should never exist." *Nation's Business* was full of discussions about partnership with labor and reported on experiments in welfare capitalism, such as the "model" Bell Telephone benefits system. The Chamber viewed vocational training as necessary to competitiveness and sought a national vocational education system; thus, in a referendum, *Nation's Business* informed the membership that half of America's children left school after sixth grade "with only the rudiments of education … and with no preparation or guidance for life work. The statistics are startling, and in sad contrast to the better practice of most of the nations of Northern Europe." The Chamber stated that, "Federal aid and encouragement is essential" to the realization of this project.[64] *Nation's Business* noted:

many of our resources are in danger of exhaustion, therefore, the thought of today is strongly directed not merely towards efficiency in securing raw resources from the soil, but also efficiency in manufacturing and in marketing both at home and abroad … The maintenance of such efficiency is to be secured only by recruiting from the younger elements, those who are prepared for the life work. This gives the reason for the present widespread and persistent agitation in favor of vocational education.[65]

Finally, the Chamber's shared NAM's frustration in securing legislation of its policy ambitions; yet, the organization also enjoyed some greater successes with Congress, due to a climate of greater receptivity to the expansion of state activism. As with NAM, the Chamber sought a national charter as the legitimate representative of business. Again reminiscent of the past, the Chamber's bid for incorporation failed to pass: In this case, Democratic opposition prevented the legislation from being reported out of the Senate Judiciary Committee.[66] Chamber members were particularly aggrieved by their inability to obtain a national charter, because agricultural interests had secured a privileged status for their own association, and employers felt thwarted by sectional opponents who blocked their efforts to coordinate business political representation. Yet, the Chamber enjoyed some successes because government was increasingly forced to cope with modern industrialism. The Federal Trade Commission legislation was passed and a system of commercial attaches was put into place. The organization also

---

[62] "Road Legislation in Present Congress," 11/18/1912, 3; David 1962; "State Income Taxation As Applied in Wisconsin," 12–16–1912, 2.

[63] Wiebe 1962.

[64] Wheeler 1913, 1; "Model Benefits for Bell Employees," 12/16/1912, 11; "Vocational Education," 1/28/1913, 4.

[65] "Vocational Education," 4/15/1913, 4.

[66] "Charter Bill Did Not Pass," 3/19/1913, 1, 4.

saw the enactment of the legislative reference bureau proposal in a $25,000 appropriation to establish a Librarian of Congress to index and compile digests of laws.[67]

The Legacy of Dueling Employers' Associations

Eventually, the U.S. Chamber of Commerce also moved away from its early support for coordination and cooperation with government and labor, but in this case, the greatest threat was the existence of the NAM and the problem of having two so-called peak associations claiming to speak for American employers. NAM and the Chamber competed to represent the business community, making it difficult for the Chamber to take stands that would alienate members, free to move to NAM. When umbrella associations lack jurisdictional monopoly, they act like sales organizations rather than decision-making bodies, defer to vocal minorities and neglect majority sentiments. The art of offending no one left peak business groups in a kind of political limbo, making it difficult to endorse cooperative policies to further long-term, collective concerns.[68]

One can see something of this dynamic in the open shop movement, which reversed the high levels of labor-management coordination during World War I and reinforced America's turn toward liberalism. Shortly after the war, the Chamber issued a stand on industrial relations that suggested a perpetuation of the labor-capital harmony that had existed during the war. Yet against this tide of good feelings went open shop campaigns at the local level, especially in geographical areas away from the industrial and unionized strongholds of the northeast. In addition, some industries fought unions, with Elbert Gary of U.S. Steel leading the open shop campaign. The movement gained enormous momentum after NAM took it on as a cause celebre: Fighting labor continued to be a niche for NAM, especially after the formation of the more coordination-oriented U.S. Chamber, and NAM perceived the open shop movement as an opportunity to capitalize on the red scare and to augment its own standing in the business community. As Clarence Whitney, the chairman of NAM's Open Shop Committee, put it to the board of directors:

[A] great many of your members are dissatisfied for one reason or another. Many claim they do not see any benefits from the Association, and that they are never approached except for donations. I believe the right field manager for the Open Shop Department will change this whole situation ... this effort will be noticed by hundreds of your members and I believe it will be difficult to calculate the benefits the Association will derive.[69]

Conclusion

A paradox is at the heart of the NAM mystery: The National Association of Manufacturers was formed to overcome the limits of laissez-faire liberalism; yet it became best known for fighting organized labor and resisting cooperation. Students of American political development may be perplexed by this dramatic shift from an

[67] "Recently Appointed Commercial Attaches," 10/15/1914, 6; "Legislative Reference Bureau Organized," 12/15/14, 7.
[68] Martin 2000;Wilson 1990.
[69] Wakstein 1964, 474.

aspiring agent of coordination with labor and the state to an organization devoted to resisting unions and government intrusion. NAM's radical policy reversal challenges our conventional understanding that Americans in general and employers in particular are deeply wedded to a synthetic Hartzian ideology of neoliberal resistance to the interventionist state and the activist working class.

We suggest that the dynamics of two-party competition in a federalist governmental system (combined with weak labor organization and sectional economic conflicts) shaped both the rise and fall of the cooperative impulse among American employers at century's turn. The 1890s – that reputed age of innocence – was in reality an era of economic conquest; many businessmen sought developmental state policies to aid in their export adventures and desired an institutional vehicle for conveying their collective support for these national policy proposals. NAM's development was part of a movement to bring the American economy and polity into the twentieth century, as the association was to be a vehicle for organizing manufacturers across sectional divides and diverse communities. The need for a national business organization supporting policies for industrial development was especially great in the Southern one-party states, where Democratic dominance required another form of organization to affirm the commonality of interests among employers, to link southern managers to their compatriots elsewhere. The McKinley campaign fostered the organization of NAM to overcome the limitations of a dysfunctional party system, and to further its political ambitions.

Yet NAM's cooperative ambitions were ultimately dashed on the shoals of the two-party system. From its inception, NAM was intimately linked to the electoral fortunes of William McKinley and to Republican desire to penetrate the solid south and to elude local networks dominated by party bosses. Consequently, NAM appeared too intimately linked to McKinley to rise up to its loftier ambitions, and this connection compromised its legitimacy in aggregating the long-term collective interests of employers. Its organizational growth was greatly hampered by the failure of Congress to legislate its agenda of economic development and NAM's concerns were viewed as Republican rather than as business issues. NAM's growth was limited by the failure of Congress to legislate a commerce department that could have added legitimacy to the new organization and its repeated efforts to gain a national charter were rejected by Congressional leaders who viewed the organization as an agent of Republican interests. NAM ultimately pushed off in a radically different, antilabor direction, and this critical juncture signaled a setback for coordination in the political economy and strengthened neoliberal views among employers.

This story offers fresh insights into the course of American political development and the "exceptional" policy positions of business from a comparative perspective. Even though American employers are often viewed as largely rejecting state intervention, the NAM story suggests a more shallow commitment to rampant free market competition by nineteenth-century employers. American employers' rejection of coordinating policy arrangements reflected not so much a deficit of imagination as a flaw in the organizational realization of the ideal.

The NAM story also illustrates how the development of national business associations and other societal groups can influence future party development: NAM's creation had a powerful impact on future trends in party competition. McKinley and Hanna held somewhat contradictory goals of modernizing and nationalizing the Republican Party on the one hand, and working around the party on the other. Ultimately, of course, these dual ambitions became less easily reconciled and the business mobilization strategy (along with other presidential efforts to side-step parties and to develop new electioneering techniques) eroded partisan politics.[70] Party leaders' efforts to organize business are part of broader presidential efforts to develop alternative sources of political power, and comprehending the origins of NAM is relevant to understanding later changes in U.S. parties and electioneering.

Finally, the U.S. case illustrates the influence of parties on the historical evolution of business organization and social class, in showing how a representation gap can give rise to interest group formation. Yet our story also demonstrates a limit to interest groups' capacities to fill gaps, as societal groups tend to mirror state structures. Weak states and parties with a limited capacity for and focus on national public policy are unlikely to give much business to national employers' organizations. Peak employer associations in countries such as Denmark were nurtured by their business parties, and their capacities and legitimacy were strengthened by their role in policy development and implementation. The electoral function of these corporatist groups remained relatively limited, in part because employers had parties to represent them and in part because electoral activities comprised only a small part of their multiple goals. As in Britain, these functions were notable weaker in the United States and NAM's creators' hopes for nonmarket coordination were dramatically limited by political institutions. Thus, NAM's desire to occupy a central, coordinating position – influenced as it was by European experiments in cooperation among business, labor, and the state – was thwarted by the very structural deficits in national bureaucracy and party that initially prompted its creation.

---

[70] Klinghard 2005; McGerr 1986; Milkis 2009.

6

The Origins of Sector Coordination in Germany

Introduction

Despite the influential estate tradition in conceptions of German society, the organization of employers is significantly weaker in Germany than in Denmark. Multisectoral encompassing peak associations are limited in both collective bargaining and policymaking, and coordination transpires at the lower level of the industrial sector. The peak associations are functionally divided, with one set devoted to industrial relations and another to political negotiations and intraindustry collaboration. Moreover, the state plays a virtually nonexistent role in institutions for nonmarket coordination but delegates authority over collective bargaining, finance-producer relations, and the provision of collective business goods to the labor market partners. Of course, the German political economy and institutions for coordination have varied tremendously across profoundly different epochs. To grasp fully the ongoing revisions of the German model, one must explore the specific historical context at critical junctures, emergent political coalitions that capture and convert older forms for shifting purposes, and the evolution of German managerial control.[1] Yet postwar business institutions share significant features with those of the Weimar Republic, and we seek to understand how sector coordination was created and renegotiated across the changing political landscape.

We argue that the structure of political competition shaped the collective articulation of business interests before and after World War I: German sectoral coordination reflects the political dimensions of multiparty competition within a federal government. Both the predemocratic elite parties and Weimar parties specialized in regions and were weakly developed at the national level; thus, no national party held most employers. Federalism reinforced regional economic diversity, sustained high levels of regional (especially Prussian) legislative power vis-à-vis the national Reichstag

---

[1] Blackbourn 1998; Berghahn 1994; Berghoff and Möller 1994; Fear 2005; Thelen 2004; Herrigel 1996; Kocka 1981; Abelshauser 2005; Anderson 2000; Katzenstein 1987; Green and Paterson 2005. This chapter constitutes something of a shadow case, as we do not have access to the archival, primary source material relied upon in other chapters.

and made it easier for industry groups (often with pronounced regional identities) to retain power at the sectoral level. The first wave of multisector groups created by the authoritarian state to compensate for the deficiencies of ineffectual, decentralized parties and the later industrial relations associations had different purposes. Absence of a robust national business party combined with employers' disgruntlement with state interventions in industrial relations during Weimar (and the Third Reich) encouraged business to resist state interference in labor market negotiations.[2] All of these contributed to torpid peak multisector associations and stronger sector coordination.

The structure of party politics in a federal system explains significant episodes in association building during the prewar German Empire and the postwar Weimar period. First, the impact of party competition on association building is apparent in the development of dueling multisector employers' associations before World War I. In the authoritarian Empire, Bismarck was motivated to use coordination to reverse late industrialization with a massive industrial push in key manufacturing sectors. But the Reich had no power of taxation, being dependent on its federal states, and because national power largely lay with the chancellor and emperor, legislation went through the parliament and could not be simply ignored. Employers had extraelectoral power in this three-class voting system (linked to property rights), and association building was a vehicle for both coordinating industrial development and aggrandizing political power.[3] The first German national multisector employers' association, the Central Association for German Industrialists (Centralverbund Deutscher Industrieller or CVDI), was created in 1876 by Bismarck's friend, Wilhelm von Kardorff (founder of the Free Conservative Party), to mobilize industry for Bismarck's tariff legislation.[4] The CVDI's major competitor, the Bund der Industriellen (BdI), was expanded into a national organization by Gustav Stresemann (Liberal Party) to represent free-trade interests and to advance the fortunes of the Liberal Party. The associations competed to represent German business until World War I.

Second, the dynamics of multiparty competition in a federal system help to explain the merger of the CVDI and the BdI into the Reich Association of German Industry (Reichsverband der deutschen Industrie or RdI) and the emergence of postwar German sectoral coordination in business-labor relations. When faced with postwar revolution, political actors on the right remained deeply divided (in the wimpish, regionally diverse party system), were unlikely to win majorities in legislative contests, sought a unitary peak employer association, and nurtured labor market coordination in policy making as an alternative to socialism.[5] Crisis prompted coordinated industrial relations and party impotence heightened demands for self-regulation, yet employers remained wary of state power without a national party to represent them. The Weimar (and Prussian) state intervened in industrial conflict when labor negotiations broke down, but the legacies of Weimar failures meant that industrial relations remained fixed at the sectoral level, largely without state involvement.

---

[2] Maier 1975, 9; Rohe 1990. We discuss the renegotiation of sector coordination after World War II in Chapter 11, but it is beyond our scope to account for the perfect storm of factors that contributed to Hitler's rise.
[3] Fear 2005; Berghahn 1994; Gershenkron 1962, Gourevitch 1986.
[4] Kardorff and Bismarck were also large landowners.
[5] Bunn 1958, 284; Kocka 1981.

The Determinants of German Sectoral Coordination

High levels of coordination are consistent with the preindustrial estate tradition in theories of German exceptionalism (Sonderweg), according to which strong organic functional groups mediate individuals' interactions with the state and overcome class antagonisms.[6] Yet contemporary scholarship questions simple ideological claims about Sonderweg, reveals the influences of the British industrial and French political revolutions, and points to the importance of liberal nation building and constitutional reform.[7] Moreover, preindustrial estates suggest institutions more encompassing than are found in sector coordination. Thus, we look beyond ideology to reflect on three possible factors for German sector coordination: patterns of industrialization, character of labor, and dynamics of federal party competition.

Characteristics of Industrialism

Several aspects of German industrialization may have shaped the country's form of employer organization and labor market coordination. Employer organization was forged in the intense heat of international economic competition and Germany's status as laggard in the race for industrialization motivated firms to seek high levels of organization and coordination. In this catch-up game, heavy industry entered into protectionist alliance with large agricultural interests (in a marriage of iron and rye) to push parliament to enact protective tariffs in 1878 and to create social reforms that would expand labor productivity.[8] Yet American industrialists – as committed as German ones to protectionist policies – failed to secure high levels of coordination and the German track toward coordination was by no means determined.[9] After the cartel movement produced high levels of concentration in some parts of German industry, firms in the monopoly capital sector became less interested in a statist-welfare solution than employers in less-concentrated sectors and even than their British counterparts.[10] Indeed, looking at Germany before World War I, one would hardly have predicted that the country would emerge as a poster child for corporatist coordination.

Germany's failure to rise above sectoral coordination, rather than the fact of coordination itself, may well reflect the deep divisions in the economy: Heavy industry/ agriculture proponents for protection had difficulty reconciling with lighter, export industries that favored free trade. Regional variations reinforced political conflicts between Junkers on big agricultural estates east of the Elbe (using unskilled labor) and Western light industry manufacturers. Conflict among diverse interests played out in bureaucratic infighting between the Imperial Office of the Interior (closer to

---

[6] This theory has also been used to explain the rejection late economic liberalism and political totalitarianism. Puhle 1978; Pois 1976; Bowen 1947, 74, 132.

[7] The aristocracy and feudalism were not any greater in Germany than elsewhere in Europe. Blackbourn 1998; Blackbourn and Eley 1984, 2–15, 56; Fear 2005; Mayer 1981; Kocka 1999, 44. The North German Federation established suffrage for men over 25 the same year as Britain expanded the franchise and before most other countries. Anderson 2000, 4–6.

[8] Gershenkron 1962; Gourevitch 1986; Hilferding 2007; Lambi 1962, 60.

[9] Fear 2005. Regulatory structural differences between the United States and Germany were faint in the late nineteenth century. Dunlavy and Welskopp 2007; Abelshauser 2005, 25–30.

[10] Fear 2005; Eley 1978, 739–42.

heavy industry) and the Treasury and Foreign Office (closer to export sectors). Yet, by the 1880s, interests became more fluid, as sectors such as iron and steel ran big trade surpluses.[11]

Close relations between banks and industry may also provide a source of cooperation: Credit banks generate high levels of industrial cooperation by funding firms' investment and by sitting on boards with interlocking directorates. Industry and agriculture were thrown into crisis by the stock market crash and economic depression beginning in 1873, and companies funded by joint-stock banks were more likely to survive and this significant industrial restructuring marked the beginning of an era of close ties between bankers and entrepreneurs.[12] Yet the features of bank-industry relations that became an organizing principle of the German model emerged slowly, and banks' role of coordinating industries was found in a number of countries in the nineteenth century. Indeed, before 1914, German banks exerted less power over their associated firms than American banks; therefore, the models that we take as a given today were much less distinctive in the prewar period.[13] Thus, the impacts of industrial structure are complicated and we turn to other determinants of coordination.

German Labor and the Industrial Relations System
The strength of the labor movement clearly drove employer organization at the sector level and motivated the merger of the early encompassing associations into the RdI after World War I, yet the initial formation of the CVDI and BdI had little to do with labor issues but reflected trade policy ambitions. Labor mobilization (in the form of union density) lagged behind Denmark and Great Britain at the turn of the century; and before World War I, the workers' movement was split among three unions identifying with a different party. But unionization rates, centralization of authority in the principal peak association (Generalkommission, or GK), and activism notably expanded between 1900 and the early 1920s.[14] In the wake of the German revolution, the unification of employers with the formation of the RdI was, indeed, a desperate attempt to use employer coordination to prevent broader radical reforms; however, labor pressures cannot explain why coordination remained fixed at the industrial sector level.[15]

A desire to cultivate workers' skills also drove associational development at the sector level; following the guilds tradition, business and labor collaborated in some industries to create skills-training institutions.[16] Yet the organizers of the encompassing associations came from industrial sectors and depended on leadership by the state. The handicraft employers (descendants of the guilds) were among the most hostile to unions; moreover, German skills were not appreciably better than those of other countries during this period. One contemporary observer felt that industrial

[11] Herrigel 1996; Gourevitch 1988; Klug 2001, 232–3; Forbes 1979, 331–9; Schonhardt-Bailey 1998, 328.

[12] Böhme 1967, 219–22.

[13] Fear and Kobrak 2010; Neuberger 1977, 192.

[14] Geary 1976. Union density expanded from 3 to 12.5 percent of the labor force between 1900 and 1925. Crouch 1993.

[15] Maier 1975; Pollock 1929.

[16] The vesting of authority over vocational training in the handicraft sectors also happened only with state intervention. Thelen 2004.

tariffs simply defended against inferior workmanship and that, "The German no longer possesses the capacity of the English manufacturer … the German executes commissions of the same kind so faultily that he is seldom able to secure a second order."[17] Thus, whereas labor activism and skills offer insights into the development of employers' organization, we also look to the political context to explain the specific form of German coordination.

Deficits of the German Party System

Even though the structures of industrialization and labor-management relations provide insights into the evolution of business representation, the story is incomplete without attention to the role of the state in forming employers' organizations and of party competition in influencing their subsequent trajectories. The German case illustrates what happens when multiparty systems exist within a federal system of government: weak, regionally diverse parties largely organized at the federal state level mean that no national unitary business party emerges to represent employers. To fill this representation gap, politicians sympathetic to business may nurture and delegate policy-making authority to interest groups, but pronounced regional variation in employers' political identities discourages robust national associations.

Before 1918, the German government did not depend on the consent of the people and parties played a limited role in governance; in addition, the national parliament held less power than regional legislative bodies, which also diminished the importance of national parties. Pre-Imperial Prussia had limited political freedoms and unification in 1871 decentralized much to the twenty-five member states of Germany, although the national Reichstag remained responsible for most domestic policy making. Some suffrage existed; nevertheless, Prussian tax-paying property owners and industrialists held greater power in a complicated three-class system of voting. The Law of Association forbade centralized political parties in Prussia until 1899 (to resist social democracy), and even though this was somewhat circumvented, feeble links united the diverse local partisan forms. Bismarck restricted the development of political parties to prevent parliamentary opposition and legislators avoided mobilizing constituents at the local level for fear of losing control.[18] Even by 1902, two-thirds of party identification was independent of "key constituency characteristics," and members of the Reichstag came from twenty-six different parties from 1879 to 1902. Sectional and religious identities rather than class typically defined German parties, although the social democrats increasingly wrested working class voters away from other parties. The Reichstag included five core parties, but these varied enormously at the regional level until the Weimar Republic finally nationalized German party politics. Vigorous public bureaucracies had developed during the absolute monarchies of the constituent states and these also enervated parties: Success of reforms imposed from above contributed to the vulnerability of reforms from below. The state's forceful role in industrial development emasculated institutions in civil society and tasks fulfilled by parties elsewhere were done by German bureaucrats.[19]

[17] Dawson 1904, 13–14.
[18] Berdahl 1972, 1, 18; Ritter 1990, 27–30, 44; Wehler 1970, 141.
[19] Schonhardt-Bailey 1998, 319, 307; Rohe 1990, 1–16; Kocka 1981, 454–5; Ritter 1990.

By the 1890s, parties were cultivating closer linkages to interest groups; for example, the Conservative Party enjoyed close ties to the Agrarian League (but also included industrialists) and the Social Democratic Party of Germany (SPD) was closely connected to organized labor. (The National Liberal and Catholic Centre parties continued to have diverse constituencies, however, with both industrialists and agrarians in the former and a range of economic interests in the latter.) Organized interests made significant financial contributions to parties; for example, the Centralverband invested over a million Marks in the 1912 Reichstag election. Yet, the bureaucratic state remained more powerful than the party system, employers remained dispersed across the regionally varied parties, and the evolution of interest groups was symptomatic of German party fragility. The decrepitude of German parties may well explain why German businessmen were less politically active than British ones. Thus, one sample finds that nearly half of British businessmen belonged to a party in the period around 1900, but that only 4 percent of German employers belonged to a party; 30 percent of British MPs came from business, compared to 15 percent in Germany.[20]

Parties were more fully institutionalized after the 1918 revolution and had higher levels of organization and more clearly defined constituent bases; yet, parties continued to encompass diverse elements. The very pure form of proportional representation introduced in 1919 led to a proliferation of parties and contributed to the impotence of the Weimar party system and by 1929, twenty-nine parties existed, although only nine had legislative influence. Programmatic distinctions between parties blurred, making it hard for parties to take stands. Thus, when employers from the Free Conservative and National Liberal parties were finally united in the German National People's Party (DNVP), the party also contained agricultural elites from the old Conservative Party (discredited during the war), moderate Christian Socialists (i.e., nonsocialist labor), and right-wing racists. The DNVP became the second largest party by 1924; yet even though various factions were unified by a common hatred of the social democrats, they were divided on issues as fundamental as parliamentary democracy and social policies (with industrialists more willing to engage in pragmatic negotiations with labor but conservatives ideologically opposed). Party leaders found it difficult to reconcile the diverse factions; for example, the RdI, industrialists, and workers within the DNVP supported the Dawes reparation payments in 1924, but right-wing extremists opposed the plan.[21] Thus, the politically weak (albeit economically strong) bourgeoisie lacked a partisan home: Severe political divisions within business and the parties' inability to represent employers interest in liberalism contributed to the decline of the Weimar democratic experiment.[22] The German party system's inability to represent specific constituency groups – reflecting the legacy of regional diversity – prompted an observer to comment in 1929:

One would naturally suppose that under a multiple party system issues and party programs would be clear-cut and easily differentiated ... With the people of the country divided into nine groups instead of two, it should be much easier for each group to contain homogeneous

[20] Blackbourn 1998, 339–44; Schonhardt-Bailey 1998, 298; Berghoff and Möller 1994, 279–80.
[21] Pollock 1929, 860–78; Kreuzer 1998; Hertzman 1958. The deep divisions contributed to its losing badly in the 1928 election and its subsequent decline. Chanady 1967, 65–71.
[22] Blackbourn and Eley 1984, 18, 26–7, 48–9.

elements which can work together. That is to say, they should be able to agree on definite principles and proposals and not write platitudinous platforms. These expectations, however, have not been fulfilled in the German multiple party system.[23]

As in other countries, parties and interest groups often evolved together: Catholics in rural areas provided the backbone of the Center Party, although the party made much more limited inroads among industrial workers, and workers played a similar role for the social democrats. In some cases, interest groups were formed to fill gaps in party coverage and government bureaucrats were leaders in these efforts. The development of the Agrarians' League and the Handicraft chambers (Allgemeiner deutscher Handwerkerbund) around the turn of the century illustrated this process of "quasi-nationalization of entrepreneurial organizations."[24] The Navy League appealed to individuals across party lines and generated popular support for imperialism, especially among skeptical agrarian Conservatives. Supporters were distributed electorally among the two Conservative parties and the National Liberals, and League secretary, Victor Schweinburg, set as a goal "the emancipation of large sections of the population from the spell of the political parties."[25]

The demand for alternative modes for political coordination to compensate for gaps in party power was accelerated during World War I, when wartime needs for economic distributive decisions taxed the already fragile Reichstag. War production requirements inspired political actors both to cede greater control over wage negotiation to labor and to delegate policy making over industrial matters to the social partners. Actors across the political spectrum – from guild socialists to old corporatist proponents of the estates to professional technocrats – supported this widespread delegation of state authority to industrial self-government.[26] Thus, the ineffectual parliamentary institutions with their feeble parties created a vacuum, in which components of civil society filled the gap, and the creation of peak employers' associations fit into this larger pattern. The following section explores the creation of the encompassing multisector employers' associations.

The Formation of Encompassing Employers' Associations

Political Challenges for Bismarck and the German Industrialists
The development of the German multisector employers' associations can be viewed as a strategic weapon in struggles over public policy and political competition. The first central employers' association was developed shortly after Germany became a nation state. The founder of the Free Conservative Party, Wilhelm von Kardorff, evidently with Bismarck's support, created the CVDI to garner societal support for industrial development goals and to compensate for the limited political influence of employers. Bismarck sought to nurture a robust industry-banking coalition as a cornerstone of the state, to be comparable to the traditional spheres of agriculture and the landed gentry.[27]

---

[23] Pollock 1929, 878.
[24] Ritter 1990; Winkler 1976, 3.
[25] Eley 1978, 332; see also Kehr 1977.
[26] Maier 1975, 9–11; Puhle 1978.
[27] Böhme 1967, 228.

Bismarck lacked an obvious partisan ally for help with his state-building and industrial development ambitions – constrained as he was by deficits of the party system – and the employers' association offered him an avenue of political power.

The backdrop for the development of the national employers' association was Bismarck's effort to create the modern Germany and to endorse industrial develop-ment economic policies.[28] Bismarck initially joined forces with the National Liberals, who sought a national, ethnically unified Germany and reduced power of the Catholic Church but ultimately broke with the party over free trade, parliamentary autonomy, and government financing. Bismarck sought an independent revenue base to emanci-pate the executive from parliamentary control, but the National Liberals wanted to preserve their legislative power.[29] The Conservative Party might have been a natural ally for Bismarck (a Prussian landowner), as 90 percent of the Conservative members of the Prussian Reichstag were nobility in 1874; yet the party resisted German nation-alism and, initially, tariff reform (even after depression hit in 1873).[30] Bismarck's closest ally in the early days of the empire was the Free Conservative Party, that helped him to shift the terms of electoral discourse, by drawing attention to tariff reform. Once a free-trade advocate, the chancellor recognized that tariffs – in addition to protecting German goods against foreign competition – offered a mechanism for raising revenue that was independent of parliamentary control and that was more hidden than direct taxes.[31]

Employers had organized at the sectoral level to push for protective tariffs, as the Great Depression of 1873–95 halved growth rates, depressed prices by about 30 per-cent in the first five years, and brought about a large-scale failure of (especially small) firms. Steel producers and bankers in the Rhine-Westphalian formed the Association of German Steel Producers to seek tariffs for their own industry, strengthen their political clout and fight labor; however, they did not launch a broader protection campaign, which they considered threatening to their own narrow tariff demands.[32] Consequently, Bismarck sought the formation of a broader coalition, and encouraged his business supporters not to undertake protest initiatives but rather to wait for cues from the government to take action. To weave together the interests of the produc-ing classes, Bismarck offered tariffs to industrialists and large landowners (Junkers) in exchange for economic and tax reform. Although none of the German parties gave Bismarck precisely what he needed, the interest groups gratified his needs in a much

---

[28] The Austro-Prussian War of 1866 left German states in a political alliance called the North German Confederation. Between 1866 and 1871 Otto von Bismarck struggled to solidify the North German Confederation into the German Empire under Wilhelm I.

[29] Claggett et al. 1982; Flynn 1988, 321–3. National Liberals resisted Bismarck's proposals for new state offices, expanded sources of imperial income, and increased military; finally, Bismarck fired Rudolph von Delbrück.

[30] Nobility were committed to the old aristocratic order that bound dynasties throughout Europe. The Prussian Conservative party reorganized as the German Conservative Party in 1876 to shore up relations with the Chancellor and to adjust to the new economic age and class system. Berdahl 1972, 3; Bohme 1967, 225.

[31] Kitchen 2006, 145–6; Dawson 1904, 15–16. Bismarck contemplated various political theories during his life. Drawn as a young man to estates theory, he considered constitutional reform as a basis for building the modern German state and proposed "orthodox liberal-democratic models" for first ten years until he "began to tire of the experiment" (Bowen 1947, 64–5).

[32] Kitchen 1978, 156–62; 2006; Böhme 1967, 224–5; Lambi 1962, 61, 66–67.

more satisfactory fashion. To secure the support of industrialists, Bismarck engineered the dismissal of Rudolf Delbrück (a statesman perceived as unsympathetic); in return, he asked employers to reconcile with the agrarians and to "affiliate 'directly' to the Chancellor."[33]

The Formation of the Central Association of German Industrialists

The creation of the Central Association of German Industrialists in 1876 must be viewed against the backdrop of the fragmented party system and Bismarck's desire to nurture an "industrial-economic" class cleavage, by rallying industrial support for trade protection policy and antisocialist legislation in advance of the "Red scare" elections of 1877 and 1878.[34] A growing contingent of industrialists, with ardent participation by Wilhelm von Kardorff of the Free Conservative Party, believed that tariffs were necessary to modernize industrial Germany. Kardorff was the author of a widely publicized pamphlet entitled, "Against the Current," which formed the basis for the Central Association's support for comprehensive tariffs and stirred sentiment against free trade.[35] Kardorff and his comrades were deeply influenced by Henry Carey, an American economist who had inspired Abraham Lincoln's nationalist economic development agenda and who was a great supporter of trade protection. Kardorff and others wrote to Carey documenting the progress of the protectionist movement.[36] When Carey wrote an essay in the *London Times*, both Kardorff and another protectionist, Stopel, translated the essay into German. Kordorff wrote to Carey in May 1876, praising his attacks on the "war kings of the British free trade policy" and stating that time was of the utmost, as Germany was about to revise its commercial treaties with a number of European countries:

> I was rejoiced by the "letters to the London Times" and the portrait you were so kind to send me. Wishing to give the full knowledge and use of your brilliant little pamphlet to my own countrymen, I began on the spot the translation of the letters ... in response to the ideas about the necessity of self defense against the theories and the agitations of the radical Manchester free trade men.[37]

Kardorff, together with Henry Axel Büeck, formed a new employers' association to unify all industrial branches behind the protectionist cause celebre. The "Central Association of German Industrialists for the Promotion and Protection of National Labor" was established in February 1876 and included iron and steel industrialists as well as lighter industry such as textile, glass, leather, chemical and paper producers. By

---

[33] Böhme 1967, 229–6. Lambi 1962, 61. The organizers of the Association of German Steel Producers were different from those of the subsequent Centralverband, yet the steel producers also had a big impact on Bismarck's thinking. When the steel producers demanded tariffs, Rudolf Delbrück (President of the Imperial Chancellor's Office) and Ludolf Camphausen (the Prussian finance minister) responded that "the iron industry ... has earned too much during recent years." The steel producers were deeply aggrieved, blamed Delbrück, and eventually won William I and Bismarck to their position. As William wrote in the margins of a report on the conflict between the warring factions that "Delbrück looks backward – Oppenheim and the steel producers look forward." Böhme 1967, 225, 227.

[34] Claggett et al. 1982, 649.

[35] Lambi 1962, 67; Craig 1978, 87.

[36] Kardorff to Carey, Letter, May 15, 1876; Craig 1978.

[37] Kardorff to Carey. 5/15/1876.

the end of 1876, most German Chambers of Commerce also endorsed protectionism. The goals of the Centralverband included advantageous tariffs, removing "London as the clearing-place of the German foreign trade" and supporting "friends and promoters of German industry" in electoral contests for the Reichstag.[38]

Even though the Central Association is generally believed to have been organized by the Free Conservatives and employers, there is some evidence that Bismarck encouraged its formation. In addition, although Bismarck is usually considered to have come late to the recognition of the advantages of protectionism, he may well have been contemplating a political economic sea change before the 1878 election. As early as 1873, Bismarck was exposed to protectionist ideas, when George Bancroft (with the American legation to Berlin) gave the chancellor a volume by Henry Carey.[39] Kardorff describes a meeting with Bismarck in 1875 in a letter to Carey: The chancellor asked Kardorff to form an employers' association to support the chancellor's tariff reform behind the rallying cry of "Solidarity."[40]

The association was extremely useful to the chancellor in the 1878 election and campaign for tariff policy. Bismarck sought support from the conservative wing of the National Liberal Party in 1877, but made limited progress as he opposed parliamentary controls on executive power and the party rejected his economic program. After the tariff bill was defeated in 1878, the chancellor set out to wrest control of parliament away from the National Liberals. In March 1878, Bismarck outlined the areas in which he desired tariff reform and the Central Association endorsed this platform. Bismarck asked Kardorff to develop a "'precise' expose on tariffs," as a foundation for political action, and requested that Kardorff "vaguely" inform the Minister of Finance, Hobrect, of the agreement. Bismarck acknowledged that he had been a free-trade oriented landowner at one point, but stated, "Now I am thoroughly converted; and in order to make up for it, I need your help and that of your friends." Protectionist voters turned out in heavy numbers in the 1878 election and the coalition of industrialist and agrarian protectionists won a majority in the Reichstag.[41] The Free Conservative Party increased its share of parliamentary seats from 10 percent in 1877 to 14.4 percent in 1878, and the Conservative Party representing protection-oriented landowners had a similar increase (from 10 to 14.9 percent). In the same period, the National Liberals dropped from 32 to 25 percent. In December 1878, Bismarck again proposed a comprehensive protective tariff, which ultimately passed. The agrarians and iron and steel industrialists negotiated a deal: Agrarians got a rate of ten marks per ton on all grains, and iron producers got ten marks per ton on pig-iron and cast iron ware.[42] A member

[38] Böhme 1967, 230–1.
[39] Bancroft to Carey, 3/30/1873.
[40] Chaitkin 2006, 66.
[41] Flynn 1988, 327–3; Klug 2001, 225, 244; Bohme 1967, 231–4. German agrarians were also becoming stronger supporters of protection, and a group of east Elbian landowners founded the Association of Tax and Economic Reformers" shortly after the formation of and worked closely with the Central Union of Industrialists.
[42] Lehmann 2009, 4; Lambi 1962, 68–9. Bismarck proposed (but failed to obtain) a National Economic Council for coordination between the CVDI and other associations and wanted this corporative body to take over the functions of parliament (Bowen 1947, 152–3).

of the Centralverband named Groethe wrote to Henry Carey outlining the campaign of the association to reduce tariffs in 1878:

The *protective* movement in Germany has very enlarged. To my Central Verband affix now the *greatest majority* of industries in Germany and a part of agriculturists. We hope now in few times to construct a good system of Protection. I send you the newest Tariff, proposed by the Central Verband, edited by my and Mr. Beutner ... The Protectionists have about 140 friends of the Reichstag, the free traders about 80–100 Members; about 200 Members are neutral and opportunistic.[43]

The Formation of the Bund der Industriellen

The CVDI did not manage to garner the support of all employers, however, as industrialists continued to be dispersed across parties (with protectionists in the Conservative and free-traders in the National Liberal Parties), to be regionally segregated and to hold diverse positions on trade. The National Liberal Party was a catch-all organization; Liberal politician Gustav Stresemann felt that free-trade-oriented employers had insufficient corporate representation and used the Bund der Industriellen to build up membership among free-trade-oriented employers.[44] Whereas the CVDI was initially controlled by heavy industrialists who favored protection, the BdI was organized in 1895 by the finishing industry and represented firms seeking to reduce tariffs and to counteract the concentration and cartelization that enabled heavy industry to raise prices on intermediate products. The Bund was not particularly vibrant and failed to wield national influence until Stresemann organized a regional chapter (the Saxony Industrial Union) in 1902 and began to use the Bund as a platform for attacking the Centralverband and its heavy industry constituents. The Bund largely represented small to medium-sized firms in light industries in Saxony, and was most powerful in regions not well-represented within the CVDI (whose power was most concentrated in Prussia).[45]

The two organizations differed in political strategies, with BdI engaging in more aggressive activism: The CVDI – with its close ties to agricultural elites – enjoyed a position privileged by the German state; however, Stresemann approached politics as something of an outsider and used the association to mobilize public opinion. The CVDI had been much closer to Chancellor Bismarck, Kaiser Wilhelm and the bureaucratic apparatus of the state, and could act as a conduit and a gatekeeper to the central powers. The BdI tended toward more progressive policy positions than its competitor because some employers in the final goods industries relied on skilled workers and worried about strikes that could interrupt worker productivity. The constituents of the BdI were outsiders during Bismarck's era; however, their focus on parliament and political mobilization became increasingly successful as the parliament grew in importance in the early Twentieth Century. The Hansabund, a quasi-party, developed in 1909 to conjure greater employer coordination and to resist hegemonic control by agrarians.[46]

---

[43] Grothe to Henry Carey, 3/26/1878.
[44] Ritter 1990, 33–41.
[45] Fear 2005; Warren 1964, 39–48; Tipton 2003.
[46] Warren 1964, 39–48; Tipton 2003; Wolff-Rohe 2001, 28–30; Blackbourn and Eley 1984,116–19.

The turn of the century also spawned the development of industry associations for coping with labor market issues, and this led to a differentiation between the associations that dealt primarily with economic and trade issues and those whose function was to prevent industrial conflict between business and labor. CVDI and BdI each created national associations to fight strikes and to cooperate with labor unions in an effort to prevent the spread of socialism: The CVDI created the "Headquarters for German Employer Unions" in 1904 after an extensive textile strike, and the BdI created the "Society of German Employers' Unions." These federations merged into the Federation of German Employers' Associations (Vereiningung der deutschen Arbeitgeberverbände) in 1913. The new federation was to work closely with the Reich Association of German Industry after the latter was established in 1919, again maintaining the functional differentiation between industrial relations and public policy.[47]

Competition between CVDA and BdI, combined with inadequate party coverage, made employers lose faith in collective solutions to social issues and many firms began developing firm-based strategies for building an internal labor market in the early 1900s, similar to those of their American counterparts. German employers felt that the absence of a dedicated business party hampered their ambitions for broader cooperative action toward collective goals, constrained business representation in parliamentary affairs and made coordination difficult. Moreover, the end of the twenty-year depression and the less radical demands of the workers' party made it easier for firm-based strategies to flourish.

Even though the CVDI became somewhat less dominated by heavy industry over time and some hoped for collaboration between the two groups, association-building efforts never produced economy-wide coordination. Large German firms turned away from coordination and experimented with segmentalist firm-based strategies for enhancing worker productivity and stability. Vertical rather than horizontal integration characterized efforts for control; firms pursued coordination by forming cartels and – much like their American counterparts – developed firm-based scientific management approaches to labor relations. Led by Carl Ferdinand von Stumm-Halberg, firms created company unions and paternalistic strategies to control labor, became less interested in social policy to secure coordination with the working class, and sought to drive wedges within labor by distinguishing the needs of skilled workers from their unskilled brethren. For their aristocratic working class, firms developed social and health programs to enhance productivity and to build skills. Large firms appealed to small producers and peasants with radical-nationalist, antisocialist appeals.[48]

Incentives for Coordination during and after World War I

Given this competition among dueling employers' associations and decentralization within the polity and economy, how did Germany come to develop significant labor market coordination? Enduring regional diversity, segmentalist strategies of large firms and the contrasting interests of large and small manufacturers might have lead

[47] Brady 1942, 78; Wolff-Rohe 2001, 31.
[48] Spencer 1979, 62; Dunlavy and Welskopp 2007; Bowen 1947, 159; Brady 1942, 73–4; Fear 2005; Chandler 1990; Sweeney 2001, 712–18.

the country to resemble the United States and to develop a more pluralist structure for business representation. In the following pages, we suggest that German corporatism unfolded in stages. First, wartime military and economic imperatives motivated high levels of labor market coordination. Second, postwar labor militancy and the coming revolution, in a context of ineffectual political parties, produced the incentives for the delegation of policymaking authority to private arrangements among the social partners. Whereas the state initially held the right to interfere in wage agreements as a measure of last resort, if arbitration did not succeed; the state's successive and unpopular interventions left a legacy of resentment against government involvement after Weimar. Without a strong party to represent them, employers concluded that they could do better on their own.[49]

The peak national employers' association, the RdI, embodied these diverse aspects of German postwar experience: It was formed to unify employers through coordination, to build economic growth after the disastrous war and to resist a militant working class, but it ultimately failed to rise above the fragmenting forces within the German economy and polity, and coordination remained largely fixed at the industrial level. Weimar party failures reinforced employers' mistrust of party politics and worked against a large state role in corporatist relations.

First, the enormous appetite of the German war machine demanded high levels of economic coordination, and during the war, bureaucrats established quasi-public corporations (Kriegswirtschaftsgesellschaften) to organize production in each industrial sector. The architect of the German war economy, Walter Rathenau, had a vision for peacetime reconstruction that lay the groundwork for Weimar experiments. Each industry was to integrate firms into an association and all associations would belong to a national group that would (sometimes with labor) engage in self-government. Although Rathenau was forced out of power and later assassinated, his ideas inspired the creation of cooperative cartels for industries to attain full employment and to incorporate demobilized soldiers. Industrial relations between labor and business became more cooperative during the war, and efforts were also made to resolve differences between the CVDI and the BdI, with Stresemann playing a crucial role in this project. In 1914, the CVDI and the BdI were brought together by the War Committee of German Industry, which became the German Industrial Council in 1918. Forced by the war effort, the Hindenburg program of 1916 introduced collective bargaining and union representation in exchange for no caps on profits and paved the way for German corporatism.[50]

Second, just as war inspired coordination, political disorder at the end of the war created a dramatic imperative for both compromise between business and labor, and the delegation of policy-making authority; the institutions of sectoral coordination were forged in the postwar chaos. Even before the war, employers continued to be highly frustrated with the offerings of the German party system, felt underrepresented in Parliament, wanted an enhanced political identity, and, consequently, sought to move policymaking to private channels. J. A. Mench proposed the formation of both a dedicated employers' party and a "League of Productive Employers"; Tille sought a

---

[49] Ritter 1990.
[50] Redlich 1944, 321; Lauterbach 1944, 29–30; Wright, 2002; Brady 1942, 78; Fear 2005; Feldman 1975.

corporatist organization that would side-step the party system and deal directly with the state. In August 1913, Leipzig employers (led by the Saar Chamber of Commerce) formed a "Cartel of Productive Estates," as an "economic parliament" to bypass the political process, and employers proposed electoral rules to guarantee parliamentary seats to businessmen.[51]

As the war ended, the employers' sense of political futility escalated enormously: Coordination and cooperation with labor were a strategy for the industrialists to resurrect their prewar power, since an outright restoration of elite domination was not possible. Employers had mixed goals, in that they assayed to roll back the regulatory expansion associated with war mobilization even while they recognized a need for order amidst the postwar chaos. Industrialists and workers shared preferences for expansionist fiscal and monetary policies. In the face of growing disunity on the right and under the extreme pressures of wartime, German industrialists recognized that they had a better chance of throwing their lot with labor than with their old agricultural allies. Jakob Reichert (Union of German Iron and Steel Industrialists) in disdain for Junkers and the middle class: "Allies for industry could be found only among the workers."[52]

Ernst negotiations for peacetime coordination between business and labor began in October 1917 to discuss postwar demobilization, and heated up in October 1918, as the end of the war and revolution seemed imminent. Hugo Stinnes, representing employers, and Carl Legien, representing labor, led the negotiations: The product was the Stinnes-Legien pact, which established committees for negotiating industrial accords (Arbeitsgemeinschaft), a central organization (Zentralarbeitsgemeinschaft or ZAG), and an eight-hour workday. German large employers accepted the ZAG to solve political problems (and pronounced regional diversity) with economic management. Organized along industrial rather than regional lines, the branch associations (Fachverband) diluted the strength of the small and medium-sized firms that identified with region over industrial sector. As a formerly antagonistic Silesian coal producer, Ewald Hilger, put it: "Unless we negotiate with the unions we can go no further… only through agreement with the unions, can we avoid anarchy, bolshevism, Spartacist rule and chaos." Germany's "corporatist revolution" unified business and labor and together the social partners recognized the benefits of collaboration in achieving collective ends.[53]

The ZAG agreement embraced the principle of Tarifautonomie, which limited the state to managing the system of labor relations and arbitration, and delegated control to the social partners.[54] Both business and labor supported self-regulation and demobilization became a battleground for the struggle over state regulatory power. Walther Rathenau and Wichard von Moellendorf had proposed a state socialist approach in a central office for economic affairs, but employers emphatically resisted this investment

[51] Feldman 1997; Sweeney 2001, 719–23; Maier 1975, 15, 40.
[52] Wolff-Rohl 2001, 39–40; Maier 1975, 45–59, 59.
[53] Maier 1975, 59–60, 70; Feldman 1997.
[54] The principle was abolished by the Nazis, but reinstated after World War II in the Basic Law of 1949 (Art. 9 Para. 3). We thank Marius Busemeyer for discussing the nuances with us. Restrictions on labor imposed during the war were ended, labor courts (Arbeitsgerichte), and mediation boards (Schlichtungsausschusse) were set up. Lauterbach 1944, 36.

of top-down authority for economic management.[55] They were joined in their opposition by Colonel Joseph Koeth, head of the War Office's Raw Materials Section and a former aid to Walter Rathenau. Koeth argued that the War Office Boards did not understand the peacetime economy, felt that the social partners had greater expertise and wisdom in these matters, and proposed allowing the Arbeitsgemeinschaft to regulate themselves. Thus, although both sides agreed that planning was necessary for postwar reemployment and demobilization of the troops, government bureaucrats engaged in a bitter battle about who should do the planning, a conflict which entailed jurisdictional infighting between leading bureaucrats and their departmental homes.[56]

Industrialists and workers (led by Stinnes and Legien) supported an empowered Demobilization Office to manage conversion and lobbied for Koeth to be appointed the head. Union leaders supported the large industrialists, as the framework for industrial cooperation would curb radicalism on the shop floor by strengthening top-down control over revolutionary shop stewards. Confronted with the twin demands of the social partners, the government ultimately caved, Koeth became head of the demobilization effort, and the new administration set up a system of self-regulation. Even though Koeth weighed in with industrialists and their labor allies to delegate economic policy making to the social partners, he asked that the associations take responsibility for ensuring appropriate decisions. Confident in Koeth and business-labor cooperation, managers sensed the revolution to be largely under control. Bringing home the troops went more or less according to plan, but demobilization's second stage – return soldiers to employment – was a grand failure. Arbeitsgemeinschaft failed to set up requisite programs and the social partners resisted Koeth's attempts to redirect work into specific sectors. Koeth lost both his job and confidence in employers' capacities for self-regulation.[57]

The Formation of the Reich Association of German Industry

The formation and evolution of the Reich Association of German Industry must be viewed against the backdrop of the economic need for coordination and the frailty of party politics: Delegating authority to the social partners was viewed as compensation for political party impotence. The CVDI and the BdI merged into the RdI on April 12,

---

[55] A scaled-back Reich Economic Office (RWA) was established in 1917 to coordinated economic planning and demobilization. In October 1918, the RWA (led by Moellendorf) began formulating plans for a public works program to reintegrate rapidly soldiers into the labor market, and the RWA sought to retain control in the hands of bureaucrats. Another key issue was the lifting of price and export controls, and Moellendorf, joined by employers in the finishing industries, feared that lifting controls would lead to a collapse of industry and inflation. Under-Secretaries Heinrich Göppert and Hans Karl Freihher von Stein also sought to continue with wartime state controls and envisioned a collaborative demobilization effort between the War Economic Office and the War Office Boards (Bessel 1993, 51–66).

[56] Bessel 1993, 51–66; Feldman 1975, 1–15.

[57] Some textile opposed this plan, fearing that it would delegate excessive power to heavy industry. Maier 1975, 61–5; Feldman 1975,1–23. In 1919 the Industrial Congress of Nürnberg also proposed a framework for industrial relations (Betriebsräte-system), in which business and labor sat on a National Economic Council and lower level District Councils (Umbreit and Scholz 1920, 65). The National Economic Council had only advisory powers but was criticized as being too expensive, duplicating the work of the Reichstag and giving equal representation to employers in the thousands and employees in the millions. Frankel 1922, 472–82.

1919. Representatives of the CVDI and the BdI began meeting in late 1918 to discuss a merger, and employers were clearly motivated to unify by the threats of the German revolution. At a meeting in early April of 1919, the secretary of the CVDI, Ferdinand Schweighoffer, pointed out that Germany had just lost the war, the socialists were on the rise and this meant that industrialists had common enemies and fairly common goals. Germany could only survive as a capitalist nation if employers could overcome the fragmentation of industry and find a mechanism to wield collective political influence. This unity of political representation was viewed with some suspicion by the smaller BdI; for example, August Weber also supported a union of the associations and self-regulation, but warned that the voice of the light industry would not be dominated by the CVDI big-business constituents.[58]

Once again, state actors were involved in the formation of the new association. Gustav Stresemann, the National Liberal MP who built up the BdI, was a major actor in the initial efforts to combine the organizations and simultaneously struggled to unify employers into the umbrella German People's Party (Deutsche Volkspartei, DVP). After leaving the Demobilization Office, Joseph Koeth was a key participant and became one of the new managers of the association. Hermann Bücher, came directly from the German Foreign Office and Ludwig Kastl worked in the Reich Finance Ministry before taking charge at the RdI, prompting the observation that the "general managers of the RdI always came from the civil service."[59]

Yet, the RdI ultimately failed to live up to expectations, and coordination was limited both by conflict between CVDI and BdI elements and by the reluctance of the industrial sectors to cede any power. A diversity of interests between CVDI and BdI led to considerable infighting both over the initial leadership of the group and over its subsequent policy platforms. Even though Stresemann was critical in conceptualizing the merger and involving the BdI, he was vetoed from the directorate by CVDI leaders Hugenberg and Stinnes (who along with Siemens and Duisberg were the strong proponents of the new Reich Association from heavy industry). Krupp's director, Wiedfeldt, worried that the RdI would be too large to control and would have interests that were too varied to generate consensus positions. The textile industry, which paid very low wages, objected to the requirements for more information sharing among sectors. Conflict arose over the organization of diverse industries and the distribution of materials. Participants feuded over the appropriate roles for the Reich Association and the ZAG; for instance, August Müller wanted the RdI to preserve the decentralized structure that appeared in the ZAG apparatus.[60]

By 1920, 70 to 80 percent of German firms were connected to the RdI and branch groups addressed twenty-five different specialities, yet the RdI failed to meet initial expectations. Heavy industry, electrotechnical industry, machine-building sectors, and chemical firms ultimately dominated the group, while small and medium-sized light industrial firms became somewhat marginalized. Karl Fritzsche wrote to Stresemann complaining that the RdI was morphing into the CVDI: A more fitting

[58] Brady 1942, 72; Wolff-Rohe 2001, 47–50.
[59] Cassis 1999, 229; Mierzejewski 2002, 202.
[60] Gatzke 1954, 51; Wolff-Rohe 2001, 44–69; Mierzejewski 2002, 202–3.

nomenclature would be the "National Union of German Heavy Industry."[61] The organization remained a rather loosely knit peak association (and it was only during the Third Reich that employer organization was to be centralized at the national level). Thus, a leader in the organization, Paul Silverberg, was to state to the press in December 1922:

> The Reich Association of German Industry? That is nothing other than a really loose peak association, which can impose very few rules on its members, branch associations and individual firms, can commit them to nothing, and in which there is a lot of talking.[62]

Moreover, the principle of *Tarifautonomie* was repeatedly violated during Weimar, as the (especially Prussian) state frequently intervened in arbitration disputes, and this negative legacy contributed to the later constitutional provision after World War II that restricted government intervention in industrial relations. The revolution was less than a sea change in other ways as well, and Rathenau claimed that no revolution had, in fact, occurred. The revolution largely reinforced positive moves toward parliamentary democracy already in progress (as most political parties had agreed to a constitutional plan and the new format for industrial relations was already largely constructed). But the revolution stopped short of curing the abuses of the former system (the civil service was not yet democratized and militarism was not significantly removed from German political life) and the revolt largely reflected the failure of elites to communicate political changes to the masses.[63]

Party politics were deeply damaging to the movement for cooperation among diverse business interests: Even though political parties were reorganized, the party system was not significantly improved. A coalition of the Social Democratic Party, German Democratic Party and German People's Party (DVP) initially formed a moderate government that included some business support for a politics of coordination. Yet, employers continued to be divided among parties, and the Democratic Party, the Catholic Center Party, the German People's Party and the German National People's Party all included business constituents; therefore, employers in each party competed with other interests and a unified business voice failed to gain ground.[64] Frustrated large employers decided to form a party dedicated to nonsocialist bourgeois interests in 1930–2, but the existing parties managed to thwart these efforts. Weimar's failure of party politics, employers' incapacities to overcome sectoral divisions, and business distrust of state efficacy contributed to a reluctance by business to embrace full-scale coordinated industrial relations. The

[61] Wolff-Rohe 2001, pp. 75, 64.
[62] Mierzejewski 2002, 202.
[63] Fear 2005; Rurup 1968, 134, 115–34.
[64] Many employers joined the German National People's Party, which constituted a broad alliance of rightist forces, joining the old Conservative agrarians and manufacturers from heavy industry with racists and others on the far ideological right. After becoming alienated from the German Democratic Party, Stresemann founded the German People's Party (Deutsche Volkspartei), building from significant constituents of the old National Liberals. This party also included major industrialists (largely, former members of the National Liberal Party) such as Stinnes. While Stresemann wanted to form an alliance with the left, the industrialists within the party (who were behind a lot of the financing) preferred to work in alliance with the German National People's Party. Gatzke 1954, 53.

failures of Weimar created lessons for the later labor market accords made in the wake of World War II.[65]

Conclusion

The significant labor market coordination found in the German political economy – that ultimately contributed to an expansion of workers' rights – was born of an author-itarian alliance to restrain radical socialism; yet this coordination has remained fixed at the industrial sector level and the state plays a very minor role in industrial rela-tions. Given the importance of the estates tradition and the nineteenth-century state in leading industrial development, one wonders how this system of sectoral coordina-tion came characterize the German model.

We suggest that economic imperatives and labor mobilization contributed to the emergence of coordination: Needs attendant to late industrialization, pressures emanating from the twenty-year depression and Bismarck's revenue and political objectives prompted the formation and shaped the evolution of the CVDI. The demands of wartime planning and postwar demobilization produced new institu-tions for unprecedented levels of cooperation between employers and labor and the formation of a unified peak association for the whole of German employers, the Reich Association for German Industry. Moreover, these economic impera-tives were reinforced by labor mobilization. Although initial employer associational activity was only indirectly impelled by early socialist party and union activity, increasing union strength – combined with prospects of growing socialist elec-toral power, radical reforms, and even revolutionary change – bolstered the case among industrialists for building institutions for cooperation with labor in the early decades of the twentieth century.

Yet, these forces cannot fully explain patterns of employer organization and the construction of sectoral coordination in turn-of-the-century Germany. First, a central motivation behind the creation of the Centralverband (and the BdI) was to solve the representational gap created by the party system. German employers were dispersed across several regionally oriented parties, and legal and historical-structural factors kept these parties organizationally weak. Bismarck's relationship with the major politi-cal parties had been uneasy: The National Liberals were ardent free-traders and the Prussian Conservatives were ambivalent about German state building. Thus, Bismarck turned to employers to overcome this shortfall in political representation, especially in the context of the push for new tariff protection, economic modernization, and nation building.

Second, the incentives for delegation of authority to private channels was great in Germany's multiparty system; with the advent of greater democracy, it was clear no business-oriented party could win outright control of the state. This political incentive, in conjunction with economic imperatives, wartime needs, and rising labor power and militancy, produced new institutions and significant levels of nonmarket

---

[65] Turner 1969, 58. The onset of the Great Depression and political frailty that enabled the successful assault by antidemocratic forces in 1929–30, were precipitating events prompting Weimar's decline and the rise of national socialism. Fear 2005; Peukert 1992; Kolb 2005.

coordination. At the same time, no dedicated business party emerged at the national level in postwar Weimar Germany; employers remained dispersed across several parties in the still fragmented, regionally grounded party system; as a result, no unified business voice existed in national government. This, in turn, reinforced the substantial distrust by employers of a robust national role in the institutions of coordination; it also reinforced the constrained capacity of the national government to assert and maintain a significant role in directing the cooperative institutions. These institutions remained in the hands of the social partners and exhibited a substantial sector-level structure.

7

Twenty-First Century Breakdown?
Challenges to Coordination in the Postindustrial Age

What we want to suggest, however, is that this era of "organized capitalism" ... has, in certain societies, come to an end, and there is a set of tremendously significant transformations which have recently been literally "disorganizing" contemporary capitalist societies (Lash and Urry 1987, 2)

Introduction

In the late twentieth century, globalization, deindustrialization, slower economic growth and the rise of neoliberal ideologies challenged countries' capacities for collective political engagement. Nations with robust collective social identities and substantial labor market coordination were considered particularly vulnerable to the assaults of a changing economy. Cooperation is always easier when resources are plentiful, and deindustrialization and depressed growth rates reduced the fiscal slack available for easing social tensions. Thus, coordinated market economies were expected to decentralize collective bargaining, and to converge on a neoliberal model of limited state intervention in the market.[1]

Naysayers rejected this convergence thesis, pointing out that economic restructuring (combined with demographic shifts) also mandates *higher* levels of social compensation and coordination to meet the human capital needs of the new economy. Moreover, countries – even within the coordinated model – diverged in response to postindustrial challenges. Continental countries with sectoral coordination, indeed, suffered notable disintegration of their coordinating capacities and adopted duelist policies that benefitted core sector employers and workers, but harmed marginal workers. Yet, macrocorporatist countries – presumably *most* vulnerable to neoliberal reforms with bloated public sectors and significant departure from the efficiencies of market competition – sustained high levels of coordination, social spending, and equality. These countries adopted neoliberal reforms, especially active labor market policies to cut passive welfare supports, yet maintained a social democratic commitment to skills.

---

[1] For critical assessments of the convergence thesis, see Berger and Dore 1996; Kitschelt et al. 1999; Hall and Sosokice 2001; Streeck 2009.

Policy makers viewed high levels of labor market coordination as key to the success of these reforms, and asked employers to provide centrist political support, to help implement the plans and to create real skills among the workforce.[2]

This chapter investigates why countries continue to diverge in their types of employers' associations and how some countries have bolstered coordination against postindustrial challenges at this new critical juncture in capitalist development. We argue that the political rules of the game – set by party system characteristics and relative centralization of government – directly influence contemporary trajectories of coordination, just as they shaped the historical emergence of peak employers' associations.[3] The structure of party competition affects the incentives of state actors today as it did a hundred years past, although politicians' concrete ambitions have changed overtime. In the nineteenth century, fears of democratization and efforts to build support for industrial policies drove state actors to nurture private associational channels of policy making. In the twentieth century, political leaders seek social partners' aide to manage the transition to postindustrial production and to cope with the negative public outcry about greater austerity. Just as politicians sometimes circle the wagons to share blame, they essay to shift the burden to social partners.[4]

Proportionality and the unity-federal divide also have long-term, indirect effects on coordination in the modern period because they promote the development of a large, capacious public sector. Higher levels of employment associated with a large public sector stimulate the economy, lower unemployment and minimize the distance between insiders and outsiders. Bureaucrats in a robust public sector are purchasers of goods, collective bargaining partners, and potential employees of low-skilled workers; therefore, they have both incentives and leverage to promote private sector coordination and attention on the human capital needs of even low-skilled workers. Private labor and business are motivated to remain coordinated to resist the jurisdictional encroachment of a growing state.[5] Thus, the very same features of the polity that enabled states to create coordinated responses to the advance of industrialized capitalism have an impact on countries' abilities to respond in a coordinated fashion to postindustrialization.

In the following pages, we assess empirically the effects of state centralization, proportionality/multipartism, and state capacity on the strength of employers' organization and the institutions of macrocorporatism in eighteen rich postindustrial democracies between the early 1970s and 2000s. We focus on employers and macrocorporatism – and not sector coordination – because our findings in Chapters 8 and 12 indicate that it is these institutions (and not sector coordination) that shape egalitarian welfare state adaptation to postindustrial pressures. Our models also account for the impacts of globalization, deindustrialization, and other explanations of the trajectories of coordination

---

[2] Martin and Thelen 2007; Thelen and Palier 2008; Busemeyer 2009; Iversen 1999.
[3] Of course, policy legacies also matter in that the structure of business representation, established during the advent of advanced industrialization also affected bureaucrats' capacities to shore up coordination and to bring employers into political coalitions for addressing the skills needs of low-skilled workers. But we believe that coordination needs to be reinvented and renewed, and the political rules of the game provide the context.
[4] Pierson 1994.
[5] Martin 2004; Martin and Thelen 2007.

in the contemporary era. After discussing the implications of coordination for employers' views of social policies in Chapter 8, we present country case studies for Denmark,
Britain, and Germany in Chapters 9–11. These illustrate how features of government
shape efforts to sustain coordination and how levels of coordination, in turn, mold governments' capacities to attend to the skills needs of marginal workers.

The Paradox of Postindustrial Capitalism

At the end of the twentieth century, globalization, deindustrialization, slower economic growth, the decline of Keynesian economics, and the rise of neoliberal ideology
all seem to threaten the institutions of social life, such as coordination, welfare state
protections, and relative equality. Deindustrialization reduces jobs for workers with
medium skills, intensifies the diversity of business interests, and scales back members'
incentives for solidaristic collective action. Technologically displaced manufacturing
workers cannot easily cross the "skills barrier" required for higher paying jobs in services, and this contributes to labor market and income inequalities. Moreover, as the
postindustrial economy produces less full-time, regular employment, interventions
targeted on the long-term unemployed and socially excluded may have fewer links to
economic production. The rise in labor market dualism threatens severely the state's
ability to respond to new welfare demands, and the institutions of coordinated markets might succumb to neoliberal reforms in the new era of "disorganized capitalism."[6]
Interests of firms have also become potentially more diverse with significant increases
in internationalization because employers and workers in sheltered and exposed sectors of the economy have different concerns. This diversification makes it difficult to
maintain solidaristic relations between segments of labor, union density, and powerful
centralized peak associations.

At the same time, the postindustrial economy creates an essential paradox because
states must also respond to "new social risks." At least during the industrial era, governments created large welfare states, in part, to compensate for the insecurities and risks
attendant to internationalization and to pursue flexible adjustment to international
openness.[7] Thus, on the one hand, the displacement of semi- and unskilled workers
generates substantial needs for short-term social assistance, sustained training, and
education; these increased welfare demands are multiplied by demographic increases
in populations of elderly, single-parent families, and immigrants. On the other hand,
slow productivity growth, episodic economic shocks, and rising fiscal stress produce
substantial pressures for welfare state retrenchment and restructuring.

The political response to these challenges has been, consequently, mixed. In the
1980s, threats associated with globalization and deindustrialization prompted policy makers across industrial countries to implement, to varying degrees, neoliberal
policy reforms that challenged welfare state generosity, relative equality, and nonmarket coordination. Inspired by new public management ideas, these reforms sought

---

[6] Lash and Urry 1987; Schmitter and Streeck 1997; Pierson 2001; Iversen and Wren 1998; Swank 2001; Scharpf
and Schmidt 2000; Armingeon and Bonoli 2006.
[7] This "compensation thesis" was initially developed by Polanyi 1944; see also Cameron 1978; Katzenstein
1985; Garrett 1998; Rodrik 1997.

to introduce market-oriented and private solutions to the welfare state, to reduce state involvement in the economy, to unleash private enterprise, and to cut taxes, regulations, and public spending. The reforms integrated user fees, accountability measures, and performance indicators into public services; and, whenever possible, they sought to turn over social provision to private sector agencies, to decentralize service delivery, and to create quasi-markets for public goods. Whereas the neoliberal governments of Margaret Thatcher and Ronald Reagan led in these reforms, similar policies were inspired by the New Public Management philosophy in Denmark and Germany.[8]

Yet a second reform wave, often advanced by center-left governments, ascended in the 1990s and this emphasized social democratic concerns (e.g., for training), even while retaining the neoliberal goal of reducing social expenditures. These reforms sought to remove the long-term unemployed from the welfare rolls with active labor market policies and Tony Blair in Britain, Bill Clinton in the United States, Poul Rasmussen in Denmark, and Gerhard Schröder in Germany converged on quite similar policy prescriptions. This second wave retained a potent dose of neoliberal thinking and relied on a curious blend of right and left ideation. The active strategy was linked to more traditionally neoliberal strategies of reducing social insurance and assistance benefits, yet it deviated greatly from the liberal belief in letting markets manage employment.[9] Active labor market policy (ALMP) had been developed in the 1960s by two Swedish economists, Gosta Rehn and Rudolf Meidner, and the 1990s variant placed even more emphasis on private sector training and jobs (and less on relocating labor).[10] The approach – heavily pushed by the European Union after the November 1997 Employment Summit in Luxembourg – aimed to be market conforming, to emphasize supply over demand, and to encourage long-term investment in worker skills. Thus, a wave of scholarship in the 1990s questioned the demise of welfare state spending and macrocorporatism, argued that postindustrialization affected CMEs and LMEs differently, and suggested more limited convergence on the liberal model.[11]

Moreover, the rise of neoliberal reforms – or defense against these changes – fails to capture the entire story because liberalization does not always merely alter formal institutions but sometimes occurs less visibly in informal institutions and in the functional performance of institutions. Changes in nonmarket coordination may occur through "drift" or "erosion" of institutions, in which small incremental changes in formal structure and practice accumulate over time.[12] Thus, politicians may respond to economic crisis in various ways: by adopting significant reforms that weaken coordination, by sustaining coordination to meet the requisites of the new economy, or by

---

[8] Huber and Stephens 2001b; Swank 2002; Scharpf and Schmidt 2000.

[9] Cox 1998.

[10] Stephens 1980. Its creators recognized that ALMP could ameliorate not only unemployment, its explicit goal, but also reduce inflation by training workers to fill jobs in tight labor markets or more particularly to ease bottlenecks. Thus, the beauty of the ALMP was its utility for macroeconomic stabilization policy (King and Rothstein 1993). See Chapters 8 to 11 on determinants and operation of ALMP.

[11] A. Martin 1979; Stephens 1980, Berger and Dore 1996, Kitschelt et al. 1999, and Hall and Soskice 2001.

[12] Baccaro and Howell 2010; Streeck 2009; Howell 2003; Glyn 2006; Hacker 2002; Martin and Thelen 2007; Streeck and Thelen 2005; Thelen 2010; Hall and Thelen 2009.

allowing more subtle changes in institutional structures that none the less threaten the foundations of coordinated market economies.

Continued Divergence of Modes of Market Coordination?

Our first order of business is to discuss the cross-national trajectories of institutions for nonmarket coordination. Large-N quantitative studies find little evidence of the convergence of institutions for nonmarket coordination (e.g., industrial relations systems) toward liberal market arrangements; and qualitative studies show surprising resiliency of tripartite concertation.[13] Moreover, where centralized wage bargaining was decentralized, scholars found strong evidence of "organized decentralization," in which high levels of cross-sectoral and economy-wide coordination were maintained.[14] Finally, there has been a resurgence of tri- and bipartite social pacts in macrocorporatist political economies and even in nations such as Ireland where coordination had been traditionally weak.[15]

Our findings concur with these portraitures and we display trends in macrocorporatism for all capitalist democracies, CMEs and LMEs in Figure 7.1.[16] We find continued divergence among CMEs and LMEs; however, the trend in nonmarket coordination in both CMEs and LMEs suggests movement toward less coordination. Yet, postindustrial capitalist democracies have had diverse experiences. Figure 7.2 captures 1974 to 2002 trajectories of macrocorporatism for eight political economies and includes our four focal cases (Denmark, Germany, the United Kingdom, and the United States) and four additional, widely discussed country cases: Australia, Italy, the Netherlands, and Sweden.

Anchoring the CME and LME groups, Denmark and the United States display surprising continuity in levels of nonmarket coordination (Figure 7.2). Denmark, along with 1970s Sweden, scores highest in macrocorporatism and sustains this level through the early 2000s. The United States scores consistently lowest among the capitalist democracies on nonmarket coordination throughout the contemporary era. Germany is moderately coordinated on the dimension of macrocorporatism and modestly less

---

[13] Wallertstein et al. 1997; Golden et al. 1999; Siaroff 1998; Berger and Compston 2002.

[14] Traxler 2003; 2004; OECD 2004. Howell and Baccaro show a near universal movement toward liberal market institutions, but with modest effects on convergence. Baccaro and Howell 2010.

[15] Rhodes 2001; Molina and Rhodes 2002; Baccaro and Simoni 2008; Hamann and Kelley 2007; Rhodes 2001; Traxler 2004; Hassel 2003. Under the pressures of continued fiscal stress and of the necessity of significant policy reforms to meet standards for EMU membership, in particular, governments and the social partners enacted numerous "social pacts." In this newer form of political exchange, relations between state, labor, and employers are more asymmetrical (in favor of the state and employers); labor is pressed for wage restraint as well as adaptation to requisites of efficiency and competitiveness in return for the right to participate in social and labor market policy making.

[16] For our overview of trends in nonmarket coordination, we simplify matters and present data on macrocorporatism alone; for the most part, trends in employers' associations parallel variations in macrocorporatism (and we discuss key national experiences in the text). For the purposes of Figures 7.1 and 7.2, we rescale our standard-score index (see measurement section below) so the lowest score in our sample of nation-years is 0.00; the new scale ranges from 0.00 to roughly 3.00. CMEs include Austria, Belgium, Denmark, Finland, France, Germany, Italy, Japan, Netherlands, Norway, and Sweden; LMEs are Australia, Canada, New Zealand, Switzerland, United Kingdom, and the United States.

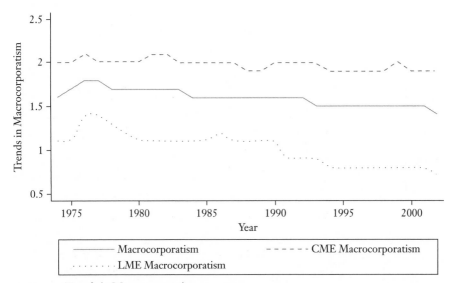

FIGURE 7.1. Trends in Macrocorporatism 1974–2002.
Note: Measurement of macrocorporatism and country composition of CME and LME categories are discussed in text.

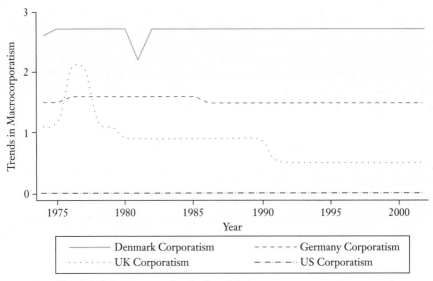

FIGURE 7.2. Trends in Macrocorporatism in Core Nations, 1974–2002.

so from the late 1980s onward. The United Kingdom exhibits periods of coordination; for example, Britain's experiment with the "social contract" in the late 1970s is a notable exception to an overall relatively low and declining level of macrocorporatism in the contemporary period.

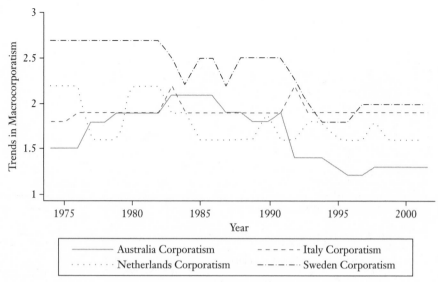

FIGURE 7.3. Trends in Macrocorporatism in Notable Nations, 1974–2002.

The picture becomes more complex with attention to some countries that evolve toward different models of coordination (Figure 7.3). Thus, Australia displays an increase in macrocorporatism in the late 1970s and 1980s with a merger of multiple employers' associations into a single national peak association and a period of greater bargaining centralization and national policy concertation. The Netherlands and Italy have also enjoyed something of a corporatist resurgence, whereas Swedish macrocorporatist institutions were initially weakened but have rebounded somewhat again.[17] As we discuss later, our political explanation contributes to an understanding of why countries that begin in one category may show movement to another.

Postindustrial Determinants of Nonmarket Coordination

Our core question is why some states have sustained high levels of nonmarket coordination in the face of postindustrial pressures; others countries have seen a decline in their capacities for collective political engagement. We investigate the explanations that underlay the rise of coordination a century before. Our first set of explanatory variables explores the exogenous threats to nonmarket coordination associated with the secular changes in the economy, and we follow with our core political hypotheses.

Postindustrial Challenges
Deindustrialization. Just as the rise of industrialization motivated nonmarket coordination, processes of deindustrialization might prompt a parallel decline in nonmarket

---

[17] The Swedish Employers Federation initially disbanded its bargaining and statistics unit, pulled representatives from tripartite forums, and discontinued its Contingency Fund in 1994, which collected money for industrial conflicts. Swenson and Pontusson 2000; Berg and Traxler 2007. On Australia, see Matthews 1991; Castles et al. 1996.

TABLE 7.1. *Relative Employment Shares, Productivity Growth, and Wage Inequalities in the
Postindustrial Economy*

	1980[a]	2005[a]	1980–2005 Change[a]	Productivity Growth[b]	Relative Wages[b]
Manufacturing jobs	28.2	16.9	−11.3	3.1	100.0
Business services jobs	6.8	13.8	7.0	0.0	106.0
Wholesale and retail trade jobs	16.5	19.1	2.6	1.2	82.0
Social and personal services jobs	28.9	33.4	4.5	−.3	70.0

[a] Sector employment shares measure a sector's wage and salary jobs as a percent of total wage and salary jobs; source OECD, *Labor Force Statistics* (various years). Data are expressed as cross-national averages for a given year for eighteen postindustrial democracies: Australia, Austria, Belgium, Canada, Denmark, Finland, France, Germany, Ireland, Italy, Japan, Netherlands, New Zealand, Norway, Sweden, Switzerland, the United Kingdom, and the United States.
[b] Productivity growth and relative wages are 1970 to 1995 means and are from Iversen (2005, ch. 6, Table 6.2).

coordination. Increases in manufacturing productivity – combined with a saturated demand for manufactures and rising private spending on services – have triggered declining manufacturing employment (especially of unskilled workers) and rising service sector employment. Table 7.1 documents these changes with data on 1980 to 2005 employment shares, productivity growth, and relative wages in high-skilled manufacturing and business services jobs and in low-skilled service sectors. The manufacturing share of total wage and salary employment has dropped from 28 to 17 percent of total employment. Even though relatively well paid jobs in business services have increased, jobs in relatively low-paid parts of the service sector have increased in comparable numbers; and even though manufacturing productivity continues to expand, service sector productivity has remained stagnant. The rich democracies have also experienced a near-universal rise in wage and total income inequality; thus, the wage ratio for full-time workers at the 90th versus 10th percentile has increased from roughly 2.7 to 3.3 between 1985 and 2005. This accompanies the growth in irregular employment such as involuntary part-time and temporary employment.[18]

Deindustrialization thwarts coordination because labor market dualism threatens business and labor cohesion. Fewer medium-skill manufacturing jobs – combined with growing nonwage costs of low-skilled employment and slow service-sector productivity growth – limit the availability of full-time, stable jobs for postindustrial workers. Even though high-skilled and low-skilled workers were securely interconnected in manufacturing production, these groups have less contact under deindustrialization, because they are increasingly located in different industries in the service economy. Expanding labor market dualism in workers' pay and job security pressure solidaristic agreements, whereas service sector employment undercuts union recruitment and

[18] As to irregular employment, involuntary part-time jobs have grown from roughly 1.7 to over 3 percent of all jobs between the mid-1980s and 2005; temporary jobs grew from roughly 7 to more than 11 percent of all employment. These changes in irregular employment are significantly larger in CMEs than in LMEs; the growth in low-wage workers in regular employment in LMEs is much greater than in CMEs (King and Rueda 2008). See ancillary materials for more data details and sources.

exacerbates divisions between white collar service sector and core manufacturing unions.[19]

Economic Performance. Slower economic growth with attendant state budgetary crises also depresses nonmarket coordination; for instance, the deterioration in economic performance diminishes the fiscal surplus required for side payments to actors to obtain compromise on tripartite bargains. Thus, economic stagnation after the oil crises brought labor and capital to question the basic principles of class compromise.[20] At the same time, some countries have used corporatist reconstruction – traditional tripartite concertation over incomes policy and new social pacts – to manage the politics of economic decline.[21] But we posit that stagnating real per capita income and higher unemployment rates will be related to declines in nonmarket coordination.

Globalization. Globalization – the increase in international integration of markets for goods, services, capital, and labor – also has potential (and complex) impacts on employers' organization and macrocorporatism within rich capitalist democracies. Trade openness was initially thought to foster nonmarket coordination because international integration, by promoting concentrated industrial sectors, encouraged robust employer and trade union organizations, centralized wage bargaining, and tripartite concertation.[22]

Yet, trade openness also makes employers' coordination more difficult to sustain due to the greater diversity of employers' and workers' interests. For unions, globalization intensifies the diversity of workers' interests across exposed and protected sectors and across skills levels; in addition, employers may use the threat of outsourcing to extract concessions from unions, and to set wage rates and employment regulations that exceed the latitude accorded by traditional collective bargains.[23] Stolper-Samuelson models of factor price convergence suggest that advanced nations have difficulty sustaining jobs for semi- and unskilled workers (a scarce factor), due to trade with developing country markets where semi- and unskilled workers are abundant.[24]

Moreover, capital mobility may foster a "race to the bottom" in social protection, because the liberalization of national financial controls enables mobile asset holders (especially firms) to pursue globally the highest rate of return on investment. Companies with an expanded exit option may opt out of cooperation with labor and the state, if they perceive the costs of compliance with negotiated bargains as too high.[25] This pressures governments to rollback social services in order to reduce labor costs, public debt, interest rates, and general disincentives to work and invest; consequently, economic globalization may force governments of all ideological stripes to pursue market-oriented welfare state reforms.[26] Thus, we anticipate that both trade openness

[19] Iversen 2001; 2005; Scharpf 2000; Pontusson 2005; Kenworthy 2008; Western 1997; Garrett and Way 1999; Iversen 2005; Burtless et al. 1998.
[20] Grote and Schmitter 2003; Anthonsen and Lindvall 2009.
[21] Visser and Hemerijck 1997; Baccaro and Simoni 2008; Hamann and Kelly 2007.
[22] Cameron 1978; Katzenstein 1985; Stephens 1980; Garrett 2000; Frieden 2006; Weiss 2003.
[23] Swank 2002, Alderson 2004; Brady and Wallace 2000; Western 1997.
[24] For reviews, see Frieden and Rogowski 1996; Burtless et al. 1998; Feenstra 2000; Ethier 2005.
[25] Traxler et al 2001; Traxler and Huemer 2007.
[26] Smith 1976[1776]; Mckenzie and Lee 1991; Strange 1996; Scharpf 2000; Hicks 1999; Huber and Stephens 1998; 2001b; Swank 2002; Hay and Rosamond 2008.

and rises in capital mobility will be negatively associated with employers' organization and macrocorporatism.

Labor: Union Density. Postindustrial declines in union density have ramifications for employers' organizations as well: Declines in unionization rates (and collective bargaining centralization) may diminish the benefits that encompassing and centralized peak associations of employers offer members, which may result in a defection of enterprises and a decline in firms' incentives to initially join employers' organizations. These encompassing associations lose leverage in relations with members, labor, and the state.[27]

Political Institutions and Agency in the Postindustrial Era

We also investigate whether the same political factors that enabled employers to develop institutions for coordination during the rise of industrial capitalism also sustain coordination today. We expect that proportionality/multipartism and the unitary-federal divide strongly shape contemporary trajectories of macrocorporatism under the challenges of postindustrialization.

Proportional Representation and Multipartism. Proportionality and multipartism sustain macrocorporatism because contemporary party elites in polities characterized by proportional representation, multiparty legislatures, and coalition governments face the same incentive structure they did in early decades of democratic competition. Representatives of business parties in this institutional context commonly have little chance of winning office outright and of realizing their distributive aims through government control. Rather, they have intensified incentives to pursue accommodative and consensus-oriented policy making, to maintain delegation of authority to tripartite or bipartite (capital-labor) private decision-making institutions, and to foster the durability and effectiveness of these cooperative institutions. Thus, a consensus-oriented, corporatist policy-making process is structurally complementary to highly proportional electoral rules and multiparty systems, whereas a competitive, pluralist policy-making style is complementary to majoritarian, winner-take-all, two-party systems. Moreover, where the electoral-party system has metamorphosed into two-party style competition between cohesive electoral blocs (such as in Sweden), party leaders have an incentive to bypass corporatist institutions.[28] We expect proportionality to be positively associated with employers' organization and macrocorporatism, and variations in the number of effective parties should be positively related to the strength of employers' organization and macrocorporatism.[29]

Federalism. Federalism should exert a disaggregating effect on cooperative institutions in the contemporary period as in the early decades of industrialized capitalism. The dispersion of policy-making authority attendant federalism should generate decentralized, geographically focused associations of capital and labor; all things equal,

---

[27] Traxler et al. 2007.

[28] See also Crepaz and Lijphart 1995, 287; Anthonsen and Lindvall 2009.

[29] We do not attempt to measure the emergence of electoral blocs, themselves; where party consolidations have not occurred, this would entail highly complex judgements about cooperation across distinct parties for many countries and elections. Instead, we simply generalize the logic of our argument (as augmented by Anthonsen and Lindvall) and assess the impact on coordination of variations in the effective number of parties.

peak associations should be weaker, sector associations should be stronger, and national cooperative institutions should be underdeveloped with federalism. Continuation of robust federalism, state decentralization, or formal transformations from unitary to federal systems (e.g., Belgium) should be negatively associated with employers' organization and macrocorporatism.[30]

Indirect Effects on Public Sector Growth. Proportionality/multipartism and centralization of government also have substantial *indirect* effects on the maintenance of cooperative institutions through their promotion of public sector growth in the twentieth century. Proportional representation (PR) is strongly associated with the predominance of center-left governance in democratic capitalism, as these systems facilitate the legislative strength and government participation of social democratic and Christian democratic parties. Whereas median parties (and voters) have an incentive to form alliances with the left to soak the rich, middle-class voters only act on this interest in multiparty systems, when they trust that their party will guarantee their interests post election. Thus, PR produces progressive party governance, which leads to higher levels of public spending. In addition, proportionality and multipartism significantly increase social spending in response to deindustrialization by amplifying the political representation of the losers in the new economy.[31]

Centralization of government is also associated with larger welfare states and public sectors because federalism fragments prowelfare coalitions and dampens national spending. Federalism has somewhat complex effects: Although it makes possible competitive, market-oriented responses to the problem of attracting mobile capital in an era of fiscal stress, it may accord opponents the opportunity to obstruct such market-oriented policy reforms. Yet on balance, federal systems experience more erosion of state capacity in the postindustrial era.[32]

A Capacious Public Sector. Large and capacious states also help to sustain high levels of social coordination against postindustrial pressures. Bureaucrats in large welfare states wear two hats: Officials in all countries serve as public guardians, who must provide some minimal level of security to marginal economic actors. In addition, in countries with large public sectors, bureaucrats also become producers of goods and services and worry about the productivity of their public enterprises. Economic stagnation in the 1980s brought into *bas relief* the contradictions inherent in these tasks, and bureaucrats searched for a non-zero-sum solution to social provision in hard times.[33] Cutting the social benefits of low-skilled workers is one solution, but improving these workers' skills is another possible response that is particularly attractive when these marginal workers might, themselves, become state employees and a potential drag on

---

[30] Related to the level of concentration of political authority, postindustrial developments such as significant transfer of authority to the supranational EU, on the other hand, should not influence national coordination dramatically: consensus-style policy making between EU-wide employers and labor association has been, to an extent, institutionalized at the EU level (Falkner 1998; Keller and Platzner 2003); transfers of monetary policy authority to the ECB has had complex – and not necessarily negative – effects on domestic corporatism (Hall and Franzese 1998).

[31] Swank 2002; Iversen and Soskice 2006; Crepaz and Birchfield 2000. One must also recognize the historical coevolution of partisan government and state size.

[32] Swank 2002; Huber and Stephens 2001b; Castles 1998.

[33] Spicker 1997.

public sector productivity. Thus, bureaucrats in large public sectors have incentives to maintain cooperative institutions among the social partners that enhance the opportunity of negotiating postindustrial transformation with efficiency and solidarism.

Large public sectors also strengthen coordination and influence the ways that claims are constructed and pressed by the social partners for a somewhat ironic reason: It gives bureaucrats greater political power in collective bargaining forums and, consequently, prompts private sector business and labor to band together to prevent intrusion by the state. A big public sector is also a much larger purchaser of goods and services than in countries with a smaller state, and the need of private sector employers – to keep their public sector consumers happy – offers the state greater leverage in its policy initiatives.

On the labor side, a high level of state employment narrows the political gap between labor market insiders and outsiders, by reducing the zero-sum distributional game between employed labor market insiders (who pay for the welfare state) and labor market outsiders (who are supported by it). Public sector employment is also often associated with higher unionization rates, and this, in turn, may offset declines in union density in the private sector, moderate insider–outsider conflicts, and otherwise bolster cooperative institutions. On the other hand, public sector unions have interests rather distinct from core private sector unions, and this undercuts the cohesiveness of encompassing labor organizations' bargaining and political strategies.[14] Yet, overall, we expect that state capacity will be positively associated with the strength of peak associations and cooperative institutions.

Partisan Government and Ideology. A final explanation of nonmarket coordination in the contemporary era stresses that left and Christian democratic governments significantly contribute to the maintenance of cooperative institutions. Christian democratic parties, with ideological roots in organic-hierarchical theories of social organization and communitarian responses to capitalism, pursue cross-class electoral strategies and promote political economic inclusion of workers. Left parties even more directly seek to promote the inclusion of workers and cooperative modes of political economic exchange (e.g., tripartite concertation and wage bargaining). Thus, we expect that left and Christian democratic governments will essay to maintain encompassing, centralized, and policy-process integrated employers' organization because employers' organization is central to the postindustrial policy strategies of progressive party governments.[15]

Empirical Analysis: Measurement and Estimation

In subsequent pages, we test our central arguments about variation in employers' organization and macrocorporatism for the developed postindustrial democracies from the 1970s to 2000s. In our case studies of postindustrial adaptation in Britain, Denmark, and Germany, we further explore the impacts of political institutions and

[14] Martin 2004; Rueda 2005; 2007; Garrett and Way 1999.
[15] Wilensky 2002; Hicks 2008; Korpi 2006; Hernandez and Rueda 2007. We also account for the impact on coordination of the ideological position of the median voter; shifts from statist to market-oriented policy preferences may be relevant to reforms of institutions for coordination.

agency on variation in coordination. Proceeding from our central theoretical claims and alternative explanations of trends in nonmarket coordination, we offer the following basic empirical models of employers' organization and macrocorporatism (where the equation for macrocorporatism is identical to Eq. 1 except for the deletion of union density).

[Eq. 1]   Employers' Organization$_{i,t}$ = α + β_1(Electoral Proportionality)$_{i,t-1}$ + β_2(Number of Effective Parties)$_{i,t-1}$ + β_3(Federalism)$_{i,t-1}$ + β_4(State Capacity)$_{i,t-1}$ + β_5(Social Democratic Government)$_{i,(t-1 \text{ to } t-3)}$ + β_6(Christian Democratic Government)$_{i,(t-1 \text{ to } t-3)}$ + β_7(Position of the Median Voter)$_{i,t-1}$ + β_8(Union Density)$_{i,t-1}$ + β_9(Deindustrialization)$_{i,t-1}$ − β_{10}(Trade Openness)$_{i,t-1}$ − β_{11}(Capital Mobility)$_{i,t-1}$ + β_{12}(Unemployment)$_{i,t-1}$ + β_{13}(Per Capita GDP)$_{i,t-1}$ + $\varepsilon_{i,t}$

[Eq. 2]   Macrocorporatism$_{i,t}$ = α + β_1(Electoral Proportionality)$_{i,t-1}$ ... + β_{12}(Per Capita GDP)$_{i,t-1}$ + $\varepsilon_{i,t}$

In these equations, α is an equation intercept, i designates nation, t designates year, and $\varepsilon_{i,t}$ is the error term.

As to our specific operationalizations of nonmarket coordination and its determinants, we use, for the most part, the same measurement procedures we did for the historical quantitative analyses of origins of employers' organization and macrocorporatism in Chapter 2. (See contemporary ancillary materials for a complete and detailed description of operationalizations and data sources for all variables used in analyses of the contemporary period.) We measure *employers' organization* as a standard score index of presence of national employers' federation, the peak federation's powers over members (i.e., appointment power, veto power over collective bargains and lockouts, own conflict funds), and policy-process integration of employers (e.g., in boards, commissions). *Macrocorporatism* is operationalized as a standard-score index of employer organization, union organization (index of union density, union peak association power, as for employers, and policy-process integration of labor), and the level of collective bargaining.[36]

For hypothesized causal factors, *proportionality* is measured as an ordinal scale of the degree of proportionality of the electoral system (0.0 = disproportional, 1.0 = semiproportional, and 2.0 = proportional). We also use a measure of the *number of effective legislative parties*, or $1/\Sigma p_i^2$, where p is the proportion of seats for the ith party. *Federalism* is measured as an 1.0 to 5.0 ordinal scale (1.0 = unity and centralized, 2.0 = unity and decentralized, 3.0 = semifederal, 4.0 federal and centralized, 5.0 = federal and decentralized). *State capacity* is operationalized as a standard-score index of government employment as a percent of total employment and government revenues as a

---

[36] Formal institutional structures (e.g., centralization of peak associations) may have declined less than informal cooperative practices and functional outcomes of coordination such as the scope of collective bargaining, association membership cohesiveness, and so forth (Thelen 2010; Baccaro and Howell 2010). Unfortunately, many of these informal practices and performances are beyond the scope of our quantitative analysis as temporal and cross-sectional data is limited or nonexistent. We do, however, expand our analysis with limited data on a few dimensions. For instance, we add a measure of collective bargaining coverage (with the loss of 1970s cases) to our core measure of macrocorporatism: Results reported below are near identical to those we obtain from this and other supplemental analysis.

percentage share of GDP.[37] State capacity, itself, becomes the focus of a succinct analysis as we assess our arguments that proportionality and federalism not only directly influence nonmarket coordination, but indirectly shape coordination through their positive impacts on the development of state capacity.

In addition, we account for prominent alternative theoretical explanations of nonmarket coordination. For partisan governance, we measure *left and Christian democratic government* as average shares of cabinet portfolios held by these party groups in the three preceding years.[38] We also control for the ideological position of the median voter (operationalized as the Kim-Fording estimate of the left-right position of the median voter based on party manifesto data and electoral choice). An accounting of the effects of the median voter is important in that median voter ideology may be significantly related to both institutional change and to variations in state capacity; that is, the absence of a control for mass ideological shifts may lead to spurious findings for the impact of state capacity on maintenance of nonmarket coordination.

In addition to electoral politics, we account for core features of postindustrial change: *deindustrialization, trade openness,* and *capital mobility* in both sets of analyses (for employers' organization and macrocorporatism) as well as *union density* in the analysis of employers' organization. We follow Iversen and Cusack and measure deindustrialization as 100 minus industrial and agricultural employment as a percentage of the working-age population.[39] Trade openness is measured as total exports and imports as a percentage of GDP, whereas capital mobility is indexed by Quinn's widely used indicator of national controls on international capital movements.[40] Union density is measured as the percentage of employed wage and salary workers that are members of unions. Finally, we control for business cycle fluctuations and fiscal capacity through inclusion of measures of unemployment and per capita real GDP. We operationalize these factors, respectively, as the percent of civilian labor force unemployed and per capita GDP in international prices (Penn World Table definitions). All variables – unless noted – are lagged one year.

For a succinct, supplemental analysis of the effects of political institutions on state capacity, we specify the following model:

[Eq. 3] $\text{State Capacity}_{i,t} = \alpha + \beta_1(\text{Electoral Proportionality})_{i,t-1} + \beta_2(\text{Federalism})_{i,t-1} + \beta_3(\text{Social Democratic Government})_{i,(mean\ t-1\ to\ t-3)} + \beta_4(\text{Christian Democratic Government})_{i,(mean\ t-1\ to\ t-3)} + \beta_5(\text{Position of the Median Voter})_{i,t-1} + \beta_6(\text{Dependent Populations})_{i,t-1} + \beta_7(\text{Unemployment})_{i,t-1} - \beta_8(\text{Trade Openness})_{i,t-1} - \beta_9(\text{Capital Mobility})_{i,t-1} + \beta_{10}(\text{Per Capita GDP})_{i,t-1} + \beta_{11}(\text{Growth})_{i,t-1} + \varepsilon_{i,t}$

[37] Recall that we seek to tap the extent to which the state can shape economic outcomes and, in turn, influence the behavior in collective bargaining, government contracting and other arenas of peak and sectoral associations of employers and labor. Alternative measures of state capacity such as an index of government consumption spending and tax revenues (both as shares of GDP) produce virtually identical results to our selected measure.

[38] In supplemental analysis, we examine the impact of long-term party legacies (i.e., years in office of Left and Christian Democratic Parties since 1950) on employers' organization and macrocorporatism. See Contemporary Ancillary Materials.

[39] Iversen and Cusack 2000.

[40] Quinn 1997.

We test for the core hypotheses that electoral proportionality and federalism have significant effects (positive and negative, respectively) on the development of state capacity. We also draw on the large literature on the twentieth-century expansion of the public economy and add several theoretically important variables to our models.[41] These determinants of size of the public sector include party government, the preferences of the median voter, the magnitude of the dependent population, unemployment rates, international openness, levels of economic development, and annual economic growth. All of the variables included in our models of state capacity and in models of nonmarket coordination are measured as described earlier for coordination models. Dependent population is measured as the total population minus population 15 to 64 years of age expressed as a percentage of the total population, and annual economic growth is measured as the percentage change in per capita GDP in international prices.

Estimation

For estimation of our models of employer organization and macrocorporatism, we initially use least squares regression with corrections for first-order autoregressive errors and panel correct standard errors.[42] Given that most of the variance in proportionality and federalism is cross-national, we do not include country fixed effects in these models. We also seek to assess a dynamic model of changes in coordination over time. To do so, we estimate Eq. 2 with inclusion of a lagged dependent variable.[43] That is, as we discussed in Chapter 2, an equation of the following form, $\text{Macrocorporatism}_{i,t} = \alpha + (1 + \varphi)(\text{Macrocorporatism})_{i,t-1} + \beta_j (X)_{i,t-1} + \varepsilon_{i,t}$, is equal to $\text{Macrocorporatism}_{i,} - \text{Macrocorporatism}_{i,t-1} = \alpha + \varphi(\text{Macrocorporatism})_{i,t-1} + \beta_j (X)_{i,t-1} + \varepsilon_{i,t}$. Thus, the β_j for independent variables are identical across equations and report the impact of variations in causal variables on changes in the dependent variable; only the coefficients for the lagged dependent variables are different.[44]

After completing analysis for a sample of 1974 to 2002 country years in all postindustrial democracies, we estimate the same sequence of models for the CMEs; based on the country classifications in the large varieties-of-capitalism literature and on previous analysis in this book, we categorize eleven nations as CMEs for this analysis: Austria, Belgium, Denmark, Finland, France, Germany, Italy, Japan, Netherlands, Norway, and Sweden. This analysis provides confidence in our overall findings on the coordination effects of political institutions and agency, and it addresses the central question of what explains variable trajectories of coordination within the CMEs.

---

[41] Cameron 1978; Swank 1988; Castles 1998; 2007. As in our models of coordination, we assess the long-term impact of party government on state capacity. See Contemporary Ancillary Materials.

[42] Beck and Katz 1995.

[43] We only use the dynamic specification for macrocorporatism, which has substantially greater temporal variation than employers' organization alone. For employers' organization, the lagged dependent variable explains current values near perfectly ($\beta = .99$) and otherwise significant variables (in Table 7.2) typically fall short of conventional levels of significance.

[44] We also wish to assess the robustness of our results to other estimators, additional model specifications, and alternative measures. For instance, we assess the sensitivity of our results to alternative measures of party government and to deletions of individual countries. See Contemporary Ancillary Materials.

Findings

Determinants of Nonmarket Coordination in the Postindustrial Era

We report the results of our analysis of the impact on coordination of political institutions and agency, partisanship and ideology, postindustrialization pressures, and economic conditions in Table 7.2. We present results for the full sample of eighteen capitalist democracies in the first column and findings for the CME-only sample of nation years in the second column of each of three sets of results. Recall that for employers' organization and the first set of results for macrocorporatism, we explain temporal and cross-national variance in levels of nonmarket coordination; for the last set of results, we focus explicitly on causes of changes in macrocorporatism. Turning first to the importance of political institutions and dynamics, we find clear support for our argument that electoral proportionality continues to bolster coordination in the postindustrial era: Proportionality has significant and substantively moderately large effects across nearly all estimators and samples.[45] Using the estimate from the first column for macrocorporatism (all capitalist democracies), one can see that a change from disproportional to proportional electoral rules (i.e., a shift in the proportionality score from 0.0 to 2.0), net of other effects, increases macrocorporatism .5 (.25 × 2). Recall that the level of macrocorporatism is measured as a standard score index and varies from roughly −1.75 to 1.75 across the sample. Thus, an impact of .5 standard deviation unit from the shift of electoral rules is arguably modestly large. In other models, impacts of a shift in electoral rules on nonmarket coordination vary in the more modest range of .1 to .2 standard deviation units.

In addition, we find that the impact on coordination of the number of effective parties – an additional test of the argument that electoral-party system change will alter incentives for maintaining coordination – is significant in each of the models of Table 7.2. Taking the model of variations in levels of macrocorporatism for all democracies, we can see that net of proportionality and other factors, a movement from a two-party to six-party system, for instance, would increase macrocorporatism by roughly .2 standard deviation units.

With respect to our hypotheses about the roles of federalism and state capacity, findings reported in Table 7.2 appear to strongly support our initial expectations. Federalism has (in all but one model) a consistently negative, substantively moderate, and significant impact on the maintenance of nonmarket coordination in the postindustrial era. With respect to the sample for macrocorporatism in all capitalist democracies, the consequence of moving from a unitary and centralized polity to a federal and decentralized one (i.e., 1.0 to 5.0 on our measure of federalism) is roughly −.2 (−.05 × 4). In addition, the impact of state capacity on coordination is positive and significant. Keeping in mind that state capacity is, itself, a standard score scale, a shift from relatively low capacity (e.g., −1.5 as in 1990 Switzerland) to a relatively high capacity (1.5 as in 2000 Sweden) would shift employers' organization by roughly .3 standard deviation units in the all-democracies sample (i.e., .0961 × 3) and

---

[45] It falls short of significance in the employers' organization equation for CMEs; but, the fact that the number of effective parties is significant in this model suggests our argument about the impacts of electoral-party systems still holds for employers in CMEs.

TABLE 7.2. *The Underpinnings of Nonmarket Coordination in Postindustrial Capitalism, 1974–2002*

Variables	Employers' Organizations		Macrocorporatism			
			Levels		Dynamic	
	All	CMEs	All	CMEs	All	CMEs
Politics & Institutions						
Proportionality $_{t-1}$	.0703***	.0144	.2515***	.2243***	.0653***	.0833***
	(.0234)	(.0154)	(.0458)	(.0452)	(.0186)	(.0209)
Number of Effective Parties $_{t-1}$	.0259***	.0212***	.0504***	.0447***	.0126**	.0201**
	(.0078)	(.0077)	(.0171)	(.0191)	(.0063)	(.0097)
Federalism $_{t-1}$	−.1323***	−.0478***	−.0523***	−.0752***	−.0069	−.0375***
	(.0199)	(.0111)	(.0211)	(.0380)	(.0057)	(.0129)
State Capacity $_{t-1}$	.0961***	.1373***	.3133***	.2775***	.0388***	.0529***
	(.0374)	(.0280)	(.0362)	(.0295)	(.0132)	(.0161)
Left Government mean, $t-1$ to $t-3$	.0009***	.0003	.0022***	.0002	.0005*	.0003
	(.0003)	(.0004)	(.0007)	(.0008)	(.0003)	(.0003)
Christian Democratic Government mean, $t-1$ to $t-3$	.0017***	−.0006	.0039***	.0011	.0003	.0004
	(.0005)	(.0004)	(.0011)	(.0099)	(.0003)	(.0004)
Median Voter $_{t-1}$	.0007	.0021**	−.0001	.0039**	.0001	.0015***
	(.0008)	(.0010)	(.0018)	(.0017)	(.0008)	(.0008)
Macrocorporatism $_{t-1}$	—	—	—	—	.8440***	.7473***
					(.0292)	(.0491)
Postindustrialization						
Union Density $_{t-1}$	.0104***	.0065***	—	—	—	—
	(.0018)	(.0014)				
Deindustrialization $_{t-1}$	−.0046	−.0121**	−.0177***	−.0421***	−.0040*	−.0154***
	(.0041)	(.0058)	(.0057)	(.0105)	(.0031)	(.0054)
Trade Openness $_{t-1}$	.0007	.0001	.0022**	.0042***	.0002	.0014**
	(.0006)	(.0006)	(.0011)	(.0013)	(.0003)	(.0007)
Capital Market Liberalization $_{t-1}$	−.0015***	−.0018***	−.0086***	−.0016	−.0030***	−.0001
	(.0007)	(.0007)	(.0022)	(.0024)	(.0009)	(.0012)
Business Cycle						
Unemployment $_{t-1}$	−.0085**	−.0047	−.0069	.0036	.0023	.0020
	(.0041)	(.0057)	(.0085)	(.0099)	(.0037)	(.0044)
Per Capita Real GDP $_{t-1}$	.0037	.0116***	.0048	.0208**	.0051**	.0094***
	(.0036)	(.0037)	(.0079)	(.0091)	(.0030)	(.0038)
Constant	.0278	.6975	1.4527	2.2427	.2771	.6930
R^2	.3292	.4659	.4261	.4611	.9490	.9144
N	494	310	493	310	493	310

Models of columns I and VI are estimated with ordinary least squares with panel correct standard errors.
* probability < .10; ** probability < .05; *** probability < .01.

by roughly .4 standard deviation unit (i.e., .1373 × 3) in the CME-only sample. We see even larger impacts of state capacity in the macrocorporatism model.[46] Generally, these results for federalism and state capacity as well as those reported earlier for electoral proportionality and the number of effective parties underscore the foundational role of political institutions and agency on the maintenance of coordination in the postindustrial era.

With regards to other political forces, recent patterns in governance by left and Christian democratic parties as well as variations in the ideological position of the median voter have selective but clear impacts on nonmarket coordination. Left party governments and, with less consistency, Christian democratic party governments are associated with maintenance of noncoordination across all capitalist democracies. In CMEs, variation in left (and Christian democratic) government does not seem to explain variation in contemporary nonmarket coordination. On the other hand, the ideological position of the median voter does: In CMEs, a shift to the right by the median voter (where 0.0 denotes strong market liberalism and 100 designates strong democratic socialism) is associated with a decline in employers' organization and macrocorporatism. Overall these findings suggest that frequent left and Christian democratic party government in CMEs help to buoy coordination above levels found in LMEs. At the same time, notable shifts toward market-conforming policy preferences by the median voter may well prompt all governments in CMEs to pursue liberalization (including policy changes such as deregulated labor markets that undermine coordination).

With respect to forces associated with postindustrialization, we find some evidence that deindustrialization, trade openness, and capital mobility directly influences the degree of nonmarket coordination. This is particularly true for deindustrialization which is consistently negative and significant in five of our six models. International variables have contradictory (but interpretable) effects. There is some evidence that trade openness bolsters macrocorporatism, especially in the CMEs. At the same time, capital mobility has negative effects on coordination; this especially true for employers' organization. These opposing findings in many ways reflect our theoretical expectations on the paradox of globalization: Internationalization fragments employers and workers and militates against coordination and simultaneously generates incentives for cooperation over incomes, labor market, and other policies.

The hypothesis that recent trends in union density will significantly shape employer's organization is also confirmed: Union density is positive and highly significant in each model of Table 7.2.[47] A fall from 60 to 40 percent in union density, for instance, would typically decrease employer organization across all the capitalist democracies by roughly .2 standard deviation units. To the extent that forces associated with postindustrialization negatively affect union density, deindustrialization and

---

[46] We recognize that state capacity and macrocorporatism co-evolve through time with increases in one causing increases in the other. (We thank Torben Iversen for pointing this out.) It is, however, particularly instructive to see that past variations in state capacity in the dynamic models of macrocorporatism are positively and significantly associated with short-term changes in national coordination.

[47] Traxler and Huemer's 2007.

globalization may indirectly further diminish the strength of employers' organization in the contemporary era.[48]

Finally, we report the effects of business cycle and fiscal capacity variables in the last set of rows of Table 7.2. As the tables indicates, per capita income, in particular, has a consistently positive and significant effect on nonmarket coordination. Overall, this result supports the view, discussed above, that economic downturn undercuts preconditions and incentives for cooperation. Generally, the importance of the effects of fiscal conditions, union density in the case of employer coordination, deindustrialization, and (selectively) internationalization are clear. Yet, the overall thrust of our findings suggests that politics and political institutions are as centrally important today in maintaining coordinated employers as they were in the formative decades of industrial capitalism.

A Note on Country Experiences in Macrocorporatism. Our model provides further insights into the widely discussed movement of key countries to less or more coordination (and from one mode to another). Macrocorporatism in Australia increased in the 1980s as a result of a (previous) merger of multiple associations into a single peak employers' organization and higher levels of bargaining centralization initiated by the Labor government. Nonetheless, Australian employers have remained less unified than Scandinavian ones and the social pact relied largely on bipartite (state and labor) negotiations on wage restraint and policy reforms.[49] Indeed, our model suggests that a combination of increased international competitive pressures and left government (as characteristic of 1980s Australia) stimulates efforts at greater cooperation; yet, Australian majoritarian institutions, federalism, and relatively low state capacity predict significant limits to these experiments with corporatism. This is, in fact, what we find for coordination in Australia.[50]

With respect to the well-known case of Sweden, the Swedish Employers Federation, as noted previously, initially disbanded its bargaining and statistics unit, pulled representatives from tripartite forums, and discontinued its Contingency Fund (for national labor conflicts) in 1994.[51] Our model suggests that the Swedish story of a relative decline in macrocorporatism reflects the importance of multipolar electoral competition. Here the electoral-party system has metamorphosed into something resembling two-party style competition between cohesive electoral blocs; consequently, party

[48] Recent surveys of the large volume of empirical research on the impact of postindustrial forces on unionization indicate that the literature is largely inconclusive (e.g., Brady et al. 2007). In our own estimates of the effects of postindustrial forces on union density (i.e., from substituting unionization rates for employer organization in the general Table 7.2 model), we find the impacts of deindustrialization, trade openness, and capital mobility are all insignificant; the negative effects of unemployment and political variables (e.g., positive effects of Left government, proportionality, and state capacity) dominate the explanation of patterns in union density.

[49] Matthews 1991; Castles, Gerritson, and Vowles 1996.

[50] As Visser and Hemerijck and others have argued, the Dutch experience of renewed macrocorporatist cooperation in the 1980s and beyond is consistent with Dutch political institutions and the challenges of international competitiveness. Visser and Hemerijck 1997. Yet, the fact that Dutch corporatism remained notably lower than Danish national cooperation is not surprising: state capacity, a key source of maintenance of national cooperation in the contemporary era, is notably lower in the Netherlands and Denmark.

[51] Swenson and Pontusson 2000; Berg and Traxler 2007.

leadership and associated interest associations have had greater incentives to bypass or weaken corporatist institutions.[52]

The Impact of Political Institutions on State Capacity

We test our arguments that proportionality and federalism have indirect effects on coordination through their impacts on state capacity by estimating Eq. 3 (by OLS with first-order autoregressive errors and panel correct standard errors). The results of this estimation are as follows (where significant coefficients [$p < .05$] are bold italicized numerals).

State Capacity$_{i,t}$ = α + **.0401** (Electoral Proportionality)$_{i,t-1}$ − **.1250** (Federalism)$_{i,t-1}$ + .0010(Social Democratic Government)$_{i,(mean\ t-1\ to\ t-3)}$ − .0002 (Christian Democratic Government)$_{i,(mean\ t-1\ to\ t-3)}$ + .0023 (Position of the Median Voter)$_{i,t-1}$ +.0001(Dependent Populations)$_{i,t-1}$ **+.0237**(Unemployment)$_{i,t-1}$ − .0002(Trade Openness)$_{i,t-1}$ − .0005(Capital Mobility)$_{i,t-1}$ + **.0201**(Per Capita GDP)$_{i,t-1}$ − **.0065**(Growth)$_{i,t-1}$ + $\varepsilon_{i,t}$

As the table suggests, both proportionality and federalism have correctly signed and significant impacts on state capacity: A change from disproportional to proportional electoral system (0.0 to 2.0) would increase state capacity by just under .1 standard deviation unit; a shift from a unitary and centralized polity to a federal and decentralized one (a change from 1.0 to 5.0) decreases state capacity by roughly .5 standard deviation unit.[53]

With respect to partisan government and other forces thought to shape state strength, Left government has a substantively positive and significant impact on the size of the public economy. An increase of three years of recent left party government control bolsters state capacity by .1 standard deviation units. One the other hand, Christian democratic parties have insignificant impacts on state capacity. In addition to left government, the ideological position of the median voter is positively related to state capacity (although only significant at the .10 level). As far as postindustrial pressures and economic conditions are concerned, we find three significant effects: Unemployment, the level of economic development, and growth are all associated with the size of public economy. Overall, this supplemental analysis confirms that proportionality and federalism do indeed influence coordination through indirect impacts on the evolution of state capacity.

Conclusion

This chapter has sought to understand the maintenance of high levels of coordination by some countries in the face of postindustrial challenges. As we will witness in greater detail in Chapters 9 to 11, policy makers across countries struggled with the transition

---

[52] Anthonsen and Lindvall 2009.

[53] It is important to note that the use of long-term legacies of party government somewhat alters these results. Whereas federalism continues to exert a strong, significant, direct effect, PR falls below conventional levels of significance in the presence of a highly significant Left Party government effect on state capacity. See ancillary materials for full results and further discussion.

to the postindustrial economy by asking employers' to aid in the task of providing collective social goods. These state efforts to coordinate employers in support of policies appropriate to the new postindustrial economy are similar, in many respects, to the historical project undertaken by government actors to create initial encompassing employers' associations (and, in turn, to mobilize support around economic development policies associated with industrial capitalism).

Political institutional characteristics – configurations of electoral and party systems and the actions of political agents – once again have been critical to trajectories of nonmarket coordination, demonstrated in our quantitative analysis of 1974 to 2002 data for eighteen nations. Proportionality and the number of effective parties have positive effects on the degree of employers' organization and macrocorporatist coordination. These findings hold for samples of all capitalist democracies and of CMEs. In addition, federalism plays an important role in determining the strength of nonmarket coordination. For both employers' associations and macrocorporatism, and for both samples of nation years, federalism exerts large negative impacts on the maintenance of nonmarket coordination.

Furthermore, the capacity of the state to foster coalitions of employers and labor in support of responses to postindustrial challenges is crucial. State capacity is positively related to maintenance of high levels of employers' organization and institutions for national coordination, for both the developed capitalist democracies as a whole, and for the CMEs in particular. We also theorized that proportionality and federalism shape the development of state capacity, itself, and thus exert long-term and indirect influence on the institutions of nonmarket coordination through state capacity. Our quantitative analysis produced clear evidence to support this claim. Finally, we also find support for the argument that net of other forces, social democratic government fosters and maintains inclusive and cooperative institutions.

For both transformational epochs of modern capitalism, politics and political institutions determined outcomes. In democracies characterized by electoral proportionality/multipartism and centralization of the national polity, employers found incentives to organize and to pursue, in consort with political actors, the development of broad structures of labor market cooperation. Where majoritarian institutions and federalism existed, pluralism and uncoordinated market economics developed and prevailed. In the modern period, a large public sector – itself a consequence of electoral systems and the federal-unitary divide – also worked to maintain coordination. Even though features of economic structure and dynamics played roles in shaping the development or maintenance of nonmarket coordination, politics and political institutions predominately explain the evolution of cooperative institutions in both eras.

8

Institutional Sources of Employers' Preferences
for Social Policy

Introduction

Government social policies are often a mixed bag for employers: Although they may enhance workers' productivity through skills training or health provision, they also add to the costs of labor. One can dwell on what the right hand giveth or what the left hand taketh away, and therein lies the difference between a business community accommodating growth in government services and one resisting expansion of the public sphere.

This chapter grapples with the deceptively simple question of what matters to the formation of employers' preferences for state social policies. In particular, we study the relative balance between economic imperative and institutional constraint in guiding human action. We ponder whether business managers – seeking to identify their social preferences – strive to fulfill objective interests grounded in the material characteristics of their firms; or whether institutions, ideas and peer pressure have an impact on how managers interpret (or socially construct) their interests? Thus, the first part of the book explores the origins and evolution of the associational forms of business, and the second part investigates how these institutions of coordination influence employers' engagement with the welfare state.

We suggest that high levels of coordination expand employers' support for the welfare state: Segments of business and labor can view their interests in diverse ways and groups shape their perception of preference. Encompassing and centralized groups focus members' attention on broader concerns more than fragmented pluralist groups: The broad scope of the groups enables them to adjudicate among the demands of diverse industrial sectors, to bind members to negotiated decisions, and to engender norms of trust so that a broad cross section of business will comply with identified goals. Corporatist organizations cultivate more intensive linkages among employers, workers and state policy experts than pluralist groups; consequently, their members both learn more about the issues and have greater opportunities to craft policies' details.

Our empirical analysis of employers' preference formation unfolds in two parts. First, we show that corporatist business organization directly increases spending on active labor market policy (ALMP) and social protection for working-age families and intensifies policy responsiveness to deindustrialization in eighteen developed democracies. Second, we reveal the underlying logic of the relationship between employer organization and ALMP by showing how a company's membership in an employers' association affects its participation in active social policy in Denmark, the United Kingdom, and Germany. We build on our own interviews with 107 randomly selected firms and cite a parallel study of Germany by Moira Nelson; we find that membership in an employer association has a strong positive effect on employer participation in ALMP programs designed to enhance the skills of marginal workers in corporatist Denmark but not in the pluralist United Kingdom (or sector-coordinated Germany). This finding confirms the expected differences between corporatist and less organized business organizations in soliciting firms' participation in social programs.

Employers and Policy Responses to Postindustrial Challenges

Active labor market policies – the most recent trend in welfare reform – provide an excellent area for investigation of cross-national differences in business preferences for the welfare state: They draw from mixed ideological inspirations; country experiments with these plans are conceptually very similar; and employers are important to program implementation. The policies address the enhanced need for skills with a social democratic emphasis on training yet also incorporate neoliberal-inspired efforts to retrench welfare spending. The central goals of ALMP are to reintegrate beneficiaries back into the core economy and to reduce individual reliance on passive assistance. To this end, ALMP links social supports to work incentives; for example, the long-term unemployed are given a "new start" in the form of access to training or to subsidized jobs.[1]

A broad range of advanced economies adopted these policies; and even though left- and right-center governmental plans differ in kind, they are surprisingly similar in their goals of reducing passive welfare, solving old welfare state traps, preparing workers for the knowledge society, and asking employers to transcend their traditional roles.[2] In social democratic welfare regimes, most training historically was provided by the state; yet ALMP depends significantly more on firm-based training. In the Christian democratic welfare regimes, the government left most activities up to the private firms, yet the new paradigm micromanages supply and demand through one-stop job centers. In liberal market regimes, training choices were largely left up to private markets, yet ALMP shifts greater responsibility to the state.

Active labor market policies involve employers and other voluntary actors far more than traditional social interventions, as employers have been important to providing centrist political support, to policy implementation, and to efforts to develop real skills among marginal workers. Yet, employer participation in ALMP has varied broadly across countries, with the social democratic countries leading the way.[3] In

---

[1] Gilbert 1992; Rhodes 2001. See ancillary materials on 1980s to 2000s levels and changes in ALMP. For a comprehensive overview of recent research on ALMP, as well as new findings on the ALMP impacts of Europeanization and globalization, see van Vliet 2011 and Swank 2011.

[2] Pontusson 1992; Manow 1998; Hemerijck and Visser 1997.

[3] Holt 1998, 12–13; Larsen and Weise 1999, 61–70; Hasluck 2000, 4; Martin 2004.

some respects, variation in the implementation of ALMP is not surprising because we expect social democratic countries to offer higher levels of social benefits and because coordinated production regimes depend on training. Yet, the social democratic enthusiasm is also somewhat baffling, in that the programs entailed significant movement away from decommodification: Denmark has been a recent leader in cutting back passive welfare supports and ALMP has been viewed by some as attacking the rights of citizenship.[4] Thus, whereas social democratic welfare regimes once were inclined to decommodify labor, they are leading in recommodifying labor once again.

The centrality of employers to the success of postindustrial social reforms presents something of a paradox: Whereas social supports to foster skills development are more important than ever and state policy makers need coordinated employers (and workers) to implement postindustrial reforms, globalization and deindustrialization have made companies more sensitive to any additional social costs. Thus, identifying the conditions under which firms engage with these policies makes a contribution to understanding the future trajectory of welfare states.

Firms' Preferences for Social Protections

Our central task is to understand why some national business communities and individual firms are more agreeable to social policy interventions than others; to this end, we consider hypotheses for why employers accept social spending increases at the national level or participate in social programs at the micro level. When very different nations are adopting quite similar policy reforms (that contradict their social policy legacies), why are these reforms picked up so differently across countries? Our core argument is that the encompassing employers' associations and nonmarket coordination have an *independent* impact on both employers' preferences and welfare state spending. Therefore, we control for the factors that contribute to the emergence and maintenance of these associations and social policies (e.g., economic pressures, challenges from labor, and politics) and then assess the independent contribution of types of coordination.

We test these hypotheses in national and firm level studies that diverge somewhat in their direct object of examination. The national-level test evaluates the determinants of ALMP spending and social protection for workers: Lacking a direct measure of business support for national policies, we use outcomes as a proxy. The firm-level study evaluates the causes of individual firms' participation in ALMP programs. Although the dependent variables differ in the two studies, the logic behind the causal mechanisms at the two levels is quite similar and we offer hypotheses for both the national and firm level studies to emphasize this correspondence. Thus, similar factors influence national ALMP spending and employers' participation in ALMP programs.

Economic Determinants of Social Spending and Preferences

An economic view of business interests has it that employers, first and foremost, are concerned about profitability, and preferences in this world are unambiguous and

---

[4] J. Martin 2000, 83, 85; Kongshøj Madsen 2000; Torfing 1999; Abrahamson 1998; Cox 1998; cf. Huo 2009, 264.

easily grasp. All things being equal, firms oppose spending that increases taxes, raises wages, diminishes profitability, or interferes with managerial control; governments are similarly wary of initiatives that might trigger business disinvestment.[5] There is undoubtedly more than an element of truth in this stylized fact; yet all things are not equal and even within this individualistic, straight-forward view of preference, firms face different economic challenges or have diverse economic characteristics that make some more amenable to social spending.

Wealth. Welfare spending has broadly risen with industrialization, as the production of wealth allowed nations to attend to social needs hitherto left unfilled and to cope with new social risks associated with modernization. Some economies and firms should be better able to afford the burdens of social spending than others, and increased affluence may promote the demand (or the willingness and capacity to pay) for social protection (i.e., Wagner's Law). For the national level, consequently, *per capita GNP* has been hypothesized to be a principal determinant of social spending.[6]

At the firm level, wealthy firms might support social policies to impose costs on their competitors, to frame policies in their own terms, or to gain political advantages from the state. Thus, companies with higher *profits as a percentage of total sales* might be more likely to participate because they have the organizational slack to devote resources to social issues. Firm *size* might be important, in that larger firms with a greater amount of organizational slack are better positioned to offer social benefits than smaller firms. Size might also matter, because larger firms are more likely to have extant programs, to match new benefits to their worker skill profiles, or to derive selective advantages in political action. Alternatively, in countries with smaller firms, managers might prefer governments to provide social benefits to assume responsibility for work-related social risks.[7]

Deindustrialization. Investment in new skills becomes most critical when economies are in transition; therefore, deindustrialization should also augment the need for new social protections (e.g., training, job placement, social transfers) particularly for semi- and unskilled workers displaced from stable, well-paying employment. Thus at the national level, one should expect to find that ALMP spending (and social protection of current workers) increases with *deindustrialization.*[8]

In addition, secular increases in *unemployment rates* automatically swell (passive) unemployment compensation and related programs and pressure policy makers to provide increased access to training, subsidized employment, and labor market services. Yet in the long term, high unemployment may force reductions in replacement rates and entitlements for passive income supports.[9]

Globalization. Trade openness has potentially complex impacts on social protections as it did on coordination. At the national level, it may foster greater social insurance against market risks, encourage more extensive ALMP for flexible adjustment

[5] Block 1977; Jacobs 1988; Lindblom 1977; and for critical appraisals, Przeworski and Wallerstein 1988; Swank 1992; Kalecki 1971.
[6] Wilensky 2002.
[7] Weinstein 1968; Ferguson 1995; Martin 1991; 2000; Gordon 1994; Jacoby 1998; Jacobs 1988; Baldwin 1990; Mares 2003, 266.
[8] Iversen and Cusack 2000; OECD 2005; Busemeyer 2009.
[9] Hicks 1999; Swank 2002; Huber and Stephens 2001.

of markets to competition, and prompt a large countercyclical public sector. Yet the "efficiency hypothesis" suggests that trade openness produces lower levels of social protection, because high taxes and redistributive social transfers may contribute to high labor costs and market distortions that undercut international competitiveness of firms. Moreover, *capital mobility* may undercut social spending by enabling capital flight and undercutting capital's willingness to engage in cooperative institutions.[10] At the firm level, companies in exposed sectors with a high level of *exports* to international markets might participate in ALMP to enhance their workers' skills or to obtain cheap labor.

Labor Determinants of National Spending and Firms' Preferences
The above arguments view employers' preferences as relatively fixed, yet managers are influenced by the power and characteristics of other social actors, especially labor. Thus, we consider factors that bring firms to acquiesce to welfare demands of other groups.

Social Democratic Party Control. Employers may accept higher social spending to appease *labor activism* or to generate workers' *skills*. At the national level, governments may expand social spending when forced to by actors, particularly workers, who seek to alter the balance of power between capital and labor. Therefore, countries with strong union organization and frequent working class participation in government through *social democratic party control* should experience welfare state expansion. Social democratic governments champion high levels of social services and frequent party control enables these governments to take action without business interference and/or to alter corporate expectations about the range of possible politics. *Union power* and organization undergirds social democratic party political power and may also directly induce higher social intervention. At the firm level, the *presence of unions* within the company may produce greater support for social programs, if unions convince managers to participate in order to reduce labor militancy or to be viewed as socially responsible.[11]

Pressures to expand social spending by *the median voter* should also have a significant impact on employers' capacities to restrain welfare state growth. Because relatively poorer voters benefit from social transfers, the magnitude of these benefits may be molded by the degree of market income inequality. Where wage differences between the top and middle earners are greater than the gap between incomes of the middle and the bottom, the middle may join the bottom to push for fiscal redistribution.[12]

Skills. Employers might also derive material benefits from social protections in their impact on skills, health, child care needs and overall productivity. Coordinated market economies foster a particularly close relationship between social protections and economic production, as these utilize manufacturing workers with *specific* as opposed to

[10] Katzenstein 1985; Rodrik 1997; Garrett 1998; Cameron 1978; Swank 2010.

[11] Hicks and Swank 1992; Korpi 1980; Stephens 1980; Esping-Andersen 1996; Huber and Stephens 2001; Swank 2002; Hacker and Pierson 2002; Swenson 1991; Castles 1978; Bowman 1985; Gordon 1991.

[12] Lupa and Pontusson 2011. Conventional median voter models emphasize the ratio of the income of mean to median voters. Meltzer and Richard 1981; Romer 1975. Alternatively, Moene and Wallerstein (2003) argue that increases in the relative income of median voters will actually generate *more* demand for social insurance.

general skills and enhance their competitive positions with information exchange and consensus. Intensive vocational training programs nurture workers' specific skills and unemployment protections make blue-collar workers feel secure in deferring employment to develop potentially redundant skills. Alternatively, in liberal market economies with contentious labor-management relations, neither workers nor employers have incentives to invest in specific skills and competitive strategies entailing a high skill-specific workforce are discouraged.[13] Thus, at the national level, CMEs should have higher levels of social spending than LMEs.

At the firm level, we should expect companies with a higher percentage of blue-collar workers to be more likely to participate in ALMP programs in order to take advantage of training opportunities or to gain cheap labor; therefore, firms with fewer *white-collar workers* are more likely to participate.[14] Because wages closely parallel skills, those with lower *average wages* are more likely to participate. We might also imagine that Danish CME and British LME firms would have different skills needs. Danish CME firms should have higher skills needs; therefore, all firms with a low proportion of *white-collar workers* (i.e., blue-collar workers at all skills levels) might be more likely to participate. In comparison, in the British LME firms with a larger proportion of *unskilled blue-collar workers* might participate in order to gain access to cheap labor.

Political Structural Determinants of National Spending and Firms' Preferences
Features of the state induce or suppress employer organization and nonmarket coordination, and these may also have a direct influence on the likelihood that employers accept or support expansions of social provision. Electoral systems affect the degree to which employers can oppose social spending because *proportional representation* systems represent a broader range of interests in national policy-making forums; in particular, losers from postindustrial change are more likely to have spokesmen in legislatures than under majoritarian systems. PR systems typically have higher levels of voter turnout, mobilization of the lower socioeconomic strata, and more frequent left-center government, which has positive effects on ALMP and social protection.[15] Governmental structures also determine the degree to which individuals with selective incentives may successfully oppose redistributive social policies. Thus, *federalism and other veto points* associated with institutional fragmentation and required legislative supra-majorities help opponents stop social reforms.[16]

At the firm level, pressures from government bureaucrats may also alter corporate preferences. Firms with a higher level of *public sector sales* may be more susceptible to governmental pressure to participate in social reforms.[17] Government policy entrepreneurs may strategically cultivate business allies to build support for their initiatives; therefore, *government outreach* to individual firms may enhance participation.[18]

---

[13] Estevez-Abe et al. 2001; Hall and Soskice 2001; Visser and Hemmerijck 1997; Manow 1998; Coates 2001; Hay 1997; Ebbinghaus and Hassel 2000; Mares 2003; Wood 2001; Regini 1995; Huber and Stephens 2001a.
[14] Burgoon 2001.
[15] Swank 2002; Crepaz and Birchfield 2000; Iversen and Soskice 2006. On turnout, see Hicks and Swank 1992; Franzese 2002; Mahler 2008.
[16] Huber and Stephens 2001b; Immergut 1992; Tsebelis 1999.
[17] Grier et al. 1994; Dobbin 1992; Mitchell 1997.
[18] Martin 1991; McConnell 1966.

Organizational Influences on Preferences and Social Policies

Network sociologists and social constructivists add a new dimension to the subject of employers' preferences. Firms have multiple goals and may choose from a range of preferences, especially because decision making occurs under conditions of bounded rationality. Companies with similar industrial structures often take divergent positions on public policy both cross-nationally and even within countries. The determinants of corporate choice transcend the material reality of the firm and the institutional context of policymaking becomes critical to understanding the formation of policy preferences by employers.[19] The following section explores how institutions for coordination contribute to employers' perceptions of their interests.

Macrocorporatism

It is our core contention that macrocorporatist forms of employer organization make employers more likely to support public social policies. These centralized and encompassing peak associations have political economic, collective action, and cognitive effects on their members, all of which expand support for social spending. First, macrocorporatist forms of association have *political economic effects* because highly organized employer (and labor) associations foster coordination in collective bargaining. Centralized bargaining produces wage compression (reducing the gap between high and low skill workers), and this motivates employers to eliminate low-skilled jobs and to support social programs (ALMP) that induce workers to make skills investments and that generally build human capital. Relations within dense networks of institutions found in CMEs reinforce close economic cooperation, long-term investment in skills, and higher rates of productivity.[20]

Second, participation in macrocorporatist groups helps to overcome the *limits to collective action*. When the provision of skills is left up to private firms, only some employers will perform this task because firms fear that free-riding companies will poach their trained employees – thus firms can secure the benefits of the good without bearing the cost. Corporatist groups bind firms to negotiated decisions and bring members to trust that they will not be punished for commitment to longer-term goals. Therefore, corporatist institutions have an economic logic (their encompassing organization of functional economic interests internalizes "externalities") and a political logic (sustained interaction enhances accommodation among social partners) that facilitate a search for the public good.[21]

Third, highly organized business associations have a *cognitive* impact on their members, in educating employers about the benefits of social policies and bringing managers into contact with policy experts from government and organized labor. Firms

[19] Granovetter 1985; Fligstein 1990; Hillman and Hitt 1999; Friedland and Robertson 1990; DiMaggio and Powell 1991; Dobbin 1992; 2009; Laumann and Knoke 1987; Mizruchi 1992; Fligstein 1990. Institutions become doubly important in the world of social policy because social benefits constitute a collective action problem and tend to be undersupplied.

[20] Iversen 2005; Pontusson 2005; Wallerstein 1999; cf., Scheve and Stasavage 2009; Hall and Soskice 2001; Kitschelt et al. 1999.

[21] Olson 1965; Streeck 1992: 265–84; Rothstein 1988, pp. 235–260; Katzenstein 1985; Visser and Hemmerijck 1997, Putnam 1993.

need to perceive that benefits of social programs outweigh costs: Highly organized employers' associations channel the ideas that influence their member's perceptions of interests, focus participants' attention on broader, shared concerns, and create norms of cooperation, trust, and "social partnership." Thus business associations not only represent their members' interests, but also shape their preferences.[22] These cognitive effects are particularly important to companies' support for social investments in marginal workers. Whereas the political economy and collective action effects of groups shed insight into why firms provide skills for core industrial workers, social protections for marginal workers have a less direct tie-in to productivity and the interpretation of social policy benefits is particularly important to broad business support.

In addition, macrocorporatism, by definition, entails densely organized and nationally centralized labor unions, and sustained interaction between these associations and employers and the state in national collective bargaining and tripartite policy-making forums. In pluralist systems, social partners provide input primarily through the legislative process, whereas in corporatist settings unions and employers are more likely to significantly instigate, if not directly develop, policies through the collective bargaining process or in tripartite advisory commissions of governmental agencies. As such, labor preferences for social protection should influence employers and be directly reflected in national policy and performance.

Pluralist systems of interest representation have fragmented, decentralized, and competing groups and bring employers to look less favorably on government social policies. First, the political economic effects are such that pluralist systems of representation fail to produce highly centralized collective bargaining, wage compression or incentives to enhance the skills of marginal workers. Second, these groups have limited capacities for collective action, as they tend to compete with one another for members, have a limited capacity to foster cooperation, and cater to the particularistic self-interests of their members. For example, the lack of strong encompassing employers' organizations has rendered American managers largely incapable politically of securing collective human capital investment policies.[23] Finally, even though all types of groups have cognitive effects in channeling information to their members, pluralist systems of representation lack the tripartite forums (found in corporatist countries) that expose employers on a regular basis to experts in labor and government. Consequently, the public and private policy communities are more intertwined through these formal institutional networks in macrocorporatist countries than in pluralist ones.

In countries with sector coordination, one is likely to find deals between business and labor at the sectoral level, which offer core workers ample social protections but which neglect the interests of labor-market outsiders. From the perspective of collective action theory, industrial sector organizations simply have few incentives to contribute to the costs of programs that address the needs of marginalized workers. Facing postindustrial pressures, social democratic and Christian democratic parties sometimes collaborate in insider–outsider strategies, by favoring their core constituency of

---

[22] Crouch 1993; Katzenstein 1985; Rothstein 2000; Martin, 2000; Turner, 1982; Grimm and Holcomb 1987, 105–18.

[23] Martin 2000. U.S. firms have, consequently, individually taken on the task of providing social benefits; for example, by 1935 firm pension plans purported to cover as much as 80 percent of the workforce. Myles 1989, 29, 12–13.

industrial workers with high social and employment protection policies, but eschewing expensive labor market policies to promote the full economic inclusion of "outsiders" (e.g., unskilled workers, the long-term unemployed).[24] In contrast, where labor organization and macrocorporatist institutions are expansive, the interests of labor market outsiders are incorporated in labor union policy preferences, recognized by employer organizations, and reflected in national policy and outcomes.

Thus, at the national level, we expect to find that higher levels of *employers' organization* and *macrocorporatism* increase ALMP spending and social protection for workers and allow national policy makers to more readily develop and implement ALMP (and social protection) in response to deindustrialization. At the firm level, membership in an *association* should make firms more likely to participate. Yet membership in an association confers a different set of benefits in corporatist countries than in pluralist ones; therefore, a firm's membership in an association will be significant to participation in corporatist countries (Denmark) but not in pluralist countries (Britain).

Policy Impacts of Employers' Organization at the National Level

We now turn to our analysis of, first, why employers might (reluctantly or even willingly) accept expansion of social provision at the national level and, second, why firms might participate in active labor market programs at the microlevel. To assess the impacts of employer organization (and institutions of nonmarket coordination) on ALMP and social protections, we develop and estimate empirical models of two specific indicators: spending on ALMP as a percentage of GDP and an index of income replacement rates, entitlement rights (e.g., waiting days, benefit duration), and population coverage rates for unemployment and sickness insurance for workers developed by Scruggs (see contemporary ancillary material for details and data sources for all variables).[25] Even though the measure of social protection for current wage earners certainly taps income support for core-sector workers, it, along with ALMP, should also capture key responses to pressures on marginal workers, the unemployed, and other labor market "outsiders" (e.g., probability of benefit coverage).

We measure employers' organization and macrocorporatism (as well as sector coordination and components of these institutional configurations) as in Chapter 7. We also test for alternative explanations of cross-national and temporal variation in social policy as discussed above. Specifically, we evaluate the policy impacts of *partisan governance* by progressive parties, the *position of the median voter*, and *union power*. While we consider alternative measures of the median voter in subsequent analysis of redistribution, we use an estimate of the ideological position of the median voter here (see Chapter 7 and ancillary material). We do so because economic measures of the median voter such as the 90:50 wage ratio are available for only a subset of the country years used here.

We also evaluate the degree to which employers can afford the welfare state by estimating the effects of *per capita real GDP*. To evaluate the extent to which employers

---

[24] Carlin and Soskice 2009; Busemeyer 2009; Rueda 2007; Martin and Thelen 2007; Palier and Thelen 2008.
[25] We explicitly limit our concerns to workers and their families. Consideration of policies for retirees adds substantial methodological complexity (e.g., Bradley et al. 2003) and extends the subject matter beyond the scope of this study (e.g., to the politics of pensions).

derive positive benefits from the postindustrial welfare state, we estimate the policy impacts of *deindustrialization, trade openness,* and *capital mobility.* The control for *unemployment* taps business cycle downturns that may call forth both automatic and discretionary ALMP spending and social protection changes. All variables are lagged one year with the exception of partisan government; for party power we use the three-year average of left and Christian democratic cabinet portfolio shares.[26]

Thus, our core models of ALMP spending and social protection takes the following form, where Eq. 2 simply adds the interaction for employers' organization and deindustrialization to Eq. 1.

[Eq. 1]   ALMP/Social Protection $_{i,t}$ = α + β_1(Employers' Organization)$_{i,t-1}$ +
β_2(Position of the Median Voter)$_{i,t-1}$ + β_3(Social Democratic
Government)$_{i,(t-1\text{ to }t-3)}$ + β_4(Christian Democratic Government)$_{i,(t-1\text{ to }t-3)}$ +
β_5(Deindustrialization)$_{i,t-1}$ – β_6(Trade Openness)$_{i,t-1}$ – β_7(Capital Mobility)$_{i,t-1}$
+ β_8(Unemployment)$_{i,t-1}$ + β_9(Per Capita GDP)$_{i,t-1}$ + $\varepsilon_{i,t}$

[Eq. 2]   ALMP/Social Protection $_{i,t}$ = α + β_1(Employers' Organization)$_{i,t-1}$ + $\cdots$ +
β_{10}(Employers' Organization × Deindustrialization)$_{i,t-1}$ + $\varepsilon_{i,t}$

In these equations, α is an equation intercept, i designates nation, t designates year, and $\varepsilon_{i,t}$ is the error term. We also assess a number of additional explanations of ALMP and social protection as indicated in our theoretical discussion. We test for direct effects on policy of macrocorporatism and sector coordination; we also assess whether a control for union organization diminishes the effects of employers' organization in Eq. 1. In addition we assess direct policy impacts of voter turnout, veto points, and proportional electoral rules (PR). We report the full results of Eqs. 1 and 2 later as well as a synopsis of these additional tests (that are fully reported in the ancillary materials). For estimation of our models, we use least squares regression with corrections for first-order autoregressive errors and panel correct standard errors.[27] Our data for eighteen nations and relatively long time series (1971 to 2002 for social protection, 1980/1985–2003 for ALMP) allow us to estimate our models with country fixed effects (and joint F-tests suggest their statistical inclusion). Finally, we use a number of alternative measures, specifications, and estimators to check the robustness of our results (see ancillary materials).

Findings: National Level Analysis of ALMP and Social Protection
Results for analysis of ALMP spending are presented in columns I and II of Table 8.1. As the table indicates, the level of employers' organization is directly related to national resources for ALMP. An increase in employers' organization of 1.0 (on our z-score scale) raises ALMP spending by .4 percent of GDP. (ALMP spending varies from 0.1 to 1.7 percent of GDP with a mean of 0.7 in the early 2000s.) In addition, as the positive interaction in column II suggests, policy makers respond to deindustrialization with greater increases in ALMP spending at high levels of employer organization. For instance,

---

[26] We use short-term measures of partisan government. Long-term cumulative years in office of left and Christian Democratic parties are strongly associated with the maintenance of macrocorporatism and, as such, our quantitative analysis cannot decisively adjudicate between party and union effects on policy.

[27] Beck and Katz 1995.

TABLE 8.1. *The Determinants of Active Labor Market and Social Protection Policies in the Postindustrial Era*

	ALMP		Social Protection	
	I	II	III	IV
Employers' organization .	.4144**	−1.4096**	.5041*	−7.4835**
	(.1670)	(.6683)	(.3189)	(2.0464)
Employers' organization	—	.0234**		.1071**
× Deindustrialization		(.0082)		(.0275)
Median voter	−.0047**	−.0046**	.0133**	.0151**
(ideological position)	(.0019)	(.0019)	(.0068)	(.0067)
Left party government	.0004	.0004	.0029*	.0031**
	(.0006)	(.0006)	(.0022)	(.0021)
Christian democratic	.0001	.0001	−.0010	−.0017
party government	(.0013)	(.0013)	(.0050)	(.0050)
Deindustrialization	.0120	.0072	.0643**	.1944**
	(.0133)	(.0129)	(.0271)	(.0550)
Trade openness	−.0029*	−.0029*	−.0012	−.0013
	(.0019)	(.0019)	(.0071)	(.0076)
Capital mobility	.0046**	.0035**	−.0043	−.0107*
	(.0018)	(.0018)	(.0070)	(.0071)
Unemployment	.0247**	.0255**	.5041*	−.1052**
	(.0117)	(.0116)	(.3190)	(.0414)
Per capita real GDP	.0034	.0061	.0628**	.0038
	(.0075)	(.0076)	(.0299)	(.0324)
Intercept	−.4566	.0370	2.5606	−3.8534
R^2	.6210	.6175	.8723	.8852
Number of observations	392	392	501	501

Models are estimated by Prais-Winston (AR1) regression with panel correct standard errors.
* Significant at the .10 level.
** Significant at the .05 level or below.

employing the mathematics of interaction terms, it is easy to see that ALMP responsiveness to a one unit change in deindustrialization at relatively high levels of employer organization (say mean 1980–2002 levels in Norway) is a substantively important and significant .03 (−.0072, the coefficient for deindustrialization, + [.0234 × .98], the coefficient for the interaction term multiplied times the value of employer's organization).[28] In other words, an increase in deindustrialization of 10 percent of the working-age population would produce an increase in ALMP spending of .3 of GDP at relatively high levels of employers' organization.

With regard to political pressures, we also find a surprising negative impact on ALMP spending of the ideological position the median voter. Specifically, in each estimation, a shift to the right by the median voter (a decrease in the median voter score where 0.0 equals strong promarket orientations, 100 equals strong collectivism) is

---

[28] On interactions, see Chapter 2; Friedrich 1982; Kam and Franzese 2009.

significantly associated with an increase in ALMP spending. This robust finding is readily interpretable in the context of our results for social protection (columns III and IV). In that analysis, a shift in the median voter to the right results in a reduction of passive social supports. Combining the two sets of findings, the evidence rather strongly suggests that where the median voter shifted right in recent years, national policy makers reduced some features of passive income supports for workers (for instance, duration of benefits) while emphasizing training and labor market integration. This electorally desirable policy mix of "activation" was also touted by the OECD and EU as a central defense against the growth of social exclusion.[29]

With respect to partisan dynamics, we find that government control by left and Christian democratic parties does not appreciably affect ALMP spending in Table 8.1 models. We do, however, find that in several alternative specifications of Eqs. 1 and 2 for ALMP, left party government does significantly and positively impact resource commitments for ALMP (see ancillary materials). We present clearer evidence of partisan government effects on social protection in columns III and IV.

With respect to socioeconomic forces in our model, we see two relatively important findings. First, capital mobility is actually associated with increased commitments of national resources for ALMP. This finding is certainly consistent with the view that greater competitiveness among postindustrial economies for mobile capital intensified concern for improving levels of work force skills as well as compensating those workers adversely affected by outward capital flows. Second, we find relatively strong business cycle effects on spending for ALMP: Increases in unemployment consistently generate greater ALMP spending.

Results for our estimation of models of social protection for workers are presented in columns III and IV of Table 8.1. In brief, employers' organization is positively and significantly related to social protection and it mediates policy responsiveness to deindustrialization. With respect to other forces, the ideological position of the median voter is – as discussed earlier– positively and significantly related to social protection for workers. In addition, governance by left parties matters: In both model estimations, government control by left parties (but not Christian democratic parties) was significantly associated with social protection. With respect to socioeconomic factors, few consistent and significant effects on social protection emerge in our analysis: Deindustrialization is the only factor to exhibit a consistent impact on policy.

A Note on Additional Findings. Several results from our tests of additional hypotheses merit comment. (Complete findings are presented in the ancillary materials.) First, the introduction of a control for union organization in the column I model does not significantly diminish the effect of employers' organization. Moreover, substitution of macrocorporatism for employers' organization in Table 8.1 equations produces near identical results: Macrocorporatism directly influences ALMP and social protection and mediates the policy effects of deindustrialization.[30] On the other hand, substitution of sector coordination for employers' organization produces null findings. Finally,

---

[29] Armingeon and Bonoli 2006; Swank 2011;
[30] The only exception is that the coefficient for the interaction of macrocorporatism and deinsdustrialization falls just short of significance at probability = .11 in the ALMP model of column II.

tests for the direct effects of voter turnout, PR, and institutional veto points produced largely insignificant or incorrectly signed coefficients.

A Study of Firms and Active Social Policy in Denmark and the United Kingdom

To evaluate how membership in an employers' association shapes firms' engagement with the welfare state, we test a model that predicts when companies' participate in the implementation of active labor market policies.[31] Some of the data were provided from a series of structured interviews (done by one of the coauthors in the winter and spring of 2001) with human resources officers and CEOs of fifty-two British firms and fifty-five Danish ones; 54 percent of the sample of two hundred companies participated. Almost all of the Danish interviews were conducted in Danish. The interview data were supplemented with Amadeus company reports and firms' annual reports. The sample was randomly drawn from the Børsen's top 500 list of employers in Denmark and the corresponding *Financial Times* list in Britain.[32]

We chose to conduct studies in Denmark and the United Kingdom to compare employer preference formation for and participation in social policy in two different institutional settings. At the same time, some of the employment conditions of the two countries were similar: At the time of the study, the two had the highest rates of employment among EU nations and were identified as among the frontrunners in active labor market policy.[33] By making two separate but parallel firm-level comparisons (comparing firms within a country but not between countries), we could isolate the significant causal factors driving firm behaviors in each country and compare significant variables across countries. (We also take advantage of recent research by Moira Nelson[34] that replicates our Danish and British firm-level analyses for Germany; we summarize Nelson's findings later.)

The dependent variable was operationalized as firms' participation in active labor market and social programs identified by the countries in their National Action Plans as mechanisms for expanding employment.[35] The dependent variable was based on data about firm positions on and participation in the programs and consisted of a scale, moving from a position entailing full participation to a position ideologically opposed to involvement.

[31] A preliminary look at firm-level preferences for social policy is provided by Martin (forthcoming). This paper offers a significant expansion of this work in evaluating the importance of sector and in investigating the role of the state.
[32] Every fifth firm was selected from the lists of the top 500 companies in each country. Whereas we anticipated some selection bias in that active companies would be more willing to participate than inactive ones, some inactive firms welcomed us as a source of additional information and some known activists had no time to see us. A size differential might indicate a comparison between Danish firms and British business units, but we chose to preserve the comparison between the largest firms and most British managers attempted to find out their business units participation. Indeed, in many British firms only a couple of units participated, thus, overstating the British participation rates.
[33] Commission of the European Communities 1999.
[34] Nelson no date.
[35] "United Kingdom Employment Action Plan" 1999; "Danmarks Nationale Handlingsplan for Beskaeftigelse" 1999.

The independent variables were operationalized as follows: An estimate of *average wages* was obtained from Amadeus company reports. The variables of *unskilled blue-collar workers*, *skilled blue-collar workers*, and *white-collar workers* were derived from data provided by the company, outlining the percentage of white-collar, skilled blue-collar, and unskilled blue-collar employees in the workforce. The *profits* measure was taken from Amadeus company reports and was calculated as the net (after tax) profit for the year divided by total sales. The *size* variable was derived from Amadeus company reports identifying firms' total revenues. A measure of *unions* was based on information supplied by the firm and was operationalized as a dummy variable, reporting whether or not the company had unions. The *exports* variable, operationalized as the percentage of total sales devoted to exports, was derived from data supplied by the firm. The variable estimating *public sector sales* represented the share of total revenues taken up by sales to the public sector and was derived from data supplied by the firm. The *sector* variable separating manufacturing from services was derived from the firm's major Standard Industrial Classification (SIC) code. The *associations* institutional variable specified membership in a peak or sector employers' association, based on data obtained from the company. It should be noted that firms joined these groups long before active labor market policy was on the public agenda and belonged for reasons other than an interest in these policies. The state *outreach* variable specified vigorous outreach by government actors, based on information provided by the firm.[36]

We estimated the hypotheses with an OLS regression method, appropriate because of the interval level quality of the dependent variable.[37] Hours of interviewing convinced us that the firms truly were distributed along an ordinal scale with interval qualities. The statistical results were supplemented and complemented by the qualitative interview evidence that provided added confidence in the assessments of the independent variables in the statistical analysis. With two separate but parallel firm-level comparisons (comparing firms within a country but not between countries), we could isolate significant causal factors driving firm behaviors in each country and compare significant variables across countries. The high correlation between some variables combined with a desire to limit the number to accommodate the small n prompted several factors. We created factors combining the *wages* and *white-collar workers* variables for the Danish study and *wages* and *unskilled blue-collar workers* in Britain, and factors of *exports* and *unions* measures in both countries.[38] Because the outreach variable

---

[36] Using firm's self-reporting is problematic because participating firms are probably more likely to recall being contacted by municipalities than nonparticipating firms, yet the issue is partially alleviated by the cross-national comparison. This approach enables us to hold constant problems of self-reporting while determining if the role of the state differs across settings. We specified the variable in both countries as the contact from municipalities and included in the British case outreach by the Blair administration, and in the Danish case contact from the regional-level Arbejdsformidlingen. Running the equation with contact only from the municipalities produced the same results.

[37] Tabachnik and Fidell 1989, 7–9. We also estimated the hypotheses with an ordered probit model that, with exception of the significance of one control variable, produced the same results.

[38] The close theoretical connection between skills and wages justified the creation of these factors. We developed slightly different wage/skills variables in keeping with our theoretical expectations for the two countries. Thus, the Danish relevant skills group was all blue-collar workers regardless of skills level (or the absence of white collar workers) while in Britain our anticipated target group constituted unskilled blue-collar workers. In Britain *wages* and *unskilled blue-collar workers* were correlated at -.47; the factor

TABLE 8.2. *Microanalysis: Firm Participation in Labor Market Policies in Great Britain*

Answer	Value	Frequency	Percent
Formal participation in job training or protected jobs program (i.e., full-blown social partnership)	5	13	25
Some limited involvement (i.e., one or two protected jobs or firm endorsed without much participation)	4	8	15
Very limited involvement – possibly someplace within the firm a line manager may have taken on a New Dealer or firm may participate in future	3	3	6
No participation, no political support, but no ideological opposition either	2	27	52
No participation and ideological opposition	1	1	2
Total		52	100

is more subjective than our other measures, we ran two equations for each case: the first with the less subjective economic and institutional variables, the second adding *outreach* by the state.

Findings
At the time of the survey, 68 percent of the Danish firms participated in subsidized jobs and training programs for the long-term unemployed; in comparison, only 40 percent of firms were involved to some extent in parallel programs in the United Kingdom. This is consistent with other studies reporting participation in active labor market programs by Danish and British firms.[39] The regression analyses demonstrate that independent variables perform differently in Great Britain and Denmark and we report findings of each study in turn. Tables 8.2 and 8.3 report values of the dependent variable in Britain and Denmark.

Turning to the first equation in the British study (without the measure of government outreach), the regression analysis surprisingly finds the *association* variable – expected to have no effect – to have a significant negative impact on participation. The findings give support for three of the control variables' influence on firms' participation: *size, public sector sales*, and the *unskilled blue-collar workers/wages* factor (See Table 8.4). A one billion pound increase in *size* produces a 0.08-point increase in participation; a 10 percent increase in *public sector sales* produces a 0.4-point increase in participation. A ten-point increase in the *unskilled blue-collar workers/wages* factor produces a four-point increase in participation. In the second equation, the addition of the highly significant variable measuring *outreach* by government makes all other measures lose

accounted for 73 percent of the variance with an eigenvalue of 1.47. The Danish *wages* and *white collar workers* variables were correlated at .4; the factor accounted for 70 percent of the variance with an eigenvalue of 1.4. The British *exports* and *unions* factor accounted for 73 percent of the variance with an eigenvalue of 1.46. The Danish factor combining *exports* and *unions* explained 60 percent of the variance and had a eigenvalue of 1.2.

[39] Holt 1998; Larsen and Weise 1999; Hasluck 2000; Snape 1998.

TABLE 8.3. *Microanalysis: Firm Participation in Labor Market Policies in Denmark*

Answer	Value	Frequency	Percent
Formal participation in job training or protected jobs program (i.e., full-blown social partnership)	5	19	35
More limited involvement (i.e., a few protected jobs or British firm signed on without much participation)	4	18	33
Very limited involvement – possibly someplace within the firm a line manager may have taken on a New Dealer or firm may participate in future	3	1	2
No participation, no political support, but no ideological opposition either	2	12	22
No participation and ideological opposition	1	5	9
Total		55	100

significance. A one-point increase in state *outreach* produces a one-point increase in firms' participation. (See Table 8.4.)

Turning next to the Danish study, the data – as expected – confirm the significance of the institutional variable measuring *association* membership on firms' participation in social programs: In both equations joining an association produces a two-point increase in participation. Two of the control independent variables have a significant effect on the dependent variable in both equations: the *size* variable and the *white-collar workers/wage* factor. In the first equation, a one-point decrease in the *white-collar workers/wage* factor has an 0.8-point increase in participation and a one-billion kroner decrease in size of sales has a 0.09-point increase in participation. In the second equation the outreach variable is also significant, but (unlike in Britain) it does not alter the other variables' performance: A on- point increase produces a 0.5-point increase in participation. (See Table 8.4.)

With respect to Germany, Nelson estimates two models of German firm participation in ALMP (identical to our Table 8.4 models without the outreach variable).[40] The first model is for firm participation in all ALMP programs; the second is for firm participation in ALMP programs for the previously unemployed. The one consistent finding to emerge for German firm participation in ALMP is that the greater the share of *low-skilled workers* in the firm's workforce, the more likely its ALMP participation. In fact, adding further context, the interview data indicate that large majorities of German firms do not believe ALMP meets their skill needs and do not feel a social responsibility for training marginalized workers. *Size, public sector sales*, and other control variables are insignificant in both of Nelson's models. With respect to membership in a peak *association*, organization membership increases participation modestly for all ALMP programs; it is insignificant in the model of firm participation in ALMP programs for the unemployed. As Nelson's work makes clear, government did not require participation in ALMP and did not strongly campaign for business association and firm involvement. Overall, these results are consistent with our expectations for a

[40] Nelson no date.

TABLE 8.4. *Microanalysis: OLS Regression Analyses of British and Danish Firms*

Variables	Britain	Britain	Denmark	Denmark
	I	II	III	IV
	B (Std. Error)	B (Std. Error)	B (Std. Error)	B (Std. Error)
Size	8.575e–11 *	2.482e–11	–8.54e–11 **	–8.05e–11**
	(.000)	(.000)	(.000)	(.000)
Profits	2.363	–.371	–4.571	–3.225
	(1.888)	(1.555)	(3.51)	(3.297)
Export/union factor	–.081	–.086	–.286	–.317
	(.184)	(.142)	(.202)	(.188)
Public sector sales	.042 **	.007	–.02	–.01
	(.014)	(.013)	(.011)	(.011)
Sector	.332	.216	.137	.089
	(.396)	(.307)	(.380)	(.353)
Unskilled blue collar/wages factor	.442 **	.311		
	(.169)	(.133)		
White collar/wages factor			–.765 ***	–.721 ***
			(.171)	(.159)
Association	(–1.374) *	–.063	2.136 **	1.667 **
	(.590)	(.537)	(.671)	(.647)
Outreach		.982 ***		.485 **
		(.195)		(.182)
Constant	3.438	1.097	.044	–.150
	(.506)	(.606)	(1.248)	(1.161)
Number of observations	44	44	43	43
R square	.422	.665	.585	.652
Standard error	1.068	.824	1.019	.946

* Significant beyond .05 level, two-tailed test.
** Significant beyond .01 level, two-tailed test.
*** Significant beyond .001 level, two-tailed test.

sector coordinated economy with high skill needs, sector-based business organization, and limited government engagement in coordination.

Several points can be gleaned from these findings (and we focus on our original analysis of Denmark and Britain). First, membership in a corporatist (as opposed to pluralist) employers' association clearly is an important determinant of involvement in ALMP programs at the firm level, just as corporatist organization is associated with greater welfare state spending at the national level. Even though membership in the Danish corporatist associations is highly determinant of participation in the ALMP programs, membership in the British employer associations not only fails to spur participation, but surprisingly works against involvement in the programs.[41]

---

[41] This finding is partially explained by the fact that joining a trade association in Britain is something of an alternative to developing a large, professional human resources department. Although firms may choose to do both, they often choose one route or the other for gaining information about policies affecting their

TABLE 8.5. *Microanalysis: Primary Source of Information for the Firm*

Source of Information	% in Denmark	% in Britain
Employers organization (formal)	31%	14%
Human resources group (formal or informal)	13%	10%
State agency or group	29%	24%
Private consultant or experts within firm	7%	14%
Newspapers, trade press, newsletters, Internet	15%	34%
Not informed	5%	4%
Total	100%	100%

Interview data overwhelmingly confirm the regression findings and suggest that the corporatist associations had strong cognitive effects. Although associations in both countries supported active labor market policies, employers groups were much more important in shaping members' preferences in Denmark than in the United Kingdom. Firms seemed to interact with their associations on a much more regular basis in Denmark than in Britain and the groups (along with the state) are vital sources of information on public policy. When asked to state their most important source of information about HR issues and social policy, 32 percent of the Danes identified an employers association, as opposed to 14 percent of the British firms, and many Danish firms mentioned associations as their second-most important source of information. British companies learned from trade press, Internet, or regular newspapers (34 percent), government or government inspired groups (24 percent), private consultants (14 percent), or formal and informal HR groups (10 percent) (see Table 8.5). Danish respondents repeatedly reported that their associations instructed them in the new policy ideas about solutions to unemployment. The high level of organization of employers allowed managers to participate in training and subsidized jobs without fear of being penalized for their altruistic behaviors.

Second, the corporatist associations in Denmark had political economic effects in offering Danish employers real skills, something that the British associations failed to deliver, and firms with different level of worker skills participated in the two programs. Danish firms with a high proportion of blue-collar workers (both skilled and unskilled) were statistically more likely to participate in active labor market programs, whereas only British firms with the least skilled workers were most likely to participate.

The interview data confirm that Danish employers were given greater opportunities to shape the policy-making process to their needs and because their associations brought employers to view the programs more positively, firms were more likely than their British counterparts to view the social protections as providing benefits for economic production. Danish employers believed that the programs would help them gain access to a more highly skilled workforce, either by enhancing the skills of their own employees or by preparing a more skilled labor pool. Despite similar vacancy rates, 31 percent of the Danish firms (as opposed to 22 percent of British managers)

workforce. Firms with developed HR departments tend to have more expertise in the HR area, in part because the alternative – membership in the association – offers so little information.

TABLE 8.6. *Microanalysis: Motivations for and Constraints against Participation*

Motivations and constraints	% in Denmark	% in Britain
Firms participated	68%	40%
Subsidies motivating participation	38%	10%
Labor needs motivating participation	31%	22%
Political pressures motivating participation	9%	31%
Need for high skills preventing participation	36%	53%
Program involving firms in a new way	50%	13%

offered labor shortages as a reason for participating. Even though the value of the subsidies was nearly equal, 39 percent of the Danish firms considered subsidies at least somewhat important to mitigating the pains of participation, compared to 10 percent of the British firms (see Table 8.6).

Lacking the programmatic benefits of providing skills, the British firms were more likely to participate to secure either good public relations or cheap labor. Because some firms engaged for philanthropic motivations or to derive political credit, it makes sense those with a higher proportion of sales to the public sector were more likely to participate. Thirty-one percent of the companies credited their participation to strong pressure from government and a desire to please the new administration (see Table 8.6). Often the political commitment to participate came from the very top, after Tony Blair had invited chief executives to Number 10 Downing Street to hear presentations about the New Deal. Whereas Danish CEOs were identified as the agent responsible for deciding to participate in the program in only 9 percent of the cases, 31 percent of British firms identified the CEO as having primary responsibility for participating in the New Deal.

Other British firms reported participating to gain access to cheap labor, as is also reflected in the statistical finding that firms with unskilled blue-collar workers were significantly more likely to participate. Firms felt that the New Deal programs did little to improve the skills of the workforce: Whereas 36 percent of the Danish firms identified skills needs as a constraint against participation, 53 percent of the British firms offered this reason.[42] The programs' limited contribution to skills enhancement is supported by vacancy rate figures. Danish vacancy rates declined with unemployment rates over the course of the 1990s, suggesting that the programs were matching skills to employment needs. British vacancy rates remained the same even while unemployment dropped and welfare reform forced people back into the workforce.[43] British employers also felt that the programs differed little from earlier government efforts to reduce long-term unemployment – these programs were old wine in new bottles. Whereas 50 percent of Danish firms believed government was asking business

---

[42] A varieties of capitalism explanation predicts that Danish firms have higher skill needs than British ones; therefore, we might expect that (all things equal) more rather than fewer Danish firms compared to British ones would decline to participate due to higher skills needs. (This is what Nelson [no date] finds for the sector coordinated Germany economy.)

[43] OECD 2001, 13–14.

to engage in the social arena in a new way, only 13 percent of British firms thought that the New Deal schemes were new.

Third, the Danish associations offered a platform for reaching out to employers, whereas the British associations did not, and this finding is supported by the quantitative analysis. Even though outreach by state actors was significantly determinative of companies' engagement with labor market programs in both countries, the statistically significant impact of government outreach on firm participation in Denmark did not diminish the significance of membership in a peak association; however, in Britain, state *outreach* supplanted other variables in Britain. As we discuss in Chapter 9, the Danish state strengthened the associations' role in active labor market policy and inspired organizational commitment to the programs. The state recently undertook steps to extend formally corporatism to social assistance policy (thus making the social arena resemble the unemployment insurance institutional track). The law required municipalities to form committees consisting of representatives from business and labor to oversee social policy in the community. Dansk Arbejdgiversforening was given the responsibility for selecting company participants to sit on these local social coordination committees. Many respondents identified these committees as vital sources of information and credited their hiring of the long-term unemployed to their committee activities. Firms also believed that the creation of company consultant positions in local municipalities greatly expanded firms' interest in active labor market policy.[44]

Compared with the Danish strategy, the British government relied much more on attracting corporate participation through market-based incentives, largely sidestepping the established national employers' associations. While Blair sought support for the New Deal programs from the Confederation of British Industries, the administration used an extensive and expensive media campaign to engage individual British firms and sought to involve employers in New Deal programs with personal appeals to the largest British corporations.[45] Yet unfortunately a vast number of companies that signed up to hire New Deal clients never actually hired anyone. The administration also developed a marketing strategy, seeking to make recipients "job-ready," to tailor the policies to corporate demands, and to reduce for firms the costs of participating. These market strategies reflected the policy legacies of a liberal welfare regime and the constraints of working with a poorly organized business community. ·

The statistical analysis did not offer support for the hypothesis that companies in the service *sector* made greater use of the programs than manufacturing firms because employers in both types of sectors participate in the programs.[46] But interview data suggest some support for a deindustrialization thesis at the firm level, namely that the programs have aided with the dislocation caused by changing skills needs. As one British manager put it, the training connected with the programs has been important to the "development of new skills for workers transferring from old industries to new industries." Many firms also pointed to the need for "soft" skills that have arisen with service sector jobs.

---

[44] Firm Interview with author, 12/12/2000.
[45] Wintour et al. 1998.
[46] It may be that the additional needs for training in service sectors are matched by the additional skills demands in manufacturing sectors with changes in the organization of work.

Conclusion

This analysis contributes to recent scholarship that emphasizes (in contrast with traditional welfare state theory) the important and positive role of employers in the development of national systems of social protection.[47] In our national-level analysis, we find strong support for our view that corporatist employers' organization plays a central role in the expansion of ALMP programs and in the maintenance of social protection for marginalized workers. Union power and social democratic government, mainstays of the power resources approach to welfare state development, also exert influence on these social policies. So, too, do shifts in the ideological position of the median voter. Yet, our empirical analyses at both the national and firm levels highlight the unique and central contribution of well-organized employers and overarching macrocorporatist institutions to the contemporary evolution of the welfare state.

We also provide new evidence on postindustrial pressures on mature welfare states. Somewhat surprisingly we find limited evidence that globalization plays a systematic role in welfare state change. Our main finding is that rises in international capital mobility have reinforced pressures for the enhancement of workforce skills and, in turn, expansion of ALMP. But we generate clear support that post–World War II deindustrialization in developed capitalism has been fundamentally important in shaping welfare policy.[48] Specifically – and somewhat novelly – we find that political institutions mediate the impact of deindustrialization: National policy makers more forcefully respond to deindustrialization with increases in ALMP spending and maintenance of social protection as the levels of employer organization and macrocorporatism rise.

In addition, our work contributes to a debate within the scholarship of business-government relations on the appropriate level of analysis for appraising corporate interests. While some scholars have studied firms' policy positions largely from the perspective of companies' industrial structure positions, others locate causality in the collective deliberative processes of national employers' associations and other types of social networks and our work endorses this sociological tradition. The following chapters offer further microlevel evidence of the importance of institutions for coordination for firms' positions on the welfare state.

---

[47] Martin 1995, 2000; Swank and Martin 2001; Swenson 2002; and Mares 2003.
[48] Iversen and Cusack 2000.

9

Employers, Coordination, and Active Labor Market Policy in Postindustrial Denmark

Introduction

In the Pantheon of European social experiments, Denmark has a privileged position. As a small open economy competing in increasingly hostile global markets, one might expect Denmark to sacrifice equality to sustain growth and employment, or to see unemployment soar due to dogged commitment to equality. Yet, it enjoys an extremely low rate of inequality and a very high GDP per capita. Danish workers receive high unemployment benefits – about 48 percent of previous earnings, compared with 24 percent in Germany, 12 percent in the United Kingdom, and 14 percent in the United States – yet unemployment is generally low. In 2009, Denmark had 6 percent unemployment – compared with 8 percent in Germany and the United Kingdom – and only 9 percent of total unemployment was considered "long-term," compared with 45 percent in Germany and 25 percent in the United Kingdom.[1] Granted, the country has experienced declining economic, employment and productivity growth rates since the global financial crisis; however, the economic malaise reflects problems associated with the neoliberal deregulation of housing mortgages rather than with social democratic investments in workers' skills.[2] It is too early to make predictions, yet from a comparative perspective, Denmark seems poised largely to persevere in addressing the skills and employment status of marginal workers.

Our puzzle is to ascertain how the Danes have sustained a commitment to social solidarity in the face of global pressures, neoliberal ideas, significant periods of right-party control, and the torments of life in the twenty-first century. With spiraling rates of unemployment and budgetary distress, Denmark was "on the edge of an abyss" in 1979, according to the Social Democratic Minister of Finance; subsequently, both bourgeois and social democratic coalition governments adopted neoliberal regulatory

---

[1] OECD, 7-6-2010. While productivity has been growing more slowly than desirable, this reflects, in part, the difficulty of measuring public sector productivity growth (OECD Economic Surveys: Denmark 2005, 23–6).

[2] We address this in greater detail in the conclusion, but see Goul Andersen 2011; Madsen 2011; Marcussen and Ronin 2011.

and social reforms, such as scaling back passive supports for the long-term unemployment. These changes led scholars to question whether Denmark would maintain universal welfare benefits, and similar pressures provoked Germany to protect core workers but largely to abandon the peripheral long-term unemployed. Yet, Danish policy makers struggled to keep everybody on the employment bus and a remarkable coalition for social solidarity defeated dualism.[3]

We argue that macrocorporatism has been a crucial source of support for continuing solidaristic policies in Denmark, as macrocorporate arrangements bring the social partners together with state policy makers to revise the lines of the welfare state in response to the shifting economic terrain. Supporting the empirical findings of Chapters 7 and 8, we show that the structure of political competition sustained macrocorporatist structures against postindustrial challenges; these structures, in turn, brought employers to support and participate in labor market programs for marginal workers. Although these macrocorporatist institutions do not deliver *permanent* or even always *functional* solutions to the challenges of economic transformation, they embody characteristic processes of decision making that allow for a wider range of interests to engage collectively in articulating and implementing updated policy interventions.

First, the same political features of the Danish state contributing to the origins of macrocorporatism helped to sustain and to reshape institutions for coordination in response to deindustrialization. There has certainly been an erosion of the central, organizing capacities of the formal labor market institutions, as these have come under severe pressure from deindustrialization in Denmark as in other advanced countries. Yet from a comparative perspective, there has been significantly less decay; for example, in 2007, around 69 percent of workers belonged to a union in Denmark, compared to 20 percent in Germany, 28 percent in the United Kingdom, and 11.6 percent in the United States.[4] In this proportional electoral system, coalition government is the norm, making for limits to wild swings in public policy; consequently, even when right parties have gained power in recent decades, the consensus orientation of coalition governments has limited the viability of neoliberal attacks on coordination. Multiparty competition and centralization both contributed to the expansion of the public sector, and this large public sector made macrocorporatist institutions more durable, in part, because private employers and workers have cooperated in order to protect their prerogatives of power.

Second, macrocorporatist employer associations and labor market coordination with unions have been crucial to employers' attitudes and behaviors toward low-skilled workers; indeed, these associations brought employers to support and to help sustain solidarity even when the bourgeois governments after 2001 tried to roll back the boundaries of the Danish welfare state. Macrocorporatist employers' associations had *cognitive impacts* on member firms in helping firms to recognize the labor market benefits of investing in low-skilled workers. Structures of macrocorporatist coordination strengthened employers' *collective capacities* to tailor the programs to business needs for an expanded labor pool. The *political economic* effects of macrocorporatism worked to employers' advantage in investing workers with real skills: High levels of

---

[3] Greve 2004; Campbell and Pedersen 2007.
[4] OECD, 7-6-2010.

coordination throughout the twentieth century had turned Denmark into a high-skills, high-employment society, and this backdrop of need for a large labor pool eased the task of finding a place in the labor market for marginal workers. Macrocorporatist structures gave social democratic party leaders a forum for building coalitions in support of solidaristic arrangements protecting a wide cross section of workers, and when the bourgeois governments sought to roll back programs to enhance the skills of marginal workers, high levels of labor market coordination checked the neoliberal reforms. Thus, we offer the Danish case as further evidence of the arguments tested at the cross-national levels in Chapters 7 and 8.

The capacity of the state to fold employers into a solidaristic coalition enables a high skills consensus: High levels of equality, security, and social solidarity are commensurate with skilled employment, investment in new technology, and labor market flexibility. According to this "flexicurity" formula, labor market regulations are low to encourage energetic economic activity and social protections are high to encourage workers to renew their skills to contribute to this rapidly changing economy. This felicitous combination inspires job growth (because employment can be terminated quite easily) and promotes productivity (because workers are retrained for changing labor market needs). When unskilled jobs declined over the course of the 1990s (and one might have anticipated higher levels of unemployment among unskilled workers), skills qualifications increased even faster due to aggressive training interventions.[5] Despite generous unemployment compensation, virtually everybody works, few work in low-skilled jobs, and this makes for high levels of income equality and social solidarity.

The Danish Model, Crises, and Reforms

The Danish Model

In the century following Niels Andersen's creation of the Confederation of Danish Employers (DA), industrial relations evolved considerably. It is beyond our scope to account for these manifold alterations, but we must take a moment to outline the essential features of the industrial relations and welfare systems during the golden age of industrialization and its aftermath.

Economic diversity poses a threat to high levels of coordination in Denmark today. Even though trade cleavages between export agriculture and protectionist industry were sharp in the early part of the twentieth century, these tensions receded as manufacturers calculated that firms in a small domestic market could best compete by producing exports with highly skilled workers. Thus, during the Golden Age, agriculture and industry jointly favored policies to nurture international competitiveness.[6] But in recent years, the tremendous growth of services – now constituting about 75 percent of the economy – has inspired new fault lines. Manufacturers (as befitting a coordinated

---

[5] Madsen 2002; Goul Andersen 2007, 73–5.

[6] Collectivist sentiments are also reinforced by the ownership pattern of firms, as a great many are family-owned or controlled by trust funds, and companies are more protected from capital markets and international competition in investment decisions (Lønroth et al. 1997; Benner and Vad 2001). A 1991 study of the 274 largest firms found only 19 percent to be diversified-owned by a large number of shareholders. Restrictions on withdrawals from funds created incentives for profits to be reinvested in the firms, causing the funds to grow over time.

market economy) strategically compete using workers with highly developed specific skills, but service sector workers typically rely on general skills; consequently, this shift has eroded the historical reliance on specific manufacturing skills that has been a hallmark of coordinated market economies. In addition, industrial firms are likely to aggressively promote exports, whereas many service enterprises (especially within the large public sector) produce for domestic markets.[7]

Yet this sectoral diversity has been mitigated by two important institutional structures: The system of industrial relations that has come to organize the political preferences and economic coordination of business and labor, and the structure of the Danish welfare state. First, corporatist peak associations bring employers and workers together in tripartite committees and in collective bargaining rounds to negotiate wages and working conditions for the entire economy. The Dansk Arbejdsgiverforening covers most industrial employers in Denmark, and Dansk Industriet (DI) is the most important member association in DA. Two other groups exist – the Finanssektorens Arbejdsgiverforening for the finance sector and the Sammenslutningen af Landbrugets Arbejdsgivere for the agricultural sector – but these groups largely coordinate with DA in channeling employers' political positions. In addition, the association for public sector municipal employers, Kommunernes Landsforeningen (KL), has been an important force in both collective bargaining and tripartite policy making in recent years. Despite recent jurisdictional attacks on DA (discussed later), cleavages separating employers been mitigated by this centralized peak association in Denmark.[8]

Labor is more fragmented than business and – as with the rest of the world – labor union membership has declined in recent years, yet the growth in white-collar and service sector employment has not significantly diminished unionization in Scandinavia as in other countries.[9] Organized along craft lines, unions often include both public and private sector workers, although many have separate divisions for the two groups. This structure reduces the distance between the public and private sphere, because the union leadership – in issuing its political positions – must consider the needs of both types of workers.

This corporatist hierarchical structure of industrial relations mutes the potential economic cleavages among segments of Danish of business and labor, and fosters universal, egalitarian protections against unemployment and other social risks. Factions of business and labor are united through encompassing collective bargaining negotiations, producing legally binding settlements that protect workers across the economy. Historically, DA and LO have passed a basic agreement that sets the framework for

---

[7] Nearly one-third of total employment was in social services while only 10 percent constituted producer services. OECD 2000b, 84–7.

[8] Recently, the Danish Commerce and Services employers organization and the Danish Chamber of Commerce formed a new association, Dansk Erhverv, to represent highly skilled firms in the export sector, which may support company-level agreements and become a competitor of DA. Jørgensen 2006.

[9] Scheuer 2007, 237–8. Three main unions include LO covering industrial workers in seventeen member unions, the Funktionærernes of Tjenestemændenes Fællesrad (FTF) covering public sector white-collar workers, and the Akademikernes Centralorganisation (AC) covering those with a university education. Large sector associations of LO include the 3F representing low-skilled workers in industry, transport, construction and public sector services, HK/Danmark representing office workers, (FOA) representing medium general-skilled workers, and Dansk Metal.

negotiating wages and other nonwage issues at the industry-level and the social part-ners are given free rein to establish the parameters of these negotiations. Tripartite committees including the social partners negotiate a broad scope of public policies; for example, agreements negotiated by the social partners cover 90 percent of labor market regulation.[10] Even in the parliamentary realm, peak associations often draft the nation's laws, especially after 1973, when the party system became severely fragmented. Legislation often only ratifies the social partners' agreements: When they have met the "consensus principle" by agreeing completely on a detailed plan, they have the right to specify labor market regulations.[11]

Second, the structure of the welfare state also helps to mute potential cleav-ages among Danish employers, as the public sector provides many universal bene-fits based on citizenship and funded by tax revenue; therefore, equality, universality, and efficiency are important organizing principles. High individual income taxes are counterbalanced by the low taxation of capital (which encourages investment), by the universal provision of cradle-to-grave services (child care, tertiary education, health care), and by the minimal use of social contributions.[12] The system for skills training also increases income equality, as Denmark spends the most on vocational training as a percentage of GDP in the European Union: Whereas Denmark spent 5 percent of the GDP on labor market programs in 1998, Britain spent only 1 percent. Thus, the macro-corporatist system of industrial relations with its "permanent social pact" and the web of state-provided social benefits have diminished social cleavages.[13]

Some anomalies disrupt this classic portraiture. Protections against the risk of unemployment depend on labor market status in this voluntary Ghent system: Whereas workers are protected by generous social insurance administered by union funds (A-kasse) marginal workers receive limited social assistance administered by munici-palities (bistand or kontanthjælp). The old-age pension system has a large private com-ponent, and a separate pension exists for elderly on social assistance. Denmark has few labor market regulations in the private sector, as firms may hire and fire at will and job mobility is about 30 percent per year.[14] The OECD found that the level of economy-wide regulation was lower than in all other OECD countries with the exception of the United Kingdom, Australia, the United States, Ireland, and Iceland.[15]

Challenges to Employer Coordination and the Welfare State

The decline of the golden age of manufacturing pressured virtually all advanced industrialized countries. Globalization made it increasingly difficult to sustain high

---

[10] Benner and Vad 2001, 411; Scheuer 1992; Due et al. 1994; Ministry of Labour 1996.

[11] Christiansen et al. 2004, 13–15; Damgaard and Svensson 1989, 731–45; Due et al. 1994.

[12] Esping-Andersen 1990; Goul Andersen 2007, 73–5; Rold Andersen 1993, 111–16. Personal taxes comprise 60 percent of total tax revenues, indirect taxes (primarily VAT), 35 percent; and corporate taxes, about 3 percent (Pedersen 1993, 241, 257). Thus, Denmark and Germany have the same level of taxation on capital income (just under 20 percent), but Denmark has a much higher individual tax rate, and Danish taxes are a much higher percentage of the GDP (at 30 percent) than are German taxes (at around 13 percent). Ganghof 2007, 1073.

[13] OECD 2001, 24; Lind 2000.

[14] Pedersen 1993, 241, 257; Hagen 1992, 153–63; Madsen 2002.

[15] OECD 2005 ,"Economic Surveys: Denmark," 37.

taxes and wage equality for low-skilled workers, and stagflation hindered the use of macroeconomic stimulation policies to balance goals of high employment and low inflation. Moreover, deindustrialization lowered productivity growth rates, making it harder to sustain macrocorporatism, universal welfare benefits, and relatively egalitarian capitalism. Denmark succumbed to very high rates of unemployment before most European countries in the 1970s, and by cutting taxes and expanding social assistance, the social democratic government developed significant budgetary deficits. Unemployment benefits allowed for a high degree of "decommodification" by allowing workers easily to escape the labor market; in addition, there were problems with the misuse of the funds as compensations for short-term layoffs, especially in seasonal industries. Unemployment soared from 0.9 percent in 1973 to 8.3 percent by 1978, and wage moderation was abandoned as unit labor costs increased by 80 percent between 1973 and 1980. In Phillips curve defying fashion, inflation hovered around 10 percent, and the national bank had to raise interest rates significantly to support the Danish krone's connection to the European currency Snake.[16]

Denmark began to resolve its economic problems in the mid 1980s, and the level of unemployment dropped (although unemployment rose again to 10 percent during the recession in the early 1990s). Most of the employment growth occurred in the private sector and was concomitant with increasing public budgetary surpluses. Reduction and better management of public debt (achieved with declining global interest rates) eased the growth of public expenditures; and increases in housing prices and a mortgage tax deduction fostered demand.[17] Nonetheless, concerns persisted about high levels of welfare state spending despite slower productivity growth.

Danes also worried about future labor shortages: Although fertility rates were among the highest in Europe in the 1990s, Danes had the second lowest life expectancy rates among EU countries. An early retirement scheme introduced in 1979 allowed insured individuals to retire at the age of 60 and increased projections of a labor deficit; moreover, high wages for low-skilled workers associated with collective bargaining restrained employment among low-skilled workers, prompting concerns about the development of a stable group of long-term and even multigenerational welfare recipients. Thus, even though economic equality actually improved over the course of the 1980s with higher levels of labor force participation, policy makers feared that this would not produce a corresponding rise in social equality among families at risk for poverty.[18]

Neoliberal Policy Reforms
Concerns about structural economic and demographic changes precipitated a turn to the right in political discourse across Europe, and Denmark was no exception. A bourgeois coalition government led by Poul Schlüter proposed broad ranging neoliberal reforms in the Modernization Plan of 1983, designed to bring public sector spending

[16] Goul Andersen 2007, 71–2; Plovsing 1998, 72; Scharpf 2000: 46–7, Scheuer 1992, 180; Iversen 1999.

[17] Scheurer 1992: 170; Goul Andersen 1997: 3–5; Madsen 2002. Schwartz adds that postindustrial manufacturing aided Danish SMEs recovery (Schwartz 2001a: 134.)

[18] Ministry of Labour, Ministry of Finance 1996; Goul Andersen 1997: 9; Mandag Morgen 1997a; Christoffersen 1996.

back under control, to jump-start the economy, to combat structural unemployment, and to address inadequate capital investment. Following the New Public Management model, Schlüter introduced budgetary reform (especially expenditure control), decentralization of welfare state spending decisions to the municipal level (with block grants), the adoption of market measures to solve social problems such as a greater reliance on outsourcing, deregulation (by making government more user-friendly to customers), and the introduction of private management strategies in government services. The government required unemployment recipients to prove their active job search and sought to reduce the levels and length of social insurance assistance. A tax reform was designed to unleash investment, to make the tax code more revenue neutral, to broaden the capital tax base, and to reduce the top individual tax rate (to 68 percent). Outsourcing was encouraged to inspire competition among service providers, to improve the provision of social service delivery and to reduce costs, although research found no evidence that private services were more productive. Municipalities were given block grants but forced to prioritize among competing goals: This served both to grant greater power and autonomy to Danish local governments and to hide budget cuts for the welfare state, and was supported by a strange bedfellows coalition of the left and right.[19]

The new public management ideas were to influence a quarter century of government reforms, and even the social democrats proposed policies that threatened the social democratic model. The package of bourgeois reforms posed obvious problems for the universal coverage of risks in terms of potential regional disparities, dualism, and reduced protections against social risks. Yet, although the reforms limited the growth in public consumption of services, they did not restrain the growth of income transfers to households and did not lead to much deregulation or contracting out.[20] Denmark sustained relatively high levels of coordination and egalitarian social policies against the various challenges and in spite of the popularity of neoliberal ideas. The following section delves into the Danish case to investigate, first, the endurance of high levels of labor market coordination and, second, the impact of macrocorporatism on solidaristic policies.

Sustaining Macrocorporatist Coordination

Stereotypes might lead one to conclude that the Danish case is fairly straightforward: Scandinavian cultural predilections for equality, macrocorporatist structures, and a universalistic welfare state should produce solutions that beget further equality and universalism. Yet, whereas deindustrialization and the problems of the Danish economy challenged macrocorporatism, high levels of coordination endured, in part, due to the structure of party competition and strategic interventions of state actors.

---

[19] Finansministeriet 1986; Scheuer 1992: 170; Ejersbo and Greve 2005; Green-Pedersen 2002; ; Viborg Andersen 1994, 15; Ganghof 2007, 1069; Christiansen 1998, 278–83; Schou 1988; Schwartz 2001.

[20] Ejersbo and Greve 2005; Campbell and Pedersen 2007; Goul Andersen 1997, 7–8; Christiansen 1998, 286; Viborg Andersen et al. 1994, 17–18. Green-Pedersen (2002) attributes the failure of market solutions in Denmark but not in Sweden to the opposition of the Danish Social Democrats, who did not hold power when New Public Management ideas arose.

Coordination came under attack in the 1980s, when sectoral divisions within DA and LO made it more difficult for the organizations to arrive at consensus about the framework for the national agreements. DA and LO signed a "declaration of intent" to decentralize aspects of work to the lowest level in order to interject greater flexibility within the Danish wage system and to achieve wage restraint (a special concern of companies in exposed sectors). The DA was decentralized and reorganized in 1994: Authority was transferred down to broad multisector associations in the areas of manufacturing, printing, construction, retail/services/ entertainment and wholesale/ transport. DA laid off a large portion of its staff and individual companies were no longer permitted to join DA, although individual employers continued to be involved with DA's many committees and other activities. The manufacturing sector organization, DI, gained enormous power with this move and retained over 50 percent of the votes. The organization retained some veto rights over bargains negotiated at the sectoral level, yet decentralization threatened to end the system of top-down concertation in incomes policy that had been a cornerstone of the Danish economy since the turn of the century.[21]

At the same time, firm-based networks were becoming more important than the old corporatist channels in areas such as industrial policy. Legislative lobbying by individual firms at times seemed to be making advances over corporatist negotiations in some policy areas. European Union directives also posed a threat to the hegemony of the social partners, since these directives largely stipulated action through legislation rather than through corporatist negotiation.[22]

The end of the Danish model seemed imminent, yet collective bargaining persisted through both Nyrup Rasmussen's social democratic government and bourgeois rule after 2001. The erosion of macrocorporatist structures was halted by governmental actions through purposeful efforts and unintended effects. Social democratic actors sought to shore up the institutions for cooperation in the sphere of collective bargaining, by threatening to intervene if the social partners couldn't reach agreement, and these threats prompted business and labor to cooperate in order to preserve their autonomy over labor market policies. Many struggles in the 1990s pitted the social partners on one side and the state on the other; for example, after a frustrating stalemate in the 1998 collective bargaining session, DA and LO tried to reassert control with a climate discussion to lay the framework for labor market policy.[23]

Threats of encroachment from the large and powerful state further bolstered business and labor determination to protect jurisdictional authority when bourgeois parties regained control of government in 2001. A rightist coalition government of the Liberal (Venstre) and Conservative (Konservative Folkeparti) parties, under the leadership of Anders Fogh Rasmussen, gained government in November 2001, aided by antiimmigrant sentiment, post-9/11 anxiety, and growing dissatisfaction with the social democrats. The new bourgeois leadership immediately sought to engineer a neoliberal makeover: Denmark would become a "welfare society" instead of a

---

[21] Due et al. 1994; Scheuer 1992; Jensen et al. 2000; Gill et al. 1998.
[22] Pedersen et al. 1992; Åkerstrom, Andersen, and Kjær, 1993; 1999; Christiansen and Nørgaard 2003; Scheuer 1992, 173; Gill et al. 1998.
[23] Jensen et al. 2000; Ugebrevet Mandag Morgen, September 1999.

"welfare state." To this end, the government sought to create greater freedom in the labor market (and to erode the social partners' control of the industrial relations system), to create more private social benefits, and, consequently, to expand dualism in social provision.[24]

The threats by Fogh Rasmussen and his new Employment Minister, Claus Hjort Frederiksen, to intervene in industrial relations strengthened the social partners' resolve to defend their terrain against a large and intrusive state. Immediately after taking office, the new government sought to roll back the jurisdictional authority of unions (and, by default, employers' associations as well) with two innovations: the establishment of a cross-sectoral public unemployment insurance fund and part-time work legislation. In both cases, unions experienced these reforms as a targeted assault, and employers' associations defended their union partners.

First, the government proposed cross-sectoral public unemployment insurance funds that would allow workers to choose to opt out of their own industries' funds in favor of the new fund. In the past, individuals had been required to belong to a fund connected to their occupation, but the reform would allow workers to shop around for the best unemployment insurance fund. This created the potential for enhanced dualism, in that individuals with a low risk of unemployment could join a fund with few unemployed members to obtain lower costs. In addition, since the unemployment funds have been a key way that unions have attracted membership, the measure threatened to erode the high union density that has long been a stable of Danish society.[25]

The government's proposal prompted immediate protest by organized labor, who viewed this move as an attack on unions (who ran the funds), a setback to the reemployment of workers, and an effort to create divisions within the ranks of labor.[26] Dansk Metal's leader, Max Bæhring, called the proposal a "declaration of war." LO, FTF, and AC submitted a joint hearing testimony to the parliament's labor market committee protesting the coalition government's interference into an arena historically left to the social partners.[27] Metal-working firms in Copenhagen and northern Jutland joined the protest and bolstered the membership of their key union, Dansk Metal, by agreeing to pay their employees' dues in Dansk Metal, as a way to discourage workers from leaving DM to join alternative funds. Even though the government ultimately created some small cross-sector funds, most LO unions refrained from raiding each others' members.[28]

Second, the bourgeois government proposed legislation to give individuals a statutory right to work part-time, which would not fall under the rules of collective bargaining and which would offer firms greater flexibility in hiring part-time workers. The right to work part-time work had hitherto been governed through collective bargains; therefore, this direct government regulation was an unusual intervention. Denmark has a relatively low rate of part-time work, compared to other European countries,

---

[24] Danmark Statsministeriet 2001.

[25] Danmark Statsministeriet 2001; Greve 2004, 164.

[26] Unions feared that the state fund would compete with private union funds (Frederiksen and Dalbro 2002) and worried that the multi-sector state fund would become a "trash can for the unemployed and inspire a rise in unemployment. LO Aktuelt 1/18/2002.

[27] Dansk Metal 12/4/2001; Frederiksen and Dalbro 2002.

[28] Scheuer 2007, 242; Hyldtoft 2002.

and Danish atypical workers enjoy more comprehensive social protections than their counterparts elsewhere.[29]

The bourgeois government's proposal to regulate part-time work was severely criticized by a broad cross section of Danish society, including the parties on the left, labor unions, and employers. Unions and employers' associations perceived the proposed legislation as an attack on their jurisdictional authority to negotiate collective agreements, as the reform declared as invalid provisions negotiated in collective bargaining that interfered with the right to work part-time. In this vein, LO Formand, Hans Jensen, protested that the law would complicate the individual wage earner's ability to protect himself or herself in a hiring relationship, would reduce the likelihood that part-time workers would receive the social benefits guaranteed to full-time employees, would force individual companies to conclude many collective bargains, and constituted an assault on the Danish model. In "the largest show of union force since the 1980s" according to LO's Harald Borsting, 154 unions met to protest the cross-sector unemployment funds and part-time work legislation. The major labor unions – LO, FTF, and AC – lodged a complaint to the International Labour Organization, that recommended that the government resume consultations with the social partners.[30]

Employers joined labor in protesting the labor market reforms: DA testified to the Folketing that a law guaranteeing the implementation of the part-time directive was acceptable only if it built on a negotiation by the labor market partners and guaranteed a directive at a minimum level. DA Director, Jørn Neergaard stated to the Danish paper, *Extra Bladet*, that the part-time legislation was an intrusion into the free system of negotiated talks and collective bargaining." Dansk Industri joined LO in signing an open letter to the parliament, protesting that politicians had no right to legislate when collective agreements had already been concluded and LO applauded Dansk Arbejdsgiverne's criticism of the reform.[31] A law on part-time work finally passed in June 2002, however, the bill precluded the replacement of collective bargaining agreements and this concession was viewed as a victory for labor.[32]

Thus, the legacies of macrocorporatist institutions and a large public sector (an outgrowth of multiparty competition and centralization) helped to sustain coordination in Denmark against postindustrial threats. The large public sector challenged private employers and workers to remain coordinated in order to protect their prerogatives of power, even when right parties gained power and employers might well have chosen to abandon coordination for the benefits of neoliberal individualism.

The Impact of Macrocorporatism on Active Labor Market Policy

We now turn to the impact of macrocorporatist institutions for coordination on employer support for and participation in active labor market policies and suggest

---

[29] Danmark Statsministeriet 2001; Buschoff and Protsch 2008, 54, 70.
[30] Deltidsansatte mister beskyttelse, LO Aktuelt 1/11/2002; LO Aktuelt 1/8/2002; LO Aktuelt 3/1/2002; Eironline 3/2003.
[31] Muntzberg 1/10/2002; LO Aktuelt 3/11/2002.
[32] Eironline 6/2002.

that high levels of coordination shaped active labor market policies in a manner that emphasized real skills development among low-skilled workers and protected solidaristic arrangements benefitting a wide cross section of workers. The Labour Market Reforms of 1994, 1996, and 1999 and the 1998 Law on Active Social Policy created ALMP in Denmark.[33] The reforms required unemployed youth to move into the 'activation' stream within six months and unemployed adults, within one year to set time limits on the receipt of passive benefits. Once activated, recipients would meet with a Public Employment Service representative to develop an individual action plan for training or for a time-limited job in the private sector (with a roughly 50 percent state subsidy). The reform created leave and job-rotation schemes, to rotate the unemployed into private sector jobs while the regular workers went on child care, education, or sabbatical leaves. The reforms also created subsidized minimum-wage jobs (fleksjob and skaanejob) for disabled individuals with "permanently-reduced working capacities."[34]

The active labor market programs seemed to go against Danish policy legacies in two important ways. First, the policies threatened the generous albeit passive unemployment benefits that had historically been a major means of guaranteeing high levels of equality. Until the 1990s, most of the Danish expenditures were on passive measures; thus, in 1985 Sweden's active component was 70 percent of total labor market spending, but Denmark's was only 21 percent. These benefits allowed for a high degree of "decommodification," allowing workers easy exit from the labor market and critics feared that the ALMP initiatives might strip citizens of their social rights and smack of social control.[35] Yet, the social democratic version of ALMP, in fact, targeted welfare reform to the real employment needs of low-skilled workers; moreover, by linking benefits reduction to greater rights to training, the ruling party sustained social democratic values.[36]

Second, despite the historical administration of most training and programs for the long-term unemployed by the state, the new active programs relied much more heavily on employers than past approaches to social assistance. Business was asked to

---

[33] The changes in the rules governing unemployment benefits were done in stages. The Labour Market Reform in 1994 limited the amount of time that a person could passively receive benefits to four years and, thereafter, required the unemployed to go into an activation period in a subsidized jobs, education, or training program. The 1994 reform also transferred control over activation to the regional labor market councils, which were mandated to match unemployed to local jobs. Subsidized jobs were created for those with reduced working capacities and leave schemes rotated the unemployed into jobs while employed persons took child-care, education, or sabbatical leaves. The 1996 Finance Act Agreement began activation after two years and created a new protected jobs scheme for those with reduced working capacities for whom no rehabilitation and reentry into ordinary work was possible. These new subsidized minimum-wage jobs (in which the state paid up to 50 percent of wages) were located in the public sector and were aimed at replacing earlier job training programs (Ministry of Labour, Ministry of Finance, 1996). A third phase of reform, passed in 1999, limited passive benefits to one year for adults and six months for unemployed unskilled youth. On the social policy side, the move toward activation had been happening within municipalities since the 1980s. The Law on Active Social Policy of September 1998 consolidated the rules on social support, rehabilitation, protected jobs, and activation by the municipalities, to emphasize early intervention, and to enhance individual responsibility. Søndergaard 2001.
[34] "Danmarks Nationale Handlingsplan for Beskaeftigelse 1999."
[35] Hagen 1992, 153–63; OECD 2001, 24; Cox 1997; Abrahamson 1998.
[36] Munk Christiansen et al. 2004; Jørgensen 2003.

implement jobs and training, based on a belief that private programs are more efficacious than public sector ones. Despite the prior absence of any business involvement with the long-term unemployed, the active labor market and social reforms received broad support from the social partners.[37] Thus, one wonders how the Danish state was able to preserve a more social democratic version of the bill and to persuade employers to participate.

We credit macrocorporatist institutions, in part, for the solidaristic orientation of the active policies and for the significant involvement of employers in the programs for low-skilled workers. First, the macrocorporatist institutions solved a *collective action* problem for employers, in allowing the social partners to have enormous input into the development of the active labor market policies; and these processes were largely responsible for enabling employers and workers to tailor the programs to real employment needs. The programs were created through tripartite processes in which business and labor peak associations played a major role. A Labor Market Commission (the Zeuthen Udvalg) composed of key politicians, bureaucrats, and representatives of the major associations had the task of bringing a more active approach to the delivery of unemployment insurance, and the bulk of its recommendations were incorporated into the Social Democrat's first labor market reform in 1994.[38] A parallel social commission issued a series of recommendations for changing the public benefits structure – in unemployment/welfare benefits area, in education reform, in early retirement, and in the creation of special job for those with reduced working capacities. There was remarkably little disagreement within the commission and perhaps 80 percent of its recommendations subsequently became regulations. In 1995, the social partners negotiated clauses in their collective bargaining agreements, called "social chapters," that committed both sides to the creation of jobs with special terms of employment. In addition, in May 1995 the Labor and Social Ministries set up a committee on protected jobs to expand and to recommend the terms of state-subsidized jobs for those individuals who had permanently reduced working capacities and could no longer be employed under normal conditions. The committee included representatives from the Labor, Social, and Finance Ministries, DA, the Farmer Employer Union, LO, KL and the County Workers Union.

The LO and DA were particularly important in the development of the third labor market reform in 1999, in developing a full-fledged proposal (fælles konklusionspapir) to lay the groundwork for this initiative. Because the two social partners had fulfilled the "consensus principle" (i.e., offering complete agreement on a detailed plan), they had the right to determine the labor market regulation; consequently, the legislature passed the bill into law virtually without changes. The government also set up the "2005 Committee" to make recommendations about Denmark's future labor market needs. Following the tradition of representatives from business and labor overseeing labor market policy, the 1999 law also required municipalities to set up corporatist committee consisting of representatives from business and labor to oversee programs for those on social assistance and to reduce unemployment in the community.[39] Dansk

[37] Madsen 1997, 8–9; J. Martin, 2000, 92 ; DA 12/171998: 7; DA, Agenda 10/2/1997.
[38] Mailand 2000, 127–9; Nørgaard 1997.
[39] Christiansen et al. 2004, 88–117.

Arbejdgiversforening is responsible for selecting company participants to sit on these local social coordination committees. Employers had formerly had responsibilities for unemployed insured workers, but the uninsured on social assistance were left to the state, and creating these committees at the local level was a significant innovation.

Our firm-level study also demonstrates that the collective action effects of corporatist employers' associations were very important to individual firms' willingness to engage in the programs. The associations made employers feel that they had influence on the creation of the active plans, especially within the municipal social coordination committees. Many of our respondents identified these committees as an important source of information about labor market policy and felt that they had significant input into the design of local programs. Thus, groups such as the Ishøj Resource Group or the Glostrup Network were crucial sources of inspiration for participation. One manager recalls efforts to generate support in the local community for welfare reform: The committee planned a "talk show" to teach firms about the programs, in which a TV star interviewed former welfare recipients who had successfully made the transition to the world of work.[40] Of course DA was unlikely to select employers as representatives who were completely hostile to the social arena, but employers usually had limited experience with social partnerships before being called to duty by DA. In fact, firms that participated in such corporatist committees (and in the association-sponsored networks described later) often ended up with positions to the left of those formally specified by their employer associations.

Second, the corporatist institutions offered a vehicle for the state to build up business support, and government policy makers made significant overtures to employers through the associations. In part, the government was able to bring the associations on board by appealing to their institutional interests and framing active labor market policies as a new growth area in an era in which collective bargaining was declining. Recognizing the pressures on collective bargaining, the associations sought to cultivate comparative advantages in other activities in order to continue to attract members and experimented with formal and informal policy study groups and networks, such as the Danish Industry's Human Resources Think Tank. One major sector organization observed that the decentralizing pressures on collective wage negotiations meant that "fewer firms will need organizations to give them advice about collective bargaining." But because "companies will still need other kinds of advice" this group expanded its functions to attract a more diversified membership, by developing informational networks:

The networks provide, along with other things, a platform from which firms can figure out what they think about issues ... Today the associations have to come up with reasons for members to pay for belonging to a group, such as to develop political positions ... Having political influence is a collective good, but you always have the free rider problem. So you have to have some individual goods as well to keep up the membership.[41]

The Danish state periodically used sticks as well as carrots to keep the business associations committed to its reform agenda. Despite the business role in designing the

---

[40] Interviews with firm respondents on 12/22/2000, 3/26/2001, and 12/20/2000.
[41] Interview with organizational representative.

programs, at periodic points in the process, both business and labor expressed reluctance to support the active policies and they were subsequently encouraged to remain committed to solidaristic positions by aggressive political leaders. The Social Ministry turned to coercion when it feared that the umbrella associations would not give sufficient support to the reforms, and reached out to individual firms with a campaign to change managers' attitudes entitled "Our Common Concern" (Det Angaar Os Alle).[42] This represented a dramatic break with tradition, because in those policy areas where the labor market partners had jurisdiction, government had refrained from excessive intervention and had left much to business and labor to work out together. One participant commented, "This new approach – of the ministry trying to intervene directly in society and trying to mobilize society – was a completely new way of doing things." Following this campaign, the Social Minister, Karen Jespersen, formed in 1996 a group of fifteen major companies, called the National Network of Firms, which was given the dual tasks of advising the Social Ministry on how to approach the private sector and of exhorting the broader business community to assume its social responsibility. This direct outreach to the firms was a major deviation from past tradition of working through the associations. An industry respondent reflected the associational view when he remarked, "DA and DI didn't like the firms getting involved with the ministry; they were worried that there would be anarchy. Individual firms could give all sorts of opinions, with one firm saying one thing and another firm saying another. But the associations speak with one voice for all business."[43] The Social Ministry's actions had the effect of prompting the Danish employers' associations to stay active in the labor market and social reforms.

State efforts to bring in the social partners periodically broke down, as happened during the encompassing labor market (den rummelige arbejdsmarked) discussions in 2000; yet unilateral action by the state quickly reminded the social partners how important it was to remain viable participants in the policy process. The negotiations fell apart over disagreement about unemployment benefits linked to the protected jobs.[44] Subsequent unilateral state action without significant social partner input gave both business and labor renewed commitment to reach future agreements in order to stay in the political game. After the negotiations on the protected jobs (and the encompassing labor market) fell apart, the social partners vowed to develop a joint proposal on improvements to the activation process before the next set of political negotiations. The social partners did not want to be excluded from the decision-making process, or as a business respondent put it, "DA and LO were like siamese twins in both needing to retain their credibility as willing participants in the political dialogue."[45]

The importance of state outreach was also obvious in the individual firms' decisions to participate in the plans. Among firms that found it necessary to contact the local

---

[42] Danish National Institute of Social Research 1997; Holt 1998, 9–10.

[43] Interviews with respondents.

[44] The LO wanted worker on protected jobs to remain in the union-controlled unemployment funds while the DA did not, and preferred that the municipalities pay extra subsidies for protected workers (Winkel 10/16/2000; DA 3/16/2000, 6). The municipal employers association, KL, also raised concerns about who would offer all of the protected jobs, and demanded a "proper ratio" between the public and private sectors (interviews).

[45] Interview with organization representative 2001.

government or labor market agency, 74 percent of the Danish firms recalled a positive experience, but only 47 percent of the British firms found the local government
response positive. Forty percent of the Danish firms had received vigorous outreach
by the local government, whereas only 27 percent of the British firms received vigorous outreach. One manager felt somewhat overwhelmed when he received "about one
application a week" from the AF, municipality, or union.[46] Many municipalities hired
"firm consultants" to visit firms and to identify potential protected jobs and many firms
felt that these consultants greatly assisted their involvement with active social policy.
Some municipalities held regular weekly or monthly sessions at large companies to
evaluate the needs of problematic employees and to give advice about state programs
to meet those needs.[47]

Third, macrocorporatism associations had *political economic effects*, in that the
plans – tailored to real economic needs by a process of social partnership – resulted
in programs with mechanisms for developing real skills and real jobs. The devices to
end long-term unemployment (the employment trial schemes and job training) were
linked to the upskilling of the general population; thus, job rotation schemes allow
firms to hire with state subsidies the long-term unemployed while their own employees receive skills training.[48] The plans also created protected jobs for disabled people
with "reduced working capacities," in an effort to bring everyone into an "encompassing labor market." With these subsidized jobs for the disabled (which required firms
to pay only two-thirds or one-half of the wage), the state addressed a problem facing
firms in companies with high wages for low-skilled workers: Demands for productivity
and flexibility made it more difficult for firms to retain workers that could not perform
at top speed, and many functions within the firm (e.g., canteen, cleaning, or security
jobs) were being outsourced. Companies could not afford to ease long-term employees
into more relaxed positions as they became less able to handle their workloads (or to
hire new workers with limited capacities to work), and such workers often ended up
on early retirement or in the social support system. Thus, the state sought to make it
easier for firms gratify their own self-interests in taking part in programs to fight social
exclusion.[49]

These political economic effects were evident in our study of individual firms'
involvement in the programs because although some Danish firms expressed concerns
about the program design, they generally believed that the programs offered real skills,
unlike their British counterparts. Firms with blue-collar workers at all skills levels (i.e.,
not white-collar workers) were significantly more likely to participate in Denmark
because they hoped with the programs to gain access to a new labor pool, whereas,
in Britain, only firms with the least-skilled workers participated to get cheap labor.
Thirty-one percent of the Danish firms offered labor shortages as a reason for participating, compared with 22 percent of the British firms, and although British firms
participated in the program for political reasons, Danish firms saw the programs as
meeting real economic needs. As one manager explained, it might "take a bit longer to

[46] Interview with industry respondent 5/15/2001.
[47] Social Ministry 1999, 23–4; Interviews with industry respondents 12/12/00, 4/19/2001; 2/20/2001.
[48] Arbejdsmarkedstyrelsen 3/16/2000.
[49] Teknologisk Institut 2000, 11.

make sure that these workers can do OK," but they often turned out to be productive employees of the firm. Many firms used the job rotation schemes to upskilled all of their low-skilled workers to an "industrial operator" qualification, which developed basic skills and flexibility of workers without specialized training. One firm reported using job rotation to reduce "the barriers between production workers and the skilled mechanics who fix the machines" so that production could move more seamlessly on the shop floor. Not all companies felt that they could derive benefits from the programs. A firm in an industry undergoing significant structural change explained that the firm "emphasizes shopfloor management, flexibility and upskilling. This makes it much harder to have weak workers in the company, since the weak workers can't live up to the higher demands of flexible production. A firm utilizing very highly-skilled white-collar workers explained: "It would be hard for an unemployed person to come into a company where everyone is so high functioning in a substantive area." Another reported, "People in our business can't make mistakes – these can lose lives. We do a lot of building on water or through the jungle. People have to work very hard and have to be able to handle stress. They can't flip out." Yet some companies using very highly educated workers were able to participate: Carl Bro, a large engineering company, created an active labor market program for unemployed immigrants, with extensive educational experiences in their countries of origin, but whose qualifications did not meet Danish standards.[50]

Finally the *cognitive* effects of belonging to an association seemed particularly important to companies' preference formation. As we saw in the quantitative analysis presented in Chapter 8, Danish firms often identified the associations as their primary source of information, and membership was a significant determinant of participation in the programs. The respondents offered repeated testimonials to the importance of corporatist employers' associations in bringing them to engage with the active social programs. Many employers identified the social coordination committees and DA sponsored networks as their entre into the realm of active social policy process and reported that these enhanced employers' understanding of social exclusion issues. The groups' informal networks or discussion groups (erfargruppe) were also important, and these task forces often took policy positions to the left of the peak groups' formal positions.

The associations also helped member firms to think in collective terms about the problems of long-term unemployment, as evidenced by respondents' frequent reference to collective goals such as achieving an encompassing labor market and corporate social responsibility. Whereas 51 percent of the Danish firms offered social responsibility as an incentive for participation in active social programs, only 26 percent of the British firms thought to mention this motivation. As one manager recalled, "The interest in participating in the social partnership for unemployed people came out of an interest in expressing social responsibility, getting new workers and retraining the workers that we currently had." Of course, not all employers shared this feeling of social responsibility or believed that the long-term unemployed required such extensive support. One manager explained, "The company pays so much tax, it should be relieved of the obligation to take care of these people," and another favored tax relief

---

[50] Interviews with industry respondents 3/29/2001; 2/20/2001; 4/24/01; 3/28/2001.

as a quid pro quo. Yet at times the desire to curb the excesses of the welfare state pushed firms to participate in the programs. Employers in a town in Northern Jutland decided:

We want to end a chronic situation of young people under 25 without education ... The firm has no concerns about labor power for itself, but is very concerned about the area. The local culture in the area cannot tolerate all of this unemployment. It is really irritating in a fishing culture to see people on unemployment sit around and smoke cigarettes and play the guitar.[51]

Macrocorporatist Impacts on Subsequent Bourgeois Reforms

The impacts of macrocorporatist institutions on active labor market programs contin-ued after the bourgeois parties regained control of government in 2001. Prime Minister Anders Fogh Rasmussen hoped to scale back welfare state spending – both active and passive – by capping municipal taxes, introducing options for private social provi-sion, and imposing user fees. In particular, Fogh Rasmussen proposed cutting back the amount spent on "activating" individuals in active labor market programs by 1.5 billion kroner.[52]

Response to the proposed changes was quite negative, and both LO and DA strongly objected to the budget cuts in active labor market policy, fearing that this would result in bottlenecks. Thus, according to DA's Tina Voldby, this move would risk putting many into long-term unemployment and could cost more in the long run. LO's consul-tant, Kim Knudsen, doubted whether private services could solve bottlenecks, increase mobility, or deal with structural unemployment. Municipal public governments pro-tested the proposal as an invasion of their jurisdiction by the national government and the newsletter, *Mandag Morgen*, observed that this moved signaled the end of activation by the municipalities.[53]

Eventually the bourgeois government backed away from many aspects of the plans. At one press conference, Claus Hjort Frederiksen, the starkly ideological employment minister, issued a stirring call for aggressive reform: It should only pay to work, it was a moral injustice that 25,000 on social assistance were passively living off the state and the government was going to rid Denmark of its passive support for unemployment. Two minutes later, however, Anders Fogh Rasmussen, prime minister and consum-mate politician, made a very different political promise: "There is one thing I want to get clear. The government has no plans to do a general reduction of the [social assis-tance] support." At the end of the day, the bourgeois actions strongly resembled the prior social democratic government's approach and both LO and DA supported the revised active labor market recommendations, with only SiD, the union for low-skilled workers, remaining opposed.[54]

After the first set of reforms, the bourgeois government set up a welfare com-mission to reform various aspects of social provision and proposed a welfare reform in April 2006. The reform aimed to expand employment activity of young people,

[51] Interviews with industry respondents 4/24/2001; 3/12/2001; 3/7/2001; 3/14/2001; 5/16/2001; 4/26/2001.
[52] Andersen 12/10/2001; Danmark Statsministeriet 2001.
[53] LO Aktuelt 1/10/2002; Winkel 3/4/2002, 8.
[54] Quote translated by C. J. Martin. Winkel 6/3/2002, 29–30; Albret 9/16/2002.

older people and immigrants and key recommendations included reducing the financial advantages of remaining on unemployment supports, speeding up the entry of
youth into employment and improving the integration of immigrants. Those younger
than 30 who lacked educational qualifications would receive only 50 percent of their
unemployment benefits if they refused to begin an educational or vocational training
program.[55]

The welfare commission's report and subsequent reform proposal drew criticism
from business, labor and the municipalities, and this served to dampen significantly
the neoliberal aspects of the plans. For example, LO argued that there were "too
many whips in the air" and too much punishment with too little positive action. The
final moderate, compromise legislation was supported by LO, DA, and political parties across the spectrum, who agreed that the legislation represented a far-reaching
reform of the protection of risks against unemployment. The compromise legislation
also marked a turning point in the bourgeois government's neoliberal ambitions to
roll back the public sector and to privatize the welfare state. At last, the government
abandoned the ambition that the private sector should grow at the expense of the public sector and recognized that Denmark's capacity to be both highly competitive and
harmonic was because of the public sector rather than despite it.[56]

Conclusion

At the end of the 1970s, Denmark was mired in skyrocketing unemployment and out-
of-control deficit, and the enormous public clambering for radical change culminated
in the electoral victory of two conservative governments in the past three decades.
Ultimately, however, Denmark managed to restructure its welfare state with active
labor market policies that preserved the spirit of social democratic solidarity and
investment in low-skilled workers, even while moving the long-term unemployed off
passive employment benefits and curing some other traps of the welfare state. This
chapter has investigated how Denmark sustained both coordination and solidarity at a
time when its highly coordinated labor market institutions and extensive welfare state
benefits were under attack.

We suggest that the features of the state responsible for the creation of macrocorporatism also contributed to sustaining high levels of coordination again postindustrial assaults. Even though deindustrialization has certainly taken its toll on the
organization of employers, from a cross-national perspective, Denmark has sustained
relatively high levels of labor market coordination. At the beginning of the twentieth
century, politicians and party leaders organized employers for political control and
policy ambition, at the end, these leaders asked the social partners to help implement social programs to address changing skills needs. Moreover, PR party systems
with centralized governments are associated with the growth of public sectors. In the
Danish case, municipal employers expanded and relied on corporatist channels to
address the needs of the long-term unemployed.

---

[55] "Fremtidens velstand og velfærd."
[56] LO Aktuelt 2006; "Drop Pisken, Fogh," 5/17/2006; "Compromise on welfare reform," *European Industrial
Relations Review* July 2006, 5; Mandag Morgen.11/2/2006, 4–5.

The macrocorporatist institutions, in turn, played a major role in the solidaristic nature of Danish active labor market policies. The social democratic government in the 1990s promoted the expansion of the core economy to include nearly all workers and used its labor market power to construct a cross-class coalition of employers' associations and unions to direct investment toward low-skilled workers. The state sought to involve these private business and labor organizations in the collective effort to expand the labor market participation of the long-term unemployed, a group that historically fell under the jurisdiction of the state. The core employers' associations and unions became active in the active labor market policy debates, in part, to preserve their jurisdictional authority over insured unemployed workers (who were handled by the insurance funds) and to expand a pool of skilled workers they viewed as necessary for remaining competitive in international markets. Macrocorporatist institutions exposed employers to the technical arguments about the economic benefits of active labor market policies and employers came to believe in the benefits of policies – to fold all workers into an encompassing labor market, which would sustain solidarity and economic growth.

The macrocorporatist structures continued to bias policy toward solidaristic outcomes even when the bourgeois parties gained power again after 2001. Business and labor associations staved off neoliberal attacks on their jurisdiction and on active labor market spending. LO and its business allies emphasized unskilled workers' rights to be integrated into the core economy over their rights to be decommodified and this points to the curious paradox of policy proposals that seem to sustain social solidarity. These policies eroded the rights of individual workers to exit the labor force, but they also expanded the labor force participation and skills of low-skill workers.[57]

Public servants in this large public sector, especially at the municipal level, also supported investments in low-skilled workers. They were both responsible for and likely to hire low-skilled workers and were motivated by productivity concerns to enhance the skills of the unemployed. Thus, the succession of reforms implemented by successive (and ideologically diverse) administrations since 1982 have been marked less by change than by continuity, because this core coalition of actors have helped to maintain solidaristic alternatives to the neoliberal reform ideas that swept through Denmark just as they captured the attention of the rest of the western world.[58] The government, ultimately, refrained from rolling back the welfare state, after municipal bureaucrats and the social partners were able to neutralize the neoliberal aims. The detailed realization of reforms was heavily shaped by this strange bedfellows coalition, which persisted through successive governments and helped to produce solidaristic, coordinated solutions to the issues at hand.

---

[57] The biggest detractors of the active labor market policies, in fact, were the unskilled workers (in SiD, which became 3F) who potentially had the most to gain from upskilling, but who resented the forcible end to decommodification. Yet the rest of organized labor within LO, FTF, and AC, and joined by the employers federation DA, believed that a permanent exclusion of marginal workers was a threat to equality and to social solidarity, and in the specific case of early retirement, praised the compromise.

[58] Christiansen 1998.

10

Employers and Active Labor Market Policy in Postindustrial Britain

Introduction

Britain offers a startling counterpoint to the Danish story of social investment in low-skilled workers. Despite extravagant claims to the contrary, the Blair administration only marginally improved the plight and skills of lower-class Brits, and ultimately did little to attract business and labor to the cause. Even though Blair's New Deal active labor market program to combat low skills and poverty was modestly social democratic, public investment actually declined and the income gap between rich and poor expanded. Employers participated in only a minimal way to enhance the human capital of low-skilled workers and few jobs for the long-term unemployed were created in the private sector by Blair's labor market initiative – about 40,000 out of 540,000 new jobs in the early years of the program. There is a tendency to conclude "plus ca change, plus la meme chose" about this story, and why would we ever expect much in the way of support for a seemingly impenetrable underclass in this land of Hobbes and Dickens? In this vein, the Blair experiments have been explained by long-standing structural constraints.[1]

Yet, Britain's fate at the end of the twentieth century may not have been quite so inevitable. After nearly two decades of Tory rule, Blair assumed office with a mandate to strike a "New Deal" between state and society, business and labor, the haves and have-nots. The New Labour government made substantial investments in programs for the long-term unemployed; indeed, Britain and Denmark spent exactly the same percentage of the GDP on improving the public employment service. In addition, Blair's promised renaissance may have come at an auspicious time. With the advent of services, jobs for blue-collar manufacturing workers with mid-range skills have greatly disappeared, vocational training programs are less important than general education programs for service workers, and general education is a more viable institution in the British liberal market economy. Blair's substantial investments in education partly paid off: Britain had lagged 14 points behind Germany in its proportion of 19–21 year olds

---

[1] Wickham-Jones 2004, 118, 115; Coates 2001; Hay 1997.

who attained Level 3, and by 2003 roughly the same percentage in each country had reached this educational level.[2] Yet these gains did little to alter the economic circumstances of the long-term unemployed.

This chapter considers why, despite some successes, Britain had such a difficult time enhancing investments in low-skilled workers and getting employers to play a major part in this effort. Even though the education system might be improving Britain's performance in the postindustrial economy, the system of business organization is constraining success. We argue that the same structure of two-party competition that worked against the evolution of corporatism at the beginning of the twentieth century (along with the consequent limited growth of the state) diminished efforts to bolster employer coordination at century's end. The Conservative Party under Margaret Thatcher easily managed to eviscerate British labor unions and the peak employers' association, as no multiparty, coalition-government consensus model worked against radical change in this two-party system; moreover, no large group of public sector bureaucrats provided a political base to withstand the neoliberal campaign to roll back the state. When "New Labour" Prime Minister Tony Blair came to power, he did little to change this state of affairs. The administration sought business and labor engagement on the New Deal, but it did not launch an offensive to strengthen unions and collective business organizations that was comparable in magnitude to Thatcher's concerted efforts to disorganize workers and employers. Although the Blair administration did a lot of shoulder tapping of individual CEOs, it largely used media outreach as a mechanism for bringing employers onto the program. The government could not threaten to invade the policy-making turf of organized business and labor – and these private sector actors did not cooperate to protect their policy-making turf – because the social partners had no prerogatives of political power. Just as business and labor efforts to gain responsibility for self-regulation were dashed by the interplay of party competition in 1918, business and labor continued to be marginal to policy wars between the two major parties in the 1980s and 1990s.

The absence of macrocorporatism, in turn, worked against employers' positive support for and involvement in programs for low-skilled workers. Pluralism has a limited institutional capacity for collective action: No collective bargaining or tripartite institutions unify the business community, and the Blair administration could not depend on a highly organized business groups to help create and to implement new programs for training low-skilled workers. Pluralism had a political economic effect in contributing to the development of a low-skills regime in Britain: Training institutions in this regime largely served to mitigate poverty rather than to generate real skills, and employers had a difficult time believing that the new active labor market policies would differ from past experiments. Finally, the absence of macrocorporatist employers' associations had a cognitive effect, in that the British pluralist associations were not an important source of information for individual firms or a vehicle for linking business to the state.

The following pages explore challenges associated with deindustrialization, efforts at reform, and the ways in which features of political competition and the institutional legacies of pluralism thwarted Blair's efforts to achieve higher levels of business

---

[2] OECD 2004; Steedman and Wagner 2006; Steedman et al. 2004, 6.

coordination. We then explore how the lack of employer organizational capacity in this pluralist system contributed to Blair's failure to escape the dysfunctional aspects of prior British labor market and social policy interventions.

Cleavages, Crises, and Reforms

The failed political struggles for coordination in the early Twentieth-Century set into place a system of pluralist business and labor organizations – that reinforced cleavages in the British economy – and contributed to the emergence of a liberal welfare state regime, with limited social investment in human capital. Financial and manufacturing concerns have never been easily reconciled in Britain: Early leadership in international banking brought financiers to resist any policies that threatened the value of the pound sterling and devaluation, whereas manufacturing interests were more interested in stimulating economic growth. As opposed to Germany, where production is funded through long-term relations with banks, most British investment capital is raised on the stock market or channeled through short-term loans and banks lacked the acute understanding of manufacturing needs demonstrated by their German brethren.[3]

Finance and service sectors have become even more dominant in the postindustrial age. The British economy still included a significant share of heavy industry (shipbuilding, textiles, and railways) in the 1960s and lighter consumer industries (cars, chemicals, energy, aircraft, and light engineering) in the 1970s; by the 1980s, however, deindustrialization redirected most economic activity into services such as banking, retailing, and knowledge-based industries. This was accompanied by other dramatic changes: mergers concentrating ownership in the largest firms, foreign purchases of British companies, and offshore production by British firms. By 1998 services constituted 71 percent of the British economy, making Britain – like Denmark – one of the more postindustrial countries in Europe.[4]

The stark economic cleavages have been reinforced by the British industrial relations system and the liberal welfare state. Britain has pluralist, weakly organized, decentralized employer associations and trade unions, and collective bargaining agreements cover only a small part of the British economy. By 1975 only about 50 percent of the workforce was covered by unions, and the peak organization, the Trades Union Congress (TUC), had limited control over its member unions. One might be tempted to conclude that the impotence of the British industrial relations system was merely endogenous to the sectoral conflict between industrial and financial sectors or to the predilections of a liberal market economy; however, the Labour Party periodically achieved higher levels of coordination between the social partners. Britain in the 1960s and 1970s had higher levels of unionization, coordination, and consultation by the state with the social partners. For example, at the "Brighton Revolution" of 1960, the Federation of British Industries organized a conference of leading employers and bureaucrats to discuss economic problems and to consider policy solutions associated with a planned economy. Inspired by French planning, the National Economic Development Council (NEDC) was set up to provide a forum for tripartite discussions

[3] Hall 1986; Zysman 1983.
[4] Coates 2001; OECD 2000b, 84–7.

within industries where employers and unions could make harmonious adjustments and learn to govern themselves.[5]

These periodic efforts at coordination failed, however, because government bureaucrats had limited capacity to organize industry, and business was insufficiently organized to consider its own long-term collective interests. A fragmentation of responsibilities among government agencies meant that no entity could claim to coordinate industrial policy, and manufacturing interests suffered as macroeconomic policy discouraged capital investment. The Treasury Department controlled fiscal policy, and the Bank of England determined monetary policy: The Bank of England sought to prevent inflation and devaluation, the Treasury sought to stimulate economic growth, and macroeconomic policy engaged in a stop-go cycle of expansion followed by restrictive monetary measures to prevent devaluation, keeping the prices of British goods higher than they would be with devaluation. The NEDC's experimentation with tripartite boards to allocate resources fostered corporatist-style negotiations, but the boards tended to indulge in "lemon socialism," allocating funds to save firms and regions. In some cases the British legacy of tripartism and compromise had sanguine results: The legacy of tripartism in the British Health and Safety Commission was to produce a consensual deliberation process in the area of health and safety regulation.[6] But despite greater moments of coordination and state efforts on their behalf, British industrial relations largely continued on the track established at the end of the first world war and never achieved the high levels of cooperation found in continental Europe.

The weakness of the industrial relations system had a powerful impact on the development of skills in British society, because employers and workers lacked the coordinating capacity to generate a high level of skills. The liberal welfare system did little to link the needs of economic production to social protection: Protections against unemployment have been very limited, and universal transfers are modest, giving workers few safeguards against the risks of investing in specific skills. A large component of social benefits is provided through the private sector, many public benefits are allocated on a means-tested basis, and both income taxes and welfare spending are low. Citizens enjoy rights to "formal" welfare state benefits (health care, education, and pensions), but the flat-rate pension system is quite small, the National Health Service is inadequately funded and the incomes policy has no pretensions for redistribution. Thus, many more Brits suffer from inadequate training and poverty than citizens in other advanced industrial nations.[7] In 2009, Britain had 8 percent unemployment and 25 percent of the total was long-term unemployment. Whereas 26 percent of the German workforce has no vocational qualifications, 64 percent of the British workforce suffers from this glaring gap. Levels of inequality in Britain were comparable to its European counterparts in the late 1970s, and they rose rapidly throughout the Thatcher years; thus, the 90–10 wage ratio for workers rose from 2.79 in 1979 to 3.38 by 1995; in 2005, the 90–10 ratio had increased to 3.5. In 2000 low-wage workers (i.e., those making less than

[5] Hall 1986; Coates 2001; Cronin 2000; Furner and Supple 1990; MacDougall 1987, 136; Middlemas 1990, 37–43.
[6] Grant 1991, 101–12; Hall 1986, 248–52; Wilson 1985, 152–3.
[7] Esping-Andersen, 1990; Rhodes 2001.

one half the median wage) constituted 20 percent of the total workforce in Britain, but only 8 percent in Denmark.[8]

The split between Britain and her continental neighbors has been especially pronounced in the area of labor market policy. Lacking the conception of a social wage, labor market policy has been relegated to residual services for the unemployed, emphasizing negative constraints against unemployment (low benefits) over positive inducements such as training opportunities. The labor exchange, responsible for both administering labor market programs and unemployment benefits, focused on managing the unemployed to the neglect of other employment concerns and became tainted as a refuge for the dregs of the labor market. Something closer to a tripartite approach to training was attempted in the 1960s with the Industrial Training Boards, which were composed of representatives from business and labor and were mandated to issue a training levy on the companies within their sectors. Yet the Labour Party was ultimately unable to garner union commitment to goals of modernization through industrial policy and incomes policy or business consensus about the delivery of training services. Thus, the training system was historically market-driven, largely voluntaristic, and limited, and firms underspent on training due to fears that trained staff would be poached by other companies.[9]

As in Denmark, the British economy came under severe strains in the 1970s and 1980s, with high unemployment and slow growth. Unemployment began to drop again in the 1990s (averaging 7.9 percent from 1988 to 1998 – compared to the EU average of 9.2 percent – and dropping to 5.5 percent in 2000) and by the later part of the decade Britain was second only to Denmark in low unemployment rates among EU countries. Yet low rates of GDP growth, somewhat skewed employment growth, productivity problems and supply-side gaps in skilled labor marred the British economy. Where the OECD Europe average economic growth rate was an annual 2.2 percent between 1988 and 1998 and the United States enjoyed 2.9 percent, Britain (like Denmark) had an annual 1.9 percent growth rate. Productivity had been a great concern for Britain for some time, and by 1993 British productivity was 71 percent of that in Germany and 57 percent of the U.S. productivity levels.[10]

The great concern over productivity motivated the formation of a joint CBI/TUC permanent committee on productivity. According to a report produced by this committee, U.S. firms operating in Britain were on average 80 percent more productive than British-owned ones in the same sector. In part, this reflected lower rates of capital investment, linked, in turn, to skill shortages and the inability of workers (especially at smaller firms) to cope with the technological advances in plant and equipment. Recommendations included increasing capital investment, expanding R&D tax incentives, encouraging the development of basic skills through the greater use of National Vocational Qualification scheme (see later) and increasing small firm participation in the Investors in People program.[11]

[8] OECD 7/6/2010; Bradley 2001, 100; OECD Employment Outlook 1996b; Hutton 1996; OECD's Earnings Database.
[9] Weir 1992; King and Rothstein 1993; Upchurch 1997, 195–6; Rhodes 2001, 30–1.
[10] OECD 2001, 12–14; Purkiss 1993.
[11] CBI & TUC 2001.

Concerns about jobs persisted despite the rebound of employment. Thatcher's policies led to an explosion of low-paid, part-time service sector jobs and a withering away of manufacturing employment. By the end of the Thatcher years, Britain had eviscerated labor market institutions to produce a cheap and poorly skilled segmented workforce available to produce "low wage, low technology, low value added products." Much improvement in employment reflected the expansion of low-skilled, low-wage jobs, especially in the entertainment and finance/insurance sectors.[12] British job growth occurred in both high-wage and low-wage sectors, with fewer jobs created in the middle-wage jobs, and manufacturing jobs continued to fall in the 1990s, by 11 percent between 1990 and 1993. Increases in female labor market participation were offset by decreases in (especially older) male employment, and young people (again especially men) continue to remain outside of school and the labor market more in Britain than in many EU countries. Regional unemployment was severe, especially in London and older industrial areas and the long-term jobless make up a larger proportion of the unemployed in Britain than elsewhere.[13]

The dreadful state of the British economy at the end of the 1970s ushered in a period in which neoliberal ideas deeply influenced political discourse. In 1979, the British Conservative Party, led by Margaret Thatcher, assumed power and immediately began to implement a broad platform of neoliberal reforms, designed to unleash market forces, to roll back the welfare state and to end all vestiges of labor market coordination. Disemboweling unions was something of a cause celebre and the Conservatives deregulated the system of labor relations with a series of anti-union laws that limited closed shop contracts, made sympathetic strikes illegal, and generally reduced the scope of legitimate industrial actions. Thatcher also attacked the major business peak association (the CBI), gutted the basic industries controlled by the state, and accelerated the economic rush into service sectors (which served to emasculate further the trade labor movement). Arguing that international competition, lower taxes, and privatization would facilitate the modernization of industry, the government reduced income taxes and spending and sold off public housing. Britain became the most deregulated economy in the OECD and the disintegration of British manufacturing produced high levels of unemployment in the 1980s.[14]

Thatcher also attacked the quasi-corporatist training system, by replacing the Industrial Training Boards in 1981 with employer-run National Training Organisations and throwing out the mandatory training levies. Conservatives launched the National Vocational Qualification (NVQ) scheme in 1986 to improve the consistency of standards across British industry; yet the NVQ standards corresponded imperfectly to real job requirements and were adopted inconsistently by firms. The conservatives also abolished the Manpower Services Commission model in 1988, replacing it with a decentralized network of Training and Enterprise Councils (TECs) to boost training through appeals to local employers; however, participation was spotty and firm training

---

[12] Nolan and Harvie 1995, 134–5; DfEE 1999, 7–8.
[13] OECD 2001, 111; Purkiss 1993; OECD, 2000a, 91–5.
[14] Nolan and Harvie 1995; Coates 2001; Cronin 2000; Rhodes 2001, 20.

fell by 26 percent between 1989 and 1993. The Conservatives launched the "Investors in People" program in 1990, but this initiative also fell far short of expectations.[15]

Despite much lip service, the Thatcher government put few resources into training and focused instead on boosting employment in low-skills jobs. The administration dramatically lowered unemployment benefits to an average 23 percent of previous earnings, shifted the balance between unemployment insurance-provided benefits to means-tested ones, and made benefits contingent on a recipients' demonstrated job search. Finally, Thatcher instituted the Youth Opportunities Scheme and other programs designed to increase the employment possibilities of school-leavers. The Thatcher legacy was one of a particularly punitive, neoliberal version of active labor market policy. Even employers expressed dissatisfaction with Thatcher's attack on skills, and the CBI pointed out that Britain ranked twentieth out of twenty-two OECD countries in skill levels, just above Turkey and Greece.[16]

When the Blair and the Labour Party regained power in May 1997, New Labour promised to follow a "third way" that avoided the mistakes of both old Labour and the Conservatives: Their proposals were built on neoliberal ideas, but with a leftist tinge. Labour's deep self-scrutiny began in 1983, after a second major loss to Margaret Thatcher, and Labour initially swung left to endorse social democratic policies, such as a compulsory training levy on firms.[17] When the party lost to John Major in 1991, the Labour Party again embarked upon a painful rethinking of its raison d'etre, but this time, moved to the center with the leadership of Blair.

Blair and his New Labour contingent rejected industrial investment, national winners, and close cooperation with trade unions, and embraced market solutions instead. Blair criticized Thatcher's policy legacy as creating a permanent strata of unemployed people (largely former industrial workers made unemployed by Thatcher's deindustrialization campaign), but he also endorsed a market philosophy that also broke with former Labour leaders. Many of his initiatives were taken from the Major administration and some interpreted this as evidence of an entrenched right-wing consensus. In a striking move, Blair granted control of monetary policy and interest rates setting to the Bank of England, and public spending actually declined from 41 percent in 1996–7 to 38 percent in 1999–2000.[18]

Thus, in both Denmark and Britain, parties on the left regained government in the mid 1990s, and both parties distanced themselves from both their progressive forebears and their conservative opponents with a leftist version of neoliberal ideas. Yet Denmark was able to make significant strides in developing the skills of low-skilled workers and to attract substantial business participation, whereas the British experiments failed both to develop skills and to entice much participation by firms. The following section explores the Blair administration's efforts to evolve greater labor market coordination with employers' support. The structure of party competition and the legacies of pluralism worked against Blair's renewed efforts to coordinate business,

[15] Upchurch 1997, 196–8.
[16] King 1995; Wood 2001, 394–5; Personnel Management Staff 1993.
[17] Giddons 1998; King 2002; Krieger 1999; Coates 2001; Hay 1997; King and Wickham-Jones 1998, 442–5.
[18] Coates 2001; Wickham-Jones 2004, 104, 108, 113–14.

and these continuing pluralist business structures diminished business support for investment in low-skilled workers.

Failed Efforts to Build Labor Market Coordination

There was some excitement at the beginning of Blair's first term that the New Labour government would redraw the boundaries between state and civil society and augment the level of organization among the social partners; but other analysts predicted failure for the Blair initiatives due to the realities of party politics. New Labour won by claiming the center space in the British two-(and a half)-party system; moreover, a large part of this winning strategy was a sturdy endorsement of the hegemonic neoliberal ideology.[19] Thus, New Labour was intrigued with the concept of "partnerships for prosperity," but it did little to promote real institutional change or to deviate from the free-market orientation of the Thatcher administration.

The administration encouraged partnerships at many levels and within many spheres, urging that employers and workers could benefit from working together to achieve the collective good. A white paper, entitled "Fairness at Work," promoted a cooperative partnership between employers and workers, that entailed a mutually beneficial trade-off: Unions would win automatic recognition when they could attract a majority of workers and employers would be guaranteed a reduction in regulatory burdens. The administration was inspired by Will Hutton's vision of stake holding, as "a principle of company relations" and a corporate strategy to fulfill firms' long-term interests in building up productive capacities and workers' skills.[20] Blair also pushed partnership in policy initiatives, between public and private actors and among networks of concerned parties.

Blair initially enjoyed friendly relations with business, and the administration was more solicitous of the major business organizations than Thatcher had been. CBI developed in 1965, as part of a merger of the two most prominent employers' associations, in part, to engage in the Labour government's tripartite experiments. Thatcher criticized tripartism and the corporatist ethic, gave preference to individual firms, and drove many members from the CBI. The CBI felt Thatcher's sting, and director-general, Terence Beckett, announced in 1980, "We have to take our gloves off and have a bare knuckle fight [with the Government] because we have to have an effective and prosperous industry."[21] By 1990, CBI had downsized by 25 percent, could no longer use its enormous headquarters, and, due to a long-term lease, had to solicit advanced subscriptions from its members to avoid near bankruptcy. Director-General Adair Turner remarked, "The CBI's role has evolved over the last 18–20 years. We've moved out of that corporatist role as part of an apex of national collective bargaining which existed in the 1970s."[22]

The Blair administration repudiated Thatcher's disdain for organized business and preached partnership with the corporate community. Blair was met with

[19] Norris 2001; Wickham-Jones 1997; Smith 1994.
[20] Fairness at Work 1998; Hutton 1998, 77.
[21] Cronin 2000; Mitchell 1990; Smith 1998, 32.
[22] Management Today Team, 1998, 32–6, 344.

considerable enthusiasm by higher-skills firms in the media, entertainment and high technology sectors, and some prominent low-skilled service sector employers, such as Lord Sainsbury, also supported the Blair agenda. Larger firms were more likely to support Blair than small ones, and many Euro-focused employers saw Blair as the man for internationalization. Smaller, low-skilled firms often remained committed to Conservative Party, free-enterprise policy positions and opposed virtually all regulation. CBI's Adair Turner calculated that three-fourths of the CBI members favored going on the euro and that the business endorsement of New Labour recognized Blair as a sympathetic voice to internationalization. Blair scored points with finance by turning the responsibility for manipulating interest rates over to the Bank of England, and underscoring that the new administration was determined to follow a fiscally sound course. Blair and Brown promised business supporters that they would not raise taxes above 40 percent of income and to restrain spending for at least a couple of years. By April 1996, Blair "told bankers and businessmen that 'errors in macroeconomic policy' by a future Labour government would be 'punished rapidly and without mercy' by the markets."[23] Blair promised that Britain would remain "one of the most lightly regulated labour markets in the world." A *Marketing Week* journalist jokingly observed how much easier it was to cover CBI conventions in the 1990s than in the 1980s, when he "wouldn't be seen alive at it, on the grounds that being seen dead" more accurately described "the state of the vast majority" of its delegates. CBI promised not to resist the government's industrial relations agenda and to aid in skills building.[24]

The Blair administration was so solicitous of employers that it was criticized for being too fond of its former enemies and too neglectful of its former friends. In the early days, Blair appointed many employers to the 320 task forces that were created to develop and to help implement policy initiatives; indeed, a study by Democratic Audit found that 71 percent of the task force members came from public or private producer interests and only 2 percent came from trade unions. The widely noted Better Regulation Taskforce was chaired by Lord Haskins (Northern Foods) and nine of the fourteen members came from private business. A business commission (sponsored by the Institute of Public Policy Research in 1996) included Lord Sainsbury (Sainsbury supermarket) and Bob Simpson (GEC), who were mandated to think about achieving greater levels of coordination in industrial relations and to reflect on the European social chapter, union recognition and the minimum wage. This cooperative sentiment struck a respondent cord in Adair Turner, director-general of the CBI, who worked closely with the administration in its early days.[25]

Yet, quickly it became apparent that the third way embraced by Blair would do little to alter the deregulated system of industrial relations that dominated Britain at least since Thatcher's rule; and in this way, New Labour differed profoundly from its old Labour predecessors. New Labour stripped the party platforms of their radicalism and did little to reverse the antiunion legislation enacted during Thatcher's rule. The administration-endorsed networks were a far cry from formal institutional engagement: The Blair model offered no coercive mechanisms to solve collective

[23] Lloyd 1999, 13; Roberts and Kynaston 2001, 17.
[24] Campbell, Taylor, and Wighton 1998, 12; Pitcher 1998, 27; Taylor 1998, 6.
[25] Weir 1999; Roberts 2003, 18; Lloyd 1999, 13–14.

action problems and no institutional alteration of voluntaristic, ad hoc industrial relations. Even though the Employment Relations Act of 1999 promoted "partnership," it stopped short of defining the term or bolstering the partners. The TUC begged the new government to create an institution for social partnership, in which the TUC, the CBI and the government would engage in formal consultation rather than ad hoc negotiations. Yet, Blair rejected this recommendation, routinely ignored the input of organized labor, and turned his back on true tripartism. The TUC felt that its views were largely ignored in the making of the National Action Plans and that the only examples of social partnership were the joint CBI-TUC productivity initiative and the Low Pay Commission. In comparison, CBI officials felt that their views were largely reflected in the NAP at least "up to a point."[26] The TUC was to observe in 1999:

> The Employment Relations Act … falls short of what we hoped to achieve on the basis of the Fairness at Work White Paper published last year. The battle over the Bill has been a long and difficult guerrilla campaign against those who would seek to minimise the influence of trade unions and weaken protection for people at work.[27]

Yet, even though Blair reached out to employers, he did not resurrect the CBI as a tripartite bargaining force any more than he altered the structural power of organized labor. Despite the early talk of partnership, the new relations did not approximate the former level of economic coordination between the CBI, organized labor, and the state found in the 1960s and 1970s. Despite the many early promises made to employers, relations between New Labour and the CBI ultimately soured, without a resurgence of the public–private alliances that seemed forthcoming at the beginning of the administration.

In part, the failure of any real institutional development reflected CBI's own difficulties in building internal consensus about the Blair offensive. The organization was split: Small business managers were particularly skeptical of the Blair plan, and resistance grew among employers who had never been entirely at ease with New Labour in the first place. Thus, *The Economist* blamed "the end of the affair" on "regulation, rather than economic management" and large employers benefitted from Blair's economic policies for economic stability and self-management by the Bank of England. But small business objected to the expanded regulatory environment, and felt that they had played an insufficient role in the formulation of the New Labour initiatives. The British Chambers of Commerce complained, "The fact that the proposals are particularly burdensome on small business we believe reflects the absence of small business representatives in the earlier social partnership exercise that helped shape the white paper."[28]

The logic of pluralist employer representation also constrained the evolution of negotiated compromises among business, labor and the state. CBI was hemmed in on the right by the Institute of Directors, a free-market association set up to act as a counterweight to CBI's earlier interest in cooperation, and competition between dueling groups reinforced CBI's difficulty in engaging in government initiatives in

---

[26] Wickham-Jones 1997; Undy 2002, 641–4; Eironline 2002.
[27] TUC 1999.
[28] *The Economist* Staff, 8/19/2000; Taylor, 8/3/1988.

a meaningful way. Adair Turner (director-general) was close to Blair, but Sir Clive Thompson (president), was much more skeptical of the New Labor line and accused the government of "bashing business" and of creating a host of new regulations which had escalated business costs. Thompson took pains to point out that "The CBI is not the business wing of the Labour party," and played "bad cop" to Turner's "good cop." The CBI could not easily cope with its divided membership and resorted to a posture of nonaction. As Dan Corry (a ministerial special advisor on transportation and industry) put it, "Members of the CBI are split on lots of issues, so they tend to lobby on the lowest common denominator stuff that everyone can agree with. If you believed what small companies say about red tape, for example, you would be amazed to find any still going at all."[29]

That employers were not forced to resolve internal disagreements, in part, reflects the broader structure of political competition. In multiparty systems with coalition governments, employers must resolve their internal disputes in order to exercise influence. Policy agreements typically endure beyond administrations and last even through ideological shifts in government, largely because at least some of the coalition partners usually endure. In two-party systems, however, employers may safely bet that the next regime will throw out many of the current government's initiatives; therefore, there are fewer incentives for managers to ensure that their views are fully represented. This too shall pass.

Thus, despite Blair's initially generous overtures to business at the dawn of his administration, he did little to change the long-term institutional profile of business and employers did very little to further the New Labour agenda. Perhaps Labour efforts to develop more social democratic policies were doomed due to changes in the global economy, and finance industrialists would always reject policies potentially favored by far-sighted industrialists.[30] Perhaps Labour's failures reflected political mishaps, the lack of encompassing labor market institutions, and the absence of a strong trade unionism.[31] Yet the story also reflects Blair's motivation to cope with the structure of two-party competition: To hone to the center and to reach out to employers was an important part of this strategy, yet, he did little to strengthen employers' collective capacities to engage in the policy-making process. Blair ultimately abandoned any attempt to imitate European social democracy and accepted as impractical any efforts to achieve coordinated capitalism in Britain.[32]

Impact of Failed Coordination on Active Labor Market Reforms

The New Deal Active Labor Market Reform
The failure of Blair to strengthen coordination among business and labor had implications for employers' engagement with New Deal policies to fight poverty and to enhance the skills of low-skilled workers. The New Deal was a central initiative in New Labour's groundbreaking ambitions and featured a set of active labor market policies designed

---

[29] Lloyd 1999, 14; Smith 1998, 32–7; Roberts 2003, 18.
[30] Coates 1999; Smith 1994.
[31] Wickham-Jones 1997.
[32] Hay 1997; King and Wickham-Jones 1998, 445–51.

to solve structural unemployment among a seemingly permanent underclass and to improve the quantity of skilled labor. For example, after six months of unemployment, young people (18–24) were required to go into the New Deal gateway program, in which they were given four options: (1) to accept a subsidized job for six months in which employers get 60 British pounds a week, (2) to work in the voluntary sector, (3) to work on the Environmental Task Force, or (4) to receive full-time education or training up to twelve months.[33] The employer subsidy constituted about 54 percent of wages.[34] The Local Employment Service oversaw the implementation of the New Deal; these public managers were expected to involve local employers and other partners in discussions about how best to implement the program, and some localities subcontracted for services or formed joint ventures with private agencies.[35] One-stop job centers permitted the unemployed to receive unemployment benefits, read about job openings and consult with employment counselors in the same location.

Despite many similarities on paper, British ALMP differed in their implementation from the Danish plans both in the target groups of the programs and in the connection to skills. In keeping with their liberal welfare antecedents, the British plans were less universal and more focused on the most marginal workers, such as adults and youth with a severe risk of unemployment. The administration hoped to further human capital development for "the learning age," recognized the enormous gaps in literacy and numerical skills among a fifth of the country's adults, and recommended that all youths be given a legal right to training. Yet it moved away from a goal of full employment toward an ambition of improving the "employability" of economically marginal individuals. The emphasis on employability partially reflected the more contingent nature of employment in Britain – with a quarter of the workforce employed in part time jobs, almost 10 percent working under temporary contracts, and the bulk of new jobs in low-skilled sectors. Enhancing the employability and skills of the unemployed also had a macroeconomic function: Building skills should expand the labor supply and diminish inflationary tendencies linked to competition over scarce labor.[36]

New Labour's mechanisms for skills development were considerably more limited than those of either their Danish counterparts or their old Labour predecessors. To critics, New Labour policies honed too closely to Thatcher's recipe for social engineering and to prevailing underclass theory that antiwork sentiments were being handed down from one generation to the next. Blair considered an expanded compulsory training system, but developed instead residual program to reduce unemployment without doing much to enhance skills. The goal of improving employability shifted focus to individual attributes and away from systemic malfunction.[37] Blair rejected a comprehensive training levy (as 75 percent of the CBI membership opposed a training levy), contemplated an employer training mandate, but ultimately developed Individual Learning Accounts (ILAs) to leave training responsibilities in the hands of the individual firms and workers. In 2001, a Skills Learning Council (to replace the Training

---

[33] United Kingdom Employment Action Plan 1999.

[34] Bell et al. 1999, 345.

[35] Finn 2000, 391–2.

[36] King and Rothstein 1993; King and Wickham-Jones 1998; Layard et al. 1991; Finn 2000, 385–7; Grover and Stewart 2000.

[37] Grover and Stewart 2000, 237–40; Finn 2000.

and Enterprise Councils) focused more directly on skills and included representation from the CBI and the TUC, but continued the traditional, voluntary, business participation in training. Critics also questioned the effectiveness of the programs.[38]

Involving Employers in the New Deal Programs

British political leaders considered employers essential for supporting and implementing their social project, yet the efforts to bring British firms into the business of implementing the welfare state met with less success than the parallel campaign in Denmark. Although employers signed up in high numbers (especially for the New Deal for Youth Unemployed People), they stopped short of actually creating jobs for this constituency. For example, the Department for Education and Employment estimated that in 1998 10 percent of a sample participated in the New Deal programs for Young People and for Long Term Unemployed People, but this figure included a big share of employers who only signed up for the program and did not actually hire New Deal clientele.[39] Despite the centrality of employers to the New Deal effort, business ultimately showed limited interest in cultivating the skills of the long-term unemployed.

The constraints of the pluralist system of business organization contributed mightily to the lack of corporate action. First, the pluralist system of business organization had *collective action effects*, in that employers had a limited organizational base to bring them into the policymaking process and to tailor the programs to real economic need. Even though individual employers participated on the task forces, Britain lacked the collective bargaining and tripartite institutions that might help employers collectively to put their imprint on the active labor market policies and to develop commitment to the outcomes. Unlike in Denmark, the British business community had limited systematic impact on or commitment to the initiatives. The Confederation of British Industry's stance toward the New Deal was characteristic of a pluralist peak business association. In Denmark, the threat of state intervention motivated employers and workers to cooperate in order to protect their policy-making prerogatives. In Britain, employers and labor had little jurisdictional turf to protect, the state did not pose much of a threat to the autonomy of the private sector and the CBI took a somewhat schizophrenic approach toward the New Labour government. Initially, the director-general of CBI, Adair Turner, waxed enthusiastic about Blair's conception of partnership between business, government, and labor, and the employers' association was accorded the prestige that it had enjoyed during the height of corporatism in the 1960s. But Sir Clive Thompson, who gained the CBI presidency in the summer of 1998, was decidedly less supportive of the partnership idea, believing that many of the New Labour initiatives decreased labor market flexibility despite claims to the contrary.

[38] Payne 2001; Heyes 2000, 154–8; Sutherland and Rainbird 2000. By January 2000, of the young people who had already left the program (85 percent), 28 percent had left to take unsubsidized jobs (usually in low-skilled sectors), 7 percent had moved into subsidized jobs, 18 percent were in training, 8 percent were in voluntary sector work, 7 percent were working in the environmental task force, and the rest had gone back on benefits, left for other known reasons or disappeared (OECD, June 2000a, 102). The absence of a control group made the program difficult to evaluate, and many participants may well have gained jobs without the intervention (Bell et al. 1999; J. Martin 2000).

[39] Hasluck 2000, 4; DfEE 2000.

Thompson's company offered services in everything from restroom maintenance to insect removal. In keeping with his firm's identity, Thompson remarked at a CBI dinner that union negotiations were best viewed as a form of "pest control." By the second Blair victory, CBI was chiding the Blair administration for its minimum wage and support for the EU Social Chapter.[40]

Because the peak employers' organization lacked the collective capacity to put an imprint on the policy and to bring its members to participate in the outcomes, Blair was left appealing to individual firms, and developed market-based inducements to entice employers to join in his campaign to expand the skills of the British people. The new prime minister campaigned to involve employers in New Deal programs with personal appeals to the largest British corporations, and the program was announced with fanfare and reference to considerable business support. Blair and the leaders of his administration including David Blunkett (secretary of state), Gordon Brown (chancellor of the exchequer), and Andrew Smith (minister for the Department for Education and Employment) roamed the country having breakfast meetings with 3,500 business leaders to introduce the New Deal and to solicit employer participation. Many employers were initially quite taken with Blair especially those in manufacturing sectors who had regretted the Thatcher program of deindustrialization, and by the launching of the program in April 1998, 3,000 firms had signed up to participate. The CBI participated in drawing up the UK's National Action Plan and the CBI, British Telecommunications, British Airways, Sainsbury, and Tesco quickly moved to endorse the New Deal. The government advertized on the New Deal Web site many companies signed employer agreements to hire New Deal clients.[41]

Business outreach was also conducted by the New Deal Task Force together with the Large Organizational Unit of the Employment Service, and although these were less press-worthy than Blair's outreach program, they engaged in serious efforts to build institutions. The Task Force was set up to advise and to provide employer input on program design, and to encourage private voluntary sector participation.[42]

Yet efforts to mobilize individual firms did not add up to an institutional commitment to the programs and British firms largely felt that they had much less input than the Danish firms into the development of the plans. This is reflected in our firm studies, as many employers were highly critical with the design and implementation of the plans and deeply pessimistic about these social interventions achieving their intended purposes. Respondents complained about the way that the New Deal programs were implemented and the Job Centre's handling of the New Deal applicants. Forty-three percent of the British firms believed that they had either never been contacted about the New Deal program at all or had only received written materials in the mail; only 27 percent reported vigorous outreach by the local employment services. Firms reported

---

[40] *Management Today* Staff 1998; CBI 2001a.

[41] Wintour et al. 1998; Bolger 1997; CBI 2001b.

[42] DfEE 1998. The Task Force and Large Organizational Unit developed more explicit market-oriented "demand-led" strategies to make workers "job-ready," to offer sector-specific programs, to increase reliance on private sector intermediaries, and to create account managers within the public sphere to handle vacancies (New Deal Task Force Working Group on Retention 1999). These market strategies reflected the policy legacies of a liberal welfare regime and the constraints of working with a poorly organized business community.

significant regional variation in the administration of the New Deal programs at the local level and few felt that the Employment Service responded adequately to companies' bid for workers. A firm that had worked with local government to create local New Deal programs reported "absolutely no follow-up" in referrals once the program was implemented. One manager in the hospitality industry recalled that despite national overtures to the company to participate, the local TECs did not want to send job candidates and that none of the company's training materials had been displayed at the local TECs. It was "a bit of a battle to get help" because "the local TEC people" felt that big companies shouldn't be participating in the New Deal and that the hotel industry was a sub-optimal placement for the clientele. British employers felt that the Job Center did not do adequate screening before sending out candidates, had "not such as the work ethic and training," and did "not know what makes the real world tick. The whole thing has been hyped by the bureaucracy, but the program has not been very good at figuring out how to get people to do work." Many who had tried to attract New Dealers reported that the job seekers had little preparation for securing employment within a private firm. Another recalled that candidates did not show up or did not have the "right specs for the job, despite the company's efforts to convey these specs to the employment service." An exasperated manager reported:

We saw a lot of young people who didn't know why they were there, didn't know what the job was, hadn't had any Gateway, and hadn't received any help in the interviews. We reported this back to the Job Center who apologized. They had also been thrown into the deep end, but they shouldn't be sending out applicants who were not prepared."[43]

Some respondents had better experiences with the local employment services, the Large Organization Unit, or private sector intermediaries; however, many criticized the national New Deal bureaucracy: One former member of the New Deal Steering group for the Employment Service stopped going to meetings because "the local government used such jargon that it was difficult for anyone outside the public sector to understand." She felt that "too much money was thrown" at the program with "too little attention to figuring out how to get people to do work." Another firm had difficulty participating because the New Dealers had to be taken on as part of the permanent head count of the firm, even though part of the salary was to be paid for by the government. British employers also felt that the programs differed little from earlier government efforts to reduce long-term unemployment – these programs were old wine in new bottles.[44]

Second, the historical *political economic* impacts of pluralism were evident: Employers' failure to develop a coordinating peak association after the first world war dampened the development of skills in the British manufacturing sector and this reinforced Britain's evolution as a liberal market economy. British manufacturers developed Fordist production processes to make use of low-skilled workers and Thatcher reinforced the low-skills orientation of the British economy with her attacks on training institutions. Therefore, expecting British programs suddenly to cultivate skills,

[43] Interviews with company respondents on February 2, 2001; June 4, 2001; June 12, 2001; January 26, 2001; April 5, 2001; June 14, 2001; May 3, 2001; January 29, 2001; January 23, 2001; June 13, 2001; June 4, 2001.

[44] Interviews on April 30, 2001; April 5, 2001; March 16, 2001; May 3, 2001; February 27, 2001.

given these past legacies, might be expecting too much. British employers viewed the programs as inadequate to immediate employment needs and ongoing institutional relations between employers and the state were limited.[45]

Evidence of these political economic effects were apparent in the firm-level analysis presented in Chapter 8: British companies, unlike their Danish counterparts, did not engage with the programs to derive real skills; rather, the British firms were more likely than Danish ones to participate to secure cheap labor. Firms believed that the New Deal programs did little to improve the skills of the workforce: Whereas 36 percent of the Danish firms identified skills needs as a constraint against participation, 53 percent of the British firms offered this reason. Managers felt that the New Deal in particular and government policies in general did little to address the pressing skills gap problem. They complained repeatedly about insufficient investment in education, training, and health, and government's lack of a long-term strategic vision to deal with the problems of long-term unemployment and social exclusion. One employer reasoned that the program had insufficient funds earmarked for training – funds would be better used by upskilling people in the industry. Another reflected that the programs:

Are the wrong end of the telescope of what the government should be doing … what the government should be asking is in what way is the educational and developmental system failing to meet the needs of business to give people jobs … If the state system isn't delivering basic competencies, then there will be people who cannot get jobs in a commercial world … This requires a long-term investment and this is a hard investment to sell. We need to address basic educational issues and economic issues. The New Deal is building a superb penthouse but this is an apartment without a foundation.[46]

Because employers felt that the New Deal did little to improve the skills of the workforce, it follows that the firms most willing to participate in the program would use workers with limited skills. Fifty-three percent of the sample said that they did not participate because they need higher skills. In the words of one manager, "the Blair government is going through the motions but it can't address the fundamentals." Another described her firms' employees as "heavy weight individuals who are too smart to be in the typical New Deal category." Another reported, "The company has been recruiting at the skilled level, but government schemes are irrelevant to this labor pool." Many employers also bemoaned the demise of apprenticeships in Britain that transpired during the Thatcher government and the dearth of engineers. Finally, government bureaucrats explicitly reached out to low skilled firms in the hospitality and retail sectors, for example, addressing on an annual basis the gathering of human resource personnel at a large hotel chain.[47]

Some firms with more highly skilled workers worried that participating in the program would hurt profitability. Thus, one manager explained that participation did not fit with the profile of this "dynamic, high flying company." Many firms were in the process of downsizing, reflecting the structural changes in the British economy; indeed, 28 percent of the sample offered not hiring as a reason for not participating. (One must

---

[45] Snape 1998, 24; Goos and Manning 2007, 128–9, found that British citizens' skills have improved and entry-level positions require higher qualifications, yet the skills content of these positions remains unaltered.
[46] Interviews on January 31, 2001; February 1, 2001; June 11, 2001; June 13, 2001; January 26, 2001.
[47] Interviews on February 1, 2001; May 2, 2001; January 22, 2001; June 11, 2001; January 24, 2001.

note that the Danish firms were in a comparable employment position, but only 20 percent offered as an excuse that the firm was not hiring at the moment. Many of the British firms reported not hiring in areas suitable for New Deal participants; which suggests that the firms might need better-trained workers.) One person remarked, "If we tried to hire the unemployed it would be an internal political nightmare." Many respondents reported that participation in the programs was limited because their firms were moving away from the conception of paternalistic responsibility for their workers' social lives. Another explained:

In a hugely competitive international environment where the criteria for job standards is increasing and every year firms have downsizing, etc., there is not a lot of room to think about programs for the socially-excluded. This sort of stuff is at odds with the philosophy of remaining competitive. Social responsibility that extends toward keeping on people who have reduced abilities goes against the survival of the fittest.[48]

The limited relevance of the British programs to skills is also revealed in vacancy rates. Danish vacancy rates declined with unemployment rates over the course of the 1990s, suggesting that the programs were matching skills to employment needs. In Britain, however, vacancy rates remained the same even as unemployment dropped as welfare reform forced people back into the workforce. In some cases managers addressed labor shortages with labor substitution technologies, thus limiting their interest in expanding recruitment. One manager captured this reality when he remarked:

The sort of people that are available are not the sort of people that we are looking for, and the sort of people that we are looking for are not available ... We need highly-skilled workers. People who have been unemployed for a long time generally are pretty unskilled. There is also the concept of the unemployable. Just because there are one million unemployed people in Britain today, doesn't mean that there are one million people on the job market.[49]

Some firms with more highly skilled workers did engage in the programs, but this was largely for philanthropic motivations or to derive political credit. The data reveals that 31 percent of the companies credited their participation to strong pressure from government and a desire to please the new administration (and recall that many CEOs had breakfasted at Number 10 Downing Street to hear presentations about the New Deal). Even though Danish CEOs were identified as the agents responsible for deciding to participate in the program in only 9 percent of the cases, 31 percent of British firms reported that the CEO had been primarily responsible for involving the firm with the New Deal. One manager reflected:

The firm signed on mainly from a public relations perspective – the CEO thought that there were kudos with being associated ... but the company did not put enough resources into making the local managers enthusiastic ... HR never really bought in.[50]

British employers also expressed a lower opinion of the program beneficiaries than their Danish counterparts, and in both countries many with the most negative preconceptions had chosen not to participate in the programs. Employers in both countries

---

[48] Interviews on February 28, 2001; June 11, 2001; January 26, 2001; January 22, 2001.
[49] OECD, 2001, 13–14; Interviews on January 29, 2001; February 1, 2001; April 4, 2001.
[50] Inverview on March 2, 2001.

doubted that entrenched poverty could be solved easily by the policies, with 53 percent of British firms believing that the socially excluded were simply "unemployable." One manager identified his firm's belief in "hire the attitude, train the person" and argued "most people with good attitudes are not on the New Deal programs." Another explained, "If people don't show up for a job, the firm does not want the responsibility of seeking them out." Another suggested:

Ideally [the firm would take social responsibility] but the problem we face at the moment is that with unemployment under 1 million, the people still unemployed are unemployable. Applicants don't want the job, but will get their benefits cut if they don't apply. Managers don't want these people ... the hard core that don't want to work."[51]

Finally, the pluralist system of business representation has *cognitive effects* on limiting employer participation in the programs for low-skilled workers: In comparison to the Danish organizations, the British employers' associations failed to be a source of information or connection to the state. The CBI and other groups did little to introduce firms to the benefits of innovation in low-skilled workers or to advertize the Blair programs. The cognitive effects of pluralism on employers' perceptions of the New Deal were apparent in the firm studies, as membership in the peak employers' had a significant negative impact on a company's participation in the programs. Thus, whereas membership in the Danish corporatist associations was highly determinant of participation in the ALMP programs, membership in the British employer associations not only fails to spur participation but also worked against involvement in the programs. This surprising finding reflected that joining a trade association in Britain was something of an alternative to developing a large, professional human resources department. Although some firms chose to do both, they often chose one route or the other for gaining information about policies affecting their workforce, and those companies with developed HR departments tended to have greater HR expertise simply because membership in the association offered so little information. When asked to state their most important source of information about HR issues and social policy, 32 percent of the Danes identified an employers association, as opposed to 14 percent of the British firms, and many Danish firms mentioned associations as their second-most important source of information. British companies learned from trade press, Internet, or regular newspapers (34 percent), government or government inspired groups (24 percent), private consultants (14 percent), or formal and informal HR groups (10 percent).

Some managers found industry associations such as the Engineering Employers Federation to be immensely important to keeping them abreast of social, employment and political issues and the British Retail Consortium. Similarly, gas companies were brought into the New Deal project by the sectoral training association, the Gas Industry and National Training Organization." Respondents also reported that formal and informal HR groups aided in their ability to understand social issues. Many such groups were linked to universities, such as the "Informal Group" developed by the University of Warwick business school and the Oxford University HR Directors'

---

[51] Interviews on March 1, 2001; January 30, 2001; March 15, 2001.

Forum. Yet a number of respondents admitted that they knew little about the programs beyond what they read in the newspapers."[52]

Conclusion

The active social policies of the Blair government were announced with great fanfare and purported to mark a major deviation from the past; yet, they are consistent in important ways with what one might expect from a liberal market economy or welfare state regime. Blair sought to expand skills, training, and the system of apprenticeships destroyed by Thatcher; however, he largely left training choices up to private markets, at least in the early years, with no one taking responsibility for ensuring that adequate training has been provided. The British plan also differed from the Danish one, in that there were no programs for workers with reduced working capacities; therefore, British interventions were largely restricted to a rather residual population, again keeping with the legacies of a liberal welfare regime. Individuals did reenter the workforce during the 1990s, but many remained under the poverty level.

The administrations efforts to bring British firms into the business of implementing the welfare state also, in many respects, resembled interventions of an earlier era. Befitting a liberal welfare regime, the government sought to use market approaches to sell the new active social programs to firms, rather than building new institutions. In part, this undoubtedly reflected a political reality that network building had less success than the parallel campaign in Denmark. The administration was later to try to address skills more explicitly and to construct business networks in each sector called "Sector Skills Councils," that were formally licensed to establish skills standards for workers in their industry.[53] Yet, in this case as well, the administration's ambitions were curtailed by the legacy of pluralist interest representation. Consequently, although many employers signed up for the New Deal, a much smaller group actually created jobs for the long-term unemployed.

---

[52] Interviews on January 23, 2001; March 2, 2001; April 3, 2001; January 26, 2001; January 22, 2001.
[53] House of Commons Education and Skills Committee. 2006, 6.

II

The Failure of Coordination and the Rise of Dualism in Germany

Introduction

Modell Deutschland was a great success during the golden age of postwar reconstruction and economic expansion and continued to inspire admiration even in the aftermath of the OPEC oil shocks and attendant global recessions and inflation.[1] In the immediate postwar decades, German growth rates were at, or above, average, unemployment and inflation rates remained below average, and economic inequality was modest to low. During the post-OPEC 1970s and 1980s, Germany continued to exhibit respectable export-led economic growth, relatively low inflation, and modest fiscal imbalances.[2]

After the oil crisis, however, unemployment appeared as a growing blight on Germany, and since the 1980s, poor employment performance has been exacerbated by rising labor market dualism and economic inequality. A series of economic shocks – together with international market competition and technological change – have racheted-up long-term levels of unemployment, engendered structural adjustments, and exacerbated labor market inequities. These shocks and structural changes have eroded the already limited capacities among the German state and employers' associations to achieve national, cooperative, and egalitarian responses to significant postindustrial challenges. The fragmented structure of the German state, coupled with its relatively weak fiscal and employment position within the political economy, has resulted in state failure to promote concertation among the social partners. Employers' associations increasingly fall short in their capacity to foster the internalization by employers of the external economic costs of employers' strategic choices and to promote a long-term perspective of employers' collective interests.

This chapter assesses the reasons for these failures. We explore the impact of economic shocks and postindustrial changes on unemployment and labor market dualism, and offer a synoptic overview of policy responses from the 1970s. We link the limited

---

[1] Giersch, Paqué, and Schmieding 1997; Kitschelt and Streeck 2003; Manow and Seils 2000; Scharpf 2000; Streeck 2009.
[2] Carlin 1996; Kitschelt and Streeck 2003; Swank 2002, ch. 5.

successes of these reforms to the dualist tendencies embedded in the logic of sector coordination and the decline in the coherence and degree of employers' organization. Unlike macrocorporatist institutions in Denmark, the German system of sector coordination is ill equipped to address these pressures and the "semisovereign" state has been unable to shore up coordinating capacity of institutions in the face of decline. We conclude with a discussion of how the German experience underscores our central arguments about employers, coordination, and maintenance of equality in the contemporary era.

The German Model, Crises, and Reforms

The postwar social market economy (*Soziale Markwirtschaft*) was, to a large extent, reconstructed on the institutional infrastructure established in the formative decades of industrialization, democratization, and state building. In contrast to national, state-mediated economic coordination in Denmark, heavily private, sector- and regionally based economic coordination prevailed in Germany and new formal-legal and informal limits on state power were enshrined. The German model was also characterized by a generous system of social insurance, multifaceted social partnership among well-organized employers and labor, and relatively consensus-oriented party competition among social democratic, Christian democratic, and liberal parties. Central to our concerns with the welfare roles of employers' organization and coordination are the labor and industrial relations system, the welfare state (*Sozialstaat*), labor market and training policies, and the interactions between these spheres.[3]

Postwar German industrial relations is a dual system of labor–management interaction. Collective bargaining over wages and conditions of work is sector-based albeit nationally coordinated across sectors. The state provides a legal framework for negotiations, and employers associations and unions bargain autonomously without direct state intervention (*Tarifautonomie*). The peak associations of employers, the Confederation of German Employer Associations (Bundesvereiningung der Deutschen Arbeitgeberverbände, or BDA), and of labor, the German Labor Federation (Deutscher Gewertschaftbund, or DGB) play limited roles in the coordination of sectoral collective bargains.[4] On the union side, the metal workers union (IGMetall) – one of (now) eight multi-industrial unions within the DGB – led every bargaining round until 2000. The metal industry employers' association (*Gesamtmetall*) leads collective bargaining for the employers.[5] Collective bargains struck in metal working, in turn, set

---

[3] Stable bank-producer relations (i.e., "patient capital") and employer cooperation for collective business goods such as R&D and technology transfer also have bearing on Germany's capacities to sustain equality against postindustrial pressures. For an extensive review of change in the German model, see Streeck 2009.

[4] Grote et al. 2007; Thelen 1991; Williams 1988.

[5] The BDA represents German employers within the areas of labor and industrial relations and social policy. The Federation of German Industry (Bunderverband der Deutschen Industrie, BDI) is the peak association of industry and trade associations, and represents German business in other areas. The BDA and BDI are joined by peak associations for the handwork sector, compulsory chambers of commerce, and miscellaneous national associations of the *Mittelstand* (primarily small and medium sized industries).

parameters for negotiations across other sectors. Until recent years, sector-negotiated collective bargains have covered roughly 80 percent of German employees. [6]

The second part of the industrial relations system involves plant- and company-level worker representation. Empowered by post–WW II statutes, works councils commonly address the organization of work, personnel issues, health and safety concerns, and wage and related matters (not covered by collective bargains); works councils representatives typically overlap with – but are elected independently of – unions.[7] Postindustrial pressures for decentralization to the firm level of key issues in collective bargaining (work hours reduction agreements) have reinforced the importance of works councils. Worker representation on company supervisory boards (*Mitbestimmung*), which mandate union representation in company board decision making (e.g., plant closings, investment), pertain primarily to iron, coal and steel companies; they have been increasingly challenged by employers in the contemporary era.[8]

The familiar German *Sozialstaat* provides social protection primarily through occupationally based social insurance.[9] Social insurance is divided into five "pillars": pensions, health and sickness, injury, unemployment, and, since 1994, long-term care. Benefit levels and eligibility conditions are largely set by government legislation although insurance funds are "self-administered" (*Selbstverwaltung*) by the social partners. Even though some consolidation has occurred, the system is characterized by substantial fragmentation (i.e., multiple funds) across regions, occupational classes, and sectors. Social insurance typically provides net income replacement rates of 60 to 80 percent (although see reforms below), and is funded primarily through equal contributions of employers and employees; total contribution rates as a percent of wages were 32.4 percent in 1980 and 42.3 percent in 2005.[10] Social insurance is compensatory in nature, designed around the needs of full-time male workers and dependents, and designed to maintain the status or achieved living standard (*Lebensstandardsicherung*) of the worker. Tax-funded social assistance (*Sozialhilfe*, until 2005), family and housing allowances and grants, and modest social services round out the *Sozialstaat*. Publically funded active labor market policies, which had been meager until the 1980s, are largely funded out of the unemployment insurance fund. In total, German social spending was 22.7 percent GDP in 1980 (two-thirds of which were cash transfers) and peaked at 27.3 percent in 2003.[11]

German education consists of a "dual structure" of general academic and skills-specific vocational training. By the age of 16, the student population has typically bifurcated into those attending academically oriented comprehensives (Gesamtschule) and grammar schools (Gymnasium) on the one hand, and those splitting their time between secondary vocationally oriented schools (Hauptschule) and workplace training. At 18, the first student pool moves into standard university education; the second group moves into technical universities and apprenticeships. National certification

[6] OECD 2004; Streeck 2009.
[7] Williams 1988; Thelen 1991.
[8] Streeck 2009.
[9] For comprehensive overviews, see, among others, Czada 2005; Hinrichs 2010; Lehmbruch 2003; Leibfried and Obinger 2003; Siegel 2004; Swank 2002, ch. 5.
[10] Hinrichs 2010.
[11] OECD 2009.

systems are administered by the relevant Chamber of Commerce or Industry. Despite weaknesses in postindustrial adaptation, large percentages of German manual workers possess high levels and quality of skills.[12]

German workers have enjoyed one of the highest levels of job protection among advanced capitalist democracies.[13] Workers in firms with more than ten employees benefit from strict requirements for advance notice of termination, strict termination criteria, mandatory training and reintegration requirements for mass layoffs and, in some cases, severance pay. Moreover, there has been substantial stability in employment protection law with most reforms altering only the firm-size thresholds.[14] Yet strong employment protection applies primarily to permanent (or regular) job contracts, rather than to the manifold "atypical" positions that have emerged since the 1980s.

Admirable postwar German economic performance is commonly attributable to the operation of these institutions.[15] The skills system undergirded manufacturing excellence and diversified quality production of consumer and industrial goods in the face of Asian and European challenges. Employment protection and generous social insurance encouraged the investment in specific skills; the generous *Sozialstaat*, despite its foundation in occupationally stratified social insurance, facilitated income equality.[16] Social partnership in sectoral wage bargaining and plant/company-level cooperation facilitated economic adjustment, wage moderation, and, in the context of pre-1970s full employment, wage equality.

In addition, some observers emphasize the positive role of an independent central bank and the limited capacity for fiscal policy intervention of a "semisovereign" state. Because collective bargaining is sectoral in focus, the system requires an external actor to force the social partners to internalize the costs of wage immoderation and the *Bundesbank* has played this role.[17] So too has the federal government who has faced constraints on Keynesian demand-side interventions from the complex divisions of fiscal responsibilities between national, state and municipal levels.[18]

Postindustrial Challenges to Sector Coordination and Social Protection

For the most part, the sector-based system of industrial relations and core features of labor market and social policy in Germany have been formally maintained during the 1990s and 2000s. Yet, a significant decline in coordinating capacity has occurred beneath this veneer of stability.[19] Union and employer association density and coherence, collective bargaining coverage and the capacity for social partnership have all significantly declined. "Smooth consolidation" of welfare state spending and fiscal imbalances has given way to more significant and inegalitarian reforms of the

[12] Gallie 2007; Upchurch 1997.
[13] OECD 2004.
[14] Ebbinghaus and Eichhorst 2006.
[15] For a synoptic statement of the German model, see Hall and Soskice 2001; Hall and Gingerich 2004; Estevez-Abe et al. 2001; and Streeck 2009.
[16] Korpi and Palme 1998.
[17] Carlin and Soskice 2009.
[18] Herrigel 1996.
[19] Hall and Thelen 2009; Thelen 2010; Streeck 2009.

Sozialstaat.[20] Atypical employment in temporary, part-time, and unstable employment
has risen as have wage and income inequalities.

Domestic and International Shocks and the Rise of Unemployment. German unemployment rates as well as economic growth and inflation performance deteriorated after
the first OPEC oil shock of 1973–4; 1970s economic expansion was further limited by
adoption of monetarism by the *Bundesbank* after 1971. Unemployment rates, in fact,
increased from a 1960–73 mean of 0.8 percent to an 1974–9 average of 3.4 percent.[21]
After improvement in economic performance, inflation accelerated after the second
(1978–9) OPEC oil shock, the trade balance worsened, fiscal deficits remained relatively high, and high interest rates in the United States prompted capital exports from
Germany and a declining Deutsche Mark (DM). Monetary policy turned decidedly
restrictive by 1980. Economic growth slipped into negative territory, unemployment
soared to over 6 percent, and the nominal government deficit approached 4 percent
of GDP.

During the 1984 to 1989 period, the trade surplus, inflation, general economic growth,
and the budget balance improved. Yet, the unemployment rate approached 8 percent
by 1985 and remained close to 6 percent through the rest of the decade. In addition,
the percentage of those unemployed for 12 months or more hovered in the range of 48
percent of all unemployed workers. From the early 1990s, long-term unemployment
has hovered at or above 50 percent; the percentage of the German labor force unemployed, itself, has stubbornly remained between 8 and 10 percent of the labor force.
(See Table 11.1.)

After the modest late 1980s recovery, the "shock" of German unification created
unprecedented challenges for Germany. Privatization of East German state-owned
enterprises, coupled with the transfer of West German wage levels, the high-quality
production model, and the (West German) DM, resulted in the loss of at least 40 percent of East German employment,[22] and swamped the capacity of newly private East
German enterprises (many of which were *Mittelstand* employers) to raise productivity levels and remain competitive.[23] The West spent 4 to 6 percent of West German
GDP annually to support privatization, infrastructure modernization, and the transfer
of social insurance pillars to the East.[24] The social insurance funds bore much of the
cost of unification: Rises in contribution rates funded subsidized employment, public
sector jobs, and training positions for over 2 million East Germans as well as extensive
early retirement for roughly 400,000 workers.[25] Total employer and employee contribution rates (as a percent of wages) increased from 35.8 to 42.1 percent between 1990
and 1998.[26]

[20] On "smooth consolidation," see Offe 1991.
[21] Sources for all data cited in the text are provided in the Ancillary Materials. For content and interpreta-
      tions of economic shocks and performance, we rely, unless otherwise noted, on Carlin 1996; Carlin and
      Soskice 2009; Giersch, Paqué, and Schmieding 1992; Manow and Seils 2000; Streeck 2009; and OECD
      (various years) *Economic Survey: Germany.*
[22] Corker et al. 1995.
[23] Manow and Seils 2000; Scharpf 2000; Streeck 2009; Wiesenthal 2003.
[24] Corker et al. 1995.
[25] Manow and Seils 2000; Hinrichs 2010.
[26] Hinrichs 2010.

TABLE II.I.   *Unemployment and Labor Market Dualism in Germany, 1980–2005[a]*

	Unemployment	Long-Term Unemployment	Part-Time Employment[b]	Temporary Work	Low-Wage Work
1981–5	6.4	36.7	11.8 (.6)	10.0	14.4
1986–90	5.8	47.9	11.7 (.6)	11.1	13.8
1991–5	6.8	39.6	12.9 (.7)	10.4	12.5
1996	8.7	47.8	14.9 (1.4)	11.1	13.6
1997	9.4	50.1	15.8 (1.7)	11.7	12.1
1998	9.0	52.6	16.6 (1.9)	12.1	12.8
1999	8.2	51.7	17.1 (1.8)	13.1	15.3
2000	7.5	51.5	17.6 (1.7)	12.7	12.9
2001	7.6	50.4	18.3 (1.8)	12.4	15.4
2002	8.4	47.9	18.8 (1.9)	12.0	15.8
2003	9.3	50.0	19.6 (2.4)	12.2	17.0
2004	9.8	51.8	20.1 (2.7)	12.4	16.9
2005	10.6	54.1	21.8 (3.8)	13.8	17.5

[a] 1981–91, West Germany only; 1992–2005, unified Germany. See the text and contemporary ancillary materials on variables and data sources.
[b] Number in parentheses is involuntary part-time workers as a percentage of total employees.

After unification, public sector borrowing costs initially increased dramatically. Wages and prices began to accelerate and, in response, the Bundesbank sifted monetary policy to a decidedly restrictive position (and the government increased taxation). Growth continued in the East; however, the aggregate economy fell into recession in 1993, and unemployment continued to rachet up. The demand shock of 1993–4 was followed closely by reinforcing pressures from the Maastricht Treaty on monetary union, which further prompted fiscal consolidation.[27] As Table II.I illustrates, general unemployment remained high through the mid-2000s (reinforced by energy price rises in 2004–5) and long-term unemployment rates rarely dipped below 50 percent of the unemployed.[28]

Three mechanisms link these shocks to the secular rise in general and long-term unemployment and dualism. First, with postindustrialization, economic shocks have produced relatively longer periods of unemployment for many workers that, in turn, have accelerated the loss of skills and human capital of the unemployed.[29] Second, recurring shocks, unification, and other structural adjustments of the economy have effectively pushed up social security contributions to unsustainable levels. In short, with social insurance (and other) taxes on wages pushing the market clearing wage to the reservation wage of the *Sozialstaat*, further contributions and taxes must be bourne by employers; yet, many potential jobs, and the relatively

[27] Carlin and Soskice 2009.
[28] German export growth – both before and after the 2007–2009 global financial crisis – has contributed to better employment performance. Many observers note, however, that export-sector success needs to be generalized to service sector and that reforms in areas such as training and education need to continue. Koske and Wörgötter 2010.
[29] Giersch, Paqué, and Schmieding 1992; Blanchard and Summers 1986.

less-skilled who seek them, are in relatively low-productivity service sectors. As a result, requisite numbers of jobs are not created and less-skilled workers increasingly fall into long-term unemployment, early retirement, or a broad class of part-time and temporary jobs.[30] Finally, these shocks are largely negative demand shocks that, in the absence of countercyclical monetary and fiscal policy, have ratcheted up the level of unemployment rate.[31]

Structural Adjustment: Employers, Labor, and the State
Pressures from global competition and technological change reinforced the adverse employment impacts of domestic and international shocks. In fact, as early as the 1960s, Germany faced challenges in heavy manufacturing from newly developed economies and producers in the automobile, machine tool, and other areas of diversified quality production encountered new competition in the 1970s and beyond from Japan and the United States, among others.[32]

The principal response of German business to these challenges – supported by German unions and facilitated by the state – was to press for significant labor productively and general efficiency enhancements. Constant if incremental technological innovation in production processes, just-in-time parts production, and other elements of lean production were implemented in core sectors of the German economy; large firms in core sectors outsourced low productivity work and pressured (small and medium-sized) suppliers for significant cost cutting.[33] Firms also shed less productive workers and demanded greater flexibility in collective bargaining that would allow company-level negotiations on structural adjustment issues, exemptions from elements of sectoral collective bargains, and, in come cases, full company-level agreements. As early as the 1960s, national policy makers had allowed expansion of elements of the social insurance funds (especially early retirement pensions) to absorb workers in heavy industrial sectors.[34]

The impacts of labor shedding on unemployment and labor market inequalities were significant. First, workers from their late 50s were able to take advantage of early, part-time, or unemployed pension provisions, but younger less-skilled workers were not. As job creation in the service sector fell notably short of job declines in the industrial core, general and long-term unemployment rates significantly increased.[35] At the beginning of the twenty-first century, the employment rate for less-skilled workers (i.e., those with less than a secondary degree) was 48.9 percent as compared to 64 percent for developed capitalist democracies as a whole.[36] Moreover, school leavers were hard pressed to find apprenticeships and job placements, and in the early 2000s, at least 200,000 school leavers were without training positions or regular employment.[37]

---

[30] Scharpf 2000; Pontusson 2005.
[31] Carlin and Soskice 2008.
[32] Herrigel 1996; Herrigel and Sabel 1999; Turner 1998.
[33] Silvia and Schroeder 2007; Turner 1998; Wiesenthal 2003; Thelen 2000.
[34] Trampusch 2005.
[35] See Scharpf and Schmidt 2000; Hinrichs 2010; and Kenworthy 2004; 2008 on Germany's poor jobs performance.
[36] OECD 2001.
[37] Hassel 2007.

A series of reforms in the 1980s and 1990s allowed the expansion of temporary contracts and a variety of forms of part-time work with lower wages and less security than full-time employment.[38] As Table 11.1 documents, part-time employment doubled from 12 to 22 percent of all German workers between the early 1980s and 2005; temporary contract work increased by 40 percent (from 10 to 14 percent of all employees) during the same period. Even for full-time workers, the percentage of employees working for less than half the medium wage increased from 14.4 to 17.5 percent between the early 1980s and 2005. Moderate increases in overall wage and income inequality also occurred. For instance, the ratio of wages of full-time workers at the 90th to 10th percentiles of the wage distribution increased from 2.88 in 1980 to 3.26 in 2005; the Gini Index of market income for working-age families increased from .388 to .473 in the same period.

Policy Responses to Postindustrialization: Neoliberalism in the German Context

The initial response of German policy makers to economic downturn, general fiscal imbalance, and the costs of labor shedding was a program of cost containment in social protection.[39] Under the 1970s and early 1980s SPD-FPD government, legislation required tighter qualifying conditions for unemployment compensation (*Arbietslosengeld*) and unemployment assistance (*Arbietslosenhilfe*), cut the duration of unemployment benefits, initiated new controls on pension and health care costs, and reduced increases in social assistance. In the SPD-FDP 1982 budget consolidation program, family allowances, housing benefits, job creation schemes, and social assistance were further limited and greater efficiencies were sought in health care.

As most observers argue, the post-1982 center-right (CDU/CSU-FPD) government led by Helmut Kohl was initially committed to a program of greater fiscal austerity, labor market deregulation, and privatization to achieve growth, competitiveness, and fiscal balance.[40] Indeed, Kohl famously declared a turnabout (*Wende*) in which market mechanisms and individual responsibility would replace state intervention and collectivism in German adaption to postindustrialization. At the same time, most observers agree with Hinrichs who points out that, in reality, Kohl's reforms constituted more of a path dependent adjustment of the Bismarckian model than radical structural reform.[41] Indeed, the Kohl government continued until the mid-1990s to commit the German state to subsidization (primarily through the social insurance funds) of the social partner's labor shedding strategy.[42]

Initially, the Kohl government followed up on the 1982 fiscal consolidation with further limitations to social insurance programs and cost control measures in health care provision; housing policy shifted from production of social housing to means-tested housing allowances. Moreover, the Kohl government liberalized restrictions on temporary and part-time employment and legislated modest restrictions on strike activity.

---

[38] Palier and Thelen 2008.
[39] For the 1970s to 2005 period, I draw upon Alber 1988; Czada 2005; Hinrichs 2010; Lawsen 1996; Lehmbruch 2003; Sigel 2004; Streeck and Hassel 2003; Swank 2002, ch. 5.
[40] Czada 2005; Hinrichs 2010; Lehmbruch 2003; Sigel 2004; Streeck and Hassel 2003.
[41] Hinrichs 2010.
[42] Leifried and Obinger 2003.

After the expansion of the *Sozialstaat* engendered by German unification, the Kohl government enacted measures to reduce benefit generosity, tighten eligibility, and induce efficiency across the *Sozialstaat*. As the costs of unification mounted, however, the Kohl government initiated even more aggressive measures. Two of these stand out.

First, the Kohl government proposed a reduction in the (employer-paid) first six weeks of sick pay from 100 to 80 percent of earnings; 350,000 citizens protested in Bonn. After heated negotiations, the legislation was passed to allow the 80 percent sick pay reduction if agreed to in employer-employee bargaining. When *Gesamtmetall* called on members to present a united front and press for implementation of sick pay reduction, BMW, Daimler-Benz, and other key employers defected from the employers' association position; for all intents and purposes, sick pay was maintained at 100 percent throughout the economy.[43] Second, the Kohl government passed (in 1997) the Pension Act of 1999. This significant legislation tightened eligibility for disability and early retirement pensions, phased out part-time and unemployed pensions, and incorporated life expectancy into the calculation of benefits. In the end, the pension act and a handful of other retrenchment measures were rescinded by the new SPD-Green coalition in 1998.

At the same time, some expansions of the *Sozialstaat* occurred during the Kohl era in addition to the adoption of long-term care insurance in 1994. First, the practice of significantly subsidizing labor shedding was maintained. Central to the state's role was the use of flexible pensions (i.e., pensions with full benefits at age 63) and unemployment pensions where workers could take unemployment at 59 (and later 57) and then move to pensions for unemployment reasons at age 60. Between 1972 and 1990, roughly 525,000 West German workers took early retirement; during the first three years of reunification close to 100,000 East Germans made use of early retirement options (Trampusch 2005).[44]

Second, ALMP policies were expanded in the 1980s to provide jobs through direct public sector employment (i.e., infrastructure), subsidized wages, and public sector training positions. In 1989, the Kohl government initiated wage subsidies of up to 80 percent for one year for employers who would issue regular employment contracts to the unemployed and these programs expanded dramatically with unification: ALMP spending averaged roughly 0.7 percent of GDP in the late 1980s, but it exploded to 1.5 percent of GDP in 1992. Resources devoted to ALMP, however, fell quickly after 1993. Yet, ALMP has typically been used as a supplement to early retirement to absorb excess labor with temporary jobs.[45] As the programs are funded in large part by the unemployment insurance fund and are crowded out by unemployment compensation spending, they are highly vulnerable to business cycles.[46] At least until the Schröder

---

[43] Thelen 2000; Streeck 2009.

[44] Ebbinghaus 2006; Trampusch 2005. As Trampusch (2005) argues, the costs of early retirement created notable pressures on the state and social partners for solutions. In 1996, after extensive bargaining, the federal government effectively transferred significant authority over early retirement to the social partners. New part-time retirement pensions would now be subject to collective bargaining and funded by employers and workers with subsidies by the state.

[45] Streeck 2005.

[46] Manow and Seils 2000; Cox 2001.

era, policy makers did not seriously consider ALMP as a mechanism for training and retraining in the face of postindustrial pressures; the 1989 wage subsidies for long-term unemployed offered employers few real incentives for employing marginalized workers in regular employment[47] Employers viewed these subsidies and other ALMP incentives as inadequate for their skill needs, felt little responsibility for marginalized workers, and were not mobilized to participate by the state.[48]

Finally, labor market and social policy entered a new stage at the end of the Kohl regime. In the wake of the dramatic rise in costs, the Kohl government embraced a strategy of informal tripartite dialogue between the government and social partners in the form of *Kanzlergespräche*; this approach was formalized with the IG Metall-initiated Alliance for Jobs (Bundis für Arbeit) in 1995 and 1996. A series of extensions to the employment promotion laws in 1997 and 1998 provided funds for new training measures to reintegrate the unemployed and wage subsidies for employers in new start-up enterprises to hire the unemployed; the reforms also tightened sanctioning measures for noncompliance by the unemployed. As such, they mark a notable turn toward the OECD's active social policy that continued during the Schröder era.

Schröder's Red-Green Governments. Gerhard Schröder's SPD-Green Party coalition essentially embraced the logic of active social policy: Reflecting an ideological trend within the SPD, the government placed an emphasis on training, reskilling, and education to combat social exclusion of marginalized workers.[49] Yet, especially after the 1999 departure from government of SPD left-wing leader Oscar Lafontaine, Schröder government policy increasingly stressed individual responsibility, removal of disincentives to work, and elements of the new public management model of contracting out, internal markets, public-private competition, and performance-based rewards.[50] Discourse on social policy reform among German elites and attentive constituencies shifted to an attack on welfare state costs and on the need for fiscal retrenchment and activation.[51]

The Schröder government initially adopted the strategy of tripartite concertation in the form of the Alliance on Jobs, Training and Competitiveness; however, this Bundis für Arbeit (like Kohl's Alliance) produced little in the way of concerted action on jobs, social policy, or dualism and the Alliance was effectively dead by 2001.[52] The government then embarked on largely unilateral policy action. As a lead-up to the famous Hartz Reforms, the government passed a series of bills that reflected the new active labor market and social policy orientation.[53] In 1999, the government passed the JUMP program for unemployed youth (Intermediate Program for Reduction in Youth Unemployment). This legislation provided wage subsidies for private sector employment, expanded public sector training and apprenticeship positions, and offered intensive job and career counseling for young people. In 2001, the government

---

[47] Wood 2001; Seeleib-Kaiser and Fleckenstein 2007; Giersch, Paqué, and Schmieding 1992.
[48] Nelson no date.
[49] Huo 2009.
[50] Seeleib-Kaiser and Fleckenstein 2007.
[51] Vail 2003; Hinrichs 2010.
[52] Grote et al. 2007; Streeck 2009; Streeck and Hassel 2003.
[53] We rely on the following sources for details of reforms: Hinrichs 2010, Huo 2009, Seeleib-Kaiser and Fleckenstein 2007, Vail 2003, and Ebbinghaus and Eichhorst 2006.

enacted the Job Rotation Program: Consciously modeled on the similar Danish initiative, the program provided subsidies from 50 to 100 percent of wages for employers who would hire unemployed workers to replace regular employees engaged in training and education. On the eve of the Hartz reforms of 2002–5, the government passed the Law for Job Activation, Qualification, Investment and Placement (or JOB-AQTIV *Gesetz*). This legislation sharpened rules for "reasonableness of work" and initiated intensive advice and counseling services for the unemployed. With these initiatives, the Schröder government also increased the federal share of ALMP financing.[54]

The Hartz reforms constituted a major effort to address welfare costs and postindustrial challenges. The Hartz Commission, chaired by Peter Hartz (personnel director at Volkswagen and IG Metall member), was appointed in the wake of the breakdown of Schröder's tripartite Alliance and of a scandal at the Federal Employment Office (Bundesanstalt für Arbeit, BA) involving the inflation of job placement numbers. The Hartz Commission report recommended 13 major sets of reforms of labor market and social policy; these were legislated between 2002 and 2004 in four packages. Hartz I and II introduced training vouchers to encourage quality and competition in training practices, new business start-up grants (Me, Inc.) for unemployed persons, and provisions to encourage work among the older unemployed; they also required immediate registration of the unemployed with the BA and tightened sanctioning provisions. Hartz III reorganized the BA to encourage effectiveness and efficiency in the "customer-oriented" delivery of employment services and to reduce the control of the social partners in BA operations; a new three-person directorate (advised by social partner representatives and experts) would run federal employment services. Hartz III also furthered the use of private service providers in employment services and, significantly, reduced the duration of unemployment insurance benefits to older workers from 32 to 18 months. In addition, Hartz I through III encouraged part-time and temporary employment as well as established consolidated job services centers for the unemployed.

The best-known component of the Hartz reforms was the 2004 Hartz IV. At the center of Hartz IV was the replacement of earnings-related unemployment assistance (taken up after entitlement to unemployment insurance expires) and *Sozialhilfe* (means-tested, flat rate social assistance for the needy) with one flat-rate, means-tested benefit (known as Arbeitslosengeld II, ALG II). This meant that beginning in 2005, workers with requisite contributions could enjoy earnings-related unemployment insurance benefits (ALG I) for 12 months (18 for older workers). After expiration of AGI (or for the unemployed who do not qualify for ALG I), able-bodied working-age individuals move to ALG II.[55] In addition, Hartz IV (coupled with Hartz I through III), establishes a significantly transformed ALMP program structure for ALG I and

---

[54] The most significant reform of social policy prior to the Hartz reforms consisted of the 2001 Pension Reform Law, which reduced average benefits from 70 to 64 percent of preretirement income; reduced benefits annually by another 0.3 percent for younger workers; and created mandatory, supplemental private accounts. In the face of significant opposition, the bill passed after the government dropped the progressive benefit cuts for younger workers and made the supplemental private accounts voluntary. Vail 2003; Hinrichs 2010.

[55] For workers who have qualified for ALG I, the transition to the lower flat-rate benefits of ALG II (less than 400 Euro in the late 2000s) is smoothed over a two-year period.

ALG II. For ALG I beneficiaries, a variety of job placement and training services are available as are revamped wage subsidies, direct job creation schemes, and special assistance for disabled and older workers. For recipients of ALG II only (typically the most marginalized, lower skilled workers), ALMP is less generous and provides fewer options. Public employment jobs (for 6 to 9 months, paying 1 to 2 Euros an hour with income topped up by ALG II), mini-jobs and other part-time or temporary jobs are also available. Yet, there is little or no programmatic efforts to substantially engage private enterprises in systematic training of marginal workers. As Nelson points out, the Hartz reforms notwithstanding, budgets for public training programs were actually significantly cut in 2002 in the wake of the placement-numbers scandal at BA.[56]

We now address the crucial questions that emerge from the empirical record: First, why did durable tripartite bargains – deals whose policy reforms potentially addressed simultaneously efficiency concerns and the rise of inequality – fail to materialize? Second, why were private employers not mobilized and engaged in policy development and implementation of ALMP in efforts to mitigate dualism?

The Failure of Cooperation: Sector Coordination, State Weakness and the Minimal Role of Employers

Despite reforms in the direction of active social policy, the level of resource commitment to ALMP in Germany as well as the numbers of workers in ALMP training appears comparatively low and in decline. For instance, average ALMP spending was 1.26 percent of GDP in the 1997–9 period and 1.21 percent for 2005–7. ALMP spending devoted to training programs has hovered between 0.35 and 0.4 percent of GDP throughout this period. The annual participation rate in ALMP programs was 5.1 percent of the labor force during the enactment of the Hartz reforms (2002–4); some three to four years later it was 4.7 percent (2005–7). Shifting to labor market surveys of employers' spending on in-career training and retraining of workers, Gallie's synthesis of multiple studies for circa 2000 suggests employers spent about 1.5 percent of labor costs on training in Germany and roughly 30 percent of workers had significant participation in (re)training; comparable figures for Denmark are 3.0 of labor costs and 55 percent of employees.[57]

Data such as these, combined with evidence presented above on the rise of irregular employment and inequality in Germany, have led some observers to conclude that policy reforms have largely failed to address dualism in any systematic way. Carlin and Soskice bluntly state that recent reforms have failed to produce anything resembling a cross-sectoral training and (re)training program to combat dualism.[58] Palier and Thelen echo these concerns and argue that Hartz IV reforms make it extremely difficult for marginalized workers in ALG II to enter regular employment and, generally, reinforce the privileged status of core sector workers.[59] Huo argues that German reforms through Hartz IV emphasize benefit conditioning and individual responsibility more

---

[56] Nelson no date.
[57] Gallie 2007.
[58] Carlin and Soskice 2009.
[59] Palier and Thelen 2008.

than effective allocation of resources for moving the low-skilled into active work.[60] It is our contention that the source of these shortcomings is the failure of the state and social partners to craft nationally encompassing policy adjustment for efficiency and equity; this failure, in turn, rests with the logic of sector coordination and the traits of the German polity.[61]

The Failure of National Cooperation: Sector Coordination and the German State

Whereas Germany experienced a brief period of successful national-level coordination in the late 1960s (Konzertierte Aktion), experiments in national concertation between the state and the social partners to address economic performance problems and dualism in the contemporary period largely failed and two, in particular, are noteworthy.[62] First, after roughly five years of "fire-side chats" between Chancellor Kohl and the social partners (*Kanzlergespräche*), IG Metall head Klaus Zwickel proposed a corporatist strategy for dealing with joblessness and problems of adjustment to postindustrial pressures: Labor would agree to wage moderation in return for new jobs and the reduction of overtime work.[63] The Kohl government wanted to lower joblessness and curb the social costs of adjustment, and enthusiastically embraced the Alliance for Jobs (Bundis für Arbeit). But employers were divided in their commitment to the new jobs and some were strongly opposed to losing control of overtime work; consequently, unions came to doubt the credibility of the pledges to create new jobs.[64] In addition, the recent election had strengthened the FPD's standing within Kohl's government and the party supported the BDI's demands for much more radical reforms in welfare state and labor market regulation. At this point, the unions walked away from further serious negotiations.[65] In this context of *Reformstau* (reform blockage), the Kohl government initiated without tripartite agreement its proposals to reduce sick pay, reform pensions, and other policies discussed above. Employer fragmentation further manifested itself with the defections of leading firms from the formal position of *Gesamtmetall* to implement the sick pay policy.[66]

The Schröder government entered office in 1998 with a commitment to end *Reformstau* and adopted a corporatist strategy of tripartite negotiations to address joblessness, economic adjustment problems, and welfare reform. In fact, Schröder

---

[60] Huo 2009.
[61] Some scholars such as Torben Iversen have suggested that the electoral strategies of Christian democratic parties, efforts to privilege core sector manufacturing workers and the middle class, play a role in dualism. Iversen 2009. Others argue that similar social democratic "insider" strategies play a role in rising inequalities. Rueda 2005; 2007. We return to these arguments in Chapter 12.
[62] The era of "concerted action" between the peak associations of labor, employers, governments at all levels and the Bundesbank produced a brief period of wage moderation, countercyclical demand management, and regularized concertation on macroeconomic problems in the late 1960s. However, with labor's more aggressive wage demands and the central bank's shift to monetarism, the era of organized cooperation ended in the early 1970s.
[63] Lehmbruch 2003; Streeck and Hassel 2003.
[64] Lehmbruch 2003.
[65] Lehmbruch 2003; Streeck 2009; Streeck and Hassel 2003.
[66] The one significant accomplishment by the Alliance, discussed earlier, is the tripartite agreement on reforming early retirement policy.

created a formalized and relatively complex structure and began peak negotiations *(Spitzengespräche)* among the core economic and social policy ministries and the social partners. Business representatives included the BDI, BDA, the chambers; labor included the DGB and the four largest sectoral associations. Modeled on a managerial process suggested by BDI president Hans Olaf Henkel, these actors would be assisted by benchmarking groups composed of leading labor, business and academic experts who would "benchmark" German economic and social performance against international standards. Finally, another level of meetings would occur among and between major sectoral and policy area actors.

Although initially promising, Schröder's Alliance for Jobs, Training, and Competitiveness quickly began to resemble its predecessor, Kohl's Alliance for Jobs. Government and employer demands to address systematically wage moderation and greater flexibility for economic adjustment met with serious union objections; such resistance was grounded in the belief in *Tarifautonomie* and in union distrust of employer commitments.[67] The unions proposed lowering the retirement age to 60 to generate more jobs, but this proposal was entirely unacceptable to the other actors.[68] Key unions such *IG Metall* and the new service sector union *verdi*, in alliance with the left-wing of the SPD in parliament, effectively acted as veto players in response to a number of government and employer proposals.[69] Fragmentation among employers played out in a conflict between the BDI and BDA: BDI president Henkel had proposed an increased role in collective bargaining for the BDI, a proposal that the BDA completely rejected.[70] To make matters worse, the SPD-led government lost control of the Bundesrat in 1999, which intensified interparty conflict and diminished confidence among the social partners that the government could credibly commit to legislate major tripartite agreements.[71] Ultimately, by the early 2000s, tripartite talks had become largely symbolic and the Schröder government strategically chose to pursue unilateral policy action.[72]

The Limits of Sector Coordination. The central question is, of course, why did these experiments fail? More precisely, why did these efforts not produce a comprehensive tripartite bargain that would effectively replace the strategy of state-supported labor shedding by core sector employers (and their unions)? In part, the answer lies in the structure of the German political economy. National-level cooperation is constrained by the vibrant sectoral organization of employers and unions (and relatively weak peak associations). This is so because the sector associations have minimal incentives to agree to comprehensive, encompassing agreements, designed to meet the needs of workers (or firms) outside the core sectors.[73] Framed in the logic of collection action,

---

[67] Siegel 2004; Lehmbruch 2003; Streek and Hassel 2003.
[68] Streeck 2009.
[69] Siegel 2004.
[70] Streeck and Hassel 2003.
[71] Czada 2005.
[72] Lehmbruch 2003; Vail 2004. Schröder's Bundis für Arbeit did enjoy a significant achievement in the 2004 vocational training agreement that committed business to create an additional 25,000 apprenticeships and associated job placements; the government, in return, committed to improve the education of school leavers, subsidize placements, and make regulations governing these operations flexible. Hassel 2007.
[73] Carlin and Soskice 2009; Huo 2009.

German employers, organized primarily across narrow sectoral lines, have little motivation to internalize the costs of their long-standing strategy of labor shedding. The *Bundesbank* overcame the logic of sectoral organization in wage-setting; however, there is no institution to directly force encompassing solutions in employment and equity. Ultimately, sector coordination of the economy, shaped historically by the regionally based, fragmented party system and federal state structure (see Chapters 2 and 7), is a big part of the explanation for rising dualism. In sum, as Grote, Lang, and Traxler recently put it, it is simply very difficult to extend German "meso-level" coordination to the national level.[74]

In addition to this limitation of sector coordination, there has been a significant decline in the organization of employers (and unions), in the scope of collective bargaining, and in strength of social partnership in recent years. Between 1992 and 2003, union density dropped from 31.3 to 19.7 percent in unified Germany and from 28.7 to 23.8 in the West.[75] Employer organization in the core metal-working sector has weakened as well: Company membership in Gesamtmetall has fallen from 54.6 to 22.5 percent between 1985 and 2003; workers covered by Gesamtmetall firms have fallen from 73.8 and 55.1 percent of metal working employees over the same period.[76] These declines in employer and union organization significantly undercut efforts at national solidaristic strategy.[77]

Industry-wide collective bargaining coverage has also fallen in recent years. Between 1995 and 2006, employee coverage has fallen from 72 to 57 percent in the West and from 56 to 41 percent in the East.[78] The percent of workplaces using an "opening clause," or the right to negotiate some features of collective bargains at the company level, has increased from 22 to 75 percent between 1999/2000 and 2004/2005.[79] In addition, the character of collective bargaining and social partnership has arguably turned much more adversarial; for instance, intense industrial conflict followed IG Metall's 1984 offensive to obtain a thirty-five-hour work week and Gesamtmetall's 1993 efforts to reconfigure the implementation of parity wages in the former East German *Länder*. Yet, even though employers, especially, seek to decentralize bargaining and otherwise obtain greater flexibility in the industrial relations system, they do not wish to abandon the system of relatively coordinated sector-based bargains.[80]

The Role of the State. Our quantitative analysis of the underpinnings national cooperation has highlighted the systematic importance of state capacity in the contemporary era. A more complete explanation of the failure of national-level concertation in Germany must also recognize the relatively modest size and limited capacity of the German state. Overall, the German state in 2005 employed roughly 12 percent of the labor force and engaged in public goods and services spending equivalent to 18.9 percent of GDP; comparable numbers for Denmark are 30 and 26 percent,

[74] Grote et al. 2007.
[75] Streeck 2009.
[76] Grote et al. 2007; Silvia and Schroeder 2007; Streeck 2009.
[77] Martin and Thelen 2007; Palier and Thelen 2008.
[78] Streeck 2009; OECD 2004.
[79] Streeck 2009.
[80] Thelen 2000; Hassel 2007.

respectively. Moreover, only a fraction of public employees are employed at the national level where broad parameters of active labor market and social policy are set, and most of these are highly skilled civil servants (*Beamte*). As Martin and Thelen point out, the relatively small size of the public bureaucracy and public social services suggests that government bureaucrats in Germany have not developed a strong interest in spearheading a solidaristic coalition as they are unlikely to employ marginal workers.[81] Local bureaucrats throughout Germany have centrally focused on managerial efficiency, contracting out, and job reductions under the pressures of fiscal imbalance, and have not expanded their activities to build extensive public-private partnerships for reintegration of large pools of long-term unemployed and lower skilled workers.[82]

In addition, the character of the German state suggests that it does not have the tools to sustain coordination and promote employer engagement in effective active social policy. First, the small size the bureaucracy and underdevelopment of cohesive public sector unions indicate that the state is unlikely to have consequential leverage over the social partners in collective bargaining arenas, especially given the sectoral character and declining scope of industry-wide bargains.[83] Second, relatively modest levels public consumption spending (versus Denmark) prevent the German state from exercising much leverage as a consumer of business goods and services. The presence of an independent central bank and limits on interventionist fiscal policy suggest that incumbent governments can not manipulate macroeconomic aggregates in order to move employers or labor to the state's preferred position.[84] Moreover, as the experience of Schröder's Alliance for Jobs brings into dramatic relief, the principle of *Tarifautonomie* significantly limits the capacity of incumbent governments to fully integrate wages (and other central collective bargaining issues) into comprehensive tripartite negotiations.[85] The same can be said with respect to the complementary principle of *Selbstverwaltung* (self-administration) in the social insurance funds: This has led to successful efforts by the social partners to block or delay some social policy reforms.[86]

In addition, contemporary analysts have build on seminal work of Peter Katzenstein and Fritz Scharpf to argue that the fragmentation of the German state plays a central role in *Reformstau* and limits on efforts of incumbent governments to foster tripartite concertation to address postindustrial challenges.[87] Generally, the fragmentation and decentralization of political authority and fiscal responsibilities in the German state create veto points in the policy process.[88] As failed tripartite concertation suggests, the diffusion of power generally and the prospect of opposition control of the Bundesrat specifically, tend to undercut the ability of federal governments to make credible commitments to enact tripartite bargains or to act unilaterally in adverse ways if social partners do not cooperate.[89] Complex fiscal relationships between federal,

---

[81] Martin and Thelen 2007.
[82] Nelson no date.
[83] Martin and Thelen 2007.
[84] On macroeconomic constraints, see Carlin and Soskice 2009.
[85] Huo 2009.
[86] Martin and Thelen 2007.
[87] Katzenstein 1987; Scharpf 1988.
[88] Tsebelis 1999; Kitschelt and Streeck 2003.
[89] Czada 2005; Streeck 2005.

state, and local governments also reduce the capacity of the federal state to use aggregate demand-oriented fiscal policy.[90] Moreover, Gerhard Lehmbruch's authoritative analysis of the failures of national coordination in the Kohl and Schröder Alliances for Jobs not only recognizes these problems, but emphasizes the centrifugal effect during tripartite concertation of overlapping yet distinctive policy communities created by federalism, the fragmentation and self-administration of social insurance funds, and associated forces.[91] Overall, the relatively modest size, notably limited capacities, and complex fragmentation of authority of the German state – in the context of structural constraints of sector coordination – helps us to explain the failure of a national, cooperative response to the economic and social challenges of postindustrialization and the mitigation of dualism.

Employers and the Rise of Dualism

In addition to the logic of sector coordination and the limits of state capacity, we must recognize that the closely related decline of employers' associations and failure of the state to engage employers in ALMP policies for marginalized workers has contributed to program weaknesses and, in turn, the rise of dualism. The national employer's association, the BDA, plays a limited, largely informal role in collective bargaining, has no strike/lockout funds, and has few other powers to control member organizations and firms; rather, *Gesamtmetall* has led bargaining rounds and the formation of important employer positions at crucial junctures.[92] Moreover, the fragmentation of employers has accelerated in recent years, and the process goes beyond the decline in company membership discussed in the previous section. Perhaps most important, the interests of larger, export-oriented firms in core sectors of the German economy have diverged from those of small and mid-size firms, often called the Mittelstand (many of whom are suppliers to large export-oriented firms). Large firms have been able to take advantage of features of bargaining decentralization and flexible adjustment that are not afforded smaller firms. For instance, large enterprises with personnel departments can take full economic advantage of company-level control over work-time reductions and they can also better afford the direct and indirect costs of labor shedding.[93] Moreover, large export-oriented firms have an interest in – and capacity to bear – the costs of higher wage increases; in return, they gain the security of uninterrupted production that is crucial for maintaining market share.[94]

   In addition, large firms, in their quest for higher productivity and lower costs have pressured their suppliers to continually reduce prices and the impact of this has been to squeeze the profit margins of smaller firms. As result, small and mid-sized firms have increasingly supported more radical reductions in social insurance costs, deregulation of markets, and related liberalizations; and they have increasingly been joined by the BDI (and FPD) in pressing the incumbent government as well as leading sectoral associations and the BDA for greater neoliberal reform.[95] Indeed, defections by

[90] Herrigel 1996.
[91] Lehmbruch 2003.
[92] Grote et al. 2007.
[93] Hassel 2007; Silvia and Schroeder 2007.
[94] Thelen and van Wijnbergen 2003.
[95] Streeck 2005.

small and mid-sized firms are one of the largest problems for the sectoral associations and BDA; a strategic response – designed to alleviate some of the burdens of industry-wide bargains on smaller firms – has been to offer firms OT -Verbände, or membership without collective bargain responsibilities.[96]

Recent work by Moira Nelson on employers and ALMP in Germany – research modeled directly on our own work on Denmark and Britain – illustrates the problems for ALMP of engaging employers in a sector-coordinated economy, in the context of organizational decline, and in the presence of limited state capacity.[97] First, our theoretical expectations about sector coordination – as discussed earlier – lead us to predict that there are few incentives for employers to significantly address the training needs of expanding pools of marginalized workers. Nelson's firm-level interviews with German enterprises provides ample support for these expectations. First, 83 percent of German firms responded "no" to the question, "Should firms take social responsibility for socially excluded people such as the long-term unemployed?" (In Denmark, only 26 percent of firms responded "no.") In addition, actual firm participation in Germany significantly lagged Denmark; there, 69 percent of firms participated in ALMP programs, and many of these at a high level of intensity (where significant numbers of marginalized workers were engaged in training and employment by a firm). In Germany, focusing on ALMP programs for the unemployed, 60 percent of German firms did not participate at all (and only 2 percent participated at a high level). Moreover, when asked why they did not participate, the most common reason – offered by 65 percent of firms – was that "the need for higher skill levels prevented participation." In fact, Nelson's analysis reveals that firms with predominately low-skilled workers were more likely to participate (for instance, to obtain cheap labor).

Second, Nelson's work reveals that the state did very little to engage employers in ALMP. Specifically, her work underscores that legislation expanding ALMP in the 1990s and 2000s did not require firms to take on new responsibilities for the low-skilled and marginalized workforce; in fact, employers have done a relatively good job in avoiding mandates such as training levies through the period of significant reform.[98] Nelson's work, in fact, highlights that the state did little to coordinate these training endeavors with market demand for skills: Despite significant subsidies for private enterprise training, large number of job seekers emerged from these training programs with no employment.[99]

Finally, any positive *cognitive* effects of employer organization on firm acceptance of public training endeavors for the reintegration of marginal workers and participation in them should also be limited. That is, firms discuss policy issues with other firms and their core workforce at the industrial sector level but are rarely brought into dialogue with a more encompassing slice of the German economy. Nelson's analysis generally confirms this expectation: Unlike macrocorporatist Denmark (see Chapter 9), membership in an employers' association did not influence whether

[96] Grote et al. 2007.
[97] Nelson no date.
[98] Hassel 2007.
[99] Nelson no date.

firms participated in ALMP programs for unemployed workers.[100] Overall, Nelson's interviews with German firms and analyses of that data reveal that unlike the impact of macrocorporatist employers' associations in Denmark, sector-based German employers' organizations did not significantly help firms see their common interests and engage them in coordinated solutions to common problems.

Conclusion

In many ways, the structure of the German political economy and its institutional infrastructure were cemented in the formative decades of industrialization. Despite efforts by state bureaucrats and business leaders, employers remained dispersed across a fragmented, regionally grounded party system before and during the Weimar Republic. The absence of a dedicated national business party sustained a substantial distrust among employers of the national state, and notably private enterprise-based sector coordination prevailed. Even though German statist traditions were reasserted during the fascist interlude, the constitutional structure of the postwar Federal Republic embraced the "semi-sovereign" state, and the institutions of sector coordination were reestablished. In the face of adverse economic impacts of post-OPEC shocks and postindustrial transformation, the institutions of the sector-coordinated economy and a constrained state produced a non-encompassing and biased response.

Core enterprises, in tacit alliance with their organized workers and with substantial subsidization by the state, pursued a strategy of modernization that included significant shedding of the least productive workers. This strategy continued to benefit its underlying coalition's members for some time. When the costs of this approach combined with the burdens of the country-specific shock of German unification proved unsustainable, the state and social partners sought a nationally coordinated solution. Yet, as we have seen, such an encompassing approach proved illusive. Unlike macrocorporatism, sector-coordinated institutions do not provide the incentives to the social partners to engage in comprehensive national bargains. This is especially true for peak employer and labor organizations with declines in cohesion and membership. Moreover, the German state, itself, lacked the capacity to forge or impose an encompassing policy solution to balance efficiency and equity goals. In the end, the state acted unilaterally to address the most pressing fiscal aspects of the crisis and to provide the economy with a modest increase in adaptive flexibility. There are no clear signs, however, that this reform track has reversed the rise of labor market dualism and inequality in contemporary Germany.

[100] Nelson no date. Nelson did find that when ALMP is defined to include programs for those in employment in Germany (e.g., minijobs), membership in an associated did modestly increase the chances of firm participation in ALMP.

The Political Foundations of Redistribution and Equality

Introduction

What is the recipe for a good society, where people pull together rather than pull apart, and material well-being seems to reflect not only the fruits of competitive markets but of cooperative endeavors to solve market failures and meet collective needs. What felicitous formula allows some nations to achieve high levels of equality even while maintaining high levels of economic efficiency and affluence? Is the quest for equality determined exclusively by the bravado, resources and organization of labor, or do strategic calculations by employers also matter to a high level of investment in human capital and a relatively egalitarian sharing of the economic pie? Why do some countries seem to have it all?

Even though countries have proposed rather similar reforms to address postindustrial stresses, the socioeconomic effects of these reforms have varied widely across advanced industrial nations, even within coordinated market economies. Macrocorporatist countries (such as Denmark) do better in simultaneously sustaining equality and growth, while continental countries with sector coordination (such as Germany) have produced dualistic policies. Employers and workers in the core economy – best prepared to withstand the vagaries of international competition and technological change – benefit from these policies, yet marginal workers are treated less kindly.

This chapter highlights the importance of employer coordination to policy makers' capacities to build broad political coalitions in support of relative equality and to the consequent divergence in redistributive outcomes. High levels of coordination ease government policy entrepreneurs' efforts to fold employers into solidaristic political coalitions to address the needs of low-skilled workers because these associations bring managers to participate in forums joining diverse sectors in discussions about the potential labor market contributions of low-skilled workers. Thus, politicians in macrocorporatist countries can entice employers into political coalitions to adopt policies that minimize negative impacts on marginal groups – even labor market actors in the Danish export sector have participated in efforts to skill and employ marginal workers – and this sustains higher levels of equality, employment, and economic growth. Countries with sectoral coordination have less luck in rallying business to the aid of marginal workers and in maintaining relative equality; for example, employers and workers in the German export sector agreed to political strategies that largely shunted aging and low-skilled workers into the unemployment system.

We document the impact of employer organization and macrocorporatism on income redistribution by the state from a broad cross-national, quantitative perspective. We assess the impact of organization and coordination on the change between pre- and postfisc income distribution for working-age families from the 1980s to 2000s in a sample of thirteen nations. We also provide systematic evidence on the relationships between employers' organization and nonmarket coordination on the one hand and income and labor market inequalities on the other. Finally, we confront the equity-versus-efficiency argument about the downside of social spending and show that high levels of employer organization and macrocorporatism have not had a negative impact on economic growth in the postindustrial era.

Class, Redistribution, and Equality

Social scientists often view relative equality as a product of social class, but many assume that employers are largely irrelevant to class coalitions in support of equality: Or to be more precise, equality increases when the right is successfully beaten down by the left, perhaps with the help of the center. To this end, scholars have noted that countries with a high degree of union organization and working-class participation in government through left parties tend to have larger welfare states and more redistribution. In countries where the right is divided, the left is more likely to gain control of government and to enact highly redistributive public policies. Employers are sometimes forced to make concessions to their workers when confronted with a powerful labor movement or leftist party and managers may begrudgingly come over time to alter their expectations about certain types of legislative outcomes.[1]

Under some circumstances, middle-class citizens may join the poor to seek redistribution from the wealthy to support policies that redistribute resources from the rich to other classes. The political positions of middle-class voters reflect electoral systems, because median voters only support redistribution parties under guarantees that their representative party will protect their interests post election. The positions of middle-class voters may reflect structures of wage compression at the bottom of the wage scale because the fortunes of the middle and bottom are less dissimilar than in countries with a larger wage gap.[2] Governmental structures influence conservative opposition to social reforms, as required legislative supra-majorities or veto points allow reform opponents (often including employers) to derail social reforms.[3] These diverse models share a common assumption: Preferences of voters on the right are relatively fixed, as

---

[1] Hicks and Swank, 1992; Korpi, 1980; Stephens, 1980; Bradley et al. 2003; Castles 1978; Huber and Stephens 2001; Hacker and Pierson 2002.
[2] Moene and Wallerstein 2003; Iversen and Soskice 2006; Lupa and Pontusson 2011.
[3] Huber, Ragin, and Stephens 2003; Immergut 1992.

employers are largely assumed to oppose redistributive social policies, even when they support social spending for their own workers.[4]

Yet we argue that government entrepreneurs often seek to bring employers into political coalitions for solidaristic reform policies, and business constitutes a critical social actor in these struggles. The system of labor market coordination is crucial to how firms engage in political coalitions to balance equality and growth, because diverse segments of capital behave quite differently under the various types of labor market coordination. Thus, we identify the cleavages separating industrial sectors and their potential interests in relatively egalitarian policies.

Industrial sectors tend to divide along two cleavages. The first pertains to the location of the industries' competitive markets and differentiates exposed, largely private sector firms from ones operating in the public and protected sectors. Firms in exposed sectors have greater difficulty passing wage costs on to consumers, which makes them adverse to government spending; however, they also have a higher need for skills for their highly productive workers, which makes them seek certain types of social programs.

The second cleavage concerns the attributes of the firm's industrial workforce and differentiates firms with more high-skilled workers (often unionized) in capital-intensive sectors from those with low-skilled workers (often nonunion) in labor-intensive sectors. Capital-intensive, unionized firms are more likely than labor-intensive, nonunionized firms to support social, labor, and Keynesian fiscal policies because associated extra wage and nonwage costs are a smaller proportion of total production costs, firms are more deeply harmed by disruptions in the production process, and the threat of labor activism is stronger.[5] In our postindustrial, service-oriented economy one tends to see a skills division between firms hiring high general-skills professionals, medium-skilled workers (often with specific skills and often in capital-intensive industries), and low general-skills workers. As we have noted, a particularly close relationship between social protections and production strategies occurs in countries that utilize manufacturing workers with *specific* as opposed to *general* skills.

These cleavages along competitive market and labor lines generate six different categories of firms, all with a different set of potential interests in social reform (see Table 12.1). First, in the upper right box of Table 12.1, one finds firms competing in exposed sectors that rely on high general-skills professional workers, and include information technology and business services companies, among others. These employers might support state-provided social benefits such as health insurance and good general education because the small firms that often populate these sectors lack the economies of scale to provide extensive social supports. Yet these employers are likely to resist spending on, training of, or wage equality for low-skilled workers because they predominantly rely on a white-collar workforce. They prefer highly competitive labor markets both because their workers derive their high general skills through the education system rather than within the firms and because labor market rigidities might restrict their competition in international markets.

---

[4] Korpi 1980; 2006.
[5] Ferguson 1995; Martin 1991, 2000.

TABLE 12.1. *Stylized Cleavages among Firms in Postindustrial Capitalism*

Skills Levels	Competitive Markets	
	Protected	Exposed
High	High (usually general) skills College/postgrad education Doctor, lawyer, bureaucrat in public and private sector	High (usually general) skills College education Information technology/business services mainly in private sector
Medium	Medium (often specific) skills Vocational training or two-year college education Teller, sec., preschool teacher Europe: many in public sector	Medium (often specific) skills Vocational training systems Core manufacturing sectors: autos, steel
Low	Low skills High school education or less Private: retail, fast food Public: nursing home aides	Low skills High school education or less Industries moved offshore & few workers left in advanced countries

Second, in the middle right box, one finds firms competing in exposed sectors that rely on medium-skilled workers in the core manufacturing sectors such as the automobile or steel industries. These employers might be drawn to solidaristic policies that expand training for lower-skilled workers when labor markets are tight; however, they are more likely to prefer segmentalist strategies that offer advantageous social benefits to their own workforce but reduce spending on the low-skilled and marginally employed persons.

Third, firms in the lower right box compete in exposed sectors with low-skilled workers. This group has largely disappeared within advanced countries, because jobs in export industries relying on low-skilled workers (e.g., textile companies) have moved offshore to countries with much lower wage structures.

Fourth, in the lower left box, one finds firms producing in protected sectors with low-skilled (mainly service) workers, such as private retail or fast-food firms. Few public sector concerns rely exclusively on low-skilled workers; however, these workers are found in corners of advanced welfare states and include nursing home aides and bus drivers. Private companies hiring low-skilled workers might be attracted to state policies that offer universal or heavily subsidized training and social benefits, because their low wages cannot sustain nonwage benefits and their low-wage workers are likely to be among the biggest beneficiaries of these public programs. But these firms may also oppose social expenditures, because they benefit from low wages and high labor market flexibility; moreover, they resist wage agreements, tax increases, and social policies that advantage nonworkers over workers. The final two boxes (middle left and upper left) include enterprises with workers in protected sectors having medium and high skills levels. These enterprises (e.g., municipal departments) may have public sector workers with responsibility for the economic condition of marginal workers and may support investment in skills-training for low-skilled workers. Yet these public sector employers might also prefer to restrain benefits for low-skilled workers to preserve state fiscal solvency.

What is striking about these various categories is that employers in several boxes have somewhat indeterminate social policy preferences: Firms may choose to see their interests as lying with (a) a *neoliberal* agenda that slashes social spending for workers generally, (b) a *segmentalist* agenda that entails investment in their own workers to the exclusion of labor market outsiders, or (c) a *solidaristic* agenda that supports investments in the skills of a broad cross-section of society that includes marginal workers.[6] The neoliberal coalition might include employers in low-skill protected and high-skill exposed industries, who wish to maintain the highest level of labor market flexibility and low social costs. Another neoliberal coalition might consist of employers in exposed sectors who unify against those in protected sectors to avoid wage and tax pressures that disadvantage firms in international markets and to lobby for neoliberal policies that foster competition.

The segmentalist coalition might unify employers who offer good benefits to their own workforce but wish to avoid the fiscal burdens or competitive disadvantages associated with extending such benefits more broadly. Here employers of manufacturing and public sector workers might support policies that benefit their own workforce, but might favor shunting off the low-skilled to passive unemployment benefits.

Finally, the solidaristic coalition might include employers in the publicly oriented protected sectors who support investments in low-skilled workers for whom they have responsibility. Private core manufacturing employers might join this coalition to seek state aide in the burdens of adjusting to a postindustrial economy, but firms with highly educated white-collar workers may not find much use in training low-skilled workers. Thus support for training and human capital enhancements might come from employers (a) in the protected public sector (who hire low-skilled workers, (b) in manufacturing firms in exposed sectors (who need an expanded labor pool and programs to facilitate industrial adjustment), and (c) in low-skilled sectors (who hire marginal workers).[7]

Determinants of Redistribution and Equality

Our central question is to understand why some countries are more likely than others to produce higher levels of redistribution and equality. We briefly review the determinants of redistribution, as our hypotheses remain close to the logic laid out in Chapter 8. We suggest that just as employers' organization and macrocorporatism influenced the strategic preferences of individual firms, so should they aid or hinder the state in constructing coalitions in support of equality and redistribution.

Economic Determinants of Redistribution

Economic and labor market conditions may motivate positive social spending on skills and other protections that enhance equality. *Economic growth* should be positively associated with better wages, more jobs and less inequality, and a generally strong fiscal basis for egalitarian policies because countries may invest heavily in practices to foster

---

[6] Martin and Thelen 2007.

[7] We assume solidaristic policies include not only ALMP and other human capital-oriented programs (e.g., health), but universalistic basic transfers (e.g., economically sufficient short-term social insurance benefits with high coverage rates). These policies, potentially supported by employers under the conditions we specify, should maintain redistribution and mitigate dualism in the face of postindustrial pressures.

equality when they are better able to afford these efforts.[8] *Deindustrialization* should foster inequality and dualism directly through the displacement from stable employment in core economic sectors and through strain on training systems that facilitate workers' transition across the skills barrier.[9] Increased service sector employment is also associated with lower productivity growth (i.e., Baumol's disease), making it more difficult for actors to fiscally maintain support for income and employment equity. *Female Labor Force Participation* may also matter, in that increases in women's labor force participation (and vulnerability to the labor market) should increase women's claims for benefits and political support of the welfare state.[10]

Trade openness should have negative impacts on inequality because industrialized countries face short- to intermediate term pressures on the incomes and jobs of semi- and unskilled workers under increased trade. Coordination might mitigate somewhat these negative effects; in the absence of cooperation among labor, capital and the state, semi- and unskilled workers become the central victims of dualism. Finally, *capital mobility* may undercut egalitarian outcomes through real (or threatened) capital disinvestment.[11]

Labor Determinants of Redistribution
National levels of redistribution should also be affected by the balance of power across countervailing societal interests. As was discussed in Chapter 8, *progressive party power* should have an impact on employers' willingness to tolerate redistribution (and associated tax increases.) Yet even though both social and Christian democratic parties have historically supported higher levels of social spending than the center-right, these parties have constructed different models of the welfare state. Christian democratic welfare and labor market regimes are governed by the principle of status maintenance (of male breadwinners). Welfare state financing structure very much promotes such an orientation, since expenditures based on social insurance contributions (preferred under Christian democracy) rather than general taxation amount to deferred wages that are politically difficult to cut. Overall, Christian democratic parties appeal to core sector workers and the middle class and, in turn, offer more centrist programs.[12] These policies effectively protect the employment and benefits of labor market insiders rather than labor market outsiders such as young workers and women.[13]

By contrast, social democratic welfare states are financed differently and in ways that do not create and feed political cleavages between insiders and outsiders. Nordic social democratic governments always emphasized activation/active labor market policies that specifically did *not* seek to insure against labor market risk by supporting stability and the enhancement of productivity of workers within the same firm or industry; rather they sought to accomplish these same goals by moving resources (including labor) to the places in the economy where they could be more productive (e.g., through

[8] Wilensky 2002.
[9] Iversen and Cusack 2000.
[10] Thus, women must act as a countervailing interest to business opposition to redistribution. Bradley et al. 2003; Huber and Stephens 2001.
[11] See Stolper-Samuelson models of factor price equalization in Frieden and Rogowski 1996; Swank 2002.
[12] Esping-Andersen 1990; Iversen and Stephens 2008; Iversen 2009.
[13] Martin and Thelen 2007.

the policies of Rehn-Meidner Sweden and of the Danish flexicurity model).[14] Thus, we expect relatively high and stable solidarism with social democratic governments, but no partisan difference from secular center-right party governments, or even some evidence of rising dualism, under Christian democratic-dominated governments.

A contrary view suggests that even social democratic parties face compelling political incentives to defend the interests of labor market insiders (skilled industrial workers) that comprise the traditional core constituencies of left parties. Social democratic parties look much like Christian democratic parties, in maintaining high levels of employment protection policies but in not supporting expansions of active labor market and related policies that benefit outsiders and impose costs (e.g., taxes) on insiders. This view questions a clear and strong positive impact of social democratic governments on contemporary patterns of solidarism.[15]

Democratic Politics and Institutions

As was discussed in Chapter 8, the economic *position of the median voter* should also matter to the power exerted by business. In the standard framework, a greater divergence between relatively affluent mean voters and less well-to-do median voters generates greater redistribution. A more recent formulation suggests that when median voters are relatively closer to the bottom than to the top, they should be more willing to ally with the poor to tax the rich.[16] In addition, PR and federalism are highly likely to have indirect effects on solidaristic policies and outcomes through their impacts on coordination. Yet, for reasons outlined in Chapter 8, we also want to assess the direct effects of democratic institutions on redistribution here.

Organizational Determinants of Redistribution

Finally, we suggest that the types of coordinating institutions of business (and labor) – most importantly macrocorporatism – should influence politicians' capacities to construct solidaristic coalitions and, in this way, should be crucial for national patterns of redistribution and inequality. Macrocorporatist institutions bring together a broad cross section of the workforce and unite high- and low-skilled workers: By definition, macrocorporatism entails densely organized and nationally centralized labor unions. Sustained and iterative patterns of interaction between these associations and employers and the state in national collective bargaining and tripartite policy-making forums create a positive sum game for business and labor. Because the groups foster a long-term perspective and guarantee compliance, each side is more willing to take positions that will benefit the broader economy.[17] Moreover, labor preferences for social protection and egalitarian outcomes are more likely to be reflected in national policy and performance, and corporatist institutions (for labor and business) should trump a labor market-insider strategy.[18]

---

[14] Katzenstein 1985; Huo 2009.
[15] Rueda 2005; 2007.
[16] Meltzer and Richard 1981; Lupa and Pontusson 2011.
[17] Wilensky 2002; Mosley et al. 1998; Streeck and Schmitter 1985; Crouch 1993; Hicks and Kenworthy 1998.
[18] Where labor organization and macrocorporatist institutions are strong, the interests of labor market outsiders are likely to be incorporated to a significant extent in union policy preferences and political

The cognitive effects of these high levels of business coordination are particularly important to employers' support for social investments in marginal workers. Whereas the political economy and collective action effects of groups shed insight into why firms provide skills for core industrial workers, social protections for marginal workers have a less direct tie-in to productivity and the interpretation of social policy benefits is particularly important to broad business support. Yet when held responsible for considering the economic needs and potential contributions of low-skilled workers in deliberative forums, labor market representatives of both business and labor assume higher levels of responsibility for these workers.

Macrocorporatist employers' associations also enhance policy entrepreneurs' capacities to bring employers into solidaristic political coalitions to enhance the human capital of low-skilled workers and to sustain higher levels of equality. Macrocorporatist employers' associations, much more than other forms of national organization, offer governments an institutional vehicle through which to build business support for social welfare initiatives. Although both macrocorporatist and sector-coordinated economies have relatively high levels of centralized collective bargaining and tripartite negotiations, macrocorporatist countries have a bigger role for the state in these processes.

Empirical Analyses

We seek to provide a systematic assessment of the importance of coordination for redistribution, equality, and dualism. We begin by estimating a model of redistribution directly analogous to that used to estimate the impact of coordination on social policy in Chapter 8. Our primary indicator of redistribution is the absolute change between pre- and posttax/transfer Gini indices for income inequality in working-wage families.[19] We estimate models of annual pooled time-series cross-section data from the early 1980s to the 2000s (typically to 2003), drawing upon data for thirteen nations from the Luxembourg Income Study (LIS). We present early 1980s and 2000s data on the magnitude of redistribution (and market income inequality) in Table 12.2.

Our central concern is to assess the impacts of *the level of employers' organization and macrocorporatism* on redistribution and labor market inequalities, and we measure these factors as well as associated forces such as sector coordination and labor organization as we did in Chapters 7 and 8. We also largely rely on the same measurement procedures for our other explanatory variables as we used in Chapters 7 and 8 (and see ancillary materials for details and data sources). Two exceptions are noteworthy. First, to evaluate the position of the *median voter* on redistribution, we use the ratio of the incomes of workers at the 90th to those at the 50th percentile[20] as well as the estimate of the ideological position of the median voter; for our one new explanatory variable,

---

strategies, recognized by employers, and, in turn, reflected in national policy and outcomes (also see Huo 2009).

[19] We also replicate all of our models with the percentage change from pre- to postfisc Gini indices. See Iversen 2009. See Contemporary Ancillary Materials.

[20] Iversen and Soskice 2006.

TABLE 12.2. *Market Inequality, Redistribution, and Dualism[a]*

	Redistribution (Gini-Market Income)		Redistribution (Gini-Market Income)		Labor Markets 50:10 Wage Ratios (Dualism)		Labor Markets 50:10 Wage Ratios (Dualism)	
	1980s		2000s		1985		2005	
Relatively high macrocorporatism								
Norway	5.3	(26.2)	9.4	(32.8)	1.4	(2.0)	1.4	(1.8)
Denmark	8.6	(30.5)	12.6	(32.8)	1.4	(2.3)	1.5	(2.3)
Sweden	10.8	(29.9)	12.9	(36.6)	1.3	(3.0)	1.4	(3.2)
Belgium	13.5	(34.7)	13.8	(37.5)	1.5	(2.6)		(3.0)
Finland	11.1	(29.9)	13.0	(36.2)	1.5	(—)	1.4	(—)
Austria						(—)		(1.2)
Moderate Macrocorporatism								
Italy	—	—	—	—	1.5	(.9)	—	(3.1)
Germany	5.5	(28.4)	10.0	(36.2)	1.7	(.7)	1.9	(3.0)
Ireland	—	—	—	—	—	—	1.8	(1.7)
Netherlands	13.2	(38.5)	8.7	(30.9)	1.6	(2.3)	1.6	(1.3)
Australia	7.7	(34.8)	11.6	(42.8)	1.7	(—)	1.7	(7.4)
Relatively low macrocorporatism								
Switzerland	1.9	(31.0)	4.1	(30.6)	1.5	(—)	1.5	(1.2)
Japan	—	—	—	—	1.7	(1.2)	1.7	(5.0)
France	10.0	(38.6)	10.6	(38.8)	1.6	(—)	1.5	(3.2)
New Zealand	—	—	—	—	1.5	(2.1)	1.6	(4.4)
United Kingdom	11.3	(41.7)	10.3	(44.3)	1.8	(1.7)	1.8	(1.6)
Canada	5.9	(33.1)	7.9	(39.3)	2.4	(4.5)	2.0	(4.9)
United States	6.4	(39.0)	6.9	(43.0)	2.0	(—)	2.1	(—)

Notes: Values for redistribution are the absolute differences in pre- and postfisc working-age family Ginis for the earliest data point in the 1980s and the closest data point to 2003. Reported Gini indices are for market income for working-age families. The second portion of the table reports the 50:10 wage ratios for full-time workers and involuntary part-time employment as a percentage of all employment.

[a] See contemporary ancillary materials for details and data sources.

we measure *female labor force participation* as the percentage of the female working-age population in the labor force.[21]

Our core model of redistribution across working-age families takes the following form, where "Coordination" represents four specifications: employers' organization, macrocorporatism, both employers and union organization, and both macrocorporatism and enterprise cooperation.

[21] We also assess a number of additional explanations of redistribution. For reasons laid out above and in Chapter 8, we examine the direct effects on redistribution of PR, federalism, and general veto points as well as voter turnout. We also assess Lupa and Pontusson's (2011) argument that the relative proximity of the median voter to the low income voter should shape redistribution. We report the results of these tests – findings that offer little or marginal support for these factors – in the Contemporary Ancillary materials.

[Eq. 1]   Redistribution$_{i,t}$ = α + β_1(Coordination)$_{i,t-1}$ + β_2(Position of the Median
           Voter) $_{i,t-1}$ + β_3(Social Democratic Government)$_{i,(t-1 \text{ to } t-3)}$ + β_4(Christian
           Democratic Government)$_{i,(t-1 \text{ to } t-3)}$ + β_5(Deindustrialization)$_{i,t-1}$ -β_6(Trade
           Openness)$_{i,t-1}$ - β_7(Capital Mobility)$_{i,t-1}$ +β_8(Unemployment)$_{i,t-1}$ + β_9(Female
           Labor Force Participation)$_{i,t-1}$ + β_{10} (Per Capita GDP)$_{i,t-1}$ + $\varepsilon_{i,t}$

where α is an equation intercept, i designates nation, t designates year, and $\varepsilon_{i,t}$ is the
error term. For redistribution, in which the dependent variable is measured at two
to six (variable) time points across thirteen nations, we initially account for uneven
measurement points with a control for years between observations; we also use a common lagged endogenous variable model where causal variables are operationalized as
means of annual observations between measurement points for inequality.[22]

We also wish to understand related features of inequality, such as wage dispersion
and dualism. In analyses of the determinants of these outcomes, we estimate a model
for all advanced capitalist democracies of the 50:10 wage ratio for full time workers, a
key indicator of labor market inequality.[23] But, labor market dualism in the coordinated
market economies has also taken the form of substantial involuntary part-time work,
temporary contract employment, and long-term unemployment in some CMEs. We
therefore refine our analysis and examine the determinants of three indicators of labor
market dualism – involuntary part-time workers as percent of total employment, temporary contract employment as a percent of total employment, and long-term unemployment of twelve months or more as a percent of total unemployment – for the
eleven CMEs from the early 1980s to 2000s. We display 1980s and 2000s mean values of
wage inequality and involuntary part-time employment in Table 12.2.

For our four measures of outcomes, we estimate the following model:

[Eq. 2]   Measure of Inequality/Dualism$_{i,t}$ = α + β_1(Macrocorporatism)$_{i,t-1}$ +
           β_2(Social Democratic Government)$_{i,(cum\ t-1\ to\ 1950)}$ + β_3(Christian Democratic
           Government)$_{i,(cum\ t-1\ to\ 1950)}$ + β_4(Deindustrialization)$_{i,t-1}$ -β_5(Trade
           Openness)$_{i,t-1}$ - β_6(Capital Mobility)$_{i,t-1}$ + β_7(Per Capita GDP)$_{i,t-1}$ + $\varepsilon_{i,t}$

where α is an intercept, i designates nation, t designates year, and $\varepsilon_{i,t}$ is the error term.
For explanatory variables, we employ a generalized model that includes macrocor-
poratism, partisan government, and postindustrial pressures. That is, to foster man-
ageability in the analyses of four dimensions of inequality/dualism, we focus on only
macrocorporatism and a simplified control model. With one exception, we use the
same measurement procedures as those discussed previously. The exception is partisan government, where we find it appropriate to use cumulative measures of years in
office for social democratic and Christian democratic parties in order to tap long-term
effects of various partisan policies on outcomes.

---

[22] The counter for years between observations is never significant and never effects findings reported later;
      thus, we drop it from the analysis. On the lagged endogenous variable/mean exogenous variable specifi-
      cation see Persson, Roland, and Tabelini 2007 and, Lupa and Ponstusson 2011.
[23] Rueda 2008; King and Rueda 2008. We also estimate models of family market income distribution and
      "low wage work," or the percentage of workers below one-half the median income. Results reported here
      for the impact of coordination are duplicated for these measures.

Estimation. We use least squares regression with corrections for first-order autoregressive errors and panel correct standard errors.[24] Because a substantial amount of variance in redistribution and its hypothesized causes is cross-national, we do not include country fixed effects in estimations for redistribution. Causal factors in our models account for a substantial portion of cross-national variation in redistribution, in any case, and we are confident that the remaining bias (from omission of relevant variables or their proxy by atheoretical unit effects) is modest.[25] Our model of wage inequality for the capitalist democracies as a whole also does well without specifying country unit effects ($R^2 > .92$); thus, we exclude them from reported results. For our second set of three outcomes of labor market dualism in CMEs, our model is less strong and we specify unit effects.

Findings for Coordination and Redistribution

Table 12.3 presents results from the estimations of our basic model of government redistribution. With respect to coordination, the first panel of the table shows that employers' organization has highly significant and positive effects on redistribution, net of other forces. The column I coefficient estimate of 2.02 for employer organization suggests that a change from the level of employers' organization in the United States (about −1.9 on our standard score scale) to that in Norway (.98) would increase redistribution by roughly 5.8 points (i.e., 2.9 × 2.02). That is, we express the Gini coefficient of inequality in percentage terms (0.0 = perfect equality, 100 = perfect inequality) and operationalize redistribution (the absolute change in the Gini index between pre- and postfisc income distributions) as a positive number. Redistribution across working-age families (the absolute change between pre- and postfisc Ginis) ranges from about 5 to 15 percent in the contemporary era; thus, the magnitude of this effect is substantial.

With respect to other features of coordination, macrocorporatism also exhibits a substantively large and positive effect on redistribution (column IV): A change from the average level of macrocorporatism in the United States to that in Norway (i.e., from −1.6 to 1.1, or 2.7) would increase redistribution by 7.6 points (2.7 × 2.8, the coefficient for macrocorporatism in column IV). The column II model estimated whether much or all of this effect is due to union organization and the associated institutional position and political power of labor. Although it is difficult to get a precise estimate between two closely related dimensions in analysis such as this, our results suggests that unique variation attributable to employers' organization is strongly, positively and significantly associated with government redistribution. Union organization, as predicted by power resource theorists, exerts a large independent effect on redistribution. Yet, both employers' and union organization matter quite a bit, net of electoral politics and socioeconomic forces. Finally, we assess the joint impact on redistribution of our aggregate index of macrocorporatism and sector coordination. As Table 12.3 demonstrates, although correctly signed, sector coordination, itself, does not significantly shape the magnitude of income redistribution by the state.

Turning to the second panel of Table 12.3, we display the findings on the independent impacts of median voters and progressive party governance on income

[24] Beck and Katz 1995.
[25] Plümper et al. 2005.

TABLE 12.3. *Determinants of Government Income Redistribution in the Postindustrial Era*

	I	II	III	IV	V
Employers and coordination		*Control for*			
Employer organization	2.0155**	1.3726**	—	—	—
	(.3640)	(.2904)			
Labor organization	—	2.2075**	—	—	—
		(.4612)			
Macrocorporatism	—	—	2.6191**	2.8416**	2.1896**
			(.4586)	(.4149)	(.5315)
Sector coordination	—	—	.5866	—	—
			(.5002)		
Electoral and party politics					
Median voter (90:50 wage ratio)	3.1734*	8.4833**	5.6768**	6.5622**	3.7053*
	(2.0173)	(1.7912)	(1.9934)	(2.2021)	(2.2894)
Left party government	−.0004	−.0030	−.0004	.0007	−.0092
	(.0061)	(.0073)	(.0075)	(.0069)	(.0084)
Christian democratic party government	.0104	.0072	.0053	.0069	.0331**
	(.0119)	(.0121)	(.0124)	(.0131)	(.0131)
Postindustrialization					
Deindustrialization	.5889**	.5642**	.5958**	.5304**	.4686**
	(.0948)	(.0803)	(.0926)	(.0880)	(.1323)
Trade openness	.0084	.0076	−.0038	.0040	−.0102
	(.0136)	(.0119)	(.0154)	(.0147)	(.0175)
Capital mobility	−.0033	.0144	.0144	.0198	−.0370*
	(.0229)	(.0214)	(.0241)	(.0232)	(.0250)
Controls					
Unemployment	.1646*	.1410*	.1834**	.2095**	.1480
	(.1168)	(.1051)	(.0986)	(.1074)	(.1314)
Female labor force participation	.1989**	.1541**	.1529**	.1688**	.1997**
	(.0313)	(.0332)	(.0361)	(.0289)	(.0450)
Per capita real GDP	−.3755**	−.3859**	−.3921**	−.3812**	−.3275**
	(.0542)	(.0473)	(.0464)	(.0605)	(.0831)
Redistribution $t-1$	—	—	—	—	.2135**
					(.0801)
Intercept	−46.2552	−51.5806	−48.6221	−47.6825	−.3675
R^2	.7719	.8253	.8106	.8185	.8593
Number of observations	57	57	57	57	44

Models are estimated with 1981–2002 data for 13 nations by ordinary least squares; equations are first-order autoregressive and are estimated with Prais-Winston regression. Panels are unbalanced where time series for each country consists of two to six annual measurements. The table reports unstandardized regression coefficients and panel correct standard errors.
* Indicates significance at the .10 level.
** Indicates significance at the .05 level or below.

distribution. In all versions of the basic model, the magnitude of difference between high and median wage earners is significantly and positively related to actual government income redistribution. The 90:50 ratio typically varies from 1.5 to 2.0 in our sample of nation years; moreover, government redistribution varies from roughly 5 to

15 points. Thus, a coefficient for the median voter variable of about 6.5 (column III) suggests that a relatively large change of .5 in the 90:50 ratio will be associated with a substantively large change in redistribution of 3.2 points (i.e., 6.5 × 0.5).[26]

With respect to recent governance by left or Christian democratic parties, neither party variable emerges as a significant determinant of redistribution in the models of Table 12.3. But long-term cumulative power of left and Christian democratic parties is strongly related to macrocorporatism in the contemporary period; long-term social democratic party governance is also significantly related to our measure of union power. Thus, we cannot (and do not) argue that party governance does not influence redistribution. Yet, our results suggest that in the early 1980s to 2000s, recent governance by progressive parties (versus center-right governments) does not exercise much of a direct effect on government redistribution independent of coordination in our sample.[27]

With regard to postindustrialization pressures, the third panel of the table illustrates that deindustrialization is especially important in calling forth increased redistribution. This factor exerts a consistently significant and substantively large effect on government redistribution. As the results we present demonstrate, deindustrialization is the most important socioeconomic force in shaping inequality and labor market dualism in recent years. But globalization – either trade openness or capital mobility – has no consistent and significant impact on redistribution in the models estimated here. With regard to other controls, both rises in unemployment and declines in affluence exert an upward effect on income redistribution. In addition, as predicted, the rise in female labor force participation is, net of other factors, associated with increases in government redistribution. Finally, it is important to point out that the results of columns I through IV are perfectly replicated by the lagged endogenous variable model of column V. With this specification the focus shifts to change in the dependent variable (see Chapters 2 and 8) and we estimate the impacts of average levels of coordination, politics, and postindustrial dynamics on the change in redistribution since the last measurement point.

Findings for Low-Wage Work, Market Inequality, and Labor Market Dualism

Table 12.4 presents results from our analysis of the impacts of coordination on inequality and dualism. As the table highlights, macrocorporatism is systematically and negatively related to market inequalities on three of our four dimensions. Higher national coordination results in less wage inequality among full-time workers; this finding also holds when we specify fixed country effects with $N-1$ dummy variables.

---

[26] As the 90:50 ratio is positively associated with coordination and other variables in the model, this positive effect might be the result of a "sign-flip" brought about by excessively high multicollinearity. (We thank John Stephens for pointing this out to us; also see Stephens [1980] and Iversen and Soskice [2009] on the relationship between market income distribution and redistribution.) Yet, the R-square delete for the regression of the 90:50 ratio on other variables in the model is only .78; thus, it is just in the range of multicollinearity where standard errors may be artificially inflated but not in an "excessive" range. Hanushek and Jackson 1977.

[27] Measures of recent left and Christian democratic party government are not beset by high multicolllinearity (e.g., as a result of the inclusion of female labor force participation); regression of either party variable on the other variables in the model (i.e., computation of the R-square delete statistics) produces R-squares of .40, at the most.

"Real proof of pudding" [handwritten]

TABLE 12.4. *The Determinants of Labor Market Inequalities in the Postindustrial Era*

	50:10 Wage Ratio All Nations	Involuntary Part-Timers CMEs	Long-Term Unemployed CMEs	Temporary Workers CMEs
Macrocorporatism	−.0431**	.0813	−3.9967**	−.7937**
	(.0092)	(.2884)	(1.6249)	(.4782)
Left party government	−.0132**	−.2568**	−1.5444**	.1145
	(.0064)	(.0455)	(.3118)	(.0864)
Christian democratic government	−.0098**	.0483	.6399*	.2238**
	(.0018)	(.0411)	(.4779)	(.1002)
Deindustrialization	.0027**	.3739**	2.7194**	.1640**
	(.0012)	(.0609)	(.3375)	(.0694)
Trade openness	.0000	−.0121	.0073	.0018
	(.0004)	(.0057)	(.0587)	(.0136)
Capital mobility	.0016**	.0159**	−.1089*	−.0043
	(.0004)	(.0069)	(.0626)	(.0132)
Growth rate in per capita real GDP	.5405	−.0330**	−.1958**	.0000
	(.8366)	(.0188)	(.1050)	(.0255)
Intercept	1.4930	−16.9433	−127.5927	−2.3105
R^2	.9242	.4071	.6005	.6588
Number of observations	404	183	272	201

[Handwritten annotations in margins: "big egalitarian effect greater", "↑ time in power SMALLER DUALISM", "Control variable that is CD associated every time → Bad. Bad news creates huge problems"]

The model of the first column is estimated with 1980s to 2000s annual data from seventeen nations by Prais-Winston (AR1) regression with panel correct standard errors. Models of the second through fourth columns are estimated for 1980s to 2000s annual data for the eleven coordinated market economies by Prais-Winston (AR1) regression with panel correct standard errors; nation fixed effects are included.
* Indicates significance at the .10 level.
** Indicates significance at the .05 level or below.

Macrocorporatism is also related to lower long-term unemployment and less use of temporary contracts within the CMEs as a group.[28] Government control by progressive parties also matters: Cumulative years in office of social and Christian democratic parties depress the magnitude of wage inequality across the capitalist democracies. When we turn to patterns of labor market dualism in CMEs, a somewhat different pattern emerges. Left parties mute the prevalence of involuntary part-time work and long-term unemployment. On the other hand, and consistent with the view that Christian democratic parties may favor core skilled worker and middle-class constituencies,[29] government control by Christian democrats results in higher long-term unemployment and more temporary workers.

With respect to postindustrial pressures, deindustrialization is consistently and significantly related to the rise of inequality and dualism. These effects are also substantively large. On the other hand, globalization has inconsistent and often insignificant impacts on inequalities and dualism. Whereas capital mobility in positively associated

[28] Estimates for the effects of employer organization produce similar results, although in some specifications the level of employers' organization falls just below statistical significance. Model results are otherwise the same as those reported in Table 12.4.
[29] Swank, Martin, and Thelen 2008; Iversen 2009.

with wage inequality, it has a marginally negative effect on long-term unemployment and is otherwise insignificantly related to inequality and dualism. Trade openness is unrelated to low-wage work and labor market dualism in CMEs. Similarly, economic growth rates are not systematically related to inequalities although low growth is associated with higher labor market dualism on two dimensions. Overall, income and labor market outcomes are vigorously driven by deindustrialization and politics: Both the institutions for national coordination and partisan government matter a good deal to the relative magnitude of inequality and dualism in the postindustrial era.

The Findings in Country Context. We have seen these dynamics in contemporary Danish and German efforts to cope with postindustrial pressures.[30] In the postindustrial era, Denmark made significant changes in some of its key institutions, such as the decentralization of bargaining and the reduction of unemployment supports. Yet the Danes made these changes in a way that was designed to support social solidarity and to locate a new equilibrium between growth and equity appropriate to the postindustrial economy. With programs to fill projected labor shortages through training and employment for the long-term unemployed, the Danes hoped to expand employment, to reduce expenditures (by getting people off the welfare rolls), to subsidize the costs of training a new labor source available to employers, and to maintain wage equality (low-wage positions for the disabled are subsidized by the state). In short, Danish policy entrepreneurs hoped to solve the trilemma of the postindustrial economy and to fix the decommodification traps of the Scandinavian welfare state[31].

The Danish state at both the national and local levels achieved high levels of success because it was able to call upon the social partners (employers and unions) in the campaign to expand employment, to reduce welfare dependency, and to solve the problems of public finances. Proponents of ALMP felt that marginal workers would stay in the workforce longer if they were given real private sector training and practice jobs. In addition to this substantive reason for engaging the private sector, municipalities wanted to avoid having to hire the entire ranks of the unemployed and vehemently maintained that the private sector had to take its fair share. Important commissions with social partner representation were appointed to formulate positions on a wide range of issues, and most reforms during the 1990s were created with the full support of both business and labor. Consequently, even employers became involved in programs to enhance the skills of the long-term unemployed, motivated by a desire to secure enhanced skills and a broader labor supply. When the bourgeois parties regained government in 2001, they again attempted to impose a neoliberal agenda on Danish society, by eroding social rights and reducing the sphere of concerted action controlled by organized business and labor. Yet, oddly, employers' associations and unions joined forces with municipalities to block the bourgeois reforms in battles over the issues of labor protections for part-time workers, the unions' control of employment funds, and the social rights of the unemployed. The peak employers' association had been an architect of the new welfare state, accepted the wisdom of investing in the skills development of marginal workers, and remained committed to high levels of government spending on active labor market policies.

---

[30] See also Martin 2004; Martin and Swank 2004; Martin and Thelen 2007.
[31] Martin 2004.

By comparison, Germany exhibits some formal institutional stability in many key realms (e.g., industrial relations and vocational training), but followed a very different strategy for dealing with marginal and unproductive workers. Recent German reforms (e.g., Hartz IV) have been less sweeping than in Denmark, but have instituted new elements of "residualism" (means-tested unemployment benefits) that reflect a trend toward greater labor market segmentation.[32] These reforms have intensified the divide between labor market insiders and outsiders and have depressed social solidarity, even as they have, paradoxically, expanded coordination at the micro (firm) level, between works councils and managers. Thus, moderate levels of coordination persist in some arenas even as solidarity declines: Core workers' interests remain sheltered, and social outsiders are less protected from the vagaries of the postindustrial economy. At the same time (as we argue in Chapter 11), the logic of sector coordination and the decline in employer organization has meant that the state had a much more difficult time eliciting material support from employers for programs to expand the skills of marginal workers. Business and labor groups in the core industrial economy have preferred to shepherd low-skilled workers onto the unemployment (and retirement) rolls and into irregular employment rather than to spend resources in preparing these workers for full-time, stable work in the postindustrial economy.

Coordination and Economic Growth

The positive impacts of coordination on public social protection, government redistribution, and equality raise the proverbial question of whether or not coordinated market economies suffer an equity-efficiency trade-off. Whereas a systematic analysis of coordination and economic performance is beyond the scope of our study, a succinct treatment of the impact of employers' organization and macrocorporatism on economic growth should be instructive. On the one hand, prevailing neoliberal theory suggests coordination and its egalitarian correlates are bad for growth. In this familiar view, relatively high levels of social protection, state intervention in labor markets, government redistribution, and relatively high tax burdens undercut work and saving incentives;[33] large public bureaucracies foster a variety of economic inefficiencies while administering redistributive and interventionist policies.[34] Relatively well-organized interests attendant coordinated institutions also foster economic inefficiencies.[35] Generally, from the neoliberal perspective, economic growth is maximized through unimpeded markets.[36]

On the other hand, some contemporary political economists suggest that high levels of nonmarket coordination are completely consistent with robust economic growth.[37] In this view, well-organized employers overcome coordination and collective goods problems facing enterprises that are not often easily solved by competitive markets; employer-labor cooperation within the industrial relation system generally complements these forms of employer-driven coordination. Hall and Gingerich explicitly

[32] Palier and Thelen 2008.
[33] Gilder 1980; Murray 1984.
[34] Okun 1975; Wolf 1990.
[35] Olson 1982; Mueller 1983.
[36] Friedman and Friedman 1979.
[37] Hall and Soskice 2001; Hall and Gingerich 2004; Hicks and Kenworthy 1998.

address the growth effects of coordinated market economies: They show that where institutional complementarities are strong – that is, where the labor and industrial relations system and corporate governance are both structured by competitive markets or both characterized by cooperative institutions – growth is higher.[38]

The institutional complementarity argument is consistent with two well-established streams of theory. First, the Olsonian view of group organization posits that as political economies experience increases in the collective organization of interests, economic efficiency is harmed.[39] Yet, at high levels of collective organization – that is where groups are encompassing and centralized – peak associations of employers and labor internalize the negative consequences of their behavior. In turn, wage restraint, innovation, and other efficiency-enhancing behaviors are fostered. Second, similar predictions flow from seminal work by Calmfors and Driffill on the centralization of wage bargaining and economic performance.[40] Employing the same logic as Olson, they argue that weak unions and decentralized bargaining is consistent with the unfettered operation of labor markets: Low inflation, high employment, and good general macroeconomic performance are to be expected. At the intermediate level of union organization and bargaining centralization, however, moderately strong union organization (and associated institutions such as sectoral bargaining) do not promote incentives to forego market-distorting behavior; and here unions assert their market power. On the other hand, at high levels of (encompassing) organization and bargaining centralization, actors have incentives to account for the macroeconomic consequences of their behavior and to promote good economic performance.[41]

In light of these debates, two competing hypotheses might be empirically assessed with respect to our central dimensions of coordination, namely, employer organization and macrocorporatism. First, standard neoliberal theory suggests that, on balance, increases in either dimension of coordination should be associated with lower economic growth. On the other hand, contemporary political economic theory suggests that initial increases of coordination (moving away from the institutions of liberal market economics) should be associated with slower economic growth but that further increases in coordination – toward encompassing associations and centralized wage bargaining and policy making – should be associated with increases in economic growth.

We test these hypotheses by estimating a basic model of 1973 to 2003 annual percentage change in real per capita GDP (in international prices) for the eighteen focal nations of this study. We use a familiar growth model that controls for past levels of real per capita GDP (i.e., catch-up processes), the previous year's inflation rate, and world demand conditions.[42] World demand conditions are measured by the annual average growth rate in all other developed democracies weighted by a country's trade

---

[38] Hall and Gingerich 2004.
[39] Olson 1982.
[40] Calmfors and Driffill 1988.
[41] Lange and Garrett (1985) and Alvarez et al. (1991), most notably, have argued that the economic growth benefits of encompassing union organization are likely to be realized in political economies with frequent governance by parties of the left. Thus, "consistent" political economics – that is, those with weak unions/decentralized labor markets and market-oriented party government or encompassing labor/centralized bargaining systems and left party government – experience the strongest economic performance.
[42] Hall and Gingerich 2004.

TABLE 12.5. *Coordination and Economic Growth in the Postindustrial Era*

	I	II	III	IV
Employer organization	−.0213		−.6867[*]	
	(.1859)		(.5356)	
Employer organization^2			.2370[*]	
			(.1805)	
Macrocorporatism		.0029		−.9441[*]
		(.1970)		(.6199)
Macrocorporatism^2				.3428[**]
				(.2106)
Per capita real GDP	−.0799[**]	−.0799[**]	−.0996[**]	−.1018[**]
	(.0367)	(.0367)	(.0415)	(.0395)
Inflation	−.0373[**]	−.0073[**]	−.0361[**]	−.0358[**]
	(.0195)	(.0195)	(.0194)	(.0194)
World demand	.0002	.0002	.0004	.0002
	(.0016)	(.0016)	(.0016)	(.0194)
Fixed effects	Yes	Yes	Yes	Yes
Intercept	3.6274	3.5799	4.4329	4.6756
R2	.3164	.3164	.3197	.3205
Number of observations	536	535	536	535

Models are estimated with 1973 to 2003 annual data from 18 nations by Prais-Winston (AR1) regression with panel correct standard errors. Models include fixed effects for years $(t-1)$.
[*] Indicates significance at the .10 level.
[**] Indicates significance at the .05 level or below.

openness. We also account for the additional growth effects of common shocks (through a test for yearly dummy variables) and of unmodeled country effects (through tests for nation dummy variables).[43] We first estimate the simple linear growth effects of employer organization and macrocorporatism and then estimate a polynomial function that tests for the hypothesized "u-shaped" effect of coordination on economic growth. Models are first-order autoregressive and estimated by Prais-Winston regression with panel-correct standard errors.

The results of our analysis are displayed in Table 12.5. First, (joint-F) tests suggest that country dummies are unnecessary; on the other hand, yearly dummy variables are, and these are included in all Table 12.5 models. (In the absence of these year dummies, world demand conditions are highly significant and positively associated with a country's growth rate in a given year.) With respect to our core concerns, the table illustrates that the linear relationship between employers' organization and macrocorporatism on the one hand, and economic growth on the other, is virtually 0.00. Different results emerge when we move to the analysis of a curvilinear relationship. For both employers' organization and macrocorporatism, we find that initial increases in coordination are associated with lower growth, whereas subsequent increases are associated with high economic growth.

[43] We also included controls for a variety of additional factors such as labor force growth and the size of the dependent population. Even though some of these additional control variables were significant, they do not change the results reported in Table 12.5 for coordination.

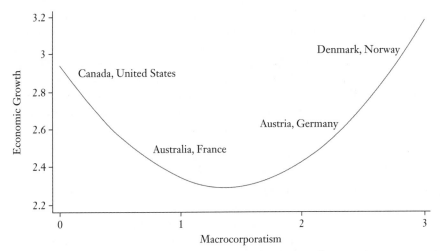

FIGURE 12.I. The Impact of Macrocorporatism on Economic Growth, 1974–2003.
Note: Estimates of economic growth at various levels of macrocorporatism when variables of Table 12.5 are at their mean levels. Representative country clusters correspond to levels of macrocorporatism.

These findings are brought into concrete relief in Figure 12.I. The "u-shaped" curve in the figure is obtained as follows: We set all (noncoordination) variables in our growth model to their sample means and allowed macrocorporatism to vary between its sample low (standardized to 0.00) and sample high. Specific growth rates were obtained by using the estimated coefficients for each variable displayed in the column IV model of Table 12.5. Thus, at levels of macrocorporatism found, for instance, in Canada and the United States in the 2000s, economic growth is just under three percent a year. At more intermediate levels of macrocorporatism (e.g., roughly 1.0 on our scale, which is typical of Australia and France in the 2000s), the economic growth rate is 2.3 to 2.4 per year. At moderately high levels of coordination (e.g., 2.0, which approximates Germany and Austria), growth is a bit better at roughly 2.5 percent a year. At high levels of macrocorporatism (i.e., 2.5 to 2.7, or the level of Norway and Denmark in the 2000s), economic growth is, again, just less than 3 percent a year. Thus, as contemporary political economy predicts, liberal market and nationally coordinated economies – net of other forces – both experience better economic growth than "intermediate" political economies.

A Note on Jobs and Coordination. Several scholars have suggested that coordinated political economies (both macrocorporatist and sector coordination) are beset by the problems of job creation.[44] The work disincentives to employees of a long-lived, generous social wage; the hiring disincentives to employers of employment taxes and protections; and related dynamics is thought to stymy job creation in CMEs. Economic growth may occur, but job creation in CMEs may well lag the competitive market environment of LMEs. Even though it is beyond the scope of this study to offer detailed analysis of this issue, we would point to a recent study by David Bradley and

[44] See, among others, Scharpf 2000; Pontusson 2005; Kenworthy 2004; 2008.

John Stephens on the determinants of employment.[45] In this work, the authors clearly show that once long-term benefit duration, social security tax burdens, and employment protection regulation are accounted, macrocorporatism (as we conceptualize and measure it here) as well as benefit generosity and ALMP spending are all positively related to employment levels in postindustrial democracies. As such, this set of findings offers additional evidence to the effect that high levels of employer organization and macrocorporatism are completely consistent with relatively good economic growth and, under specific conditions, job creation.

Conclusion

Deindustrialization has fueled greater income inequality and labor market dualism and, in combination with pressures on mature welfare states from demography, macroeconomic crises, and neoliberal orthodoxy, has created unprecedented challenges for national policy makers seeking to sustain efficiency with egalitarianism. We argue that high levels of employer organization and, more broadly, the institutions of macrocorporatist coordination bolster equality and work against dualism in labor markets. Employers' capacities to grasp the benefits of and to support a policy approach that sustains investment in low-skilled workers counteracts the drift toward greater inequality and dualism. Employers' capacities to act collectively on these preferences are greatly influenced by their organization: When employers have high levels of organization, their supportive positions on social policies can contribute to the maintenance of relatively high levels of equality, redistribution, and equitable jobs. In addition, we have argued that the combination of highly organized employers, densely organized and centralized unions movements, and their sustained interaction in collective bargaining and national policy forums offers an especially powerful bulwark against potent inegalitarian trends. The institutional legacies arising from the bargains concluded at the beginning of the twentieth century, once established, work to sustain the impulse for coordination among the social partners and have a profound impact on the struggles to cope with the challenges of the twenty-first century.

Thus, our analysis contributes to an understanding of the social and coalitional underpinnings of equality and redistribution in democratic capitalist political economies. Extant analyses of the coalitional bases for redistribution and equality largely assume that preferences of voters on the right are relatively fixed, and that employers generally oppose redistributive social policies in both majoritarian and proportional systems. We differ from these analyses in highlighting how employers' organization and preferences matter enormously to the political bases of equality. Well-organized union movements and social democratic governments are central to the determination of patterns of equality and redistribution in contemporary democratic capitalism. Yet, the quest for equality is not determined exclusively by the bravado, resources, and organization of the left; rather, the strategic calculations by business managers also matter to a high level of investment in social capital and a relatively egalitarian sharing of the economic and social pie. When organized at a high level, employers can also be persuaded to develop strategic preferences for public policies that seek to

---

[45] Bradley and Stephens 2007.

balance economic growth and social equality, rather than to view the world as a stage for pitched economic strife.

Moreover, our analysis demonstrates that the gains from coordination in greater equality are not tarnished by significant declines in economic growth, stagnant job creation, and intensification of problems of postindustrial economies. High levels of employer organization and macrocorporatist coordination produce economic growth rates that are comparable to liberal market political economies. With the reform of notably long benefit duration, high social security taxes, and restrictive employment protection regulations, macrocorporatism and attendant egalitarian policies (generous shorter term benefits coupled with significant and effective active labor market programs) appear to be consistent with employment growth. This suggests that a successful adaptation to the significant challenges of postindustrialization is possible and, when success is defined as the maintenance of social solidarity with economic efficiency, highly organized employers and institutions for national cooperation may, indeed, be part of the solution instead of part of the problem.

Conclusion

Social Solidarity after the Crisis of Finance Capitalism

Introduction

Bringing to mind the old Chinese curse, we have the dubious privilege of living in interesting times. The global financial crisis of 2008 set off a new attack on economic truisms and political leadership, thrust advanced industrial nations into a new period of soul searching and suggested that economic well-being may well be doomed by the fits and starts associated with outrageous fortunes. Public opinion seems insecure, both condemning the folly of unregulated markets yet questioning the wisdom of governmental oversight. At this dark and terrible moment, one wants a lantern to guide us through the chaos.[1]

This final chapter reflects on how the global economic crisis might affect governments' capabilities for sustaining the social democratic model and abilities to draw employers into coalitions in support of social investments. Earlier chapters explore two transitional moments in industrial relations, the rise of advanced industrial capitalism and the advent of the postindustrial economy. We show that some governments' efforts to create and to sustain institutions for coordination among the social partners had a major impact on the evolution and survival of programs to enhance skills and to reduce long-term unemployment. But the financial crisis may well usher in a new era of economic constraint: Major service sectors (in particular finance and real estate) have faltered badly and globalization seems in remission. Thus, one wonders if the institutional structures that sustained economic and social coordination against globalization, deindustrialization, and neoliberalism continue to have the same impact in the new economic climate. Will the havens of security gain the upper hand or does the old logic break down? Crises of capitalism can lead to new openings: new forms of policy regimes, new institutions and new relations among nations; and with this in mind, we speculate about the possible outcomes in a new world order.[2]

---

[1] Martin used some of this paragraph in her call for papers for the Society for Advancement of Socio-Economics (SASE) International Conference in Paris, 2008.
[2] Gamble 2009, 7.

In the following pages, we recap the major themes of the book and contemplate some weaknesses in the finance capital growth model revealed by the crisis. We then reflect on the impact of the economic crisis on our models of coordination – their resiliency in responding to the new economic challenges and in sustaining equitable policy making – and consider how processes of collective political engagement might shape national responses to the new era.

The State, Institutions for Coordination, and Equality

At the heart of our book has been the desire to understand why coordinated capitalism emerges in some countries but not others, and how the institutions for coordination influence employers' perceptions of their social identities. As a vehicle for understanding these broader issues, we focus on the state's efforts to construct peak employers' associations at the beginning of the twentieth century, the political interventions to sustain these associations against postindustrialization at the end of the twentieth century, and the impact of these associations on employers' preferences for social policies.

First, the book emphasizes the causal importance of the structure of political competition – party structure and degree of centralization of government – to the development of institutions for employer coordination. Peak encompassing associations were formed by politicians and bureaucrats for political purposes; employers shared a desire for coordination across countries, yet institutional outcomes reflected the differential incentives for politicians to delegate policy-making authority to private channels for negotiation. Party leaders had greater incentives to delegate authority in multiparty systems than in two-party systems, and this led to corporatism; the structure of business representation, in turn, molded employers' support for the evolution of the welfare state.

Second, we show that features of the state – multipartism and state centralization – so critical to peak employers' organizations at the end of the nineteenth century continued to sustain employer organization against the challenges of globalization and deindustrialization at the end of the twentieth century. Moreover, highly centralized governments with multiparty competition tended to produce large public sectors, and these worked to sustain high levels of macrocorporatist coordination among peak business and labor associations. A large and capacious public sector helps governments to sustain high levels of labor market coordination by creating higher levels of employment (and easing the task of employing low-skilled workers), providing supply-side benefits of training, and reducing reliance on social assistance (thus reducing zero-sum conflicts between skilled and unskilled labor). A large public sector makes both public and private sector employers more likely to employ the low-skilled, and more interested in developing the skills of these workers; in addition, because public sector workers are predominantly female, both women and their employers recognize the special needs for welfare state services for women and prefer that these services not be linked to employment status. A capacious public sector gives the state the means to push social groups into coalitions for social solidarity because public sector unions and sectoral employers' associations accord state actors greater political power in collective bargaining forums. Private employers and workers become more willing to cooperate to preserve their jurisdiction against the intrusion of a large state. Thus, countries with large public sectors have a greater capacity to sustain high levels of coordination in the postindustrial world.[3]

Third, we suggest that highly organized corporatist business associations aid government policy entrepreneurs in their efforts to reintegrate marginal groups into the core economy and make firms more likely to support social protection, redistribution, and relative levels of equality. Macrocorporatist employers' associations, in particular, enhance business concerns about marginal workers because the groups have political economic, collective action, and cognitive effects. The political economic effects under macrocorporatism are such that highly coordinated, centralized bargaining produces wage compression and a narrow wage gap between the most and least skilled blue collar workers. Wage compression motivates employers to eliminate low-skilled jobs and provides a rational for business to support high levels of vocational training and unemployment insurance to encourage workers to invest in specific skills. Macrocorporatist associations also have collective action effects: Only some employers will provide collective benefits such as skills training, but encompassing employers' and labor associations can foster collaboration on the provision of these benefits with, for example, highly coordinated vocational training systems. Support for social protections for core workers has a quite different logic than support for redistributive policies geared to address the needs of marginal workers; therefore, it is also important to note the cognitive effects of macrocorporatist associations. Employers have a range of possible interests, and highly organized business associations help employers recognize the profit-maximizing benefits of social policies and bring them into contact with policy experts from other realms.

Our political story does not account for all variation in employer organization and preference formation. For example, as we show empirically in Chapter 2, our political variables have a independent, significant effect on employer organization and macrocorporatist coordination, but labor mobilization, the legacies of skills formation systems, and religious and ethnic cleavages also have significant effects. In Chapter 8, we demonstrate that employer organization, levels of deindustrialization, left party control, unemployment, and in some equations per capita real GDP and capital mobility all have a significant, independent impact on levels of social protection.

Nevertheless, we differ from some political economist experts on varieties of capitalism, in that we assume that interests are constructed and that politics plays an important causal role in shaping business interests. We agree that employers often organize and support social policies in reaction to an aggressive labor movement; yet we point to the less well-known story of political intervention by right party leaders to organize and mobilize business. We share economic sociologists' fascination with group impacts on the construction of preference, but highlight the importance of structures of the state in the evolution of business networks. We admire business historians' attention to agency at critical junctures and perceptions of individual variation in the emergence of capitalist forms, but pay rather more attention to the impact of party politics on these processes.

[3] See also Martin 2004; Martin and Thelen 2007.

Structuralist

Finally, we offer a model of institutional change that emphasizes the importance of processes of collective political engagement. Historical institutionalists convincingly highlight two somewhat different types of institutional and policy evolution: Change can occur at critical junctures when new arrangements create policy legacies for future initiatives, but change can also transpire through incremental alterations as shifting political coalitions adapt institutions for new purposes. We argue that processes of collective political engagement are vital to both of these types of institutional change: Modes of deliberation delimit both the range of new institutional arrangements possible at critical junctures and the types of political coalitions that subvert institutions to new policy ends. Processes of collective political engagement themselves change over time and do not always deliver functional solutions, yet nations' characteristic ways of engaging in social deliberation have a somewhat enduring quality and diverse types have distinctive capacities for institutional reinvention and policy renewal at critical junctures.

The Logic of Postfinance Capitalism and Politics of Solidarity

We have some sense of what helps to sustain social solidarity during the ideological rise of neoliberalism, globalization, and deindustrialization, but the new economic climate is characterized by deglobalization and the vulnerability of major service sectors (in particular finance and real estate). In fact, the financial crisis has created somewhat mixed legacies for future trajectories in public policy.

First, the global crisis of finance capitalism has had somewhat mixed impacts on conceptions of governmental regulation. The downturn initially called into question the legitimacy of the growth model based on the deregulation of finance capital, the validity of neoliberal ideology, and the appropriate role of the state in the economy. The growth model based on the deregulation of finance capital enabled major economic restructuring, but ultimately it appeared that much of the apparent success of the new regulatory regime stemmed from successive national bubbles. Finance capital drove growth through assets bubbles in shares, housing, and commodities such as oil, and this was facilitated by an expansion of credit, decline of the savings ratio, and conspicuous consumption. The "financialization" of markets created fictitious financial wealth, strengthened international financial capital over productive capital, and reinforced exchange-value over use-value. Moreover, a beggar thy neighbor dynamic allowed a string of ascendent model countries to claim success at the expense of its close competitors. Thus, Japan in the 1980s rose in Germany's ashes, and the United States became the standard bearer of economic renewal in the 1990s.[4]

Many pundits initially celebrated the death knoll to deregulation and neoliberalism in the wake of the downturn and called for systemic solutions and state intervention to solve market externalities. While the prior financial regime put a high priority on depoliticized economic management, the crisis encouraged revisiting debates on the appropriate role of states and a return to repoliticized forms of financial management. Given the interdependence of institutions, systemic regulation seemed necessary to

---

[4] Gamble 2009, 7–15; Jessop, 2010, 43; Brenner 2001.

monitor financial instruments. The Obama victory gave a sense of excitement on the left that progressive ideas would gain salience in political circles and 70 percent of Americans polled supported greater governmental aid to those who could not care for themselves. *Newsweek* – hardly a radical rag – declared that "Big Government Is Back – Big Time."[5] The crisis prompted a big jump in expansionary Keynesian fiscal policies and government stimulus programs, and a seeming break with the monetarist policies of Thatcher and Reagan. In a moment reminiscent of Nixon's famous declaration "We are all Keynesians now," Sarkozy remarked, "Am I a socialist? Perhaps."[6]

Yet, neoliberal ideology has had remarkable staying power despite its seeming unpopularity immediately after the crisis. "Deregulation" only imperfectly captures the regulatory approach of the past quarter century and the era is better characterized as one of "reregulation" in which firms were allowed to renege on worker commitments and to create new risky derivatives markets. There has also been a decoupling of economic policy from other policy-making realms; consequently, macroeconomic stabilization policies with firm commitments to enhancing employment are unlikely to emerge with this crisis as they did during the Great Depression.[7] Moreover, the public is fickle and has a short-term memory: One can't document a move to the left because the parties in charge at the crisis point have been blamed for the crisis by a citizenry that seems to be moving right again. Labour Prime Minister Gordon Brown was the man of the hour in October 2008, when the British press nicknamed him "Flash Gordon," but the bailout quickly ran into trouble, and Brown lost the subsequent election to Conservative David Cameron, who promised to roll back Tony Blair's New Deal initiatives.[8]

Second, the financial crisis has had profound budgetary impacts, and even though the failures of finance capitalism may have undercut neoliberal ideology, they also have undercut social investments. Bubble economies created fiscal slack for social solidarity and high rates of employment created a labor market need for the low-skilled workers; yet after the fall, financial woes have both reduced economic slack and increased unemployment. Thus, a year after the crisis, the *Economist* announced that "a leaner and fitter state should emerge" from the crisis, and recommended various forms of "liposuction" to trim the fat.[9] While GDP growth rates have begun to rebound in some countries, nations with sovereign debt crises, such as Greece, have been forced to adopt significant austerity measures, causing massive civil unrest. Although the crisis prompted budgetary deficits everywhere, cross-national variations reflect the size of automatic stabilizers, fiscal positions in advance of the crisis, and the severity of the crisis in the country.[10]

The crisis has hurt core advanced countries less than their less-wealthy counterparts and has given rise to fears about economic nationalism and trade protectionism. The WTO calculated that seventeen out of the G20 had created new trade barriers, and 80 percent of categories of good and services were affected by trade-distorting measures.

So true!

---

[5] Burnham 1999; Seabrook 2009; *Newsweek* 2/16/2009.

[6] *The Economist* 2/21/09, 56, 441.

[7] Block 2009; Lindvall 2009.

[8] *The Economist* 2/21/2009, 56.

[9] *The Economist* 9/26/2009, 29–32.

[10] Cameron, forthcoming.

Coordinated winners may be able to sustain coordinated capitalism at home, but they may well handle the profound fiscal crisis by beggaring their debtors in less-developed countries. In the years before the crisis, coordinated countries were like college under-graduates on spring break in Eastern Europe, encouraging risky financial ventures with low-interest loans. The heavy investment in Eastern Europe by Austria, Italy and Sweden came to a screeching halt with the financial crisis.[11] Countries haven't taken much responsibility for these problems; instead, they moved capital from foreign mar-kets back to home ones. Thus, even if coordinaion survives in some rich countries, the politics of austerity is likely to be a fact of life for peripheral countries outside of the northern European core, there may be a dangerous drying up of credit across borders and a resurgence of economic nationalism.

So econ ntlsm = bad?

Implications for Regimes of Coordination

The crisis seems to have somewhat mixed ideological and economic implications for the future of coordinated capitalism, equality, and social solidarity; therefore, one wonders whether the truisms of the neoliberal period will continue to hold up in the future. Will the havens of security continue to support solidaristic, relatively egalitar-ian social policies or will their coordinating capacities be scaled back? When the rules of the game change, will the old logic still apply?

It is immediately apparent that the financial crisis has had a quite powerful negative impact on economic growth, employment and exports across the advanced industrial democracies, and that even the cozy corners of coordinated capitalism were, at least initially, hit hard. Miracles often seem to become less miraculous over time, and the flexicurity phenomenon is no exception. Nevertheless, social partners in countries that maintained a large welfare state against the pressures of deindustrialization and globalization have struggled to sustain coordination and to support somewhat solida-ristic solutions to economic malaise.

The economic situation after the global financial crisis has been bleak. With a sharp contraction of private consumption, GDP growth in 2011 was projected to be 3.2 per-cent in Sweden, 2.0 percent in Denmark, and 2.5 percent in Finland; compared to 3.2 percent in the United States and Canada and 2.5 percent in the United Kingdom. Celebrated as employment miracles a few years before, unemployment also increased precipitously in Scandinavia, although the new levels were comparable to postcrisis rates of unemployment among liberal countries as well. Unemployment was projected in 2011 to be 6.9 percent in Denmark, 8.7 percent in Sweden, 9.0 percent in Finland, 8.9 percent in the United States, and 7.9 percent in the United Kingdom.[12]

Yet whereas the immediate figures on economic growth and unemployment have inspired pessimism, many of the macrocorporatist countries' specific economic prob-lems harken back to neoliberal policies. For example, recent economic problems in Denmark partially reflect the neoliberal reforms imposed by the bourgeois government

---

[11] *Financial Times* 9/14/2009.
[12] The continental countries – with the worst rates of unemployment in the precrisis part of the decade – did not fare significantly worse during the downturn: Germany was projected to have rates of 8.0 percent in 2011; France, 9.5 percent; Italy, 8.7 percent; and Austria, 4.9 percent. OECD 2010.

since 2001. The housing bubble was enabled by massive credit expansions, low interest rates and amortization loans. The bourgeois government's expansionary fiscal policy was highly criticized because it largely constituted tax cuts targeted to the highest income brackets.[13] Faith in government reached a 30 year low in 2011 and the social democrats regained the government in the November 2011 election.[14]

Moreover, the highly coordinated countries with the largest public sectors have surprisingly waged the best defense against budgetary deficits. High support for the tax state has meant that these countries largely enjoyed budget surpluses before the crisis; since 2008, these countries have had much lower deficits than liberal countries. In 2011, Sweden was projected to have a deficit of −1.7 percent of GDP; Denmark, −4.8; Finland, −3.8; United States, −8.9; United Kingdom, −10.3; Germany, −4.5; and France, − 6.9.[15]

Even though employment has declined, there has been less pain than one might have predicted; indeed, the Danish model of "flexicurity" was intended to work precisely as macroeconomic events have predicted. In a flexible labor market with very few labor market regulations, firms can hire and fire at will: This flexibility tends to elevate employment during periods of rapid economic growth but depresses employment more rapidly during recessions. Thus, Steen Bocian, the chief economist of Den Danske Bank, noted that although employment in Denmark fell more rapidly than the EU average in 2009, production levels fell in other countries at a similar rate, but labor market rigidities prevented the layoffs.[16] The active labor market policies have a more difficult time working in an economy dominated by high unemployment, but many Danes have continued to receive high levels of worker retraining, and the safety net remains secure. In the face of the economic crisis, Danes are much more optimistic about getting another job than citizens of other countries, and brief periods of unemployment have a more limited significance. Danes feel more secure in their work; even though they lack job security, they have broader employment security: Thus, 67 percent of Danes believe that they would find a new job within six months if they got laid off, compared to only 45 percent of all EU citizens.[17]

Flexicurity has advantages in advocating a spirit of Schumpeterian creative destruction, and some parts of the Scandinavian economies are making the most of the crisis with industrial restructuring. With limited labor market rigidity, there are weaker impulses to succumb to lemon socialism. A movement has been afoot in Denmark to take advantage of the crisis by restructuring and making the economy more "green," both to cut back damage to the environment and to boost the economy with a more efficient use of energy. The social partners have been more proactive than the bourgeois government and criticized its lending policy proposal (which included no "green" aspect) and environmental bill (which ignored energy). Aggressive interventions were advocated by The Environmental Economic Council (Det Miljøøkonomiske Råd), an advisory board made up of business, labor,

[13] Goul Andersen 2011; Madsen 2011.
[14] Synovate/Mandag Morgen 7/27/2011. Thanks to Jørgen Goul Andersen for providing this to us.
[15] OECD 2010.
[16] Elmer and Hansen 2010.
[17] Hansen 2010.

environmentalists and government representatives, which considered the government's interventions to be insufficiently ambitious and largely covered by EU directives.[18] Danish firms are benefitting from robust institutions for business-government coordination during these troubled times; thus, the Danish Ministry of Foreign Affairs declared the crisis good for Danish energy companies because the vibrant public-private cooperation would improve firms' competitive positions.[19]

The structures for coordination have continued to act as a bulwark against growing inequality, as the highly coordinated Danish social partners have advocated creative non-zero-sum policy solutions to the new climate of economic scarcity. Even though the significant industrial restructuring prompted by the crisis has certainly put stress on industrial relations, the social partners have largely managed to sustain processes of negotiated bargaining. The most recent collective bargaining round was more stressful than the prior one (concluded during economic prosperity), but the centralized bargaining model endured. Employers and workers explored job-sharing arrangements rather than advocated major welfare state cutbacks; in this vein, the DA and LO jointly asked the government to take the lead in developing more flexible work-sharing rules so that companies could be protected from making deeply invasive cuts. In March 2009, the government proposed faster access to training, a national alert system, expanded monitoring of labor market trends and more flexible rules for work-sharing; for example, employees would be permitted to work for two weeks and then take one- or two-week leaves. But both employers and workers expressed dissatisfaction that government's efforts to create more flexible work-sharing rules did not go far enough.[20]

Conclusion

The financial crisis seems to confirm our beliefs about the institutional benefits of coordinated capitalism and a large, vibrant state. Coordinated countries with high levels of macrocorporatism, infrastructure bolstering social investments, and large states seem best equipped to survive the storm, and social democratic, continental, and liberal countries seem to be learning rather different lessons from the crisis. Although the new British government is moving to cut spending to the bone, the Scandinavians believe that Keynesian anticyclical spending continues to be the appropriate course of action and their strong fiscal positions enable them to hold to this policy course. Rather than seeking to prevent private employers from laying off excess workers, these countries are permitting much higher rates of unemployment but are trying to ease the burdens of those temporarily cast out of the labor market with continuing high levels of training and generous unemployment benefits. The jury is still out, but it is likely that model countries will continue to diverge in their chosen policy paths after the crisis in much the same way that they did before.

We often take as a given the current spirit of atomistic individualism in the United States, yet the reconstruction of our institutions for coordination could also improve

---

[18] Jørgensen 9/18/2009.
[19] "Financial Crisis is Good for the Danish Energy Companies," 10/28/2008.
[20] Jørgensen 2010; Jørgensen. 2009.

our capacities for collective action. We are in the midst of political, economic, social, and geographical change, and the first decade of the twenty-first century imposed massive costs on civil liberties, the working poor, human capital, and social solidarity. The complaints about excessive government that played so well during the 1980s and 1990s may be an indulgence that we cannot afford to take in our current age of financial economic crisis, religious wars, and natural disasters. This book suggests that social solidarity will, perhaps, continue in some small countries of Western Europe, but one worries about the broader cross section of humanity. Thus, it is important to understand the construction of coalitions that support economic efficiency and social solidarity.

Bibliography

Academic, Government, Interest Group Publications

Abelshauser, Werner. 2005. *The Dynamics of German Industry.* New York: Berghahn Books.

Abrahamson, Peter. 1998. "Efter velfærdstaten: Ret og pligt til aktivering." *Nordisk Sosialt Arbeid* 3 (18): 133–42.

Achen, Christopher. 2000. "Why Lagged Dependent Variables Can Suppress the Power of Other Independent Variables." Political Methodology Working Paper.

Ackers, Peter and Adrian Wilkinson. 2003. *Understanding Work and Employment* (eds), Oxford: Oxford University Press.

Adams, W. S. 1953. "Lloyd George and the Labour Movement." *Past and Present* 3 (February): 55–64.

Agerholm, Sophus and Anders Vigen. 1921. *Arbejdsgiver Foreningen Gennem 25 Aar, 18961921.* Copenhagen: Langkjaers bogtrykkeri.

Ahmed, Amel. 2010. "Reading History Forward: The Origins of Electoral Systems in Advanced Democracies." *Comparative Political Studies* Special Issue on The Historical Turn in Democratization Studies. August/September 43: 1059–88.

Akdemikernes Centralorganisation. 2000. *Rapport om Akademikernes Erfaringer Med IT – Forløb.* Copenhagen: Akademikernes Centralorganisation (October).

Åkerstrom Andersen, Niels and Peter Kjær. 1993. "Private Industrial Policy in the Danish Negotiated Economy," in Jerzy Hausner, Bob Jessop, and Klaus Nielsen, eds., *Institutional Frameworks of Market Economies.* Avebury.

Alber, Jens. 1988. "Germany," in Peter Flora (ed.), Growth to Limits: The Western European Welfare States Since World War II. 2 Germany, United Kingdom, Ireland, Italy. New York: Walter de Gruyter, 1–154.

Albret, Poul. 2002. "Venstres udfordring: Skal være venner med alle." *Mandag Morgen,* 31 (September 16): 22.

Alderman, Geoffrey. 1984. Pressure Groups and Government in Great Britain. New York: Longman.

Alderson, A. S. 2004. "Explaining the Upswing in Foreign Direct Investment: A Test of Mainstream and Heterodox Theories of Globalization." *Social Forces* 83: 81–122.

Alestalo, Matti and Stein Kuhnle. 1987. "The Scandinavian Route: Economic, Social, and Political Developments in Denmark, Finland, Norway, and Sweden," in Robert Erikson et al., eds., *The Scandinavian Model.* Armonk, NY: M. E. Sharpe.

Alestalo, Matti and Hannu Uusitalo. 1992. "Social Expenditure: A Decompositional Approach," in Jon Eivind Kolberg, eds., *The Study of Welfare State Regimes.* Armonk, NY: M. E. Sharpe, 37–68.

Alkestrup, Per. Lederne Hovedsorganisation. Memo to Beskæftigelseministeriet hearings. "Høring om udkast til forslag til lov om gennemførelse af dele af arbejdstidsdirektivet." 7 (January 2002).

Allardt, Erik. 1986. "The Civic Conception of the Welfare State in Scandinavia," in Richard Rose and Rei Shiratori eds., *The Welfare State East and West*. New York: Oxford University Press.

Allen, Christopher. 1990. "Trade Unions, Worker Participation, and Flexibility." *Comparative Politics* 22 (3 April): 253–72.

Almond, Gabriel A. 1958. "Research Note: Comparative Study of Interest Groups in the Political Process," *American Political Science Review*, 52 (March 1958): 270–82.

Alvarez, R. Michael, Geoffrey Garrett, and Peter Lange. 1991. "Government Partisanship, Labor Organization, and Macroeconomic Performance." *American Political Science Review* 85 (2): 539–56.

Amable, Bruno. 2003. *The Diversity of Modern Capitalism*. Oxford: Oxford University Press.

Amorin, Octavio and Gary Cox. 1997. "Electoral Institutions, Cleavage Structures, and Number of Parties." *American Political Science Review* 41: 149–74.

Amoroso, Bruno. 1990. "Development and Crisis of the Scandinavian Model of Labour Relations in Denmark," in Guido Baglioni and Colin Crouch, eds., *European Industrial Relations*. Newbury Park, CA: Sage, 71–96.

Andersen, Bent Rold. 1993. "The Nordic Welfare State Under Pressure." *Policy and Politics* 21 (2): 109–20.

Andersen, Lars. 2006. Fra fattighjælp til velfærdsstat. I Lars Andersen m.fl.: Fra verdenskrig til velfærd. Gyldendal 2006. side 48–62.

Andersen, Lars Schädler. 2010. "Ulykkesforsikringens tilblivelse," in Jørn Henrik Petersen, Klaus Petersen & Niels Finn Christiansen, eds., *Frem mod socialhjælpsstaten. Dansk Velfærdshistorie*, vol. 1. Odense, DK: Syddansk Universitetsforlag, chapter 7.

Andersen, Niels. to DSF. Letter. 7/12/1897. DA – Korrespondance, General udgående 1896 6 30 til 1899 9 21. 1897_52 12/7/1897. Erhvervsarkivet, Aarhus, DK.

Andersen, Steen and Kurt Jacobsen. 2008. *Foss*. Copenhagen.

Andersen, Torben K. 2001. "Regering og kommuner I opgør om skattestop." *Mandag Morgen* 42 (December 10): 10–16.

Anderson, Margaret Lavinia. 2000. *Practicing Democracy*. Princeton, NJ: Princeton University Press.

Ansell, Ben W. 2008. "Traders, Teachers, and Tyrants: Democracy, Globalization, and Public Investment in Education." *International Organization*, 62 (2 Spring): 289–322.

Anthonsen, Mette and Johannes Lindvall. 2009. "Party Competition and the Resilience of Corporatism." *Government and Opposition* 44 (2): 167–87.

Arbejdsgiverforeningen af 1896. "Til Bestyrelsen for." 8/3/1897. 1897_26. p 1–2, DA–Korrespondance, General udgånde 1896 6 30 til 1899 9 21.

Arbejdsmarkedstyrelsen. no date. *Benchmarking af privat jobtraening*. Copenhagen: Arbejdsmarkedstyrelsen.

——— 2000. "AF Mål og rammer." *Arbejdsmarkedstyrelsen*. (February 16).

——— 2000. "Midtvejsstatus for handlingsplan til fremme af privat jobtraening." *Arbejdsmarkedstyrelsen* (March 16).

Arbødigst, DA to Hr. Grosserer, letter. 25 Marts 1914. folder: "Foreningen af Arbejdsgivere I aarhus, 1916 incl., 06158; Box, "Dansk Arbejdsgiverforening Regnskabsafd/Administrationss1913–1954 Korrespondance med foreninger. Erhvervsarkivet, Aarhus, DK.

Armingeon, Klaus and Giuliano Bonoli. 2006. *The Politics of Post-Industrial Welfare States: Adapting Post-war Social Policies to New Social Risks*. London: Routledge.

Atkinson, A. B. and Gunnar Viby Mogensen, eds. 1993. *Welfare and Work Incentives: A North European Perspective*. Oxford: Clarendon Press.

Baccaro, Lucio and Chris Howell. 2010. "Institutional Change in European Industrial Relations" Reformulating the Case for Neoliberal Convergence." Paper presented at the Seventeenth International Conference of the Council of European Studies, Montreal, April 15–17.

Baccaro, Lucio and Marco Simoni. 2007. "Centralized Wage Bargaining and the 'Celtic Tiger' Phenomenon." *Industrial Relations* 46 (3): 426–55.

Baccaro, Lucio and Macro Simoni. 2008. "Policy Concertation in Europe: Understanding Government Choice." *Comparative Political Studies* 41 (10): 1323–48.

Bach, Hans and Anne-Birte Kylling. 1997. "New Partnership for Social Cohesion: the Danish Partnership Concept." Copenhagen: Socialforskningsinstitutted.

Bacote, Clarence. 1959. "Negro Officeholders in Georgia under President McKinley," *The Journal of Negro History* 44 (3 July): 217–39, 220.

Baldwin, A. H. 1912."The New 'Chamber of Commerce of the United States of America,'" *American Industries* XII (10).

Baldwin, Peter. 1990. *The Politics of Social Solidarity* Cambridge: Cambridge University Press.

Bancroft, George (American Legation, Berlin) to H. C. Carey. March 30, 1873. Historical Society of Pennsylvania, Edward Carey Gardiner Collection, Collection 227A. Series 5. Correspondence of H.C. Carey. Box 11, Folder 5.

Barnett, Antony. 1998. "Is Labour's love-in with the CBI over?" *The Observer* (May 31): 4.

Bartolini, Stefano. 2000. *The Political Mobilization of the European Left, 1860–1980.* NewYork: Cambridge University Press.

Beaverbrook, Lord. 1963. *The Decline and Fall of Lloyd George.* New York: Duell, Sloan and Pearce.

Beck, Nathaniel and Jonathan Katz. 1995. "What To Do (and Not To Do) with Time-Series-Cross-Section Data in Comparative Politics." *American Political Science Review* 89 (September): 634–47.

1996. "Nuisance versus Substance: Specifying and Estimating Time-Series-Cross-Section Models." *Political Analysis* 6: 1–36.

Becker, Uwe. 2001. "The U.S., Danish and Dutch Routes to Employment Growth." Paper presented at APSA, San Francisco.

Beer, Samuel. 1957. "The Representation of Interests in British Government: Historical Background," *The American Political Science Review* 51 (3 September): 613–50.

Bell, Brian, Richard Blundell, and John van Reenen. 1999. *International Tax and Public Finance* 6: 339–60.

Bell, Richard. 2008 (initially 1901). *Trade Unionism.* Charleston, SC: BiblioBazaar.

Benner, Mats and Torben Bundgaard Vad. 2001. "Sweden and Denmark Defending the Welfare State," in Fritz Scharf and Vivien Schmidt, eds., *Welfare and Work in the Open Economy*, New York: Oxford University Press. Vol. 2.

Bennett, Robert. 2000. "The Logic of Membership of Sectoral Business Associations." *Review of Social Economy* LVIII (1 March): 17–42.

Bensel, Richard. 2000. *The political economy of American industrialization.* New York: Cambridge University Press.

Beramendi, Pablo and Christopher Andersen, eds. 2008. *Democracy, Inequality, and Representation.* New York: Russel Sage Foundation.

Berdahl, Robert. 1972. "Conservative Politics and Aristocratic Landholders in Bismarckian Germany." *The Journal of Modern History* 44 (1 March): 1–20.

Beretningen om Dansk Arbejdsgiversforenings Virksomhed 1927–1928. 1928. Erhvervsarkivet, Aarhus, DK.

Berg, Annika and Franz Traxler. 2007. "Sweden," in Franz Traxler and Gerhard Huemer, eds., *Handbook of Business Interest Associations, Firm Size and Governance: A Comparative Analytical Approach.* New York: Routledge, 299–314.

Berger, Stefan and Hugh Compston, eds. 2002. Policy Concertation and Social Partnership in Western Europe: Lessons for the 21st Century. New York: Berghahm Books.

Berger, Suzanne. 1981. "Regime and Interest Representation," in S. Berger, ed., *Organizing Interests in Western Europe*. Cambridge: Cambridge University Press, 83–101.

Berger, Suzanne and Ronald Dore, eds. 1996. *National Adversity and Global Capitalism*. Ithaca, NY: Cornell University Press.

Berghahn, Volker. 1994. *Imperial Germany 1871–1914*. New York: Berghahn Books.

Berghoff, Hartmut and R. Möller. 1994. "Tired Pioneers and Dynamic Newcomers?" *Economic History Review* XLVII (2): 262–87.

Berk, Gerald. 1994. *Alternative Tracks*. Baltimore: Johns Hopkins University Press.

Berk, Gerald and Marc Schneiberg. 2005. "Varieties in Capitalism, Varieties of Association." *Politics and Society* 33 (March): 46–87.

Berman, Sheri. 2006. *The Primacy of Politics: Social Democracy and the Ideological Dynamics of the Twentieth Century*. New York: Cambridge University Press.

Bermeo, Nancy and Ugo Amoretti, eds. 2004. *Federalism and Territorial Cleavages*. Baltimore: Johns Hopkins University Press.

Bernhagen, Patrick. 2007. *The Political Power of Business*. London: Routledge.

Bessell, Richard. 1993. *Germany After the First World War*. Oxford: Clarendon Press.

Best, Michael 1990. *The New Competition*. Cambridge, MA: Harvard University Press.

Billie, Lars. 1998. *Dansk partipolitik 1987–1998*. Copenhagen: DJØF Forlag.

Bindslev, Alfred. 1937–8. *Konservatismens Historie i Danmark*. Bd. 2–3.

Blackbourn, David. 1998. *The Long Nineteenth Century: A History of Germany, 1780–1918*. New York: Oxford University Press.

Blackbourn, David and Geoff Eley. 1984. *The Peculiarities of German History*. New York: Oxford University Press.

Blanchard, Oliver and Lawrence Summers. 1986. "Hysteresis and the European Unemployment Problem." *NBER Macroeconomics Annual* 1: 15–78.

Blangstrup, Christian, ed. 1915. "Salomonsens Konversations Leksikon." Bind 1, 2. Copenhagen: J. H. Schulz Forlags Boghandel.

Blank, Stephen. 1973. *Industry and Government in Britain*. Lexington, MA: Lexington Books.

Block, Fred. 1977. "The Ruling Class Does Not Rule: Notes on the Marxist Theory of the State." *Socialist Revolution* 33 (May–June): 6–27.

Block, Fred. 2009. "A New Era of Regulation?" *States, Power, and Societies* (Fall).

Blyth, Mark. 2001. "The Transformation of the Swedish Model." *World Politics* 54 (1 October): 1–26.

Böhme, Helmut. 1967. "Big-Business Pressure Groups and Bismarck's Turn to Protectionism, 1873–79." *The Historical Journal* 10 (2): 218–36.

Boix, Carles. 1999. "Setting the Rules of the Game: the Choice of Electoral Systems in Advanced Democracies." *American Political Science Review* 93 (3): 609–24.

Bolger, Andrew. 1997. "CBI to Endorse Scheme for Jobless." *Financial Times* (October 9): 11.

Bond, James T. "The Impact of Childbearing on Employment," in Dana Friedman, Ellen Galinsky, and Veronica Plowden, eds., *Parental Leave and Productivity*. New York: Families and Work Institute.

Bonoli, Giuliano. 2003. "Two Worlds of Pension Reforms." *Comparative Politics* 35 (4): 399–416.

Bonoli, Giuliano and Hedva Sarfati. 2002. "Conclusions: The Policy Implications of a Changing Labour Market-Social Protection Relationship," in G. Bonoli and H. Sarfati, eds., *Labour Market and Social Reforms in International Perspective*. Burlington, VT: Ashgate.

Bowen, Ralph. 1947. *German Theories of the Corporatist State*. New York: McGraw-Hill.

Bowman, John. 1985. "The Politics of the Market: Economic Competition and the Organization of Capitalists." *Political Power and Social Theory* 5: 35–88.

Bradley, David. *The Political Economy of Employment Performance: Testing the Deregulation Thesis.* Doctoral dissertation. Chapel Hill: University of North Carolina.

Bradley, David and John D. Stephens. 2007. "Employment Performance in OECD Countries: A Test of Neoliberal and Institutionalist Hypotheses." *Comparative Political Studies* 40 (12): 1486–1510.

Bradley, David, Evelyne Huber, Stephanie Moller, Francois Nielson, and John D. Stephens. 2003. "Distribution and Redistribution in Postindustrial Democracies. *World Politics* 55 (2): 193–228.

Brady, David and M. Wallace. 2000. "Spatialization, Foreign Direct Investment and LaborOutcomes in the American States." *Social Forces* 79: 67–100.

Brady, David, Jason Bechfield, and Wei Zhao. 2007. "The Consequences of Economic Globalization for Affluent Democracies. *Annual Review of Sociology* 33: 313–34.

Brady, Henry and David Collier 1994. *Rethinking Social Inquiry: Diverse Tools, Shared Standards.* Berkeley, CA: Rowman and Littlefield and Berkeley Public Policy Press.

Brady, Robert. 1942. "Modernized Cameralism in the Third Reich." *The Journal of Political Economy* 50 (1 February): 65–97.

1943. *Business as a System of Power.* New York: Columbia University Press.

Bramsen, Bo. 1964. *Ludvig Bramsen.* Copenhagen: Ny og Nordisk Forlag.

Brandes, Stuart. 1976. *American Welfare Capitalism.* Chicago: University of Chicago Press, 99.

Brandolini, Andrea and Timothy Smeeding. 2008. "Inequality Patterns in Western Democracies: Cross-Country Differences and Changes over Time," in Pablo Beramendi and Christopher J. Anderson, eds., *Democracy, Inequality, and Representation: A Comparative Perspective.* New York: Russel Sage Foundation, 25–61.

Braunthal, Gerard. 1965. *Federation of German Industry in Politics.* Ithaca, NY: Cornell University Press.

Brebmen, J. Bartlet. 1948. "Laissez Faire and State Intervention in Nineteenth-Century Britain." *Journal of Economic History* Supplement VIII: 59–73.

Brenner, Robert. 2001. "The World Economy at the Turn of the Millennium toward Boom or Crisis?" *Review of International Political Economy* 8 (Spring 1): 6–44.

Bristow, Edward. 1975. "The Liberty and Property Defence League and Individualism." *The Historical Journal* XVIII 4: 761–789.

British Iron Trade Association. 1899. *The Times* (June 8): 12.

British Workers League. 10/11/1917. "Minutes of Meeting," 4–5.

Brøndsted, K. G. 1925. *J. B. S. Estrup: Mindeskrift I Anledning af Hundredaarsdagen for hans Føddel.* Copenhagen: Udgivet af "Hørjes Fond."

Brown, Gordon. 2000. "Why the party still needs its soul." *New Statesman* (February 28).

Bruun, Henry. 1938. *Den faglige arbejderbevægelse I Danmark indtil år 1900.* Copenhagen: Nordisk Forlag.

Buck, Col AF to McKinley. Letter. January 8, 1896. McKinley Papers. Series 2 P1 V87-P90.

Büeck, Henry Axel. 1906. 1906. Der *Centralverband deutscher industrieller und seine dreissigjährige arbeit von 1876 bis 1906.* Berlin: Guttentag.

Bureau of Industrial Research. 1919. *The Industrial Council Plan in Great Britain: Reprints of the Report of the Whitley Committee.* Washington, DC: Bureau of Industrial Research.

Bureau of Labor, 1911. *Industrial Education.* Washington: Government Printing Office.

Burgess, Keith. 1975. The Origins of British Industrial Relations. London: Croom Helm.

Burgoon, Brian. 2001. "Globalization and Welfare Compensation: Disentangling the Ties That Bind." *International Organization* 55 (3): 509–51.

Burk, Addison, ed. 1904. *Republican Club Book 1904.* Philadelphia: Dunlap Printing Company, 10.

Burnham, Peter. 2001. "New Labour and the Politics of Depoliticisation." *British Journal of Politics and International Relations* 3 (2): 127–49.

Burtless, Gary, et al. 1998. *Globaphobia: Confronting Fears about Open Trade.* Washington, DC: Brookings Institution.

Buschoff, Karin Schulze and Paula Protsch. 2008. "(A-)typical and (In-)secure? Social Protection and "Non-standard" Forms of Employment in Europe." *International Social Security Review* 61 (4): 51–73.

Busemeyer, Marius. 2009. "Asset Specificity, Institutional Complementarities and the Varieties of Skills Regimes in Coordinated Market Economies." *Socio-Economic Review* 7 (3): 375–406.

Busemeyer, Marius and Christine Trampusch. 2011. "Introduction." in Busemeyer and Trampush eds. *The Political Economy of Skill Formation.* Oxford: Oxford University Press.

Bussière, Eric. 1997. "Banks, Economic Development and Capitalism in France," in Alice Teichova, Ginette Kurgan-Van Hentenryk, and Dieter Ziegler, eds., *Banking, Trade and Industry: Europe, America, and Asia from the Thirteenth to the Twentieth Century.* New York: Cambridge University Press, 113–30.

Buun, Ronald. 1958. "Codetermination and the Federation of German Employers' Associations." *Midwest Journal of Political Science* 2 (3): 278–297.

Cable, Vincent. 1995. "The Diminished Nation-State: A Study in the Loss of Economic Power." *Daedalus* 124 (2): 23–53.

Cain, P. J. and A. G. Hopkins. 1980. "The Political Economy of British Expansion Overseas, 1750–1914." *The Economic History Review* New Series 33 (4): 463–90.

Calmfors, Lars and John Drifill. 1988. "Centralization of Wage Bargaining." *Economic Policy* 3 (April): 13–61.

Cameron, David. 1978. "The Expansion of the Public Economy: A Comparative Analysis." *American Political Science Review* 72 (4): 1243–61.

Cameron, David. Forthcoming. European Responses to the Economic Contradiction of 2008–9," in Nany Bermeo and Jonas Pontusson, eds., *Coping with Crisis.* New York: Russell Sage Foundation.

Campbell, John and Leon Lindberg. 1990. "Property Rights and the Organization of Economic Activity by the State." *American Sociological Review* 55 (5): 634–47.

Campbell, John and Ove K. Pedersen, 2007. "The Varieties of Capitalism and Hybrid Success." *Comparative Political Studies* 40 (3): 307–32.

Campbell, John and Ove Kaj Pedersen. Forthcoming. *The War of Ideas in Advanced Political Economies.* Princeton, NJ: Princeton University Press.

Campbell, John, Rogers Hollingsworth, and Leon Lindbergh, eds. 1991. *Governance of the American Economy.* Cambridge: Cambridge University Press.

Campbell, Katharine, Robert Taylor, and David Wighton. 1998. "Blair Moves to Head Off Business Criticism." *Financial Times* (May 22): 12.

Capoccia, Giovanni and Daniel Ziblatt. 2010. "The Historical Turn in Democratization Studies." *Comparative Political Studies* 43 (8/9): 931–68.

Carey, Sonia. 2000. "The Organisation of the Training Function in Large Firms," in Helen Rainbird, ed., *Training in the Workplace.* New York: St. Martin's Press.

Carlin, Wendy. 1996. "West German Growth and Institutions, 1945–90," in Nicholas Crafts and Gianni Toniolo, eds., *Economic Growth in Europe since 1945.* New York: Cambridge University Press, 455–97.

Carlin, Wendy and David Soskice. 2009. "German Economic Performance: Disentangling the Role of Supply-Side Reforms, Macroeconomic Policy, and Coordinated Economy Institutions." *Socio-Economic Review* 7 (1): 67–100.

Cassis, Youssef. 1999. *Big Business: the European Experience in the Twentieth Century.* Oxford: Oxford University Press.

Castles, Francis G. 1978. *The Social Democratic Image of Society.* London: Routledge & Kegan Paul. 1993. *Families of Nations.* Brookfield, VT: Dartmouth Press.

1998. *Comparative Public Policy: Patterns of Post-war Transformation.* Northampton, MA: Edward Elgar.

Castles, Francis G. 2004. *The Future of the Welfare State: Crisis Myths and Crisis Realities.* New York: Oxford University Press.

Castles, Francis G. 2007. "Testing the Retrenchment Hypothesis: An Aggregate Overview," in F. G. Castles, ed., *The Disappearing State? Retrenchment Realities in an Age of Globalization.* Northanpton, MA: Edward Elgar, 19–43.

Castles, Francis G., Rolf Gerritsen, and Jack Vowles, eds. 1996. *The Great Experiment: Labour Parties and Public Policy Transformation in Australia and New Zealand.* St. Leonards, NSW: Allen and Unwin.

CBI (Confederation for British Industry). 2001a. Manifesto. (On 2001 election).

2001b. "Issue Statements: New Deal for the Unemployed" (Updated March 23). http://www.cbi.org.uk.

CBI & TUC (Confederation for British Industry and Trades Union Congress). 2001. *The UK Productivity Challenge.* www.tuc.org.uk/economy/tuc-3928-fo.cfm.

Cecil, Lord Robert to Arthur Stanley. July 31, 1917. GD193/115/1/74. Arthur Steel Maitland Collection. Edinburgh: National Archives of Scotland.

Chaitkin, Anton. 2006. "How Carey and Bismarck Transformed Germany." *EIR* (April 28).

Chanady, Attila. 1967. "The Disintegration of the German National People's Party 1924–1930." *The Journal of Modern History* 39 (1): 65–91.

Chandler, Alfred. 1962. *Strategy and Structure.* Cambridge, MA: MIT Press.

1990. *Scale and Scope.* Cambridge, MA: Harvard University Press.

Chapman, Herrick. 2007. "France's Liberation Era, 1944–47," in *Revisiting the Liberation,* Andrew Knapp, ed. New York: Palgrave, 2007.

Chhibber, Pradeep and Ken Kollman. 2004. *The Formation of National Party Systems.* Princeton, NJ: Princeton University Press.

Childs, Harwood. 1930. *Labor and Capital in National Politics.* Columbus: Ohio State University Press.

Christensen, Jørgen Grønnegård. 1997. "The Scandinavian Welfare State: The Institutions of Growth, Governance, and Reform. Review Article." *Scandinavian Political Studies* 20 (4): 367–86.

Christiansen, Peter Munk. 1997. "Er det nødvendigt bade at styre og ro – og er det overhovedet godt?" in Torben Fridberg, ed., *Hvem løser opgaverne I fremtidens velfærdssamfund?* Århus: Århus Universitetsforlag, 63–92.

1998. "A Prescription Rejected: Market Solutions to Problems of Public Sector Governance." *Governance* 11 (3): 273–95.

1999. "Det fælles bedste?" in Jørgen Goul Andersen, Peter Munk Christiansen, Torben Beck Jørgensen, Lise Togeby, and Signild Vallgårda, eds., *Den demokratiske udfordring.* København, Denmark: Hans Reitzels Forlag, 247–66.

Christiansen, Peter Munk, Birgit Møller, and Lise Togeby. 2001. *Den danske elite.* Copenhagen: Hans Reitzels Forlag.

Christiansen, Peter Munk and Asbjørn Sonne Nørgaard. 2003. "Faste forhold – flygtige forbindelser. Stat og interesseorganisationer i Danmark i det 20. århundrede." Aarhus: Aarhus University Press.

Christiansen, Peter Munk, Asbjørn Sonne Nørgaard, and Niels Christian Sidenius. 2004. *Hven Skriver Lovene?* Aarhus: Aarhus Universitetsforlag.

Christiansen, Peter Munk and Hilmar Rommetvedt. 1999. "From Corporatism to Lobbyism?" *Scandinavian Political Studies* 22 (3): 195–220.

Christoffersen, Mogens Nygaard. 1996. "Opvækst of arbejdsløshed." Copenhagen: Socialforskningsinstituttet.

Claggett, William, Jeffrey Loesch, w. Phillips Shively, and Ronald Snell. 1982. "Political Leadership and the Development of Political Cleavages: Imperial Germany, 1871–1912." *American Journal of Political Science* 26 (4): 643–63.

Clarke, P. F. 1972. "The End of Laissez Faire and the Politics of Cotton." *The Historical Journal* 15 (3): 493–512.

Clegg, Hugh, Alan Fox, and A. F. Thompson. 1964. *A History of British Trade Unions since 1889.* Oxford: Clarendon Press.

Cleveland Press. 1896. (March 25): 6.

Cline, Peter. 1970. "Reopening the Case of Lloyd George Coalition and the Postwar Economic Transition 1918–1919." *Journal of British Studies* 10 (1): 162–75.

Coates, David. 2001. "Capitalist Models and Social Democracy: The Case of New Labour." The British Journal of Politics & International Relations. 3 (3 October): 284–307.

1999. "Models of Capitalism in the New World Order." *Political Studies* XLVII: 643–60.

Coats, A. W. 1968. "Political economy and the Tariff Reform Campaign of 1903." *Journal of Law and Economics* 11 (1): 181–229.

Coen, David. 1997. "The Evolution of the Large Firm as a Political Actor in the European Union." *Journal of European Public Policy* 41 (1): 91–108.

Coleman, William D. 1987. "Federalism and Interest Group Organization," in Herman Bakvis and William M. Chandler, eds., *Federalism and the Role of the State.* Toronto: University Of Toronto Press, 171–87.

1988. *Business and Politics.* Toronto: University of Toronto Press.

Coleman, William D. and Wyn Grant. 1988. "The Organizational Cohesion and Political Access of Business." *European Journal of Political* Research 16: 467–87.

Coleman, William D. and Henry Jacek. 1989. *Regionalism, Business Interests and Public Policy.* Beverly Hills: Sage.

Commission of the European Communities. 1999. "Employment Package I: Commission Adopts Draft Report on Member States Employment Policies." *RAPID* (September).

Committee on Commerce and Industry. 1898. Proceedings of the Third Annual Convention of the National Association of Manufacturers. New York: NAM Bureau of Publicity, 46–7.

Compston, Hugh and Per Kongshøj Madsen. 2001. "Conceptual Innovation and Public Policy: Unemployment and Paid Leave Schemes in Denmark." *Journal of European Social Policy* 11 (2): 117–32.

Cord, Trap. 1902. *The Danish Accident Law for Workers.* Copenhagen: J. Jørgensen and Co.

Corker, Robert, et al. 1995. *United Germany: The First Five Years. Performance and Policy Issues.* Washington, DC: International Monetary Fund.

Cox, Robert Henry. 1997. "The Consequences of Welfare Retrenchment in Denmark." *Politics & Society* 25 (3): 303–26.

1998. "From Safety Net to Trampoline." *Governance* 11: 397–414.

2001. "The Social Construction of an Imperative: Why Welfare Reform Happened in Denmark and the Netherlands but Not in Germany." *World Politics* 53: 463–98.

Craig, Gordon Alexander. 1978. *Germany, 1866–1945.* Oxford: Oxford University Press.

Crepaz, Markus. 1992. "Corporatism in Decline?" *Comparative Political Studies* 25 (2): 139–68.

Crepaz, Markus and Vicki Birchfield. 2000. "Global Economies, Local Politics: Globalization and Lijphart's Theory of Consensus Democracy and the Politics of Inclusion," in Markus Crepaz et al., eds., *Democracy and Institutions.* Ann Arbor: University of Michigan Press, 197–224.

Crepaz, Markus and Aaron Lijphart. 1995. "Linking and Integrating Corporatism and Consensus Democracy." *British Journal of Political Science* 25: 281–8.

Croly, Herbert 1912. *Marcus Alonzo Hanna.* New York: The Macmillan Co, 184.

Cronin, James. 2000. "Convergence by Conviction: Politics and Economics in the Emergence of the 'Anglo-American Model.'" *Journal of Social History* XXXIII (4): 781–804.

Crouch, Colin. 1990. "Trade Unionism in the Exposed Sector," in Renato Brunetta and Carlo Dell'Aringa, eds., *Labor Relations and Economic Performance*. New York: New York University Press, 68–91.

——. 1993. *Industrial Relations and European State Traditions*. New York: Oxford University Press.

Crouch, Colin, David Finegold, and Mari Sako, eds. 1999. *Are Skills the Answer?* New York: Oxford University Press.

Culpepper, Pepper. 2003. *Creating Cooperation: How States Develop Human Capital in Europe*. Ithaca, NY: Cornell University Press.

Cusack, Thomas, Torben Iversen, and David Soskice. 2007. "Economic Interests and the Origins of Electoral Institutions." *American Political Science Review* 101 (August): 373–91.

Cuthbert, D. D. 1971. "Lloyd George and the Conservative Central Office," in A. J. P. Taylor, ed., *Lloyd George: Twelve Essays*. London: Hamish Hamilton: 182–6.

Czada, Roland. 2005. "Social Policy: Crisis and Transformation," in Simon Green and William E. Paterson, eds., *Governance in Contemporary Germany: The Semisovereign State Revisited*. New York: Cambridge University Press, 165–89.

DA. 8/25/1897. "Vedtægter for Arbejdsgiverforeningen af 1896" (Vedtagne pågeneralforsamlingen 25/8/ 1897) DA – lovmateriale underskrevne love 1896–1914. DA (06158). Erhvervsarkivet, Aarhus, Denmark.

DA Arbødigst to Hr. Grosserer. Letter. Marts 25, 1914. folder: "Foreningen af Arbejdsgivere I aarhus, 1916 incl., "06158; Box, Dansk Arbejdsgiverforening Regnskabsafd/Administrations 1913–1954 Korrespondance med foreninger, Erhvervsarkivet, Aarhus, DK.

DA to DSF. March 1898. DA – Korrespondance, 1898_138 22/3/1898, General udgående 1896 6 30 til 1899 9 21.

DA to Hr. Grosserer, "Foreningen af Arbejdsgivere I Aarhus," 28 Oktober 1915, folder: "Foreningen af Arbejdsgivere I aarhus, 1916 incl.," 06158; Box, Dansk Arbejdsgiverforening Regnskabsafd/ Administrations 1913–1954 Korrespondance med foreninger, Erhvervsarkivet, Aarhus, DK.

DA Hovedkontoret, 1928. *Beretning om Dansk Arbejdsgiver Forenings Virksomhed*, København Langkjærs Bogtrykkeri, pp. 62–6.

"DA – Korrespondance, General udgående 1896 6 30 til 1899 9 21." 1897_46–48, 23/6/1897. Erhvervsarkivet, Aarhus, DK.

"DA – Korrespondance, General udgående 1896 6 30 til 1899 9 21." 1897_71 10/9/1897. Erhvervsarkivet, Aarhus, DK.

"DA – Korrespondence, General udgående 1896 6 30 til 1899 9 21." 1897_25 (20/2/1897). Erhvervsarkivet, Aarhus, DK.

"DA-Korrespondence 1897_25 (20/2/1897), General udgående 1896 6 30 til 1899 9 21," Erhvervsarkivet, Aarhus, DK. DA 06158.

Daadler, Hans. 1966. "Parties, Elites and Political Development in Western Europe," in Joseph LaPalombara and Myron Weiner, eds., *Political Parties and Political Development*. Princeton, NJ: Princeton University Press, 43–77.

Dall, Villy. 2008. Den conservative bastion in Thy. (December 29). http://arkiv.thisted-bibliotek. dk/artikler/den_konservative_bastion_i_thy.htm.

Damgaard, Bodil. 2000. *Kommunerne, virksomhederne og den aktive socialpolitik*. Copenhagen: Socialforskningsinstituttet.

Damgaard, Erik and Palle Svensson. 1989. "Who Governs? Parties and Policies in Denmark." *European Journal of Political Research*. 17: 731–45.

Dando, W. Elbert. Memo. No date. "Details of a Plan for Creation of a Banking Organization, to Deal Especially with Government Loan Requirements Incidental to the War," GD193/164/3/ 1/2. Arthur Steel Maitland Collection. Edinburgh: National Archives of Scotland.

Danish National Institute of Social Research. 1997. *New Partnership for Social Cohesion*. Copenhagen: Ministry of Social Affairs.

Danmark Statsministeriet 2001. "Regeringsgrundlag 2001: Vækst, velfærd – fornyelse." Copenhagen: Statsministeriet.

"Danmarks Nationale Handlingsplan for Beskaeftigelse 1999." 1999. Kobenhavn: Arbejdesministeriet. (May).

Dansk Arbejdsgiverforening. October 2, 1997. "Fynske kommuner skaber flest skånejob." *Agenda*. Copenhagen: Dansk Arbejdsgiverforeningen, 8.

March 12, 1998. "Høj vækst i privat efteruddannelse." *Agenda* 6. Copenhagen: Dansk Arbejdsgiverforeningen, 1–5.

June 1998. "Få indflydelse på arbejdsmarkeds-politikken I dit lokalområde." Copenhagen: Dansk Arbejdsgiverforeningen.

December 17, 1998. "Privat jobtræning klart mest effektiv." *Agenda*. Copenhagen: Dansk Arbejdsgiverforeningen, 7.

1999. "Kommunerne stopper brug af AMU-kurser." *Agenda*. Copenhagen: Dansk Arbejdsgiverforeningen, 3.

2000. "Mundigheder informerer for dårligt." *Agenda*. Copenhagen: Dansk Arbejdsgiverforeningen.

June 2000. *Arbejdsmarkeds Rapport*. Copenhagen: Dansk Arbejdsgiverforeningen.

March 16, 2000. "Kommuner giver fleksjob til mange unge." *Agenda*. Copenhagen: Dansk Arbejdsgiverforeningen, 6.

2001. "Ledige formidles ikke til ledige job." *Agenda*. Copenhagen: Dansk Arbejdsgiverforeningen, 8.

October 21, 2001. "Kommunerne bruger ikke effektiv adtivering." *Agenda*. Copenhagen: Dansk Arbejdsgiverforeningen, 5.

October 24, 2002. "Kontanthjælpsmodtagere dropper jobsøgning." *Agenda* 17. Copenhagen: Dansk Arbejdsgiverforeningen: p. 1.

December 24, 2002. "Virksomheder kan nemmere få arbejdskraft." *Agenda*.17 Copenhagen: Dansk Arbejdsgiverforeningen, 6.

Dansk Metal. December 4, 2001. "Den danske model er vejen til vækst og velfærd," *Metalbladet* 12. April 23, 2002. "Nej til brugerbetaling på efteruddannelse."

April 6, 2006. "Hellere uddannelse end pisk og prygl."

Daunton, M. J. 1989. "'Gentlemanly Capitalism' and British Industry 1820–1914." *Past and Present* 122 (1): 119–58.

1996. "How to Pay for the War." *The English Historical Review* 111 (443): 882–919.

Davenport-Hines, R. P. T. 1984. *Dudley Docker: The Life and Times of a Trade Warrior*. NewYork: Cambridge University Press.

1988. "The Modernization Crisis of British Industry," in Hiroaki Yamazuki and Matuo Miyamoto, eds., *Trade Associations in Business History*. Tokyo: University of Tokyo Press, 205–26.

David, G. Cullom. 1962. "The Transformation of the Federal Trade Commission, 1914–1929," *Mississippi Valley Historical Review* 49: 437–55.

Davis, Mike. 2000. *Prisoners of the American Dream*. New York: W. W. Norton.

Dawes, Charles. *A Journal of the McKinley Years*. Chicago: Lakeside Press.

Dawson, William. 1904. "The Genesis of the German Tariff." *The Economic Journal* 14 (53): 11–23.

Deeg, Richard & Gregory Jackson. 2007. "Towards a More Dynamic Theory of Capitalist Diversity." *Socio-Economic Review* 5 (1): 149–80.

Deloitte & Touche. 1999. "The Employment Service: Proposal to Provide a Mechanism to Control the Demand for the Large Organisation Unit's Services." Unpublished paper. (January).

Denny, Charlotte. 1999. "Private firms fail New Deal." *The Guardian* (May 17).

de Swaan, Abram. 1992. "Perspectives for Transnational Social Policy." *Government and Opposition* 27 (1): 33–51.

DfEE (Department for Education and Employment). 1999. *United Kingdom Employment Action Plan*. London: DfEE.

1998. "Employer coalitions to advise and promote New Deal – Smith." *M2 Presswire* (May 22).

2000. "Learning and Training at Work 1999."*Research Brief* 202 (May).

DiMaggio, Paul and Walter Powell. 1991. "Introduction," in Walter Powell and Paul DiMaggio, eds., *The New Institutionalism in Organizational Analysis.* Chicago: The University of Chicago Press, 1–38.

Djelic, Marie-Laure, Sigrid Quack. 2003. *Globalization and institutions.* Cheltenham, UK: Edward Elgar.

Dobbin, Frank. 1992. "The Origins of Private Social Insurance: Public Policy and Fringe Benefits in America, 1920–1950." *American Journal of Sociology* 97 (March): 1416–50.

2004. *The Sociology of the Economy.* New York: Russell Sage Foundation.

2009. *Inventing Equal Opportunity.* Princeton, NJ: Princeton University Press.

Docker, Dudley to Arthur Steel Maitland. no date. GD193/128/231. Arthur Steel -Maitland Collection. Edinburgh: ASM Collection.

November 30, 1911. GD193/153/4/68. Arthur Steel -Maitland Collection. Edinburgh: ASM Collection.

Letter. 7/29/1915. ASM GD193/165/1/179. Arthur Steel -Maitland Collection. Edinburgh: ASM Collection.

November 13, 1915. GD193/165/2/124. Arthur Steel -Maitland Collection. Edinburgh: ASM Collection.

Downs, Anthony. 1957. *An Economic Theory of Democracy.* New York: Harper.

Due, Jesper and Jørgen Steen Madsen. 2008. "The Danish Model of Industrial Relations: Erosion or Renewal?" *Journal of Industrial Relations* 5 (3): 513–29.

"Hvorfor er den danske aftale model anderledes en denSvenske?" FAOS Forskningsnotat, #26: 1–17.

2006. "Fra storkonflikt til barselsfond. Den danske model under afvikling eller fornyelse." DJØF's Forlag.

Due, Jesper, Jørgen Steen Madsen, Carsten Strøby Jensen, and Lars Kjerulf Petersen. 1994. *The Survival of the Danish Model.* Copenhagen: DJOEF Publishing.

Dunleavy, Colleen and Thomas Welskopp. 2007. "Peculiarities and Myths: Comparing U.S. and German Capitalism," *German Historical Institute Bulletin* 41 (Fall): 33–64.

Dutton, D. J. 1981. "The Unionist Party and Social Policy 1906–1914." *The Historical Journal* 24 (4): 871–84.

Duverger, Maurice. 1954. *Political Parties, Their Organization and Activity in the Modern State.* New York: Wiley.

Dybdahl, Vagn. 1969. *Partier og Erhverv.* Aarhus: Universitets Forlaget i Aarhus.

Ebbinghaus, Bernard. 2006a. "The Politics of Pension Reform: Managing Interest Group Conflicts," in Gordon L. Clark, Alicia H. Munnell, and J. Michael Orszag, eds., *The Oxford Handbook of Pensions and Retirement Income,* Oxford: Oxford University Press, 759–77.

Ebbinghaus, Bernhard. 2006b. *Reforming Early Retirement in Europe, Japan, and the USA.* New York: Oxford University Press.

Ebbinghaus, Bernhard and Werner Eichhorst. 2006. "Employment Regulation and Labor Market Policy in Germany, 1991–2005." Institute for the Study of Labor (IZA) Discussion Paper No. 2505.

Ebbinghaus, Bernhard and Anke Hassel. 2000. "Striking Deals: Concertation in the Reform of Continental European Welfare States." *Journal of European Public Policy* 7 (1): 44–62.

Economist Staff. 1993. "Business Lobbies: Reversal of Fortune." *The Economist* 328 (7827): 57.

November 6, 1999. "Britain: Revolting." *The Economist* 353 (8144): 59.

August 19, 2000. "The End of the Affair." *The Economist.*

September 26, 2009. "Deflating the State." *The Economist* 30.

February 2, 2009. "Britain: Thanks, Gordon." *The Economist* 390 (8619): 56–7.

February 28, 2009.

Economy Watch. "Top Ten Economies in the World." http://www.economywatch.com/economies-in-top/top-ten-economies.html.

Edelman, Lauren. 1990. "Legal Environments and Organizational Governance." *American Journal of Sociology* 95: 1410–40.

Eironline. 1999. "Early Retirement Scheme Finally Concluded." *Euroline* (February). http://www.eurofound.europa.eu/eiro/1999/02/inbrief/dk9902111n.htm

    2003. "ILO criticizes government over new part-time work legislation." *Eironline* (March).

    1998. "Third reform of labour market policy is underway." *Eironline*.

    1998. "Tripartite agreement reached on content of new labour market reform." *Eironline*.

    1999. "Social Democrats Propose Obligatory Supplementary Training Funds." *Eironline* (June).

    2001. "DA and LO Make Joint Proposal on Labour Market Activation Reform." *Eironline*.

    2001. "New Government Challenges Trade Union Movement" *Eironline* (December).

    2002. "New Act on part-time work adopted after lengthy debate." *Eironline* (June).

    2002. "Low-Wage Workers and the 'Working Poor'," *Eironline* (August).

Ejersbo, Niels and Carsten Greve. 2005. "Public Management Policymaking in Denmark 1983–2005." Unpublished paper for the IIM/LSE Workshop on Theory and Methods for Studying Organizational Processes. London: London School of Economics.

Eldersveld, Samuel. 2000. *Political Parties in American Society.* New York: St. Martin's Press.

Eley, Geoff. 1978. "Reshaping the Right: Radical Nationalism and the German Navy League, 1989–1908." *The Historical Journal* 21 (2): 327–54.

Elmer, David and Morten Bjørn Hansen. April 22, 2010. "Dansk beskæftigelse falder mere end EU's." *Agenda* 7.

Engineering Employers Federation. 7/19/1917. inute Book. No. 13. Meeting of Management Committee, 19th June, 1917, p. 20. MSS.237/1/1/13. Modern Records Centre, Warwick University, Warwick, UK.

    1917. Minute Book. No. 13. Meeting of the Management Committee on 27th July, 1917, p. 59. MSS.237/1/1/13. Modern Records Centre, Warwick University, Warwick UK.

    1918. Minute Book. No. 13. Meeting of the Management Committee 25th January, 1918, p 200. Modern Records Centre, Warwick University, Warwick, UK.

Esping-Andersen, Gosta. 1985. *Politics Against Markets,* Princeton, NJ: Princeton University Press.

    1990. *Three Worlds of Welfare Capitalism.* London: Polity Press.

    1996. *Welfare States in Transition.* Thousand Oaks, CA: Sage.

Estevez-Abe, Margarita. 2008. *Welfare and Capitalism in Postwar Japan.* Cambridge: Cambridge University Press.

Estevez-Abe, Margarita, Torben Iversen, and David Soskice. 2001. "Social Protection and the Formation of Skills," in Peter A. Hall and David Soskice, eds., *Varieties of Capitalism: The Institutional Foundations of Comparative Advantage.* New York: Oxford University Press, 145–83.

Ethier, W. J. 2005. "Globalization, Globalization: Trade, Technology, and Wages." *International Review of Economic Finance* 14: 237–58.

European Information Service. 1997. "Training: Three Initiatives to Improve Continuing Training." *European Report* (May 3).

"Fairness at Work." 1998. London: House of Commons Library Research Paper 98/99.

Falkner, Gerda. 1998. EU Social Policy in the 1990s: Toward a Corporatist Policy Community. London: Routledge.

FBI Bulletin. August 15, 1918, 385. Modern Records Centre, Warwick University, Warwick, UK.

FBI. 1916. "Minutes of the Organization Sub-Committee of the Executive Council" (October 31), MSS200/F/3/DA/A/12. Modern Records Centre, Warwick University, Warwick UK.

FBI. 1917. "Minutes of the Meeting of the Organization and Management Committee of the Federation of British Industries" (February 23). MSS200/F/3/DA/A/13. Modern Records Centre, Warwick University, Warwick, UK.

Fear, Jeffrey. 2005. Organizing Control: August Thyssen and the Construction of German Corporate Management. Cambridge, MA: Harvard University Press.

1995. "German Capitalism," in Thomas McCraw, ed., *Creating Modern Capitalism*. Cambridge, MA: Harvard University Press.

Fear, Jeffrey and Christopher Kobrak. 2010. "Banks on Board: Banks in German and American Corporate Governance, 1870–1914." *Business History Review* 84: 703–36.

Federation of British Industries. 1916. "The Chairman's Report for the Organization Sub-Committee. 12/5/1916," p. 1. MSS200/F/3/DA/A/12. Modern Records Centre, Warwick University, Warwick UK.

Federation of British Industries. 1917. "Company Meeting." (March 12): 12. Modern Records Centre, Warwick University, Warwick, UK.

Feenstra, R. 2000. *The Impact of International Trade on Wages*. Chicago: University of Chicago Press.

Feldman, Gerald. 1975. "Economic and Social Problems of the German Demobilization, 1918–19." *Journal of Modern History* 47 (1): 1–47.

1992. Army, Industry, and Labor in Germany 1914–1918. London: Berg Publishers.

1997. *The Great Disorder*. New York: Oxford University Press.

Fellman, Susanna, Martin Iversen, Hans Sjögren, and Lars Thue, eds. 2008. *Creating Nordic Capitalism: The Business History of a Competitive Periphery*. New York: Palgrave Macmillan.

Fererra, Maurizio, Anton Hemerijck, and Martin Rhodes. No Date. "The Future of Social Europe." Report for the Portuguese Presidency of the European Union.

Ferguson, Thomas 1995. *Golden Rule*. Chicago: University of Chicago Press.

Ferleger, Louis and William Lazonick. 1993. "The Managerial Revolution and the Developmental State: The Case of U.S. Agriculture." *Business and Economic History* 22 (2): 67–98.

Ferrera, Maurizio, Anton Hemerijck, and Martin Rhodes. 2000. *The Future of Social Europe: Recasting Work and Welfare in the New Economy*. Lisbon: CELTA/Ministerio do Trabalho eda Solidariedade.

Financial Times Staff. 9/14/2009. "G20 nations break 'no protectionism' vow." *Financial Times*.

Finansministeriet. 1986. *Finansredogørelsen 1987*. Copenhagen: Ministry of Finance.

1991. *Udlicitering – effektivitet gennem konkurrence*. Copenhagen: Ministry of Finance.

1992. *Den offentlige sektor 1982–1992*. Copenhagen: Ministry of Finance.

Fink, Jørgen. 1991–1993. "Den danske industris historie." *History / Royal Academy Collections*, New series, 19: 2.

1988. *Middelstand I Klemme?* Aarhus: Universitetsforlaget i Aarhus.

2000. *Storindustri eller Middelstand*. Aarhus: Aarhus Universitetsforlag.

Finn, D. 2000. "From Full Employment to Employability: A New Deal for Britain's Unemployed?" *International Journal of Manpower* 21 (5): 384–99.

Fisher, Victor to Arthur Steel Maitland. Letter. 11/22/1917. GD193/99/2/149.

Fligstein, Neil. 1990. *The Transformation of Corporate Control*. Cambridge, MA: Harvard University Press.

Flynn, John. 1988. "At the Threshold of Dissolution: the National Liberals and Bismarck 1877/1878." *The Historical Journal* 31 (1): 319–40.

Forbes, Ian. 1979. "Social Imperialism and Wilhelmine Germany." *The Historical Journal* 22 (2): 331–49.

Frankel, Emil. 1922. "Germany's Industrial Parliament: The National Economic Council." *Political Science Quarterly* 37: 472.

Franzese, Robert J. Jr. 2002. *Macroeconomic Policies of Developed Democracies*. New York: Cambridge University Press.

Fraser, Neil. 1999. "How Strong Is the Case for Targeting Active Labour Market Policies?" *International Journal of Manpower* 20 (3/4) 1999: 151–64.

Fraser, Peter 1962a. "The Liberal Unionist Alliance: Chamberlain, Hartington, and the Conservatives, 1886–1904." *The English Historical Review* 77 (302): 53–78.

1962b. "Unionism and Tariff Reform: The Crisis of 1906." *The Historical Journal* V (2): 149–66.

Frederiksen, Claus Hjort and Vibeke Dalbro. 2002. Memo plus attachment. Arbejdsmarkedsudvalget 2. Samling L122-bilag 5 (offentligt) (March 1).

Fridberg, Torben. 1997. "Hvem løser de sociale opgaver?," in T. Fridberg, ed., *Hvem løser opgaverne I fremtidens velfærdssamfund?* Copenhagen: Socialforskningsinstituttet.

Frieden, Jeffry A. 1988. "Sectorial Conflict in U.S. Foreign Economic Policy, 1914–1940." *International Organization* 42 (1): 59–90.

2006. *Global Capitalism: Its Fall and Rise in the Twentieth Century.* New York: W. W. Norton.

Frieden, Jeffry and Ronald Rogowski. 1996. "The Impact of the International Economy on National Politics: An Analytical Overview," in *Internationalization and Domestic Politics*, Robert Keohane and Helen Milner, eds. New York: Cambridge University Press, 25–47.

Friedland, Roger, and A. F. Robertson, eds. 1990. *Beyond the Market Place: Rethinking Economy and Society.* New York: Aldine de Gruyter.

Friedman, Gerald. 2000. "The Political Economy of Early Southern Unionism: Race, Politics, and Labor in the South, 1880–1953." *Journal of Economic History* 60 (2): 384–413.

Friedman, Milton and Rose Friedman. 1979. *Free to Choose.* San Diego: Harcourt Brace Jovanovich.

Friedrich, Robert J. 1982. "In Defense of Multiplicative Terms in Multiple Regression Analysis." *American Journal of Political Science* 26 (4): 797–833.

Friis, Henning. 1969. "Issues in Social Security Policies in Denmark," in Shirley Jenkins, ed., *Social Security in International Perspective.* New York: Columbia University Press, 129–46.

Fulcher, James. 1991. "Labour Movements," in *Employers, and the State: Conflict and Cooperation in Britain and Sweden.* Oxford: Clarendon Press.

1997. "Did British Society Change Character in the 1920s or the 1980s." *British Journal of Sociology* 48 (3): 514–21.

Furner, Mary and Barry Supple, eds. 1990. *The State and Economic Knowledge: The American and British Experiences.* Cambridge: Cambridge University Press.

Gable, Richard. 1959. "Birth of an Employers' Association." *Business History Review* 33 (4): 535–45.

Galenson, Walter. 1952. *The Danish System of Labor Relations.* Cambridge, MA: Harvard University Press.

Gallagher, Michael. 1991. "Proportionality, Disproportionality and Electoral Systems." *Electoral Studies* 10 (1): 33–51.

Gallie, Duncan. 2007. "Production Regimes and the Quality of Employment in Europe." *Annual Review of Sociology* 33: 85–104.

Gamble, Andrew. 2009. *The Spectre at the Feast.* Basingstoke: Palgrave Macmillan.

Ganghof, Steffen. 2007. "The Political Economy of High Income Taxation." *Comparative Political Studies* 40 (9): 1059–84.

Garon, Sheldon. 1987. *The State and Labor in Modern Japan.* Berkeley: University of California Press.

Garrett, Geoffrey. 1998. *Partisan Politics in the Global Economy.* New York: Cambridge University Press.

2000. "The Causes of Globalization." *Comparative Political Studies* 33 (6/7): 941–91.

Garrett, Geoffrey and Christopher Way. 1999. "Public Sector Unions, Corporatism, and Macroeconomic Performance. *Comparative Political Studies* 32 (4): 411–34.

Garst, W. Daniel, 1999, "From Sectoral Linkages to Class Conflict," *Comparative Political Studies* 32 (7): 788–809.

Gatzke, Hans. 1954. "The Stresemann Papers." *Journal of Modern History* 26 (1): 49–59.

Geary, Dick. 1976. "The German Labour Movement." *European Studies Review* 6: 297–330.

Gershenkron, Alexander. 1962. *Bread and Democracy in Germany.* Berkeley: University of California Press.

Gessner, Dieter. 1977. "Agrarian Protectionism in the Weimar Republic." *Journal of Contemporary History* 12 (4): 759–78.

Geyer, Robert and Beverly Springer. 1998. "EU Social Policy After Mastricht," in Pierre-Henri Laurent and Marc Maresceau, eds., *The State of the European Union*. Boulder CO: LynneRienner, 207–23.

Giddons, Anthony. 1998. *The Third Way*. Cambridge: Polity.

Giersch, Herbert, Karl-Heinz Pacqué, and Holger Schmieding. 1992. *The Fading Miracle: Four Decades of Market Economy in Germany*. New York: Cambridge University Press.

Gilbert, Bentley. 1965. "The British National Insurance Act of 1911 and the Commercial Insurance Lobby."; *Journal of British Studies* 4 (2): 127–48.

Gilbert, Neil. 1992. "From Entitlements to Incentives: the Changing Philosophy of Social Protection." *International Social Security Review* 45 (3): 5–17.

Gilder, George. 1981. *Wealth and Poverty*. New York: Basic Books.

Gill, Colin, Herman Knudsen, and Jens Lind. March 1, 1998. "Are There Cracks in the Danish Model of Industrial Relations?" *Industrial Relations Journal* 29: 30.

Glass, Hon. Carter. April 15, 1913. "Banking and Currency Reform." *Nation's Business* 1 (10).

Glyn, Andrew. 2006. *Capitalism Unleashed*. New York: Oxford University Press.

Golden, Miriam. June 2, 1993. "The Dynamics of Trade Unionism and National Economic Performance." *American Political Science Review* 87: 439–454.

Golden, Miriam, Michael Wallerstein, and Peter Lange. 1999. "Postwar Trade-Union Organization and Industrial Relations in Twelve Countries," in Herbert Kitschelt, Peter Lange, Gary Marks, and John Stephens, eds., *Continuity and Change in Contemporary Capitalism*. New York: Cambridge University Press, 194–230.

Goldthorpe, John. 1984. *Order and Conflict in Contemporary Capitalism*. Oxford: Clarendon Press.

Gollin, Alfred. 1976. "Historians and the Great Crisis of 1903." *Albion: A Quarterly Journal Concerned with British Studies* 8 (1): 83–97.

Gollin, Alfred. 1983. "Review of British Economic and Strategic Planning 1905–1915," *Albion: A Quarterly Journal Concerned with British Studies* 15 (3): 259–65.

Goodin, Robert and Martin Rein. 2001. "Regimes on Pillars." *Public Administration* 79 (4): 769–801.

Goodin, Robert. 2001. "Work and Welfare: Towards a Post-productivist Welfare Regime." *British Journal of Political Science* 31: 13–39.

Goos, M. and A. Manning. 2007. "Lousy and Lovely Jobs: The Rising Polarization of Work in Britain." *Review of Economics and Statistics* 89 (1): 118–33.

Gordon, Colin. 1994. New Deals: Business, Labor, and Politics in America, 1920–1935. New York: Cambridge University Press.

Goul Andersen, Jørgen. 1997. "The Scandinavian Welfare Model in Crisis? Achievements and Problems of the Danish Welfare State in an Age of Unemployment and Low Growth." *Scandinavian Political Studies* 20 (1): 1–31.

2008. "Public Support for the Danish Welfare State," in Erik Albæk, Leslie Eliason, Asbjørn Sonne Nørgaard, and Herman Schwartz, eds., *Crisis, Miracles and Beyond*. Aarhus: Aarhus University Press.

2007. "The Danish Welfare State as 'Politics for Markets' Combining Equality and Competitiveness in a Global Economy." *New Political Economy* 12 (1): 71–8.

2011. "Økonomiske kriser," in Martin Marcussen and Karsten Ronit, eds., *Kriser, politik og forvaltning*. Copenhagen: Hans Reitzels Forlag, 84–112.

Gourevitch, Peter. 1986. *Politics in Hard Times*. Ithaca, NY: Cornell University Press.

Gourevitch, Peter and James Shinn. 2005. *Political Power and Corporate Control: the New Global Politics of Corporate Governance*. Princeton, NJ: Princeton University Press.

Granovetter, Mark. 1985. "Economic Action and Social Structure: The Problem of Embeddedness." *American Journal of Sociology* 91 (3): 481–510.

Grant, Wyn. 1989. *Government and Industry*. Brookfield, VT: Gower Publishing.

————. 1991. "Government and Manufacturing Industry since 1900," in Geoffrey Jones and Maurice Kirby, eds., *Competitiveness and the State*. Manchester, UK: Manchester University Press, 100–19.

————. 2000. "Globalisation, Big Business and the Blair Government." CSGR Working Paper No. 58/00. Warwick, UK, August.

Grant, Wyn and David Marsh. 1977. *The Confederation of British Industry*. London: Hodder and Stoughton.

Green, Simon and William E. Paterson. 2005. *Governance in Contemporary Germany: The Semisovereign State Revisited*. New York: Cambridge University Press.

Green-Pedersen, Christoffer. 2001. "Minority Governments and Party Politics: The Political and Institutional Background to the 'Danish Miracle.'" *Journal of Public Policy* 21 (1): 53–70.

Green-Pedersen, Christoffer. 2002. "New Public Management Reforms of the Danish and Swedish Welfare States: The Role of Different Social Democratic Responses."; *Governance* 15 (2): 271–94.

Green-Pedersen, Christoffer, Kees van Kersbergen, and Anton Hemerijck. 2000. *How Politics Still Matters*. Aarhus: Aarhus University Doctoral Dissertation.

Green-Pedersen, Christoffer, Kees van Kersbergen, and Anton Hemerijck. 2001. "Neoliberalism, the 'Third Way' or What? Recent Social Democratic Welfare Policies in Denmark and the Netherlands." *Journal of European Public Policy* 8 (2): 307–25.

Greenwood, Justin. 2002. *Inside the EU Business Associations*. New York: Palgrave.

Greenwood, Justin, Jurgen Grote, and Karsten Ronit, eds. 1992. *Organized Interests and the European Community*. Thousand Oaks, CA: Sage.

Greve, Bent. 2004. "Denmark: Universal or Not So Universal Welfare State." *Social Policy & Administration* 38 (2): 156–69.

Grier, Kevin, Michael Munger, and Brian Roberts. 1994. "The Determinants of Industry Political Activity, 1978–1986." *American Political Science Review* 88 (4): 911.

Grimm, Curtis and John Holcomb. 1987. "Choices Among Encompassing Organizations," in Alfred Marcus, Allen Kaufman, and David Beam, eds., *Business Strategy and Public Policy*, New York: Quorum Books. 105–118.

Grønnegård Christensen, Jørgen. 1997. "The Scandinavian Welfare State: The Institutions of Growth, Governance, and Reform." *Scandinavian Political Studies* 20 (4): 367–86.

Grote, Jürgen and Philippe Schmitter. 2003. "The Renaissance of National Corporatism: Unintended Side-Effect of European Economic and Monetary Union, or Calculated Response to the Absence of European Social Policy?," in Fritz van Waarden and Gerhard Lehmbruch, eds., *Renegotiating the Welfare State*. London: Routledge, 279–302.

Grote, Jürgen, Achim Lang, and Franz Traxler. 2007. "Germany," in Franz Traxler and Gerhard Huemer, eds., *Handbook of Business Interest Associations, Firm Size and Governance: A Comparative Analytical Approach*. New York: Routledge, 141–76.

Grothe to Henry Carey. March 26, 1878. Box 13, Folder 5, letter from Grothe to Henry Carey. Historical Society of Pennsylvania, Edward Carey Gardiner Collection, Collection 227A. Series 5. Correspondence of H. C. Carey.

Grover, Chris and John Stewart. 2000. "Modernizing Social Security?" *Social Policy & Administration* 34 (3): 235–52.

Grosvenor, G. H. to William R. Holloway. March 21, 1896. Holloway Papers.

Haahr, Jens Henrik and Søren Winter. 1996. *Den Regionale Arbejdsmarkedspolitik*. Århus: Systime.

Hacker, Jacob. 2002. *The Divided Welfare State*. Cambridge: Cambridge University Press.

Hacker, Jacob and Paul Pierson. 2002. "Business Power and Social Policy." *Politics and Society* 30 (June): 277–325.

Hagen, Kåre. 1992. "The Interaction of Welfare States and Labor Markets," in Jon Eivind Kolberg, ed., *The Study of Welfare State Regimes*. Armonk, NY: M. E. Sharpe, 124–68.

Hall, Alex. 1976. "The War of Words: Anti-socialist Offensives and Counter-propaganda in Wilhelmine Germany." *Journal of Contemporary History* 11: 11–42.

Hall, Peter. 1986. *Governing the Economy.* Oxford: Oxford University Press.

1993. "Policy Paradigms, Social Learning, and the State: the Case of Economic Policymaking in Britain." *Comparative Politics* 25 (3): 275–96.

1997. "The Political Economy of Adjustment in Germany," in Frieder Naschold, David Soskice, Bob Hancke, and Ulrich Jurgens, eds., *Okonomische Leistungsfähigkeit und institutionelle Innovation.* Berlin: WZB-Jahrbuch, 295–317.

Hall, Peter A. and Robert Franzese. 1998. "Mix Signals: Central Bank Independence, Coordinated Wage-Bargaining, and European Monetary Union." *International Organization* 52 (3): 505–35.

Hall, Peter A. and Daniel W. Gingerich. 2004. "Varieties of Capitalism and Institutional Complementarities in the Macroeconomy: An Empirical Analysis." Max Planck Institute for the Study of Societies Discussion Paper 04/5.

Hall, Peter and Michèle Lamont, eds. 2009. *Successful Societies.* Cambridge: Cambridge University Press.

Hall, Peter A. and David Soskice, eds. 2001. *Varieties of Capitalism: The Institutional Foundations of Comparative Advantage.* New York: Oxford University Press.

Hall, Peter and Rosemary Taylor. 1996. "Political Science and the Three New Institutionalisms." *Political Studies* 44: 936–57.

Hall, Peter A. and Kathleen Thelen. 2009. "Institutional Change in Varieties of Capitalism." *Socio-Economic Review* 7: 7–34.

Hamann, Kerstin and John Kelly. 2007. "Party Politics and the Reemergence of Social Pacts in Western Europe." *Comparative Political Studies* 40 (8): 971–94.

Hancke, Bob, Martin Rhodes and Mark Thatcher. 2007. *Beyond Varieties of Capitalism.* Oxford: Oxford University Press.

Hansen, J. A. 1922. "De Samvirkende Fagforbund Gennem 25 Aar." *National Economic Journal* 3, 30 (1922) Foredrag i Nationaløkonomisk Forening d. 26. October 1922.

Hansen, Hal. 1997. *Caps and Gowns: Historical Reflections on the Institutions That Shaped Learning for and at Work in Germany and the United States.* Unpublished Dissertation. University of Wisconsin.

Hansen, Hanne Foss. 2005. "Evaluation in and of Public-sector Reform: The Case of Denmark in a Nordic Perspective." *Scandinavian Political Studies* 28 (4): 323–47.

Hansen, Morten Bjørn. 2010. "Danskerne frygter ikke at miste jobbet." *Agenda* 8 (April 6).

Hansen, Svend Aage and Ingrid Henriksen. 1984. *Dansk Social Historie 1914–39.* Copenhagen: Gyldendalske Boghandel.

Hanushek, Eric and John E. Jackson. 1977. *Statistical Methods for the Social Sciences.* New York: Academic Press.

Harris, Richard. 1989. "Politicized Management," in Richard Harris and Sidney Milkis, eds., *Remaking American Politics.* Boulder, CO: Westview Press, 2161–285.

Hart, Jeffrey. 1992. "The Effects of State-Societal Arrangements on International Competitiveness." *British Journal of Political Science* 22: 255–300.

Hartz, Louis. 1955. *The Liberal Tradition in America.* New York: Harcourt Brace.

Hasluck, Chris. 2000. *The New Deal for Young People, Two Years On.* Sheffield: Research Management Employment Service (February).

2001. "Lessons from the New Deal: Finding Work, Promoting Employability." *New Economy* 8 (4): 230–4.

Hassel, Anke. 2003. "The Politics of Social Pacts." *British Journal of Industrial Relations* 41 (4): 707–26.

Hassel, Anke. 2007. "What Does Business Want? Labor Market Reforms in CMEs and Its Problems," in Bob Hancké, Martin Rhodes, and Marl Thatcher, eds., *Beyond Varieties of Capitalism.* New York: Oxford University Press.

Hassel, Anke. 2009. "Policies and Politics in Social Pacts in Europe." *European Journal of Industrial Relations* 15 (1): 7–26.

Hassel, Anke and Bernhard Ebbinghaus. 2000. "Concerted Reforms." Europeanists Conference, Chicago, April 1.

Hatting, Jørgen. 1966. *Fra Piper til Christmas Møller 1915–1929*. København: Nyt Nordisk Forlag.

Hawley, Ellis. 1966. *The New Deal and the Problem of Monopoly*, Princeton, NJ: Princeton University Press.

Hay, Alexander. 2000. "It's All in Your Best Interests, Sonny." *New Statesman*, July 17.

Hay, Colin. 1997. "Anticipating Accommodations, Accommodating Anticipations: The Appeasement of Capital in the 'Modernization' of the British Labour Party, 1987–1992." *Politics and Society* 25 (2): 234–56.

Hay, Colin and Ben Rosamond. 2008. "Globalization, European integration, and the Discursive Construction of Economic Imperatives," *Journal of European Public Policy*, 9: 147–68.

Hayes, Carlton. 1937. Review of "Wilhelm von Kardorff, ein nationaler *Parliamentarier im Zeitalter Bismarcks und Wilhelms II, 1828–1907.*" *The American Historical Review* 43 (1): 126–8.

Hearing on L122 – bilag 5 to create cross-section unemployment funds.

Hearings on L83, Law to Regulate Part Time Work.

Hazlehurst, Cameron. 1971. *Politicians at War July 1914–May 1915*. London: Jonathan Cape.

Hegel, G. W. F. 1929. "Philosophy of History," in Jacob Loewenberg, ed., *Hegel: Selections*. New York: C. Scribner's Sons, 388–9.

Hemerijck, Anton and Philip Manow. 1998. "The Experience of Negotiated Social Policy Reform in Germany and the Netherlands," prepared for Varieties of Welfare Capitalism conference, Cologne, Germany, June 11–13.

Hemerijck, Anton and Martin Schludi. 2000. "Sequences of Policy Failures and Effective Policy Responses," in Fritz Scharpf and Vivien Schmidt, eds., *Welfare and Work in the Open Economy*. Oxford: Oxford University Press.

Hemerijck, Anton and Jelle Visser. 1997. *"A Dutch Miracle": Job Growth, Welfare Reform, and Corporatism in the Netherlands*. Amsterdam: Amsterdam University Press.

Henderson, Sir A., to Arthur Steel Maitland. June 12, 1912. Letter with enclosed letter from Docker.

Henley, Andrew and Euclid Tsakalotos. 1992. "Corporatism and the European Labour Market after 1992." *British Journal of Industrial Relations* 30 (4): 567–86.

Henriksen, Victor. 1910. "Industriforeningen og den danske Industri." *Arbejdsgiveren* 45 (11): 569–72.

Hernandez, Marco A. and David Rueda. 2007. "The Political Economy of Coordination in Industrial Democracies." Paper presented at the Annual Meetings of the American Political Science Association, August 30–September 2.

Herrigel, Gary. 1996. *Industrial Constructions: The Sources of German Industrial Power*. New York: Cambridge University Press.

Herrigel, Gary and Charles Sabel. 1999. "Craft Production in Crisis: Industrial Restructuring in Germany during the 1990s" in Pepper Culpepper and David Finegold, eds., The German Skills Machine: Sustaining Comparative Advantage in a Global Economy. Providence: Berghahn Books, 77–114.

Hertzman, Lewis. 1958. "The Founding of the German National People's Party (DNVP), November 191–January 1919." *Journal of Modern History* 30 (1): 24–36.

Heyes, Jason. 2000. "Workplace Industrial Relations and Training," in Helen Rainbird, ed., *Training in the Workplace*. New York: St. Martin's Press.

Hicks, Alex. 1999. *Social Democracy and Welfare Capitalism*. Ithaca, NY: Cornell University Press.

    2008. "Getting Back to Business." Paper presented at the Annual Meetings of the American Sociological Association, Boston, August 1–4.

Hicks, Alexander and Lane Kenworthy. 1998. "Cooperation and Political Economic Performance in Affluence Democratic Capitalism." *American Journal of Sociology* 103 (6): 1631–72.

Hicks, Alexander and Duane Swank. 1984. "Governmental Redistribution in Rich Capitalist Democracies." *Policy Studies Journal* 13 (December): 265–86.

1992. "Politics, Institutions, and Welfare Spending in Industrialized Democracies, 1960–1992." *American Political Science Review* 86 (September): 659–74.

Hiley to Nugent. February 20, 1917. MSS200/F/3/D1/2/8. Modern Records Centre, Warwick University, Warwick, UK.

Hilferding, Rudolf. 2007. *Finance Capital.* New York: Routledge.

Hillman, Amy and Michael Hitt. 1999. "Corporate Political Strategy Formulation." *The Academy of Management Review* 24 (October): 825–42.

Hillman, Amy, G. Kleim, and Doug Schuler. 2004. "Corporate Political Activity." *Journal of Management* 30: 837–57.

Hinrichs, Karl. 2010. "A Social Insurance State Withers Away: Welfare State Reforms in Germany – Or; Attempts to Turn Around in a Cul-de-Sac," in Bruno Palier, ed., *A Long Goodbye to Bismarck? The Politics of Welfare Reforms in Europe.* Amsterdam: Amsterdam University Press, 45–72.

Holnen, Pernille. 2001. "When Work Is Like a Gift." Working Paper 11 (2001). Danish National Institute of Social Research.

Holt, Helle. 1998. *En kortlægning af dansk virksomheders social ansvar* [A Summary of Danish Firms' Social Responsibility]. Copenhagen: Danish National Institute of Social Science Research.

Hooghe, Liesbet and Gary Marks. 1999. "The Making of a Polity: The Struggle over European Integration," in Herbert Kitschelt, Peter Lange, Gary Marks, and John Stephens, eds., *Continuity and Change in Contemporary Capitalism.* New York: Cambridge University Press, 70–100.

Höpner, Martin. 2007. "Coordination and Organization: The Two Dimensions of Nonliberal Capitalism." Paper presented at the Annual Meetings of the American Political Science Association, August 30–September 2, Chicago.

Hornemann Møller, Iver. 1992. *Den danske velfaerdsstats tilblivelse.* Frederiksberg: Samfundslitteratur, 55–125.

1994. *Velfaerdsstatens udbygning,* Frederiksberg: Samfundslitteratur.

Horwitz, Morton, *The Transformation of American Law, 1780–1860.* Cambridge, MA: Harvard University Press, 1977).

Hounshell, David Allen. 1978. *From the American System to Mass Production: the Development of Manufacturing Technology in the United States, 1850–1920.* Unpublished dissertation, University of Delaware.

House of Commons Education and Skills Committee. 2006. *Higher Standards, Better Schools for All.* HC 633-I. London: House of Commons, The Stationery Office Limited.

Howell, Chris. 2003. "Varieties of Capitalism: and Then There Was One?" *Comparative Politics* 36: 102–24.

Huber, Evelyne and John D. Stephens. 1998. "Internationalization and the Social Democratic Welfare Model: Crises and Future Prospects." *Comparative Political Studies* 33 (3): 353–97.

2001a. "Welfare State and Production Regimes in the Era of Retrenchment," in Paul Pierson, ed., *The New Politics of the Welfare State.* New York: Oxford University Press, 107–45.

2001b. *Development and Crisis of the Welfare State.* Chicago: University of Chicago Press.

Huber, Evelyne, Charles Ragin, and John D. Stephens 1993. "Social Democracy, Christian Democracy, Constitutional Structure and the Welfare State." *American Journal of Sociology* 99 (3): 711–49.

Huo, Jingjing. 2009. *Third Way Reforms: Social Democracy after the Golden Age.* New York: Cambridge University Press.

Hutton, Will. 1996. *The State We're In.* London: Vintage.

1998. *The Stakeholding Society.* Cambridge: Polity Press.

Hyldtoft, Lene Askgaard. 2002. "Government Liberalises Unemployment Insurance Funds." *Eironline* (September).

Hyldtoft, Ole. 1999. Danmarks Økonomiske historie 1840–1910. Aarhus.

Hyman, Richard. 2011. Understanding European Trade Unionism: Between Market, Class and Society (London: Sage).

Immergut, Ellen. 1990. "Institutions, Veto Points, and Policy Results: A Comparative Analysisof Health Care." *Journal of Public Policy* 10 (4): 391–416.

1992. The Political Construction of Interests: National Health Insurance Politics in Switzerland, France, and Sweden. New York: Cambridge University Press.

Inman, Phillip. 1999. "35 % of New Dealers leave for 'Unknown Destination.'" *The Guardian*, August 13.

"Industrifagene under Arbejdsgiverforeningen." 1906, October 17. *Arbejdsgiveren* 42 (7): 325–6.

"Industrifagenes Fælleskommission." 1906, December 5. *Arbejdsgiveren* 42: 384–5.

Ioakimoglou, Elias and Eva Soumeli. 2002. "Low Wage Workers and the 'Working Poor.'" *Eironline* (September 17).

Irwin, Douglas. 1994. "The Political Economy of Free Trade." *Journal of Law and Economics* 37 (1): 75–108.

Iversen, Martin Jes. 2011. *Economic Orders and Formative Phases: A Business Historical Journey through Danish Capitalism, 1850–2000.* Copenhagen: Copenhagen Business School.

Iversen, Torben. 1999. *Contested Economic Institutions.* New York: Cambridge University Press.

2001. "The Dynamics of Welfare State Expansion," in Paul Pierson, ed., *The New Politics of the Welfare State.* New York: Oxford University Press, 45–79.

2005 *Capitalism, Democracy and Welfare.* Cambridge: Cambridge University Press.

2009. "Dualism and Political Coalitions: Inclusionary versus Exclusionary Reforms in an Age of Rising Inequality." Typescript, Department of Government, Harvard University.

Iversen, Torben and Thomas Cusack. 2000. "The Causes of Welfare Expansion: Deindustrialization or Globalization?" *World Politics* 52 (April): 313–49.

Iversen, Torben, and David Soskice. 2001. An Asset Theory of Social Policy Preferences. *American Political Science Review* 95 (4):875–93.

2006. "Electoral Institutions and the Politics of Coalitions: Why Some Democracies Redistribute More Than Others."; *American Political Science Review* 100 (2): 165–81.

2009. "Distribution and Redistribution: In the Shadow of the Nineteenth-Century." *World Politics* 61 (3): 438–86.

Iversen, Torben and John Stephens. 2008. "Partisan Politics, the Welfare State and Three Worlds of Capital Formation." *Comparative Political Studies* 41 (4/5): 600–37.

Iversen, Torben and Anne Wren. 1998. "Equality, Employment, and Budgetary Restraint: The Trilemma of the Service Economy." *World Politics* 50 (July): 507–46.

Iversen, Torben, Jonas Pontusson, and David Soskice, eds. 1999. *Unions, Employers, and Central Banks.* New York: Cambridge.

Jacobs, David. 1988. "Corporate Economic Power and the State: A Longitudinal Assessment of Two Explanations." *American Journal of Sociology* 93 (January): 852–81.

Jacobsen, Hans Thyge. 1937. "Sociallovgivningen," in Alfred Bindslev, ed., *KonservatismensHistorie I Danmark.* Odense: Kulterhistorisk Forlag, 149–58.

Jacobsen, Kurt and Dorthe Pedersen, 2009. *Kampen om den danske model.* Copenhagen: Informations Forlag, 8.

Jaccoby, Sanford. 1998. *Modern Manors: Welfare Capitalism Since the New Deal.* Princeton, NJ: Princeton University Press.

Jason Boyle to W. R. Holloway. April 5, 1895. Letter. Holloway. William Robeson, *Papers, 1795–1903*, Microfilm ILL:CLIO0104.

Jensen, Carsten Strøby, Jørgen Steen Madsen, and Jesper Due. 2000. "Arbejdsgiverorganisering I Danmark – et institutionssociologisk perspektiv på arbejdsgiverorganiseringens betydning for den danske arbejdsmarkedsmodel," in Carsten Strøby Jensen, ed., *Arbejdsgivere i Norden*. Copenhagen: Nordisk Ministerråd, 83–154.

Jensen, Jane. 2002. "Social Policy and Citizenship Regimes: Redesigning to a Common Theme?" Prepared for the Workshop on Transforming the Democratic Balance among State, Market and Society. Center for European Studies, Harvard University (May 17–18).

Jensen, Lise Møller and Jens Holger Laursen. 2000. "Det besværlige sociale ansvar." *Politiken* (October 11): III.1.

Jensen, Per. 1999. "From Welfare to Workfare – New Perspectives or New Realities. The Danishcase." Paper for the Fourth European Conference of Sociology, August 18–21, Amsterdam.

Jensen, Per H. 2005. "Reversing the Trend from "Early" to "Late" Exit." *The Genevia Papers* 30: 656–73.

Jensen, Richard. 1971. *The Winning of the Midwest*. Chicago: University of Chicago Press.

Jessop, Bob. 1992. "From Social Democracy to Thatcherism," in N. Abercrombie and A Ward, eds., *Social Change in Contemporary Britain*. Cambridge: Polity Press, 14–39.

2010. "The 'Return' of the National State in the Current Crisis of the World Market." *Capital & Class* 34(1)38-43.

John Myles. 1989. *Old Age and the Welfare State*. Lawrence: University Press of Kansas.

Jones, Geoffrey. 2000. *Merchants to Multinationals*. Oxford: Oxford University Press.

Jones, Geoffrey and Maurice Kirby. 1991. "Competitiveness and the State In International Perspective," in G. Jones and M. Kirby, eds., *Competitiveness and the State*. Manchester, UK: Manchester University Press, 1–19.

Jonker, Joost. 2003. "Competing in Tandem: Securities Markets and Commercial Banking Patterns in Europe During the Nineteenth Century," in Douglas J. Forsyth and Daniel Verdier, eds., *The Origins of National Financial Systems: Alexander Gerschenkron Reconsidered*. New York: Routledge, 64–86.

Jørgensen, Carsten. 1999. "Considerable Discrepancies Identified in State Subsidies for Training." *Eironline* (September).

2006. "New Employer Organisation Favours More Company-Level Agreements." *Eironline* (November).

2009. "Economic Crisis Leads to Extensive Use of Work-Sharing." *Eironline* (June 1).

2010. "Difficult Collective Bargaining in Light of Economic Crisis." *Eironline* (February 3).

Jørgensen, Harald. 1962. *Tre Venstremænd*. Copenhagen: Udgiverselskab for Danmarks Nyeste Historie.

Jørgensen, Henning. 1994. "De menneskelige resourcer – om udvikling af erhvervs – og velfærd-spotentialer." Aalborg: Institut for Økonomi, Politik go Forvaltning.

2003. "Aktivgørelse af aktiveringen kommer ikke af sig selv – betydningen af institution-elt design for udvikling af ledighedsinstanser," in P. K. Madsen and L. Pedersen, eds., *Drivkræfter bag arbejdsmarkedspolitikken*. København: Socialforskningsinstituttet, 164–200.

Josephson, Matthew. 1940. *The President Makers*. New York: Harcourt, Brace and Co., 6.

Journal of meeting notes of the NUM. No page numbers or dates. MSS.200/N/1/1/1. Modern Records Centre, Warwick University, Warwick, UK.

Kalecki, Micha. 1971. "Political Aspects of Full Employment (Revised Version)," in Micha Kalecki, ed., *Selected Essays on the Dynamics of the Capitalist Economy*. New York: Cambridge University Press, 138–45.

Kam, Cindy D. and Robert Franzese. 2009. *Modeling and Interpreting Interactive Hypotheses in Regression Analysis.* Ann Arbor: University of Michigan Press.

Kardorff, Siegfried von. 1936. *Wilhelm von Kardorff, ein nationaler Parliamentarier im Zeitalter Bismarcks und Wilhelms II, 1828–1907.* Berlin: E. S. Mittler & Sohn.

Kardorff Wabnitz, Wilhelm von to Henry Carey. Letter. May 15, 1876. Historical Society of Pennsylvania. Box 19, Folder #2, Historical Society of Pennsylvania, Edward Carey Gardiner Collection, Collection 227A. Series 5. Correspondence of H. C. Carey.

Katz, Harry. 1993. "The Decentralization of Collective Bargaining: A Literature Review and Comparative Analysis." *Industrial and Labor Relations Review* 47 (1): 3–22.

Katzenstein, Peter. 1978. *Between Power and Plenty.* Madison: University of Wisconsin Press.

    1985. *Small States in World Markets: Industrial Policy in Europe.* Ithaca, NY: Cornell University Press.

    1987. Policy and Politics in Germany: The Growth of the Semisovereign State. Philadelphia: Temple University Press.

Kaufman, Burton. 1971. "United States Trade and Latin America: the Wilson Years." *The Journal of American History* 58 (2): 342–63.

    1972. "The Organizational Dimension of United States Foreign Economic Policy, 1900–1920." *Business History Review* XLVI (Spring): 17–44.

Keep, Ewart. 1999. "Skills And Training Policies Reviewed." *Eironline* (June) www.eironline.org.

Kehr, Eckart. 1973. *Battleship Building and Party Politics in Germany 1894–1901.* Chicago: Anderson.

    1977. *Economic Interest, Militarism, and Foreign Policy.* Berkeley, CA: G. A. Craig.

Keller, Berndt and Hans-Wolfgang Platzer. 2003. *Industrial Relations and European Integration.* Burlington, VT: Ashgate.

Kendix, Michael and Mancur Olson. 1990. "Changing Unemployment Rates in Europe and the USA," In Renato Brunetta and Carlo Dell'Aringa, eds., *Labor Relations and Economic Performance.* New York: New York University Press, 68–91.

Kenworthy, Lane. 2001. "Wage-Setting Measures: A Survey and Assessment." *World Politics* 54 (October): 57–98.

    2004. *Egalitarian Capitalism.* New York: Russell Sage Foundation.

Kenworthy, Lane. 2008. *Jobs with Equality.* New York: Oxford University Press.

Kenworthy, Lane and Leslie McCall. 2007. "Inequality, Public Opinion and Redistribution." *Socio-Economic Review* 6 (1): 35–68.

Kenworthy, Lane and Jonas Pontusson. 2005. "Rising Inequality and the Politics of Redistribution." *Perspectives on Politics* 3 (3): 449–71.

Kiilerich, Ole. 1975. *Politikeren Estrup og hans konge.* Denmark: Gyldendal.

Kim, Hee Min and Richard Fording. 2003. "Voter Ideology In Western Democracies: An Update." *European Journal of Political Research* 42: 95–105.

King, Anthony. 2002. "Tony Blair's First Term." in A. King, ed., *Britain at the Polls, 2001.* Chatham, NJ: Chatham House, 1–44.

King, Desmond. 1995. *Actively Seeking Work.* Chicago: University of Chicago Press.

    1997. "Employers, Training Policy, and the Tenacity of Voluntarism in Britain." *Twentieth Century British History* 8 (3): 383–411.

    2007. *Separate and Unequal: African Americans and the US Federal Government.* Oxford: Oxford University Press.

King, Desmond and Bo Rothstein. 1993 "Institutional Choices and Labor Market Policy." *Comparative Political Studies* 26 (2): 147–77.

King, Desmond and David Rueda. 2008. "Cheap Labor." *Perspectives on Politics* 6 (2): 279–97.

King, Desmond and Mark Wickham-Jones. 1998. "Training Without the State: New Labour and Labour Markets." *Policy and Politics* 26 (4): 439–55.

King, Gary, Robert Keohane, and Sidney Verba. 1994. *Design Social Inquiry: Scientific Inference in Qualitative Research.* Princeton, NJ: Princeton University Press.

Kirchheimer, Otto. 1966. "The Transformation of Western European Party Systems," in La J. Palombara and M. Weiner, eds., *Political Parties and Political Development*. Princeton, NJ: Princeton University Press, 177–99.

Kitchen, Martin. 1978. *The Political Economy of Germany 1815–1914*. London: Croom Helm.

2006. *A History of Modern Germany 1800–2000*. Malden: Blackwell Publishers.

Kitschelt, Herbert. 1993. "Class Structure and Social Democratic Party Strategy." *British Journal of Political Science* 23 (3): 299–337.

Kitschelt, Herbert and Wolfgang Streeck. 2003. "From Stability to Stagnation: Germany at the Beginning of the Twentieth-First Century." *West European Politics* 26 (4): 1–36.

Kitschelt, Herbert, Peter Lange, Gary Marks, and John Stephens, eds. 1999. *Continuity and Change in Contemporary Capitalism*. New York: Cambridge University Press.

Kjærgaard, Carsten. 2001 "New Roles for the Social Partners – and for Business," in Carsten Kjærgaard and Sven-Åge Westphalen, eds., *From Collective Bargaining to Social Partnerships*. Copenhagen: The Copenhagen Centre.

Kjærgaard, Carsten and Sven-Åge Westphalen, eds. 2001. *From Collective Bargaining to Social Partnerships*. Copenhagen: The Copenhagen Centre.

Klinghard, Daniel. 2005. "Grover Cleveland, William McKinley and the Emergence of the President as Party Leader." *Presidential Studies Quarterly* 35 (December): 736–60.

Klug, Adam. 2001. "Why Chamberlain Failed and Bismarck Succeeded." *European Review of Economic History* 5: 219–50.

Knudsen, Tim. 1991. "State Building in Scandinavia," in T. Knudsen, ed., *Welfare Administration in Denmark*. Copenhagen: Publikationscentralen.

Knudsen, Tim, ed. 2002. *Den nordiske protestantisme og velfærdsstaten*. Århus: Aarhus Universitetsforlag.

Knudsen, Tim and Bo Rothstein. 1994. "State Building in Scandinavia." *Comparative Politics* 26 (3): 203–20.

Kocka, Jürgen. 1981. "Capitalism and Bureaucracy in German Industrialization before 1914." *The Economic History Review* 34 (3): 453–68.

Kocka, Jurgen. 1999. Asymmetrical Historical Comparison: The Case of the German Sonderweg." *History and Theory* 38 (1): 40–50.

Kohlsaat, H. H. 1923. *From McKinley to Harding*. New York: Charles Scriber's Sons, 33–36.

Kolb, Eberhard. 2005. *The Weimar Republic*. New York: Routledge.

Korpi, Walter 1980. "Social Policy and Distributional Conflict in the Capitalist Democracies." *West European Politics* 3: 296–315.

Korpi, Walter. 2006. "Power Resources and Employer-Centered Approaches in Explanations of Welfare States and Varieties of Capitalism." *World Politics* 58 (January): 167–206.

Korpi, Walter and Joakim Palme. 1998. "The Paradox of Redistribution and Strategies of Equality: Welfare State Institutions, Inequality, and Poverty in the Western Countries." *American Sociological Review* 63 (3): 661–87.

2001. "New Politics and Class Politics in Welfare State Regress." Presented at the APSA annual meeting, San Francisco, August 30–September 3.

2003. "New Politics and Class Politics in the Context of Austerity and Globalizsation: Welfare State Regress in 18 Countries, 1975–95." *American Political Science Review*, 97 (3): 425–46.

Korpi, Walter and Michael Shalev. 1979. "Strikes, Industrial Relations and Class Conflict in Capitalist Societies." *British Journal of Sociology* 30: 164–87.

Koske, Isabell and Andreas Wörgötter. 2010. "Germany's Growth Potential, Structural Reforms and Global Imbalances." OECD Economics Department Working Papers, No. 780.

Kraft, Kornelius. "An Evaluation of Active and Passive Labour Market Policy." *Applied Economics* 30 (1998): 783–93.

Kreuzer, Marcus. 1998. "Electoral Institutions, Political Organizations, and Party Development."
    Comparative Politics 30 (3): 273–92.
    2010. "Historical Knowledge and Quantitative Analysis: The Case of the Origins of
    Proportional Representation." *American Political Science Review* 104 (2): 369–92.
Krieger, Joel. 1999. *British Politics in the Global Age.* New York: Oxford University Press.
Kristensen, Ole P. 1987. *Vaeksten i den offentlige sektor. Institutioner of politik.* Kobenhavn: Jurist- og
    Okonomforbundets Forlag.
Kruhøffer, Anette and Jan Høgelund. 2001. *Virksomheders sociale engagement.* Copenhagen:
    Socialforskningsinstitutted.
Kuo, Alexander. 2010. "Political Origins of Firm Strategies." Paper presented at the Seventeenth
    International Conference of Europeanists, April 15–18, Montreal.
Kurth, James. 1979. "The Political Consequences of the Product Cycle." *Industrial Organization*
    33 (1): 1–34.
Kwon, Hyeok Yong and Jonas Pontusson. 2010. "Globalization, Labour Power and Partisan
    Politics Revisited." *Socio-Economic Review* 8 (2): 251–82.
Kylling, Anne-Birte, Hans Bach, and Morton Kjær. 1996. *Initiativer på private virksomheder.* Aarhus:
    Formidlings Center.
Labour Ministry. 1997. *Adult Vocational Training* Copenhagen: Labour Ministry.
    1998. *Videreførelse af den aktive arbejdsmarkedspolitik.* Copenhagen: Labour Ministry.
Labour Ministry, Social Ministry. 1995. *Rapport fra udvalget om skånejobs.* Copenhagen: Labour
    Ministry.
Labour Research Department. 1923. *The Federation of British Industries.* London: Labour Publishing
    Company.
Lambi, Ivo. 1962. "The Protectionist Interests of the German Iron and Steel Industry, 1873–1879."
    Journal of Economic History 22 (1): 59–70.
Landsorganisationen I Danmark og Dansk Arbejdsgiverforening. 2000. Fælles mål for LO og DA
    I forbindelse med videreudvikling af den sociale indsats for et mere rummeligt arbejds-
    marked. Copenhagen: LO and DA.
Lane, Christel and Geoffrey Wood. 2009. "Introducing Diversity in Capitalism and Capitalist
    Diversity," *Economy and Society,* 38 (3).
Lang, Louis, ed. 1910. *The Autobiography of Thomas Collier Platt.* New York: BW Dodge & Co.
Lange, Peter and Geoffrey Garrett. 1985. "The Politics of Growth: Strategic Interaction and
    Economic Performance in the Advanced Industrial Democracies, 1974–1980." *Journal of
    Politics* 47: 792–827.
Lange, Peter, Michael Wallerstein, and Miriam Golden. 1995. "The End of Corporatism?," in
    Sanford Jacoby, ed., *Workers of Nations.* Oxford: Oxford University Press, 76–100.
Larsen, Mona and Hanne Weise. 1999. *Virksomheders sociale engagement* [Firms' Social Engagement].
    Copenhagen: Danish National Institute of Social Science Research, 16.
Larsen, Morten and Scott Lash. 1985. "The End of Neo-Corporatism." *British Journal of Industrial
    Relations* 23 (2): 215–39.
Lash, Scott and John Urry. 1987. *The End of Organized Capitalism.* Oxford: Polity Press.
Lasonick, William. 1983. "Industrial Organization and Technological Change: The Decline of
    the British Cotton Industry." *British History Review* 57 (2): 195–236.
Lauer, Solon. 1901. *Mark Hanna.* Cleveland: Nike Pubishing House.
Laumann, Edward and David Knoke. 1987. *The Organizational State.* Madison: University of
    Wisconsin Press.
Lauterbach, Albert. 1944. "Economic Demobilization in a Conquered Country." *Journal of Politics*
    6 (1): 28–56.
Lawson, Kay and Peter Merkl. 1988. *When Parties Fail.* Princeton, NJ: Princeton University
    Press.

Lawson, Roger. 1996. "Germany: Maintaining the Middle Way," in Vic George and Peter Taylor-Gooby, eds., *European Social Policy: Squaring the Welfare Circle.* New York: St Martin's Press, 31–50.

Layard, Richard, Stephen Nickell, and Richard Jackman. 1991. *Unemployment: Macroeconomic Performance and the Labor Market.* New York: Oxford University Press.

Leech, Margaret. 1959. *In the Days of McKinley.* New York: Harpers.

Lehmann, Sibylle H. 2009. *The German Elections in the 1870s: Why Germany Turned from Liberalism to Protectionism.* Bonn: Max Planck Institute for Research on Collective Goods 2009/34.

Lembruch, Gerhard. 1984. "Concertation and the Structure of Corporatist Networks," in John Goldethorp, ed., *Order and Conflict in Contemporary Capitalism.* New York: Oxford University Press, 60–80.

Lehmbruch, Gerhard. 2003. "Welfare State Adjustment between Consensual and Adversarial Politics," in Fritz van Waarden and Gerhard Lehmbruch, eds., *Renegotiating the Welfare State.* London: Routledge, 142–68.

Leibfried, Stephan and Herbert Obinger. 2003. "The State of the Welfare State: German Social Policy between Macroeconomic Retrenchment and Microeconomic Recalibration." *West European Politics* 26 (4): 199–218.

Leibfried, Stephan and Paul Pierson. 1995. "Semisovereign Welfare States," in S. Liebfried and P. Pierson, eds., *European Social Policy.* Washington, DC: Brookings Institution, 43–77.

Lescure, Michel. 1995a. "Banks and Small Enterprises in France," in Youssef Cassis, Gerald D. Feldman and Ulf Olsson, eds., *The Evolution of Financial Institutions and Markets in Twentieth-century Europe.* Aldershot: Scholar Press, 31531–50 328.

1995b. "Banking in France in the Inter-war Period," in Charles H. Feinstein, ed., *Banking, Currency and Finance Between the Wars.* Oxford: Clarendon, 31531–50336.

2008. "Banking and Finance," in Geoffrey Jones and Jonathan Zeitlin, eds., *The Oxford Handbook of Business History.* New York: Oxford University Press.

Levi, Margaret. 1998. "A State of Trust," in Valerie Braithwaite and Margared Levi, eds., *Trust & Governance.* New York: Russell Sage Foundation.

Levine, Daniel. 1978. "Conservatism and Tradition in Danish Social Welfare Legislation, 1890–1933," *Comparative Studies* 20 (1): 54–69.

Lieberman, Ben. 1997. "Turning against the Weimar Right: Landlords, the Economic Party and the DNVP," *German History* 15 (1): 56–79.

Lieberman, Evan. 2005. "Nested Analysis as a Mixed-Method Strategy for Comparative Research." *American Political Science Review* 99 (3): 435–52.

Lijphart, Arend. 1999. *Patterns of Democracy: Government Forms and Performance in Thirty-Six Countries.* New Haven, CT: Yale University Press.

Lijphart, Arend and Markus Crepaz. 1991. "Corporatism and Consensus Democracy in Eighteen Countries." *British Journal of Political Science* 21: 235–56.

Lind, Jens. 2000. "Recent Issues on the Social Pact in Denmark," in Giuseppe Fajertag and Philippe Pochet, eds., *Social Pacts in Europe.* Brussels: European Trade Union Institute, 135–59.

Lindblom, Charles. 1977. *Politics and Markets: The World's Political Economic Systems.* New York: Basic Books.

Lindvall, Johannes. Forthcoming. "Politics and Policies in Two Economic Crises." In Nancy Bermeo and Jonas Pontusson, eds., *Coping with Crisis.* New York: Russell Sage Foundation.

Lipset, Seymour Martin and Stein Rokkan. 1967. "Cleavage Structures, Party Systems, and Voter Alignments," in S. M. Lipset and S. Rokkan, eds., *Party Systems and Voter Alignments.* New York: Free Press, 488–509.

Lloyd, John. 1999. "The Story of a Strange Romance," *New Statesman* 12 (580): 13.

LO Aktuelt. November 11, 2002. "Deltidsansatte mister beskyttelse." LO Aktuelt.

March 1, 2002. "En samlet fagbevægelse mod regeringen," LO Aktuelt.

January 10, 2002. "LO og DA enige i kritik af besparelser," LO Aktuelt.

January 8, 2002. "LO rystet over lovforslag om deltid," LO Aktuelt.

March 11, 2002. "LO tilfreds med DA's kritik af deltidsforslag," LO Aktuelt.

January 18, 2002. "Statslig akasse bliver skraldespand for ledige," LO Aktuelt.

Locke, Richard. 1990. "The Resurgence of the Local Union: Industrial Restructuring and Industrial Relations in Italy." *Politics and Society* 18: 347–79.

Lønroth, Helle, Hanne Nørreklit, and Poul Erik Sørensen. 1997. "Capital Market Pressure, Corporate Governance and their Influence on Long-term Investments: The Case of Denmark." Working Paper 97–3. Aarhus School of Business.

Lowe, Rodney. 1978. "The Failure of Consensus in Britain: The National Industrial Conference." *The Historical Journal* 21 (3): 649–75.

Lowe, Rodney and Richard Roberts. 1987. "Sir Horace Wilson, 1900–1935." *The Historical Journal* 30 (3): 641–62.

Lowe, Rodney and Neil Rollings. 2000. "Modernising Britain, 1957–64," in R. A. W. Rhodes, ed., *Transforming British Government* Vol. 1. London: Macmillan.

Luebbert, Gregory. 1991. *Liberalism, Fascism, or Social Democracy.* New York: Oxford University Press.

Lupa, Noam and Jonas Pontusson. 2011. "The Structure of Inequality and the Politics of Redistribution." *American Political Science Review* 105 (2) : 316–36.

Lynn, Leonoard and Timothy McKeown 1988. *Organizing Business: Trade Associations in America and Japan.* Washington, DC: American Enterprise Institute.

Macara, Sir Charles. 1921. *Recollections.* London: Cassell and Company.

MacDougall, Donald. 1987. *Don and Mandarin.* London: John Murray.

MacRosty, Henry. 1907. *The Trust Movement in British Industry.* London: Longmans, Green and Company.

Madsen, Per Kongshøj. 1997. "Employing the Hard-to-Place." Paper prepared for the New Partnership for Social Cohesion Conference, October 16–18, Copenhagen, Denmark.

2002. "The Danish Model of Flexicurity: A Paradise – With Some Snakes," in Hedva Sarfatiand Giuliano Bonoli, eds., *Labour Market and Social Protections Reforms In International Perspective.* Aldershot: Ashgate, 243–65.

2011. "Flexicurity i modvind – En analyse af den danske flexicuritymodel under den økonomiske krise." Unpublished manuscript. Center for arbejdsmarkedsforskning (CARMA), Aalborg Universitet.

Mahler, Vincent. 2008. "Electoral Turnout and Income Redistribution by the State: A Cross-National Analysis of the Developed Democracies." *European Journal of Political Research* 47: 161–83.

Mahler, Vincent and David Jesuit. 2006. "Fiscal Redistributon in the Developed Countries: New Insights from the Luxembourg Income Study." *Socio-Economic Review* 4 (3): 483–511.

Mahoney, James. 2010. "After KKV: The New Methodology of Qualitative Research." *World Politics* 62 (1): 120–47.

Maier, Charles. 1975. *Recasting Bourgeois Europe.* Princeton, NJ: Princeton University Press.

Mailand, Mikkel and M. M. Simonsen. 2002. "Denmark in the 1990: Status Quo or a More Self-Confident State?," in Stefan Berger and Hugh Compston, eds., *Policy Concertation and Social Partnership in Western Europe.* Oxford: Berghahn Books, 83–95.

Mailand, Mikkel. 2000. *Den danske model lokalt og regionalt.* Copenhagen: Copenhagen University FAOS.

Maisel, Ephraim. 1989. "The Formation of the Department of Overseas Trade, 1919–1926." *Journal of Contemporary History* 24 (1): 169–90.

Maitland, Arthur Steel to Bonar-Law. Letter. September 17, 1917. GD193/115/1/81.

Maitland, Arthur Steel to Bonar Law. Memo attachment. November 16, 1917. GD193/99/2/147–8. Steel-Maitland to Bonar Law date 1916.

Maitland, Arthur Steel to "Pele" Lieut-Colonel R.A. Sanders MP. Letter. June 6, 1916. GD193/170/1/490. See correspondence in ASM GD193/GD166/2; Letter from ASM's secretary to BS Townroe at the War Office 11/9/1915 GD193/164/3/14/135.

Maitland, Arthur Steel to McKenna. Letter. August 16, 1915. GD193/164/3/1/54.

Maitland, Arthur Steel to Lord Milner. February 19, 1910.

Maitland, Arthur Steel to Victor Fisher. December 14, 1917.

Maitland, Arthur Steel to Gerald A Steel. June 8, 1916. GD193/170/1/29.

Maitland, Arthur Steel to Dudley Docker. January 10, 1916. GD172/1/3.

Maitland to Dudley Docker. May 24, 1915. GD193/165/1/538.

Maitland, Arthur Steel to Dudley Docker. December 3, 1911. GD193/153/4/70.

Maitland, Arthur Steel's secretary to Townroe, War Office. November 9, 1915.

Maitland, Arthur Steel to WGS Adams. July 4, 1916.

Maitland, Arthur Steel. 1919. "Scheme for the Reform and Development of the Consular and Commercial Diplomatic Services," in D. Cameron Watt, ed., *British Documents on Foreign Affairs: Reports and Papers from the Foreign Office Confidential Print* Volume I, Part II, Series K, University Publications of America Doc. 7, p. 32.

Mallalie, W. C. 1950. "Joseph Chamberlain and Workmen's Compensation." *Journal of Economic History* 10 (1): 45–57.

Management Services. 2001. "Shortage of the Right People for the Right Job Says Survey." *Management Services* 45 (3): 4.

Management Today Team. 1998. "Will Clive Split the CBI?" *Management Today* (November): 32–6.

Mandag Morgen. 1997. "Velfærdsparadokset: Social polarisering trods økonomisk lighed." *Ugebrevet Mandag Morgen* 43 (December 8): 5–9.

Mannische, Peter. 1939. Denmark, *A Social Laboratory*. Copenhagen: G. E. C. Gads, 74–135.

Manow, Philip. 1998. "Welfare State Building and Coordinated Capitalism in Japan and Germany." Prepared for the Conference on Varieties of Welfare Capitalism, June 11–13, Cologne, Germany.

2001. "Comparative Institutional Advantages of Welfare State Regimes and New Coalitions in Welfare State Reforms," in Paul Pierson, ed., *The New Politics of the Welfare State*. New York: Oxford University Press, 146–64.

Manow, Philip and Eric Seils. 2000. "Adjusting Badly: The German Welfare State, Structural Change, and the Open Economy," in Fritz Scharpf and Vivian Schmidt, eds., *Welfare to Work in the Open Economy, Volume II*. New York: Oxford University Press, 264–307.

Manow, Philip and Kees van Kersbergen, 2009. *Religion, Class Coalitions, and Welfare States*. Cambridge: Cambridge University Press.

Mansbridge, Jane. 1980. *Beyond Adversary Democracy*. Chicago: University of Chicago Press.

Mares, Isabela. 2003. *The Politics of Social Risks: Business and Welfare State Development*. New York: Cambridge University Press.

Marcussen, Martin and Karsten Ronit. 2011. *Kriser, politik og forvaltning* Copenhagen: Gyldendal Academic.

Margo, Robert. 1990. *Race and Schooling in the South*. Chicago: University of Chicago Press.

Marmefelt, Thomas. 1998. *Bank-Industry Networks and Economic Evolution; An Institutional-Evolutionary Approach*. Aldershot: Ashgate.

Marrison, A. J. 1983. "Businessmen, Industries and Tariff Reform in Great Britain, 1903–1930." *Business History* 25 (2 July): 148–78.

Marrison, Andrew. 1995. *British Business and Protection, 1903–32*. Oxford: Oxford University Press.

Martin, Andrew. 1979. "The Dynamics of Change in a Keynesian Political Economy," in Colin Crouch, ed., *State and Economy in Contemporary Capitalism*. London: Croom Helm, 88–121.

Martin, Cathie Jo. 1991. Shifting the Burden: The Struggle over Growth and Corporate Taxation. Chicago: University of Chicago Press.

1994. "Business and the New Economic Activism." *Polity* 27 (1) 49–76.

Martin, Cathie Jo. 1995. "Nature or Nurture? Sources of Firm Preferences for National Health Care Reform." *American Political Science Review* 89 (December): 898–913.

Martin, Cathie Jo. 2000. Stuck in Neutral: Business and the Politics of Human Capital Investment Policy. Princeton, NJ: Princeton University Press.

    2004. Reinventing Welfare Regimes. *World Politics* 57 (1): 39–69.

    2006. "Sectional Parties, Divided Business," *Studies in American Political Development* 20 (2): 160–84.

Martin, Cathie Jo and Duane Swank. 2004. "Does the Organization of Capital Matter?" *American Political Science Review* 98 (4): 593–611.

    2008. "Does the Organization of Capital Matter?" *American Political Science Review 98* (4 November): 593–611.

Martin, Cathie Jo and Kathleen Thelen. 2007. The State and Coordinated Capitalism. *World Politics* 60 (October): 1–36.

Martin, John. 2000. "What Works Among Active Labour Market Policies: Evidence from OECD Countries' Experiences," *OECD Economic Studies.* 20: 83, 85.

Matthew, H. C. G. 1995. *Gladstone: 1875–1898.* Oxford: Clarendon Press.

Matthews, John. 1919. "Political Parties and the War." *American Political Science Review* 13 (2): 213–28.

Matthews, Trevor. 1991. "Interest Group Politics: Corporatism without Business," in Francis G. Castles, ed., *Australia Compared: People, Policies, and Politics.* North Sydney, NSW: Allen and Unwin.

Matuo, Miyamoto, ed. 1988. *Trade Associations in Business History.* Tokyo: University of Tokyo Press, 139–72.

Matzner, Egon and Wolfgang Streeck. 1991. "Introduction," in *Beyond Keynesianism.* Brookfield, VT: Edward Elgar, 1–20.

Mayer, Arno. 1981. *The Persistence of the Old Regime.* New York: Pantheon Books.

McCartney, John and Paul Teague. 1997. "Workplace Innovation in the Republic of Ireland." *The Economic and Social Review* 28 (October): 381–99.

McConnell, Grant. 1966. *Private Power and American Democracy.* New York: Alfred Knopf.

McDonald, G. W. and Howard F. Gospel. 1973. "The Mond-Turner Talks, 1927–1933: A Study in Industrial Co-Operation." *The Historical Journal* 16 (4): 807–89.

McDougall, Thomas. 1896. "The Home Market," Proceedings of the First Annual Convention of the National Association of Manufacturers of the United States. January 21–23, Chicago, 3–8.

McGerr, Michael. 1986. *The Decline of Popular Politics.* New York: Oxford University Press.

McGill, Barry. 1974. "Lloyd George's Timing of the 1918 Election." *The Journal of British Studies* 14 (1): 109–24.

McKinley to Col. JF Hanson. Letter. February 27, 1896. McKinley Papers. Series 2 P1 V87-P90.

McKinley to RE Wright. Letter. January 4, 1896. McKinley Papers. Series 2 P1 V87-P90.

McKinley to McDougall. Letter. December 19, 1894. McKinley Papers. Series 2 P1 V87-P90.

McKinley to Rev. I Dawson. April 15, 1895. Letter. McKinley Papers. Series 2 P1 V87-P90.

McKinley to W. Heath. Letter. February 5, 1895. McKinley Papers. Series 2 P1 V87–90.

McKenzie, R., and Lee, D. 1991. Quicksilver Capital: How the Rapid Movement of Wealth Has Changed the World. New York: The Free Press.

Melling, Joseph. 1992. "Welfare Capitalism and the Origins of Welfare States." *Social History* 17 (3): 453–78.

Meltzer, Allan and Scott Richard. 1981. "A Rational Theory of the Size of Government." *Journal of Political Economy* 89 (5): 914–27.

Mendalen, Charles. 1978. "State Monopoly Capitalism in Germany." *Past and Present* 78 (February): 82–112.

Michie, Randald. 2003. "Banks and Securities Markets 1870–1914," in Douglas J. Forsyth and Daniel Verdier, eds., *The Origins of National Financial Systems: Alexander Gerschenkron Reconsidered.* New York: Routledge, 43–62.

Middlemas, Keith. 1990. *Power, Competition and the State, Vol. 2.* London: MacMillan.

Mierzejewski, Alfred. 2002. "Der Reichsverband der Deutschen Industrie 1919–1924/25." *Enterprise & Society* 3 (1): 202–3.

Miles, Robert. 1982. *Coffin Nails and Corporate Strategies.* Englewood Cliffs, NJ: Prentice-Hall.

Milkis, Sidney. 2009. Theodore Roosevelt, the Progressive Party, and the Transformation of American Democracy. Lawrence: Kansas University Press.

Millar, Jane. 2000. "Keeping Track of Welfare Reform: The New Deal Programmes." Joseph Rowntree Foundation (June).

Milner, Lord to Arthur Steel Maitland. November 1, 1916. In folder titled "Arrangement with Labour Party 1916–1917." GD193/99/2/106. Arthur Steel Maitland Collection. Edinburgh: National Archives of Scotland.

Ministry of Labour and Ministry of Finance, Denmark. 1996. "Labour Market Policy in Transition," May.

Ministry of Labour. 1996. *The Danish Labour Market Model.* Copenhagen: Ministry of Labour (June).

Mitchell, Neil. 1990. "The Decentralization of Business in Britain." *Journal of Politics* 52: 628–37. 1997. *The Conspicuous Corporation.* Ann Arbor: University of Michigan Press.

Mizruchi, Mark 1992. *The Structure of Corporate Political Action.* Cambridge, MA: Harvard University Press.

Mjøset, Lars and Tommy H. Clausen, eds. 2007. "A Symposium on Methodology in Comparative Research." *Comparative Social Research* 24: 261–391.

Moe, Terry. 1987. "Interests, Institutions, and Positive Theory." *Studies in American Political Development* 2: 277.

Moene, Karl Ove and Michael Wallerstein. 2003. "Earnings Inequality and Welfare Spending: A Disaggregated Analysis." *World Politics* 55 (July): 485–516.

Molina, Oscar and Martin Rhodes. 2002. "Corporatism: The Past, Present, and Future of a Concept." *Annual Review of Political Science* 5:305–31.

Moore, Barrington. 1966. *Social Origins of Dictatorship and Democracy.* Boston: Beacon Press.

Morgan, Glenn, Richard Whitley, and E. Moen, eds. 2005. *Changing Capitalisms.* Oxford: Oxford University Press.

Morgan, Glenn. 2005. "Introduction." in Morgan et. al. *Changing Capitalisms.* Oxford: Oxford University Press.

Morgan, Kenneth. 1970. "VII. Lloyd George's Premiership." *The Historical Journal* XIII (1):130–57.

Mork, Gordon. 1971. "Bismarck and the 'Capitulation' of German Liberalism." *Journal of Modern History* 43 (1): 59–77.

Morley, Chris. 1998. "Breakfast Date with Minister." *Birmingham Evening Mail* (March 17): 15.

Mosley, Hugh, Tiziana Keller, and Stefan Speckesser. 1998. *The Role of the Social Partners in the Design and Implementation of Active Measures.* Geneva: International Labour Office.

Mueller, Dennis C. 1983. *The Political Economy of Growth.* New Haven, CT: Yale University Press.

Muntzberg, Steen to the Employment Ministry. Memo. January 10, 2002. "Høring om udkast til forslag til lov om gennemførelse af dele af arbejdstidsdirektivet (j. nr. 6234–0006). Hearing on L83.

Murray, Charles. 1984. *Losing Ground: American Social Policy, 1950–1980.* New York: Basic Books.

Myles, John. 1989. *Old Age and the Welfare State.* Lawrence: University of Kansas Press.

Myles, John and Paul Pierson. 2001. "The Comparative Political Economy of Pension Reform," in P. Pierson, ed., *The New Politics of the Welfare State.* New York: Oxford University Press, 305–33.

Møller, Iver Hornemann. 1994. *Velfaerdsstatens udbygning.* Frederiksberg: Samfundslitteratur.

NAM Proceedings.1901. p. 8, 66, 109.

NAM. "Proceedings of the First Meeting of the Executive Committee of the National Association of Manufacturers of the United States of America," *National Industrial Review* 1 (3 April 1, 1895), 67.

1902. Proceedings of the Seventh Annual Convention of the National Association of Manufacturers of the United States (New York: NAM Bureau of Publicity, April 15, 16, and 17.)

1896. Proceedings of the First Annual Convention of the National Association of Manufacturers of the United States, Chicago, January 21–23.

1898. Proceedings of the Third Annual Convention of the National Association of Manufacturers of the United States of America. New York: NAM, 35.

1926. "Reports of Officers: Annual Address of President Edgerton." *Proceedings of the Thirty-first Annual Convention of the National association of Manufacturers of the United States of America.* New York: NAM.

National Association of Manufacturers. 1895, May. *The National Industrial Review* 1 (4).

1895, July. "Advice from the South." *National Industrial Review* II (6): 154.

1895, July. *The National Industrial Review* II: 148.

1896, August. *National Industrial Review* VI (7).

Neergaard, N. "Niels Andersen." Salmonsens konversationsleksikon. http://runeberg.org/salmonsen/2/1/0764.html.

Nelson, Moira. No date. "An Analysis of Firm Support for Active Labor Market Policies in Denmark, Germany, and the Netherlands." Manuscript, Bremen International Graduate School of Social Sciences.

Neuberger, Hugh. 1977. "The Industrial Politics of the Kreditbanken, 1880–1914." *Business History Review* 51 (2): 190–207.

New Deal Task Force Working Group on Retention. 1999. *Lasting Value: Recommendations for Increasing Retention within the New Deal.* London: New Deal Task Force.

Nielsen, Charles. Ydby skriver i Sydthy Årbog om: Polarforskeren Knud Rasmussen, Etatsråden og Ydby Missionshus. Cites Niels Andersen letter to "De kongelige ordenes kapitel." http://www.cmi.dk/Charles.html.

Nolan, Peter and David Harvie. 1995. "Labour Markets: Diversity in Restructuring," in David Coates, ed., *Economic and Industrial Performance in Europe.* Aldershot: Edward Elgar, 125–52.

Nørgaard, Asbjørn Sonne. 1997. *The Politics of Institutional Control.* Aarhus: Forlag Politica.

1999. "Arbejdsmarkedspolitik: Korporatisme til alle tider og alle sider," in Jens Blom-Hansen and Carsten Daugbjerg, eds., *Magtens Organisering.* Aarhus: Forlaget Systime.

Nørregaard, Georg. 1943. "Arbejdsforhold inden for dansk håndværk og industri 1857–1899." Nationaløkonomisk Tidsskrift, Bind 81.

Norris, Pippa. 2001. "New Labour and Public Opinion: The Third Way as Centrism?," in Stuart White, ed., *New Labour: The Progressive Future?* New York: Macmillan, 32–44.

Northcott, Clarence. 1917. "The Organization of Labor in War Time in Great Britain." *Political Science Quarterly* 32 (2): 209–23.

Nugent to Sir Vincent Caillard. Letter. March 14, 1917. MSS200/F/3/D1/2/2–3. Modern Records Centre, Warwick University, Warwick, UK.

March 20, 1917. MSS200/F/3/D1/2/13. Modern Records Centre, Warwick University, Warwick, UK.

Nugent to H.M. Cleminson. Letter. June 1, 1917. MSS200/F/3/D1/2/17. Modern Records Centre, Warwick University, Warwick, UK.

Nugent to Dixon. Letter. February 8, 1917. MSS200/F/3/D1/2/7. Modern Records Centre, Warwick University, Warwick, UK.

Nugent to Dixon. Letter. May 29, 1917. MSS200/F/3/D1/2/7. Modern Records Centre, Warwick University, Warwick, UK.

Nugent to Dixon. June 7, 1917, MSS200/F/3/D1/2/7. Modern Records Centre, Warwick University, Warwick, UK.

Nugent. "Excerpt from letter to Mr. Docker of 28th Oct., 1916." MSS.200/F/3/D1/2/2–3. Modern Records Centre, Warwick University, Warwick, UK.

"Exerpt from letter to Mr. Docker of 27th March, 1917. Reconstruction Scheme." MSS200/F/3/D1/2/2–3. Modern Records Centre, Warwick University, Warwick, UK.

"Excerpt from letter to Mr. Docker of 30th Jan., 1917. "Trades Union Congress, and Employers' Parliamentary Association." MSS200/F/3/D1/2/1. Modern Records Centre, Warwick University, Warwick, UK.

Nugent to Sir Robert Hadfield. May 14, 1917. MSS200/F/3/D1/2/9. [Addressed to "Dear Sir" but in the Hadfield folder.] Modern Records Centre, Warwick University, Warwick, UK.

Nugent to Mr. E. V. Hiley. Letter. February 19, 1917. MSS200/F/3/D1/2/8. Modern Records Centre, Warwick University, Warwick, UK.

Nugent to Fitzjohn Oldham. March 20, 1917. MSS200/F/3/D1/2/5. Modern Records Centre, Warwick University, Warwick, UK.

Nugent to Sir Wm. B. Peat. Letter. February 8, 1917. MSS200/F/3/D1/2/4. Modern Records Centre, Warwick University, Warwick, UK.

Nugent to Peter Rylands. Letter. December 19, 1919. MSS20/F/3/D1/2/1. Modern Records Centre, Warwick University, Warwick, UK.

Nugent to Peter Rylands January 11, 1918. MSS200/F/3/D1/2/1. Modern Records Centre, Warwick University, Warwick, UK.

Nugent to Peter Rylands. Letter. January 18, 1917. MSS200/F/3/D1/2/1. Modern Records Centre, Warwick University, Warwick, UK.

Nugent to Sir R.V. Vassar-Smith. Letter. October 26, 1917. MSS200/F/3/D1/2/19. Modern Records Centre, Warwick University, Warwick, UK.

Octavio, Amorin and Gary Cox. 1997. "Electoral Institutions, Cleavage Structures and Number of Parties." *American Political Science Review* 41: 149–74.

OECD. 1994. *The OECD Jobs Study*. Paris: Organization for Economic Co-operation and Development.

1996. The OECD Jobs Strategy: Enhancing the Effectiveness of Active Labour Market Policies. Paris: Organization for Economic Co-operation and Development.

1996. *Employment Outlook 1996*. Paris: Organization for Economic Co-operation and Development.

2004. *Education at a Glance*. Paris: Organization for Economic Co-operation and Development.

2001. *OECD Employment Outlook*. Paris: Organization for Economic Co-operation and Development.

2000a. *United Kingdom*. Paris: Organization for Economic Co-operation and Development.

2000b. *OECD Employment Outlook*. Paris: Organization for Economic Co-operation and Development.

2004. *OECD Employment Outlook*. Paris: Organization for Economic Co-operation and Development.

2005. *Economic Surveys: Denmark*. Paris: OECD.

2006. *Economic Surveys: Denmark*. Paris: OECD.

2010 . *Economic Outlook 87. Annex Tables*. Paris: OECD.

Various years. *Economic Surveys: Germany*. Paris: OECD.

July 26, 2010. "How do OECD labour markets perform?" http://www.oecd.org/document/22/0,3746,en_2649_39023495_43221014_1_1_1,00.html.

Offe, Claus. 2003. "The European Model of 'Social' Capitalism: Can I Survive European Integration?" *Journal of Political Philosophy* 11 (4):437–69.

1991. "Smooth Consolidation of the West German Welfare State: Structural Change, Fiscal Policies, and Populist Politics," in Frances Fox Piven, ed., *Labor Politics in Postindustrial Societies.* Cambridge: Polity Press, 124–46.

Okun, Arthur M. 1975. *Equality and Efficiency: The Big Tradeoff.* Washington, DC: Brookings.

Olcott, Charles. 1916. *William McKinley* Vol. 1. New York: Houghton Mifflin.

Olson, Mancur 1965. *The Logic of Collective Action.* Cambridge, MA: Harvard University Press.

1982. *The Rise and Decline of Nations.* New Haven, CT: Yale University Press.

Orloff, Ann Shola and Eric Parker. 1990. "Business and Social Policy in Canada and the United States, 1920–1040." *Comparative Social Research* 12: 295–339.

Orren, Karen and Stephen Skowronek. 2004. *The Search for American Political Development.* New York: Cambridge University Press.

Osborne, W. M. to McKinley. Letter. Series 1, Reel 1 "1847 Sept 6 1987 Feb 22."

Osterman, Paul. 1995. "Work/Family Programs and the Employment Relationship Paul Osterman." Administrative Science Quarterly 40: 681–700.

Palier, Bruno, ed. 2010. *A Long Goodbye to Bismarck? The Politics of Welfare Reforms in Europe.* Amsterdam: Amsterdam University Press.

Palier, Bruno. 2001. "How to Characterise the Pattern of Reforms in Bismarckian Welfare Systems?" Paper presented for the 2001 annual APSA meeting, August 30–September 1.

Paster, Thomas. 2011. German Employers and the Origins of Unemployment Insurance." MFIfG Discussion Paper 11/5. Cologne: Max Planck Institute for the Study of Social Sciences.

Palier, Bruno and Kathleen Thelen. 2010. "Institutionalizing Dualism." *Politics & Society* 38 (1 March): 119–148.

Payne. Jonathan. 2001. "New Learning and Skills Council Faces Tough Challenges." *Eironline.* www.eiro.eurofound.ie/2001.

Pedersen, Ove Kaj, Niels Andersen, Peder Kjær, and John Elberg. 1992. *Privat Politik.* Frederiksberg: Samfundslitteratur.

Pedersen, Peder. 1993. "The Welfare State and Taxation in Denmark," in A. B. Atkinson and G. V. Mogensen, eds., *Welfare and Work Incentives: A North European Perspective.* Oxford: Clarendon Press.

Pedersen, Ulrik. 2000. Interview. Kommuner Landsforeningen (December).

Penrose, Edith. 1959. *The Theory of the Growth of the Firm.* Oxford: Basil Blackwell.

Perez, Sofia. 2000. "From De-centralization to Re-organization: Explaining the Return to National-Level Bargaining in Italy and Spain." *Comparative Politics.* 32: 437–58.

Personnel Management Staff. 1993. "UK Skills Are Damagingly Low." *Personnel Management* 25 (8): 63.

Persson, Torsten, Gérand Roland, and Guido Tabellini. 2007. "Electoral Rules and Government Spending in Parliamentary Democracies." *Quarterly Journal of Political Science* 2 (2): 155–88.

Petersen, Jan Nørgaard. 1979. "Brydninger i Højre 1894–1901." *Historie/Jyske Samlinger*, Bind Ny række, 13 (1979–1981): 4.

Peukert, Detlev. 1992. *The Weimar Republic: The Crisis of Classical Modernity.* New York: Hill and Wang.

Pfaller, Alfred, Ian Gough, and Goran Therborn. 1991. *Can the Welfare State Compete?* London: Macmillan.

Phillips, Gregory. 1981. "The Whig Lords and Liberalism, 1886–1893." *The Historical Journal* 24 (1): 167–73.

Pierson, Paul. 1994. *Dismantling the Welfare State?* New York: Cambridge University Press.

2001. "Coping With Permanent Austerity," in Paul Pierson, ed., *The New Politics of the Welfare State.* New York: Oxford University Press, 410–56.

Pierson, Paul and Theda Skocpol. 2002. "Historical Institutionalism in Contemporary Political Science," in Ira Katznelson and Helen Milner, eds., *Political Science: State of the Discipline.* New York: W.W. Norton, 693–721.

Pike, Alan. May 24, 1999. "Training Reforms May Spur Revolt on New Deal for Jobs." *Financial Times*, p. 18.

Piore, Michael and Charels Sabel. 1984. *The Second Industrial Divide.* New York: Basic Books.

Pitcher, George. 1998. "CBI Should Try Self-Improvement before Calling for Wider Reform." *Marketing Week* 21 (36): 27.

Platt, D. C. M. 1968. *Finance, Trade, and Politics in British Foreign Policy 1815–1914.* Oxford: Clarendon Press.

Ploug, Niels and Jørgen Søndergaard. 1999. *Velfærdssamfundets fremtid.* Copenhagen: Social-forskningsinstituttet.

Plovsing, Jan. 1998. *Socialpolitik.* Copenhagen: Handelshøjskolens Forlag.

Plümper, Thomas and Vera Troeger. 2007. "Efficient Estimation of Time-Invariant and Rarely Changing Variables in Finite Sample Panel Analyses with Unit Fixed Effects." *Political Analysis* 15 (2): 124–39.

Plümper, Thomas, Vera Troeger, and Philip Manow. 2005. "Panel Data Analysis in Comparative Politics: Linking Method to Theory." *European Journal of Political Research* 44: 327–54.

Pois, Robert. 1976. "The Bourgeois Democrats of Weimar Germany." *Transactions of the American Philosophical Society* New Series 66 (4): 1–117.

Polanyi, Karl. 1943. *The Great Transformation.* New York: Rinehart.

Pollock, James. 1929. "The German Party System." *American Political Science Review* 23 (4): 859–91.

Pontusson, Jonas. 1992. "Introduction: Organizational and Political-Economic Perspectives on Union Politics," in Miriam Golden and J. Pontusson, eds., *Bargaining for Change.* Ithaca, NY: Cornell University Press, 277–306.

  1995. "From Comparative Public Policy to Political Economy: Putting Institutions in Their Place and Taking Interests Seriously." *Comparative Political Studies* 28 (April): 117–47.

  1997. "Between Neo-Liberalism and the German Model," in Colin Crouch and Wolfgang Streeck, eds., *Political Economy of Modern Capitalism.* Thousand Oaks, CA: Sage, 55–70.

  2005. Inequality and Prosperity: Social Europe versus Liberal American. Ithaca, NY: Cornell University Press.

Pontusson, Jonas and Peter Swenson. 1996. "Labor Markets, Production Strategies, and Wage Bargaining Institutions," *Comparative Political Studies* 29 (2): 223–50.

Porter, Michael and Elizabeth Olmsted Teisberg. 2006. *Redefining Health Care.* Boston: Harvard Business School Press.

Post, James, Edwin Murray, Jr., Robert Dickie, and John Mahon. 1983. "Managing Public Affairs." *California Management Review* 26 (Fall): 135–50.

Prime Minister Office. 2006. "Fremtidens velstand og velfærd." Copenhagen: Schultz Grafisk.

Przeworski, Adam and Michael Wallerstein. 1988. "Structural Dependence of the State on Capital." *American Political Science Review* 82 (March): 11–30.

Puhle, Hans-Jurgen. 1978. "Conservatism in Modern German History." *Journal of Contemporary History* 13 (4): 689–720.

Purkiss, Alan. 1993. "Revolution in Reverse." *Accountancy* 111 (February): 3034.

Putnam, Robert. 1993. *Making Democracy Work.* Princeton, NJ: Princeton University Press.

Quinault, Roland. 1985. "John Bright and Joseph Chamberlain," *The Historical Journal* 28 (3): 623–46.

Quinn, Dennis. 1997. "The Correlates of Change in International Financial Markets."; *American Political Science Review* 91 (3): 531–52.

Raess, Damian. 2006. "Globalization and Why the 'Time is Ripe' for the Transformation of German Industrial Relations." *Review of International Policy Economy* 12 (3): 449–79.

Ragin, Charles 1987. The Comparative Method: Moving Beyond Qualitative and Quantitative Strategies. Berkeley: University of California Press.

Rambusch, Sigurd. 1988. *Jacob Scavenius.* Aarhus: Universitetsforlaget is Aarhus.

Raymond, Lesley. 2001. "A Targeted Approach." *Catalyst* (August) www.newdeal.gov.uk.

Redlich, Fritz. 1944. "German Economic Planning for War and Peace." *Review of Politics* 6 (3): 315–35.

Regalia, I. and Marino Regini. 2004. "Collective Bargaining and Social Pacts in Italy," in H. C. Katz, W. Lee, and J. Lee, eds., *The New Structure of Labor Relations*. Ithaca, NY: Cornell University Press, 59–83.

Regini, Marino. 1995. "Firms and Institutions: The Demand for Skills and their Social Production in Europe." *European Journal of Industrial Relations* 1 (2): 191–202.

Rein, Martin. 1997. *Enterprise and Social Benefits after Communism*. New York: Cambridge University Press.

Rempel, Richard. 1972. *Unionists Divided*. London: Archon Books.

Rhodes, Martin. 2001a. "Restructuring the British Welfare State," in Fritz Scharf and Vivien Schmidt, eds., *Welfare and Work in the Open Economy*. New York : Oxford University Press, 19–68.

  2001b. "The Political Economy of Social Pacts," in Paul Pierson, ed., *The New Politics of the Welfare State*. New York: Oxford University Press, 165–96.

Rhodes, R. A. W. 1999. "Traditions and Public Sector Reform: Comparing Britain and Denmark." *Scandinavian Political Studies* 22 (4): 341–70.

Ridings, Eugene. 2001. "Chambers of Commerce and Business Elites in Great Britain and Brazil in the Nineteenth Century." *The Business History Review* 75 (4): 739–73.

Ringe, Astrid and Neil Rollings. 2000. "Responding to Relative Decline." *Economic History Review* LIII (2): 331–53.

Ritter, Gerhard. 1990. "The Social Bases of the German Political Parties, 1867–1920," in Karl Rohe, ed., *Elections, Parties and Political Traditions*. New York: Berg, 27–52.

Roberts, Dan. 2003. "Many Industrialists and Entrepreneurs Who Worked with the Government in Its First Term Now Feel Disillusioned." *Financial Times*, (April 10), p. 18.

Roberts, Richard and David Kynaston. 2001. "The Rout of the Stakeholders." *The New Statesman* (September 17).

Rodgers, Terence. 1988. "Employers' Organizations, Unemployment and Social Politics in Britain during the Inter-War Period." *Social History* 13 (3): 315–41.

Rodrik, Dani. 1997. *Has Globalization Gone to Far?* Washington, DC: Institute for International Economics.

  1998. "Why Do More Open Economies Have Bigger Governments?" *Journal of Political Economy* 106: 997–1032.

Rogaczewska, Anna Patrizia, Henrik Holt Larsen, and Carsten Skovbro. 1999. *HRM i Danske Virksomheder*. Cranet-E Undersøgelsen. Gylling, DK: Narayana Press.

Rogers, Lindsay and W. R. Dittmar. 1935. "The Reichswirtschaftsrat." *Political Science Quarterly* 50 (4): 481–501.

Rohe, Karl. 1990. "German Elections and Party Systems in Historical and Regional Perspective: An Introduction," in K. Rohe, ed., *Elections, Parties and Political Tradition*. New York: Berg, 1–25.

Röhl, J. C. G. 1966. "The Disintegration of the Kartell and the Politics of Bismarck's Fall from Power, 1887–90." *The Historical Journal* 9 (1): 60–89.

Rokkan, Stein. 1999. *State Formation, Nation-Building, and Mass Politics in Europe*, Peter Flora, Stein Kuhnle, and Derek Urwin, eds. Oxford: Oxford University Press.

Rollings, Neil. 2008. "Private Transnational Governance in the Heyday of the Nation-State." *Economic History Review* 61 (2): 409–31.

Romer, Thomas. 1975. "Individual Welfare, Majority Voting, and the Properties of a Linear Income Tax." *Journal of Public Economics* 4 (2): 163–85.

Ronit, Karsten. *Interesseorganisationer i dansk politik*. Copenhagen: Jurist- og Økonomforbundets Forlag.

Rosdahl, Anders. 2001. "The Policy to Promote Social Responsibility of Enterprises in Denmark." Paper prepared for the European Commission. Copenhagen: Socialeforskningsinstitute.

Rosholm, Michael. n.d. *Is Labour Market Training a Curse for the Unemployed?* Copenhagen: Socialforskningsinstitut.

Ross, George. 1995. *Jacques Delors and European Integration.* New York: Oxford University Press.

Ross, Duncan. 2004. "Industrial and Commercial Finance in the Inter-war Years," in R. Floud and P. Johnson, eds., *The Cambridge Economic History of Modern Britain vol. 2: Economic Maturity 1860–1939.* Cambridge, UK/New York: Cambridge University Press.

Rothstein, Bo. 1988. "State and Capital in Sweden." *Scandinavian Political Studies* 11 (3): 235–60.

    2000. Just Institutions Matter: The Moral and Political Logic of the Universal Welfare State. New York: Cambridge University Press.

    2005. *Social Traps and the Problem of Trust.* New York: Cambridge University Press.

Rothstein, Bo and Jonas Bergström. 1999. *Korporatisms fall och den svenska modellens kris.* Stockholm: SNS Förlag.

Rubin, Gerry. 1984. "Law, War and Economy." *Journal of Law and Society* 11 (3): 317–33.

Rueda, David. 2005. "Insider-Outsider Politics in Industrialized Democracies." *American Political Science Review* 99: 61–74.

    2007. Social Democracy Inside Out: Partisanship and Labor Market Policy in Industrialized Democracies. New York: Oxford University Press.

    2008. "Left Government, Policy, and Corporatism: Explaining the Influence of Partisanship on Inequality." *World Politics* 60 (3): 349–89.

Rueschemeyer, Dietrich, Evelyn Huber, and John Stephens. 1992. *Capitalist Development & Democracy.* Chicago: University of Chicago Press.

Runciman, W. G. 1993. "Has British Capitalism Changed since the First World War?" *British Journal of Sociology* 44 (1): 53–67.

Runciman, W. G. 1995. "New Times or Old? A Reply to Fulcher." *British Journal of Sociology* 46 (4): 708–14.

Rurup, Reinhard. 1968. "Problems of the German Revolution 1918–19." *Journal of Contemporary History* 3 (4): 109–35.

Salamon, Lester and John Siegfried. 1974. "Economic Power and Political Influence." *American Political Science Review* 71 (4): 1026–43.

Sandholtz, Wayne and John Zysman. 1989. "1992: Recasting the European Bargaining." *World Politics* 42 (1): 95–128.

Scharpf, Fritz. 1988. "The Joint Decision Trap: Lessons from German Federalism and European Integration." *Public Administration* 88: 239–78.

    2000. "Economic Changes, Vulnerabilities, and Institutional Capabilities," in Fritz Scharpf and Vivian Schmidt, eds., *Work and Welfare in the Open Economy, Volume 1: From Vulnerability to Competitiveness.* New York: Oxford University Press, 21–124.

Scharpf, Fritz and Vivian Schmidt, eds. 2000. *Welfare to Work in the Open Economy.* New York: Oxford University Press.

Scheinberg, Stephen. 1973. "Invitation to Empire: Tariffs and American Economic Expansion in Canada." *Business History Review* 47 (2): 218–38.

Scheuer, Steen. 1992. "Denmark: Return to Decentralization," in Anthony Ferner and Richard Hyman, eds., *Industrial Relations in the New Europe.* Oxford: Blackwell, 168–97.

    2007. "Dilemmas of Collectivism: Danish Trade Unions in the Twenty-First Century." *Journal of Labor Research* 28 (2): 233–54.

Scheve, Kenneth and David Stasavage. 2009. " Institutions, Partisanship, and Inequality in the Long Run." *World Politics* 61 (2): 215–53.

Schmidt, Vivian. 2002. *The Futures of European Capitalism.* Oxford: Oxford University Press.

Schmitter, Philippe. 1981. "Interest Intermediation and Regime Governability in Contemporary Western Europe and North America," In Suzanne Berger, ed., *Organizing Interests in Western Europe.* New York: Cambridge University Press, 287–327.

Schmitter, Philippe and Wolfgang Streeck. 1991. "From National Corporatism to Transnational Pluralism." *Politics and Society* 19 (2): 133–64.

Schneiberg, Mark. 2007. "What's on the path?" *Socio-Economic Review* 5: 47–80.

Schneider, Ben Ross. 2004. *Business Politics and the State in Twentieth-Century Latin America.* Cambridge: Cambridge University Press.

Schonhardt-Bailey, Cheryl. 1998. "Parties and Interests in the 'Marriage of Iron and Rye." *British Journal of Political Science* 28 (2): 291–332.

Schou, Bent. 1988. "Udgiftsstyring eller fornyelse?," in Karl Henrik Bentsen ed., *Fra Vækst til Omstilling.* Copenhagen: Frederiksberg Bogtrykkeri, 333–63.

Schrank, Andrew. 2009. "Understanding Latin American Political Economy" *Economy & Society* 38 (1 Feb): 53–61.

Schwartz, Herman. 2000a. "Round up the Usual Suspects!," in Paul Pierson, ed., *The New Politics of the Welfare State.* New York: Oxford University Press, 17–44.

— 2001b. "The Danish 'Miracle' Luck, Pluck, or Stuck?," *Comparative Political Studies* 34 (2):131–55.

Scruggs, Lyle. 2001. "Is There Really a Link between Neo-Corporatism and Environmental Performance?" *British Journal of Political Science* 31 (4): 686–92.

Scruggs, Lyle and Peter Lange. 2002. " Where Have All the Members Gone? Globalization, Institutions, and Union Density." *Journal of Politics* 64 (1): 126–53.

Seabrooke, Leonard. 2009. *The Warwick Commission.* Coventry: Warwick University.

Search, Theodore. 1898. "To the Executive Committee and Members of the National Association of Manufacturers," *Proceedings of the Third Annual Convention of the National Association of Manufacturers.* New York: NAM Bureau of Publicity, 3–32.

— 1900. "President's Report." *Proceedings of the Fifth Annual Convention of the National Association of Manufacturers,* April 24 -26, Boston, Philadelphia: NAM Bureau of Publicity.

— 1901. "President's Report." *Proceedings of the Sixth Annual Convention of the National Association of Manufacturers.* New York: NAM Bureau of Publicity, 23–4.

— 1902. "Annual Report of the President." *Proceedings of the Seventh Annual Convention of the National Association of Manufacturers of the United States.* New York: NAM Bureau of Publicity, 15.

Seeleib-Kaiser, Martin and Timo Fleckenstein. 2007. "Discourse, Learning, and Welfare State Change: The Case of German Labour Market Reforms." *Social Policy and Administration* 41 (5): 427–48.

Shefter, Martin. 1986. "Trade Unions and Political Machines," in Ira Katznelson and Aristide Zolberg, eds., *Working Class Formation.* Princeton, NJ: Princeton University Press.

Shonfield, Andrew. 1965. *Modern Capitalism.* New York: Oxford University Press.

Shreve, Earl. 1949. *The Chamber of Commerce of the United States of America.* New York: Newcomen Society in North America, 1949.

Siaroff, Alan. 1998. "Corporatism in Twenty-Four Industrial Democracies: Meaning and Measurement." *European Journal of Political Research* 36: 175–205.

Siegel, Nico A. 2004. "EMU and German Welfare Capitalism," in Andrew Martin and George Ross, eds., *Euros and Europeans: Monetary Integration and the European Model of Society.* New York: Cambridge University Press, 103–25.

Silvia, Stephen J. and Wolfgang Schroeder. 2007. "Why Are German Employers Associations Declining? Arguments and Evidence." *Comparative Political Studies* 40 (12): 1433–59.

Sisson, Keith. 1987. *The Management of Collective Bargaining.* New York: Blackwell.

Skidelsky, Robert. 1979. "The Decline of Keynesian Politics," in Colin Crouch, ed., *State and Economy in Contemporary Capitalism.* New York: St. Martin's Press, 55–87.

Sklar, Martin. 1988. *The Corporate Reconstruction of American Capitalism, 1890–1916.* New York: Cambridge University Press.

Skocpol, Theda. 1985. "Bringing the State Back In: Strategies of Analysis in Current Research," in Peter Evans, Dietrich Rueschemeyer, and Theda Skocpol, eds., *Bringing the State Back In.* New York: Cambridge University Press, 3–37.

1995. *Social Policy in the United States.* Princeton, NJ: Princeton University Press.

Skov Christensens, Poul Erik. 2007. "Beretning til 3F's 1. ordinære kongres" (September 15).

Skowronek, Stephen. 1982. *Building a New American State.* New York: Cambridge University Press.

Smith, Adam. 1976 (1776). *An Inquiry into the Nature and Causes of the Wealth of Nations.* Oxford: Clarendon Press.

Smith, David. 1998. "Will Clive Split the CBI?" *Management Today* (November): 32–7.

Smith, Martin. 1994. "Understanding the 'Politics of Catch-Up.'" *Political Studies* XLII: 708–15.

Smith, Mark. 2000. *American Business and Political Power.* Chicago: University of Chicago Press.

Snape, Dawn. 1998. *New Deal for Young Unemployed People: A Good Deal for Employers?* Sheffield: Research Management Employment Service (December).

Snow, David, E. Burke Rochford, Jr., Steven Worden, and Robert Benford. 1986. "Frame Alignment Processes, Micromobilization, and Movement Participation." *American Sociological Review* 51:464–81.

Socialeforskningsinstitut. 1997. *New Partnership for Social Cohesion.* Copenhagen: Ministry of Social Affairs.

Social Ministry. 1999. "Det angaar os alle." Copenhagen: Social Ministry (January).

Søndergaard, Jørgen. 2001. Interview with the author (June).

Soskice, David. 1990. "Wage Determination: the Changing Role of Institutions in Advanced Industrialized Countries." *Oxford Review of Economic Policy* 6 (4): 36–61.

Soskice, David. 1999. "Divergent Production Regimes: Coordinated and Uncoordinated Market Economies in the 1980s and 1990s," in Herbert Kitschelt, Peter Lange, Gary Marks, and John Stephens, eds., *Continuity and Change in Contemporary Capitalism.* New York: Cambridge University Press, 101–34.

Spencer, Elaine Glovka. 1979. "Rulers of the Ruhr." *Business History Review* 53 (1): 40–64.

Spicker, Paul. 1997. "The Welfare State and Social Protection in the United Kingdom," in Maurice Mullard and Simon Lee, ed., *The Politics of Social Policy in Europe.* Lyme, NH: Edward Elgar, 90–106.

Stanley, Arthur to Lord Robert Cecil. July 25, 1917.

Stanley, Arthur to Lord Robert Cecil. August 2, 1917.

Steedman, H. and K. Wagner 2006. "Changing Skill Needs in Europe and Responsiveness of Apprenticeship/Work-based Learning." Unpublished paper.

Steedman, H., S. McIntosh, and A. Green. 2004. *International Comparisons of Qualifications: Skills Audit Update.* London: Centre for Economic Performance and Department for Education and Skills. Research Report 548.

Steigerwalt, Albert. 1964. *The National Association of Manufacturers 1895–1914.* Grand Rapids: University of Michigan.

Steinmo, Sven and Caroline Tolbert. 1998. "Do Institutions Really Matter?" *Comparative Political Studies* 31 (2): 165–87.

Stephens, John D. 1980. *The Transition from Capitalism to Socialism.* Atlantic Highlands: Humanities Press.

Stern, Clarence. 1963. *Resurgent Republicanism.* Ann Arbor, MI: Edwards Brothers.

Stevens, Beth. 1986. *Complementing the Welfare State.* Geneva: International Labor Org.

Stone, Nathan. 1978. Promotion of Foreign Commerce in Europe and the United States (Washington, 1907).

Strachey, Loe to Arthur Steel Maitland. February 24, 1916.

Strange, S. 1996. *The Retreat of the State: The Diffusion of Power in the World Economy.* New York: Cambridge University Press.

Streeck, Wolfgang. 1992. *Social Institutions and Economic Performance.* Beverly Hills, CA: Sage.

    2001. "High Equality, Low Activity: The Contribution of the Social Welfare System to the Stability of the German Collective Bargaining Regime." *Industrial and Labor Relations Review* 54 (3): 698–706.

    2005. "Industrial Relations: From State Weakness as Strength to State Weakness as Weakness. Welfare Corporatism and the Private Use of the Public Interest," in Simon Green and William E. Paterson, eds., *Governance in Contemporary Germany: The Semisovereign State Revisited.* New York: Cambridge University Press, 138–64.

    2009. *Re-Forming Capitalism: Institutional Change in the German Political Economy.* New York: Oxford University Press.

Streeck, Wolfgang and Anke Hassel. 2003. "The Crumbling Pillars of Social Partnership." *West European Politics* 26 (4): 101–24.

Streeck, Wolfgang and Philippe Schmitter. 1985. *Private Interest Government.* Beverly Hills, CA: Sage.

    1991. "From National Corporatism to Transnational Pluralism." *Politics and Society* 19 (June): 133–64.

Streeck, Wolfgang and Kathleen Thelen. 2005. *Beyond Continuity: Institutional Change in Advanced Political Economies.* New York: Oxford University Press.

Stubbs, J. O. 1972. "Lord Milner and Patriotic Labour, 1914–1918." *The English Historical Review* 87 (345): 717–54.

Sturges, Kenneth. 1915. *American Chambers of Commerce.* New York: Moffat, Yard and Co.

Suarez, Sandra. 2000. *Does Business Learn?* Ann Arbor: University of Michigan Press.

Sunley, Peter, Ron Martin, and Corrine Nativel. 2001. "Mapping the New Deal." *Transactions of the Institute of British Geographers* 26 (4): 484–512.

Sutherland, Jim and Helen Rainbird. 2000. *Training in the Workplace*, ed., Helen Rainbird. New York: St. Martin's Press, 189–209.

Swank, Duane. 1988. "The Political Economy of Government Domestic Expenditure in the Affluent Democracies." *American Journal of Political Science* 32 (4): 1120–50.

    1992. "Politics and the Structural Dependence of the State in Democratic Capitalist Nations." *American Political Science Review* 86 (March): 38–54.

    2000. "Social Democratic Welfare States in a Global Economy," in Robert Geyer, Christine Ingrebritsen, and Jonathon Moses, eds., *Globalization, Europeanization, and the End of Scandinavian Social Democracy?* London: Macmillan, 85–138.

    2001. "Political Institutions and Welfare State Restructuring," in Paul Pierson, ed., *The New Politics of the Welfare State.* New York: Oxford University Press, 197–237.

    2002. *Global Capital, Political Institutions, and Policy Change in Developed Welfare States* Cambridge Studies in Comparative Politics. New York: Cambridge University Press.

    2003. "Withering Welfare? Globalization, Political Economic Models, and the Foundations of Contemporary Welfare States," in Linda Weiss, ed., *States and Global Markets: Bringing Domestic Institutions Back In.* Cambridge: Cambridge University Press.

    2010. "Globalization," in Herbert Obinger, Francis Castles, Stephan Leibfried, and Jane Lewis, eds., *Oxford Handbook on Comparative Welfare States.* New York: Oxford University Press.

    2011. "Activating Change? The Political Economy of Active Social Policy in Developed Capitalist Democracies," in David Brady, ed., *Comparing European Workers Part B: Policies and Institutions*, Research in the Sociology of Work, Volume 22. Bingley, UK: Emerald Group Publishing.

Swank, Duane and Cathie Jo Martin. 2001. "Employers and the Welfare State." *Comparative Political Studies* 34 (October): 889–923.

Swank, Duane, Kathleen Thelen, and Cathie Martin. 2008. "Institutional Change and the Politics of Social Solidarity in the Advanced Industrial Democracies," Paper presented at the Annual Meetings of the American Political Science Association, Boston.

Sweeney, Dennis. 2001. "Corporatist Discourse and Heavy Industry in Wilhelmine Germany." *Comparative Studies in Society and History* 43 (4): 701–34.

Swenson, Peter. 1991. "Bringing Capital Back In, or Social Democracy Reconsidered: Employer Power, Cross-Class Alliances, and Centralization of Industrial Relations in Denmark and Sweden." *World Politics* 43: 513–44.

2002. *Capitalists against Markets: The Making of Labor Markets and Welfare States in the United States and Sweden.* New York: Oxford University Press.

Swenson, Peter and Jonas Pontusson. 2000. "The Swedish Employer Offensive against Centralized Bargaining," in Torben Iversen, Jonas Pontusson and David Soskice, eds., *Unions, Employers, and Central Banks.* New York: Cambridge University Press, 77–106.

Synovate/Mandag Morgen. 2011. "1971–2007: Valgundersøgelserne" (July 27).

Tabachnik, Barbara and Linda Fidell. 1989. *Using Multivariate Statistics.* New York: Harper.

Taylor-Gooby, Peter. 1991. "Welfare State Regimes and Welfare Citizenship." *Journal of European Social Policy* 1 (2): 93–105.

Tedlow, Richard. 1988. "Trade Association and Public Relations," in Hiroaki Yamazuki and Matuo Miyamoto, eds., *Trade Associations in Business History.* Tokyo: University of Tokyo Press, 139–72.

Teknologisk Institut. 2000. *Fleksjob på fremtidens arbejdsmarked.* Teknologisk Institut (May).

Thelen, Kathleen. 1991. *Union of Parts: Labor Politics in Postwar Germany.* Ithaca, NY: Cornell University Press.

2000. "Why German Employers Cannot Bring Themselves to Dismantle the German Model," in Torben Iversen, Jonas Pontusson, and David Soskice, eds., *Unions, Employers, and Central Banks.* New York: Cambridge University Press, 138–72.

2001. "Varieties of Labor Politics in the Developed Democracies," in Peter Hall and David Soskice, eds., *Varieties of Capitalism: The Institutional Foundations of Comparative Advantage.* New York: Oxford University Press, 71–103.

2004. *How Institutions Evolve.* Cambridge: Cambridge University Press.

2010. "Presidential Address: Economic Regulation and Social Solidarity: Conceptual and Analytical Innovations in the Study of Advanced Capitalism." *Socio-Economic Review* 8: 187–207.

Thelen, Kathleen and Christa van Wijnbergen. 2003. "The Paradox of Globalization: Labor Relations in Germany and Beyond," *Comparative Political Studies* 36 (8): 859–80.

Tipton, Frank. 2003. *A History of Modern Germany since 1815.* New York: Continuum.

Titmuss, Richard. 1958. *Essays on the Welfare State.* London: Unwin Books.

Tolliday, Steven and Jonathan Zeitlin. 1991. *The Power to Manage.* New York: Routledge.

Tomlins, Christopher. 1985. *The State and the Unions.* Cambridge: Cambridge University Press.

Torcal, Mariano and Scott Mainwaring. 2003. "The Political Recrafting of Social Bases of Party Competition." *British Journal of Political Science* 33: 55–84.

Torfing, Jacob. 1999. "Workfare with Welfare: Recent Reforms of the Danish Welfare State." *Journal of European Social Policy* 9 (1): 5–28.

Trampusch, Christine. 2005. "Institutional Resettlement: The Case of Early Retirement," in Wolfgang Streeck and Kathleen Thelen, eds., *Beyond Continuity: Institutional Change in Advanced Political Economies.* New York: Oxford University Press, 203–28.

2010. "Co-evolution of Skills and Welfare in Coordinated Market Economies?" *European Journal of Industrial Relations* 16 (September).

Traxler, Franz. 1999. "The State in Industrial Relations." *European Journal of Political Research* 36: 55–85.

2000. "Employers and Employer Organisations in Europe." *Industrial Relations Journal* 31 (4): 308–16.

2003. "Bargaining (De)centralization, Macroeconomic Performance and Control over the Employment Relationship." *British Journal of Industrial Relations* 41 (1): 1–27.

2004. "The Metamorphoses of Corporatism: From Classical to Lean Patterns." *European Journal of Political Research* 43: 571–98.

Traxler, Franz and Gerhard Huemer, eds. 2007. *Handbook of Business Interest Associations, Firm Size and Governance: A Comparative Analytical Approach.* New York: Routledge.

Traxler, Frans, Sabine Blaschke, and Bernhard Kittlel. 2001. *National Labour Relations in Internationalized Markets.* New York: Oxford University Press.

Traxler, Franz, Bernd Brandl, and Susanne Pernika. 2007. "Business Associability, Activities, and Governance: Cross-National Findings," in Franz Traxler and Gerhard Huemer, eds., *Handbook of Business Interest Associations, Firm Size and Governance: A Comparative Analytical Approach.* New York: Routledge, 351–406.

Trentmann, Frank. 1996. "The Transformation of Fiscal Reform." *The Historical Journal* 39 (4): 1005–48.

2008. *Free Trade Nation.* Oxford: Oxford University Press.

Treu, Tiziano. 1992. *Participation in Public Policy-Making: The Role of Trade Unions and Employer Associations.* New York: Walter de Gruyter.

Trubowitz, Peter. 1998. *Defining the National Interest.* Chicago: University of Chicago Press.

Tsebelis, George. 1999. "Veto Players and Law Production in Parliamentary Democracies: An Empirical Analysis." *American Political Science Review* 25 (3): 591–608.

TUC (Trade Union Congress). 1999. General Council Report. http://www.tuc.org.uk/congress/ index.cfm?mins=97&minors=67.

Turner, Henry. 1969. "Big Business and the Rise of Hitler." *American Historical Review* 75 (1 October): 56–70.

Turner, John. 1982. "Towards a Cognitive Redefinition of the Social Group," in Henri Tajfel, ed., *Social Identity and Intergroup Relations.* New York: Cambridge University Press.

1984. "The Politics of Business," in J. Turner, ed., *Businessmen and Politics.* London: Heinemann, 33–49.

Turner, Lowell. 1998. *Fighting for Partnership: Labor and Politics in Unified Germany.* Ithaca, NY: Cornell University Press.

Umbreit, Paul and Karl Scholz. 1920. "The Program of German Socialized Industrial Managements." *Annals of the American Academy of Political and Social Science.* 92: 61–5.

Undy, Roger. 2002. "New Labour and New Unionism, 1997–2001." *Employee Relations* 24 (6): 638–55.

United British Industries Association. 1916. *Proceedings.* July 20. MSS.200/F/3/D1/1/6.

Unwin, George. 1966. *The Gilds and Companies of London,* London: Frank Cass & Co.

Upchurch, Martin. 1997. "'Social Partnerships,' The Market and Trade-Union Involvement in Training." *Journal of European Social Policy* 7 (3): 191–208.

Vail, Mark I. 2003. "Rethinking Corporatism and Consensus: The Dilemmas of German Social-Protection Reform." *West European Politics* 26 (3): 41–66.

Van Vliet, Olaf. 2011. *Convergence and Europeanization: The Political Economy of Social and Labour Market Policies.* Leiden: Leiden University Press.

Velfærdskommissionen. 2005. *Fremtidens velfærd og globaliseringen: Analyserapport.* Copenhagen: Velfaærdskommissionen.

Verdier, Daniel. 2003. "Explaining Cross-National Variations in Universal Banking in Nineteenth-Century Europe, North American, and Australasia," in Douglas J. Forsyth and Daniel Verdier, eds., *The Origins of National Financial Systems: Alexander Gerschenkron Reconsidered.* New York: Routledge, 23–42.

Viborg Andersen, Kim, Carsten Greve, and Jacob Torfing. 1994. "Reorganizing the Danish Welfare State: 1982–93." Working Paper 1994/1. Copenhagen University, Institute for Political Studies.

Vigen, Anders. 1946. *Arbejdsgiver Foreningen Gennem 50 Aar 1896–1946.* Copenhagen: Langkjærs Bogtrykkeri.

Visser, Jelle. 1992. "Trade Union Membership Database," Typescript. Sociology of Organizations Research Unit, Department of Sociology, University of Amsterdam (March).

Visser, Jelle and Anton Hemerijck. 1997. *"A Dutch Miracle": Job Growth, Welfare Reform, and Corporatism in the Netherlands.* Amsterdam: Amsterdam University Press.

Vitols, Sigurt. 2001. "The Origins of Bank-Based and Market-Based Financial Systems: Germany Japan, and the United States," in Wolfgang Streeck and Kozo Yamamura, eds., *The Origins of Non-Liberal Capitalism: Germany and Japan in Comparison.* Ithaca, NY: Cornell University Press, 171–99.

Wakstein, Allen. 1964. "The Origins of the Open-Shop Movement, 1919–1920." *Journal of American History* 51 (3): 460–75.

Walker, Jack. 1983. "The Origins and Maintenance of Interest Groups in America." *American Political Science Review* 77.

Wallerstein, Michael. 1989. "Wage-Setting Institutions and Pay Inequality in Advanced Industrial Societies." *American Journal of Political Science* 43 (2): 649–80.

Wallerstein, Michael and Miriam Golden. 1997. "The Fragmentation of the Bargaining Society: Wage Setting in Nordic Countries, 1950–1992." *Comparative Political Studies* 30 (6): 699–731.

Wallerstein, Michael, Miriam Golden, and Peter Lange. 1997. "Unions, Employers' Associations, and Wage-Setting Institutions in Northern and Central Europe, 1950–1992." *Industrial and Labor Relations Review* 50: 379–401.

Walles, Malcolm. 1988. *British and American Systems of Government.* Oxford: Philip Allan Publishers.

Warren, Jr., Donald. 1964. *The Red Kingdom of Saxony.* The Hague: Martinus Hijhoff.

Watt, D. Cameron. 1997. "Economic Affairs, Cultural Propaganda, and the Reform of the Foreign Office, 1910–1939," *British Documents on Foreign Affairs*, Part II, Series K. Washington, DC: University Publications of America.

Wehler, Hans-Ulrich. 1970. "Bismarck's Imperialism 1862–1890." *Past and Present* 48: 119–55.

Weinstein, James. 1968. *The Corporate Ideal in the Liberal State, 1900–1918.* Boston: Beacon Press.

Weir, Margaret. 1992. *Politics and Jobs.* Princeton, NJ: Princeton University Press.

Weir, Margaret, Ann Shola Orloff, and Theda Skocpol. 1988., *The Politics of Social Policy in the United States.* Princeton, NJ: Princeton University Press.

Weir, Stuart. 1999. "The City Has Taken Over the Quangos under New Labour." *The Independent* (November 23).

Weiss, Linda, ed. 2003. *States in the Global Economy: Bringing Domestic Institutions Back In*, L. Weiss, ed. New York: Cambridge University Press.

Wellesley, Sir Victor. 1918. "Principles of British Commercial Policy Abroad," in *British Documents on Foreign Affairs*, Part II. Series K. Vol. I. Doc. 12. Appendix VI. (June): 51–59.

Werking, Richard. 1977. *The Master Architects.* Lexington: University of Kentucky.

Werking, Richard Hume. 1978. "Bureaucrats, Businessmen, and Foreign Trade." *Business History Review* LII (3): 321–41.

Westergaard-Nielsen, Niels. 2001. "Danish Labour Market Policy: Is It Worth It?," Centre for Labour Market and Social Research Working Paper 01–10 (November).

Western, Bruce. 1997. *Between Class and Market.* Princeton, NJ: Princeton University Press.

Wheeler, Harry. 1913. "Three Great Elements," *Nation's Business* 1 (6): 1.

White, William Allan. 1928. *Masks in a Pageant.* New York: MacMillan.

Whitley, Richard. 1999. *Divergent Capitalisms: The Social Structuring and Change of Business Systems.* Oxford: Oxford University Press.

Wickham-Jones, Mark. 1997. "Social Democracy and Structural Dependency." *Politics & Society* 25 (2): 257–65.

2004. "The New Left," in R. Plant, M. Beech, and K. Hickson, eds., *The Struggle for Labour's Soul: Understanding Labour's Political Thought since 1945.* New York: Routledge, 24–46.

Wiebe, Robert. 1962. *Businessmen and Reform.* Cambridge: Harvard University Press.

1967. *The Search for Order.* New York: Hill and Wang.

Wiesenthal, Helmut. 2003. "German Unification and 'Model Germany': An Adventure in Institutional Conservatism." *West European Politics* 26 (4): 37–58.

Wighton, David. 1998. "MPs Call for Changes to New Deal Plan for Joblessness." *Financial Times* (February 5) p. 10.

Wilensky, Harold. 1975. *The Welfare State and Equality.* Berkeley: University of California Press.

1976. *The "New Corporatism," Centralization, and the Welfare State.* Beverly Hills, CA: Sage.

2002. *Rich Democracies: Political Economy, Public Policy, and Performance.* Berkeley: University of California Press.

William McKinley to J. F. Hanson. Letter. February 27, 1896. McKinley Papers. Series 2 V87-P90.

Williams, Karen. 1988. *Industrial Relations and the German Model.* Brookfield, IL: Avebury.

Wilson, Graham. 1985. *The Politics of Safety and Health.* Oxford: Clarendon Press.

1986. "American Business and Politics," in Allan Cigler and Burdett Loomis, eds., *Interest Group Politics.* Washington, DC: CQ Press, 227–31.

1990. *Business and Politics,* 2nd ed. Chatham, NJ: Chatham House.

Wilson, E. P. 1898. "The Cincinnati Convention," *American Trade* II (5): 1.

Windmuller, John and Alan Gladstone, eds. 1984. *Employers Associations and Industrial Relations.* New York: Oxford University Press.

Winkel, Jasper Steen. 2000. "Fireparts-krig om det rummelige arbejdsmarked." *Ugebrevet Mandag Morgen* 36 (Oktober 16): 5–8.

March 4, 2002. "Regeringen vil tage aktiveringen fra kommunerne." *Mandag Morgen* (9), 5–8.

Winkel, Jasper Steen. June 3, 2002. "Hjort Frederiksen kopierer SR-politik." *Mandag Morgen* 21: 29–33.

Winkler, Heinrich. 1976. "From Social Protectionism to National Socialism." *Journal of Modern History* 48 (1): 1–18.

Wintour, Patrick, William Keegan, and Anthony Browne. 1998. "Soaring Pound Casts Doubt on Welfare Plans." *The Observer* (April 5) p. 2.

WM Osborne letter to McKinley, *McKinley Papers* Series 1, Reel 1 "1847 Sept 6 1987 Feb 22."

Wolf, Charles Jr. 1990. *Markets or Governments: Choosing Between Imperfect Alternatives.* Cambridge, MA: MIT Press.

Wolff-Rohe, Stephanie. 2001. *Der Reichsverband der Deutschen Industrie 1919–1924/25.* Frankfurt am Main: Peter Lang.

Wood, Adrian. 1994. *North-South Trade, Employment, and Inequality.* Oxford: Clarendon Press.

Wood, Stewart. 2001. "Labour Market Regimes Under Threat?," in Paul Pierson, ed., *The New Politics of the Welfare State.* New York: Oxford University Press.

Wright, Jonathan. 2002. *Gustav Stresemann.* New York: Oxford University Press.

Zeitlin, Jonathan. 1990. "The Triumph of Adversarial Bargaining: Industrial Relations in British Engineering, 1880–1939." *Politics and Society* 18 (3): 381–404.

Zysman, John. 1983. *Governments, Markets and Growth: Finance and the Politics of Industrial Change.* Cornell University Press.

Østergård, Uffe. 1992. "Peasants and Danes: The Danish National Identity and Political Culture." *Comparative Studies in Society and History,* 34 (1): 3–27.

Newspaper Articles/Anonymous Periodical Articles

"$10,000 to bet on M'Kinley." *Atlanta Journal* (July 15, 1896) p. 9.
"A High-Tariff Republican President," *New York Times* (January 25, 1895) p. 1.
"A Ninth Cabinet Member: A Contingent Offer Made." *New York Times* (February 23, 1897) p. 1.
"A Centre Coalition Party." *The Times* (May 14, 1919) p. 13.
"Army Of Industry." *The Times* {January 22, 1917) p. 6.
"Businessmen to Be Brought into Closer Touch with Government." *Nation's Business* (1912).
"Charter Bill Did Not Pass." *Nation's Business* I (9) (March 19, 1913) pp. 1, 4.
"Commercial Counsellors." *The Times* (December 167, 1916) p. 5.
"Committees on National Legislation." *Nation's Business* I (1) (September 2, 1912) p. 2.
"Company Meeting. Federation of British Industries." *The Times* (March 12, 1917) p. 12.
"Compulsory Vocational Education." *Nation's Business* II (11) (November 15, 1914) p. 15.
"Concern about Indemnities," *The Times* (May 15, 1919) p. 14.
"Conciliation and Trade Disputes," *The Times* (March 22, 1899) p. 14.
"Delegates Got Down to Business." *Cincinnati Enquirer* (January 24, 1895) p. 8.
"Den ekstraordinære Hovedgeneralforsamling den 19. December." 20 (52) *Arbejdsgiveren* (December 26, 1920) pp. 450–1.
"Dixie the Toast." *Atlanta Constitution* (January 28, 1895) p. 7.
"Employers' body makes cutbacks." 1996 *European Industrial Relations Review* 268 (May) p. 4–5.
Employers' Parliamentary Association. 1914. The Times (March 27) p. 13.
"For the McKinley Monument," *New York Times* (October 6, 1901) p. 3.
"Historisk Tilbageblik I glimt." *KF Blandet* 2 (September): Aargang 125.
"Home Interests and Foreign Trade." *American Statesman* II (12) (March 15, 1899) p. 92.
"Industrifagene under Arbejdsgiverforeningen." *Arbejdsgiveren* 42 (7) (October 17, 1906) p. 325.
"Industrifagenes Fælleskommission." *Arbejdsgiveren* 49 (7) (December 5, 1906) pp. 384–5.
"It's President Dolan." *Cincinnati Commercial Gazette* (January 25, 1895) p. 1.
"Legislative Reference and Bill Drafting Bureau," *Nation's Business* I (17) (November 15, 1913) p. 4.
"Legislative Reference Bureau Organized." *Nation's Business* II (12) (December 15, 1914) p. 7.
"M'Kinley's Tour," *Macon Telegraph* (March 27, 1895) p. 1.
"Manufacturers in Convention." *Atlanta Constitution* (January 24, 1895) p. 2.
"Manufacturers Cheer for McKinley." *New York Times* (January 22, 1896) p. 1.
"McKinley for President." *New York Times* (March 1, 1895).
"Membership Map of the National Chamber," *Nation's Business* I (11) (5/15/1913) p. 8.
"Metropolitan Cash Used for M'Kinley." *New York Times* (April 4, 1908).
"Model Benefits for Bell Employees." *Nation's Business* I (5) (December 16, 1912) p. 11.
"Mr. Quay Takes a Stand." *New York Times* (December 9, 1896) p. 5.
"Mr. Chamberlain on His Proposals." *The Times* (October 5, 1903) p. 6.
"Need for Shells." *The Times* (5/14/1915) p. 8.
"No Federal Support," *Nation's Business* I (1) (September 22, 1912) p. 1.
"Opinions of Leaders in Business World and in Education." *Nation's Business* I (4) (November 18, 1912) p. 2.
"Organization and Purposes of the Chamber of Commerce of the United States." *Nation's Business* I (1) (September 2, 1912) p. 8.
"Our Trade Future." *The Times* (January 11, 1917) p. 5.
"Overseas Trade Departmental Differences." *The Times* (July 26, 1919) p. 8.
"Permanent Trade Commission." *Nation's Business* I (7) (January 28, 1913) p. 3.
"Promoting Foreign and Domestic Commerce." *Nation's Business* I (17) (May 15, 1913) p. 3.
"Recently Appointed Commercial Attaches." *Nations' Business* II (10) (October 15, 1914) p. 6.
"Reciprocity Convention Meets in Washington." *The New York Times* (November 20, 1901) p. 8.

"Referendum on Banking and Currency." *Nation's Business* I (16) (October 15, 1913) p. 1.

"Resignation of Sir Charles Macara." *The Times* (November 14, 1914) p. 12

"Road Legislation in Present Congress." *Nation's Business* 1 (4) (November 18, 1912) p. 3.

"San Francisco Industrial Convention." *The National Industrial Review* 1 (May 3, 1895) p. 94.

"Secretary Charles Nagel Speaks Encouragingly." *Nation's Business* 1(7) (Jan 28, 1913) p. 3.

"State Income Taxation As Applied in Wisconsin." *Nation's Business* 1 (5) (December 16, 1912) p. 2.

"The Centre Group." *The Times* (July 17, 1919) p. 13.

"The Method for Selection of Committees in the Chamber of Commerce of the United State of America." *Nation's Business* I (6) (January 20, 1913) p. 8.

"The Chamber's Field." *Nation's Business* 1 (1) (September 2, 1912) pp. 1–2.

"The National Association of Manufacturers and other Organizations." *American Trade* II (19) (July 1, 1899): p. 148.

"The Cincinnati Convention." *Atlanta Constitution* (January 27, 1895) p. 19.

"They Welcomed M'Kinley." *Macon Telegraph* (March 18, 1895) p. 1.

"To Cotton Mill Men." *Atlanta Constitution* (January 27, 1895) p. 19.

"Tomorrow in Odd Fellow's Temple." *Cincinnati Enquirer* (January 21, 1895) p. 8.

"Two Important Decisions." *Nation's Business* 1 (12) (June 16, 1913) p. 1.

"Union of Employers. Terms of National Combination Settled." *The Times* (January 20, 1917) p. 3.

"Vocational Education." *Nation's Business* I (7) (January 28, 1913) p. 4.

"Vocational Education." *Nation's Business* I (April 15, 1913) p. 4.

"Will Discuss Reciprocity." *The New York Times* (August 17, 2001) p. 7.

"Woodmansee Is Once More Chosen." *Cincinnati Enquirer* (February 13, 1895) p. 8.

Index

British Chambers of Commerce, 71, 198
British Electrical and Allied Manufacturers'
    Association (BEAMA), 78
British Employers Confederation, 69, 70
British Manufacturers' Association (BMA), 78, 83
Brown, Gordon, 202, 252
Brown, W.W., 94
Bücher, Hermann, 124
Buck, Colonel A.F., 96
Büeck, Henry Axel, 117, 261
Bund der Industriellen (BdI), 110, 112, 119, 120, 121, 123,
    124, 126, 209
Bureau of Manufactures, 101, 102, 103
Burke, Edmund, 71
business associations, i, 2, 7, 8, 9, 11, 23, 26, 28, 29, 37, 107,
    155, 182, 250, *See also* employers' organizations
business organizations, 1, 16, 37, 38, 104, 150, 190, 196,
    See also employers' organizations
business preferences, 150, *See* preferences

Calmfors, Lars, 243
Cameron, David, 252
Canada, 19, 31, 32, 98, 132, 135, 235, 245, 253, 288, 291
capital mobility, 136, 141, 145, 146, 153, 158, 160, 169,
    232, 239, 240, 250
capitalism, 4, 5, 9, 10, 12, 13, 15, 22, 26, 27, 28, 29, 44, 48,
    49, 72, 76, 90, 105, 128, 129, 130, 137, 138, 139, 142,
    146, 148, 167, 169, 175, 199, 246, 248, 249, 250,
    251, 252, 253, 255, *See also* coordinated market
    economy; liberal market economy; varieties
    of capitalism
Carey, Henry C., 32, 117, 118, 119, 259, 262, 263, 272, 278
CDU (Christian Democratic Union, Germany), 215
Cecil, Lord Hugh, 76, 84, 263, 293
Central Association for German Industrialists
    (Centralverbund Deutscher Industrieller or
    CVDI), 110
Central Association of German Industrialists for
    the Promotion and Protection of National
    Labor, 117
centralization of government, 129, 138, 249,
    See also federalism
Centralverband, 32, 45, 114, 117, 118, 119, 126
Chamberlain, Joseph, 71, 75, 79, 80, 88, 283, 289
Chamberlain, Neville, 80
Christian Democratic parties, 25, 37, 138, 139, 141, 145,
    147, 156, 158, 232, 233
    Christian Democratic government, 140, 141, 147,
    158, 236
Churchill, Winston, 76
Cincinnati Manufacturers' Association, 95
cleavages (ethnic and religious), 12, 21, 34, 36, 37, 38, 39,
    41, 43, 44, 56, 70, 172, 173, 174, 191, 229, 232, 250
Cleveland Business Men's Marching Club, 94
Clinton, Bill, 131

collective action, 12, 23, 27, 35, 53, 58, 72, 89, 130, 155,
    156, 181, 182, 190, 198, 201, 234, 250, 256
collective bargaining, 7, 12, 16, 17, 23, 32, 50, 51, 54,
    59, 62, 63, 70, 109, 121, 128, 129, 137, 139, 140, 141,
    155, 156, 173, 175, 177, 178, 179, 181, 182, 190, 191,
    196, 201, 209, 210, 211, 214, 216, 221, 222, 223,
    224, 233, 234, 246, 249, 255, *See also* labor and
    industrial relations; country headings
Confederation of British Industry (CBI), 69, 88, 193,
    194, 195, 196, 197, 198, 199, 200, 201, 202, 206,
    259, 260, 272, 283, 289, 293, 295
Confederation of Danish Business, 60
Confederation of Danish Employers (Dansk
    Arbejdsgiverforeningen or DA), 50, 54,
    172, 266
Confederation of German Employers' Associations
    (BDA), 209, 221, 224, 225
Conservative parties (Konservative Folkeparti), 177
Conservative Party (Britain), 70, 73, 74, 76, 77, 79, 83,
    190, 194
Conservative Party (Germany), 114, 116, 118
Conservative People's Party, 65, 66
Converse, John, 99
coordinated market economies (CMEs), 9, 25, 128,
    132, 173, 227, 236, 240, 243
coordination, i, 2, 4, 5, 7–8, 10, 12, 13–18, 19, 20, 21,
    22, 23, 24, 25, 26, 27, 28–35, 36, 37, 38, 39, 40,
    41, 42, 43, 44, 45, 46, 48, 49, 50, 51, 53, 54,
    62, 64, 67, 68, 69, 70, 71, 72, 73, 75, 76, 77,
    79, 81, 85, 88, 89–90, 91, 92, 98, 101, 106–08,
    109–113, 115, 118, 119–121, 122, 123–24, 125–27,
    128–131, 132–36, 137, 138–143, 145–48, 149, 151,
    152, 154–55, 156, 157, 158, 160, 165, 169, 171, 172,
    173, 176, 179, 187, 190, 191, 192, 194, 195, 197, 198,
    199, 209, 220, 222, 223, 224, 225, 226, 227, 228,
    229, 233, 234, 236, 237, 239–47, 248–49, 250,
    253, 255, *See also* employers' organizations;
    macrocorporatism; sector coordination;
    pluralism
    nonmarket coordination, 20, 29, 30, 33, 34, 38, 49,
    67, 89, 132, 134, 135, 136, 140, 141, 143, 145, 148,
    228, *See also* coordinated market economies;
    employers' organizations; macro-
    corporatism, sector coordination; pluralism
corporatism, 7, 9, 10, 12, 15, 16, 17–21, 22–23, 24, 25, 26,
    28, 30, 32, 34, 35, 37, 38, 39, 40–43, 45,
    47–49, 50, 59, 69, 70, 74, 79–80, 87, 88, 89, 90,
    98, 100, 108, 111, 115, 120–22, 128, 129, 131, 132,
    133, 134, 136–37, 138, 139, 140, 141, 142, 143–47,
    148, 149, 150, 155–57, 158, 160, 166, 169, 171–72,
    173–75, 176–77, 179, 181, 182, 184, 185, 186, 187, 188,
    190–91, 194, 196, 201, 206, 209, 220, 225–26, 227,
    228, 231, 233–39, 240, 242, 243–47, 249, 250, 253,
    255, 272, *See also* macrocorporatism
Corry, Dan, 199

Lily Lee Tsai, *Accountability without Democracy: How Solidary Groups Provide Public Goods in Rural China*

Joshua Tucker, *Regional Economic Voting: Russia, Poland, Hungary, Slovakia, and the Czech Republic, 1990–1999*

Ashutosh Varshney, *Democracy, Development, and the Countryside*

Jeremy M. Weinstein, *Inside Rebellion: The Politics of Insurgent Violence*

Stephen I. Wilkinson, *Votes and Violence: Electoral Competition and Ethnic Riots in India*

Jason Wittenberg, *Crucibles of Political Loyalty: Church Institutions and Electoral Continuity in Hungary*

Elisabeth J. Wood, *Forging Democracy from Below: Insurgent Transitions in South Africa and El Salvador*

Elisabeth J. Wood, *Insurgent Collective Action and Civil War in El Salvador*

Is financial crisis a likely critical juncture point? Or are political and econ instit. more subject to instrumental shifts set in place b/f crises, making the crisis a reinforcement of instit. rules? prev.